Clashing Views
on Controversial
Economic Issues

6th edition

Clashing Views
on Controversial
Economic Issues

6th edition

Edited, Selected, and with Introductions by

Thomas R. Swartz
and
Frank J. Bonello
University of Notre Dame

The Dushkin Publishing Group, Inc.

This book is dedicated to the thousands of students who have persevered in the "Bonello/Swartz-B.S." introductory economics course sequence at the University of Notre Dame. It is also dedicated to our children and grandchildren. In order of their birthdates, they are:

Mary Elizabeth, Karen Ann, Jennifer Lynne, John Anthony, Anne Marie, Rebecca Jourdan, David Joseph, Stephen Thomas, Chelsea Margaret, and Kevin Joseph.

Photo Acknowledgments

Part 1   USDA/Soil Conservation Service
Part 2   Raymond Juschkus/The Chase Manhattan Bank
Part 3   REUTERS/BETTMANN

Library of Congress Catalog Card Number: 92–71145

Manufactured in the United States of America

Sixth Edition, Second Printing
ISBN: 1–56134–059–6

 Printed on Recycled Paper

The Dushkin Publishing Group, Inc.
Sluice Dock, Guilford, CT 06437

PREFACE

> Where there is much desire to learn, there of necessity will be much arguing.
> —John Milton (1608–1674), English poet and essayist

Presented here are 18 debates on important and compelling economic issues, which are designed to stimulate critical thinking skills and initiate lively and informed discussion. These debates take economic theory and show how it is applied to current, real-world public policy decisions, the outcomes of which will have an immediate and personal impact. How these debates are resolved will affect our taxes, jobs, wages, educational system, and so on; in short, they will shape the society in which we live.

It has been our intent throughout each of the six editions of *Taking Sides: Clashing Views on Controversial Economic Issues* to select issues that reveal something about the nature of economics itself and something about how it relates to current, everyday newspaper headlines and television news stories on public policy issues that deal with economic considerations (and almost all do these days). To assist the reader, we begin each issue with an *issue introduction*, which sets the stage for the debate as it is argued in the YES and NO selections. Each issue concludes with a *postscript* that briefly reviews the arguments and makes some final observations. The introduction and postscript do not preempt what is the reader's own task: to achieve a critical and informed view of the economic issue at stake. Certainly, the reader should not feel confined to adopt one or the other of the positions presented. The views presented should be used as starting points, and the *suggestions for further reading* that appear in each issue postscript offer additional resources on the topic. At the back of the book is a listing of all the *contributors to this volume*, which provides information on the economists, policymakers, political leaders, and commentators whose views are debated here.

Changes to this edition The sixth edition of *Taking Sides* represents a major revision of this book. Twenty-eight of the 36 selections and 13 of the 18 issues are new. Thus, as we rush toward the dawn of the twenty-first century, this heavily revised book will help us understand the implications of a changing set of economic issues that were not part of our world just a few short years ago. The newly raised issues are: *Should American Farmers Be Forced to Face Market Competition?* (Issue 2); *Is National Service at Odds With American National Interest?* (Issue 3); *Are Women Paid Less Than Men Because Their Working Conditions Are More Favorable?* (Issue 4); *Are Rent Controls the Cause of America's Homelessness?* (Issue 5); *Do Hostile Takeovers Harm Society?* (Issue 6); *Is Mass Transit the Answer to Improving U.S. Energy Efficiency?* (Issue 7); *Is Choice a Panacea for the Ills of Public Education?* (Issue 8); *Did Reaganomics Fail?* (Issue 9); *Should the Federal Reserve Target Zero Inflation?* (Issue 11); *Does the United States Save Enough?* (Issue 12); *Is Japan a Threat to America's*

Economic and National Security? (Issue 16); *Does Global Warming Require Immediate Government Action?* (Issue 17); and *Should a New Military-Industrial Complex Be Developed?* (Issue 18). In addition, the NO readings for Issue 1 on profits and Issue 10 on federal budget deficits have been replaced in order to bring a fresh perspective to each issue.

As with all of the previous editions, the issues in the sixth edition can be used in any sequence. Although the general organization of the book loosely parallels the sequence of topics found in a standard introductory economics textbook, you can pick and choose which issues to read first, since they are designed to stand alone.

A word to the instructor An *Instructor's Manual with Test Questions* (multiple-choice and essay) is available through the publisher. The manual includes a grid that correlates the individual issues in this edition of *Taking Sides* with chapters of 10 standard textbooks often used in introductory economics courses. And a general guidebook, called *Using Taking Sides in the Classroom*, which discusses methods and techniques for integrating the pro/con approach into any classroom setting, is also available.

Acknowledgments We have received many helpful comments and suggestions from our friends and readers across the United States and Canada. As always, their suggestions were very welcome and have markedly enhanced the quality of this edition of *Taking Sides*. If as you read this book you are reminded of an essay that could be included in a future edition, we hope that you will drop us a note. We very much appreciate your interest and help, and we are always pleased to hear from you.

Our special thanks go to those who responded with suggestions for the sixth edition:

Tony Barrett
College of St. Scholastica

A. L. Buddy Brockman
Central Piedmont Community
  College

Karl E. Burgher
Montana College of Mineral
  Science and Technology

Stephen D. Casler
Allegheny College

Leo M. Corbaci
University of Notre Dame

Robert M. Edmondson
Barton College

Joyce Gleason
Nebraska Wesleyan University

Garland R. Hadley
Midwestern State University

Montey Holloway
University of Notre Dame

John Homer
Olivet College

John Houck
University of Notre Dame

Douglas Houston
University of Kansas

Richard Johnston
Lafayette College

Robert Otto
Western Kentucky University

Peter W. Replogle
Orange County Community
    College

Dave Thiessen
Lewis–Clark State College

Kenneth Weiher
University of Texas at San
    Antonio

We are also indebted to Mimi Egan, our editorial advisor at The Dushkin Publishing Group. She provided excellent council, suggested material, and gave us much needed support as we approached our publication deadlines. Those who suffered most in the preparation of this manuscript were those who had to read Swartz's tortured handwriting—our typists: Frank J. Bonello, Cheryl Dial, and Sherry Reichold. Finally we owe much to our graduate assistant here at the University of Notre Dame: Amy Quist. She was always able to maintain a wonderful smile even when our requests to run to the library were outrageous.

To all those mentioned above, we owe a huge debt, many thanks, and none of the blame for any shortcomings that remain in this edition of *Taking Sides*.

Thomas R. Swartz
Frank J. Bonello
University of Notre Dame, Indiana

CONTENTS IN BRIEF

CONTENTS

Free-market economist Milton Friedman contends that the sole responsibility of business is to increase its profits. Philosopher Christopher D. Stone
insists that the time for corporate social responsibility has come and
considerations other than profit making sometimes take precedence in a
business.

Former economics professor and current congressman Dick Armey (R-
Texas) asserts that government farm programs are costly, reduce productivity, decrease competitiveness, and only hurt those they are intended to
help. Economics professor Andrew Larkin argues that lawmakers need to
radically rethink U.S. farm policy so as to address the consequences of low
farm prices and high farm costs that cause both farmers and the environment to suffer.

Doug Bandow, a former special assistant to President Reagan, argues that the Nunn-McCurdy proposal on national service represents an objectionable intrusion of the state into the affairs of individual members of society—an intrusion that will weaken our future military preparedness. Professor of sociology Charles Moskos, who advises the conservative-leaning Democratic Leadership Conference, characterizes this proposal as "bold legislation" and "a GI Bill without the GI."

Associate professor of economics Randall K. Filer maintains that comparable worth policies are unnecessary since wage differentials simply reflect differences in workers' preferences for jobs with varying degrees of pleasantness. Associate professors of sociology Jerry A. Jacobs and Ronnie J. Steinberg argue that empirical evidence proves that wage differentials cannot be explained by worker employment choices.

Journalist William Tucker analyzes the problem of homelessness across the United States and suggests that rent controls and homelessness are correlated. Sociologist Richard P. Appelbaum and his research associates submit that Tucker's statistical analysis is flawed and that he ignores the real causes

Political scientists John E. Chubb and Terry M. Moe believe that the United States must free public schools from "political and bureaucratic control" and instead rely upon "markets and parental choice" in the quest for quality education. Public school superintendent Bill Honig replies that privatizing public schools through a system of choice is both unnecessary, given the school reforms of the 1980s, and dangerous, in light of the expected market consequences.

Economists Samuel Bowles, David M. Gordon, and Thomas E. Weisskopf believe that the economic policies of the Reagan administration failed to reverse the long-term deterioration of the U.S. economy due to the inability of Reaganomics to escape the contradictions of right-wing economics. The policies created an economic environment that hindered rather than stimulated investment. Paul Craig Roberts, an economist and former government policymaker, believes that Reaganomics was a success: it was not the cause of increased government budget deficits; careful analysis of the data suggests that the United States does not save or invest too little; it created an improved investment environment; and some 20 million jobs were created during the Reagan era.

Federal Reserve chairman Alan Greenspan believes that federal government budget deficits, in the long run, hurt the economy. The deficits crowd out or reduce net private domestic investment, which means a reduction in the rate of growth in the nation's capital stock. This, in turn, means less capital per worker and a reduction in labor productivity, the result of which is that the output of goods and services is smaller and persons are worse off. Economics professor Robert Eisner believes that if the budget position of the government is measured appropriately, then, in "a fundamental, long-run sense, . . . the total budget is now in balance." The real problems of the U.S. economy are not budget deficits but a lack of expenditures on "human capital and in public investment."

Former Cleveland Federal Reserve Bank president W. Lee Hoskins supports House Joint Resolution 409, which calls for the Federal Reserve to pursue policies to eliminate inflation. Hoskins believes zero inflation would "help markets avoid distortions and imbalances, stabilize the business cycle, and promote the highest sustainable growth in our economy." Economics professor Michael Meeropol opposes House Joint Resolution 409. He believes that a move to zero inflation will not reduce unemployment and reduce the risk of inflation, it will not produce a higher possible rate of saving and investment, and it may increase income inequality by redistributing income to high-income people from low-income people.

Sociology professor Fred Block argues that savings should be calculated using the Federal Reserve's flow of funds data rather than the conventional National Income and Product Accounts data, and that the former data indicate that savings are adequate. Economics professor William D. Nordhaus believes that increased amounts of saving and investment are necessary if the United States is to avoid a substantial decrease in its standard of living.

Senator Robert W. Kasten, Jr. (R-Wisconsin) wants to reduce the tax rate on capital gains because such a reduction will increase government revenues, stimulate the economy and the job market, and bring the U.S. economy more in line with "European and Asian competitors." Professor of economics John Miller is against a cut in the tax rate on capital gains because he believes that the benefits will primarily go to the rich and that it will not stimulate investment. Instead, he proposes an increase in the tax rate on short-term capital gains.

Associate professor of politics Lawrence M. Mead, an advocate of the work ethic, urges Congress to make work a fundamental condition of receiving welfare assistance. Attorney Morton H. Sklar rejects Mead's contention that work must be a key ingredient in any welfare system. His experience suggests that a work requirement is inappropriate for many welfare recipients and not cost-effective for those who would be asked to work.

Columnist Robert Kuttner alleges that David Ricardo's eighteenth-century view of the world does not "describe the global economy as it actually works" in the twentieth century. He says that, today, "comparative advantage" is determined by exploitative wage rates and government action; it is not determined by free markets. Social critic Michael Kinsley replies that we do not decrease American living standards when we import the products made by cheap foreign labor. He claims protectionism today, just as it did in the eighteenth century, weakens our economy and only "helps to put off the day of reckoning."

Professor of international economic relations Stephen D. Cohen concludes that a continuation of our "inferior industrial performance relative to Japan" is a threat to both the "economic [and] national security interests of the United States." Philip H. Trezise, a senior fellow of the Brookings Institution, replies that "on any rational calculation, economic competition from Japan does not threaten America's national security" or its long-run economic vitality.

Cynthia Pollock Shea, a senior researcher with the Worldwatch Institute, pleads with governments and industries to initiate a "crash program" designed to halt emissions of chemicals that deplete the ozone, such as chlorofluorocarbons, before irreparable damage is done to world agriculture, marine life, and human health. Professor of economics Lester B. Lave warns against drastic solutions that could themselves be harmful or, at a minimum, "costly if the greenhouse consequences are more benign than predicted."

Mackubin T. Owens, a professor of defense economics, warns that the
industrial base would be "hard-pressed to support our military needs"
without substantial lead time, and, therefore, a strategic trade and investments policy should be "enacted as soon as possible." Associate professor of
international affairs William J. Long attacks Owens's military-industrial
complex and proclaims that "defense protectionism, like other forms of
protectionism, is unnecessary, ineffective, and even dangerous."

INTRODUCTION

Economics and Economists: The Basis for Controversy

Thomas R. Swartz

Frank J. Bonello

> I think that Capitalism, wisely managed, can probably be more efficient for attaining economic ends than any alternative system yet in sight, but that in itself it is in many ways extremely objectionable.
> —Lord John Maynard Keynes, *The End of Laissez-Faire* (1926)

Although more than 60 years have passed since Lord Keynes (1883–1946) penned these lines, many economists still struggle with the basic dilemma he outlined. The paradox rests in the fact that a free market system is extremely efficient. It is purported to produce more at a lower cost than any other economic system. But in producing this wide array of low-cost goods and services, problems arise. These problems—most notably a lack of economic equity and economic stability—concern some economists. Other economists choose to ignore or minimize these issues. These problems form the foundation of this book.

If the problems raised and analyzed in this book were merely the product of intellectual gymnastics undertaken by eggheaded economists, then we could sit back and enjoy these confrontations as theoretical exercises. Unfortunately, we are not afforded that luxury. The essays contained in this book touch each and every one of us in tangible ways. They are real-world issues. Some focus upon *macroeconomic* topics, such as the current state of the U.S. economy and the underlying causes, effects, and cures for inflation, unemployment, and recession. Another set of issues deals with *microeconomic* topics. We refer to these issues as "micro" problems not because they are small problems but because they deal with small economic units, such as households, firms, or individual industries. The third set of issues concerns international aspects of economic activity. This area has grown in significance as the volume of international transactions has grown and as U.S. society has come to realize the importance of international interdependence. This final set of issues also touches on our future directly and forces us to consider whether or not we should make fundamental changes in our economic policy.

For each of the 18 issues considered in this book we have isolated those areas that currently generate the most controversy among economists. In a few cases, this controversy represents a confrontation between extreme positions, where the views of the "free-market" economist are contrasted with the views of the "radical reformist" economist. In other cases, the conflicts are not as extreme. Rather they represent conflicts between one extreme and economists with more moderate views. Finally, we could not ignore the conflicts that occur among economists who generally agree on most other issues. Economists, even those who identify strongly with the same philosophical perspective, rarely agree on all issues. Thus, these otherwise like-thinking economists sometimes differ on specific topics.

The underlying reason for this apparent conflict and disagreement among economists can be explained, at least in part, in terms of Lord Keynes's 1926 remark. How various economists will react to the strengths and weaknesses found in an economic system will depend upon how they view the relative importance of efficiency, equity, and stability. These are central terms, and we will define them in detail in the following pages. For now the important point is that some economists may view efficiency as the overriding quality. In other cases, the same economists may be willing to sacrifice the efficiency generated by the market in order to ensure increased economic equity or increased economic stability or both. Determining when efficiency should be given a high priority and when efficiency should give way to other considerations occupies a large portion of the professional economist's time.

Given this discussion of conflict, controversy, and diversity, it might appear that economists rarely, if ever, agree on any economic issue. We would be misleading the reader if we allowed this impression to stand. Economists rarely challenge the internal logic of the theoretical models that have been developed and articulated by their colleagues. Rather, they will challenge either the validity of the assumptions used in these models or the value of the ends these models seek to achieve. For example, it is extremely difficult to discredit the internal logic of the microeconomic models employed by the free-market economist. These models are elegant and their logical development is persuasive. However, these models do get challenged. The challenges typically focus upon such issues as the assumption of functioning, competitive markets, and the desirability of perpetuating the existing distribution of income. In this case, those who support and those who challenge the operation of the market agree on a large number of issues. But they disagree most assuredly on a few issues that have dramatic implications.

This same phenomenon of agreeing more often than disagreeing is also true in the area of economic policy. In this area, where the public is more acutely aware of the differences that exist among economists, these differences are not generally over the kinds of changes that will be brought about by a particular policy. Again, the differences more typically concern the timing of the change, the specific characteristics of the policy, and the size of the effect or effects.

ECONOMISTS: WHAT DO THEY REPRESENT?

Newspaper, magazine, and television commentators all use handy labels to describe certain members of the economics profession. What do the headlines mean when they refer to the "Chicago School," the "Keynesians," the "antitrusters," or the "radical economists"? What do these labels stand for? Since we, too, use our own labels throughout this book, we feel obliged to identify the principal groups or camps in our profession. Let us warn you that this can be a misleading venture. Some economists, perhaps most economists, defy classification. They float from one camp to another, selecting a gem of wisdom here and another there. These are practical men and women who believe that no one camp has all the answers to all the economic problems confronting society. As a consequence, they may be ardent supporters of a given policy recommendation of one philosophical group but vocal critics of other recommendations emanating from the same philosophical group.

Recognizing this limitation, four major groups of economists can be identified. These groups are differentiated on the basis of three criteria: how they view efficiency relative to equity and stability; what significance they attach to imperfectly competitive market structures; and how they view the evolution of an economic society. Before describing the views of the four groups based on these criteria, it is essential to understand the meaning of certain terms to be used in this description.

Efficiency, equity, and stability represent goals for an economic system. *Efficiency* reflects the fact that the economy produces those goods and services that people want and that it does so without wasting scarce resources. *Equity* in an economic sense has several dimensions. It means that income and wealth are distributed according to accepted principles of fairness: that those who are unable to care for themselves receive adequate care, and that mainstream economic activity is open to all persons. *Stability* is the absence of sharp ups and downs in business activity, in prices, and in employment. In other words, stability is marked by steady increases in output, little inflation, and low unemployment.

When the term *market structures* is used, it refers to the number of buyers and sellers in the market and the amount of control they exercise over price. At one extreme is a *perfectly competitive market*, where there are so many buyers and sellers that no one has any ability to influence market price. The other extreme is a market that has only one seller or one buyer, who obviously could have great control over price. This market structure, which we call *pure monopoly*, and other market structures that result in some control over price are grouped under the broad label of *imperfectly competitive markets*. That is, imperfect competition is a situation in which the number of market participants is limited and, as a consequence, the participants have the ability to influence price. With these terms in mind, we can begin to examine the various schools of economic thought.

Free-Market Economists

One of the most visible groups of economists and perhaps the easiest group to identify and classify is the *free-market economists*. These economists believe that the market, operating freely without interference from government or labor unions, will generate the greatest amount of well-being for the greatest number of people.

Economic efficiency is one of the priorities for free-market economists. In their well-developed models, "consumer sovereignty"—consumer demand for goods and services—guides the system by directly influencing market prices. The distribution of economic resources caused by these market prices not only results in the production of an array of goods and services that are demanded by consumers, but this production is undertaken in the most cost-effective fashion. The free-market economists claim that at any point, some individuals must earn incomes that are substantially greater than those of other individuals. They contend that these higher incomes are a reward for greater efficiency or productivity and that this reward-induced efficiency will result in rapid economic growth, which will benefit all persons in the society. They might also admit that a system driven by these freely operating markets will be subject to occasional bouts of instability (slow growth, inflation, and unemployment). However, they maintain that government action to eliminate or reduce this periodic instability will only make matters worse. Consequently, government, according to the free-market economist, should play a minor role in the economic affairs of society.

Although the models of free-market economists are dependent upon functioning, competitive markets, the lack of these competitive markets in the real world does not seriously jeopardize their position. First, they assert that large-sized firms are necessary to achieve low per unit costs; that is, a single large firm may be able to produce a given level of output with fewer scarce resources than a large number of small firms. Second, they suggest that the benefits associated with the free operation of markets are so great compared to government intervention that even a "second-best solution" of imperfectly competitive markets still yields benefits far greater than any that would result from government intervention. Lastly, the free-market economists clearly view the market as the highest form of economic evolution. The efficiency of the system, the simplicity of the system, the power of the system, and, above all, the personal freedoms inherent in the system demonstrate its superiority.

These advocates of the free market have been given various labels over time. The oldest and most persistent label is *classical economists*. This is because the classical economists of the eighteenth century, particularly Adam Smith (1723–1790), were the first to point out the virtues of the market. Smith captured the essence of the system with the following words:

> Every individual endeavors to employ his capital so that its produce may be of greatest value. He generally neither intends to promote the public interest nor knows how much he is promoting it. He intends only his own security, only his

own gain. And he is in this led by an invisible hand to promote an end which was no part of his intention. By pursuing his own interest he frequently promotes that of society more effectively than when he really intends to promote it.

—Adam Smith, *The Wealth of Nations* (1776)

Since free-market economists and those who echo their views resist most forms of government intervention, they are also sometimes referred to as *conservatives* or *libertarians*. These labels are as much political labels as they are economic characterizations. It must be recalled that the classical economists of the eighteenth century not only embraced the political philosophy of laissez-faire—roughly translated to "leave it (the economy) alone"—but developed a set of economic theories that were totally consistent with this political theory. These "political economists" were, as a result, called libertarians because they espoused political and economic policies that maximized personal freedoms or liberties. The nineteenth-century libertarians are not to be confused with twentieth-century liberals. Modern-day liberals, as we shall explain shortly in more detail, are often willing to sacrifice some freedoms in the marketplace in order to ensure the attainment of other objectives.

Still other labels are sometimes attached to the free-market economists, such as *monetarists*, the *Austrian School*, *public choice* economists, *Chicago School* economists, and the *rational expectations* school. With regard to the modern-day practitioners of free-market economics, the most notable is Nobel laureate Milton Friedman (b. 1912), formerly a professor of economics at the University of Chicago. He and others argue that the government's attempts to promote economic stability through the manipulation of the money supply actually cause more instability than would have occurred if the government had not intervened. As a consequence, these monetarists advocate a policy that would allow the money supply to grow at a reasonable, steady rate.

In the 1980s, a new group of free-market economists was formed: the *supply-siders*. These economists, led by Arthur Laffer, also believe strongly in the market. What makes them unique is the specific proposals they offer to reduce government intervention in the economy. They contend that reductions in marginal tax rates will stimulate private activity.

Supporters of rational expectations are also a relatively new group of free-market economists. They claim that government monetary and fiscal actions will have no effect on economic activity unless the actions are unanticipated; that is, unless the government actions are surprises. They argue that since government is unlikely to consistently surprise the public, monetary and fiscal policies will not have much effect on economic activity.

Before turning our attention to the other major camps of economists, we should note that the free-market economists have been very successful in influencing the development of economics. Indeed, most introductory economic textbooks present major portions of the basic theoretical concepts of the free-market economists, especially in those chapters dealing with microeconomics. It is because of this influence over long periods of time that so many labels are used to describe them, so much is written about them, and so much is written by these conservative economists. Of the 18 issues that are considered in this book, the free-market position is represented in a substantial number.

Liberal Economists

Probably the single largest group of economists in the United States in one way or another can be classified as *liberal economists*. Liberal in this instance refers to the willingness to intervene in the free operation of the market. These economists share with the free-market economists a great respect for the market. However, the liberal economist does not believe that the explicit and implicit costs of a freely operating market should or can be ignored. Rather, the liberal economist maintains that the costs of an uncontrolled marketplace are often borne by those in society who are least capable of bearing them: the poor, the elderly, and the infirm. Additionally, liberal economists maintain that the freely operating market sometimes results in economic instability and the resultant bouts of inflation, unemployment, and slow growth. Thus, although liberal economists believe that economic efficiency is highly desirable, they find the attainment of economic efficiency at any cost to be unacceptable and perhaps even "extremely objectionable."

Consider for a moment the differences between free-market economists and liberal economists at the microeconomic level. Liberal economists take exception to the free market on two grounds. First, these economists find a basic problem with fairness in the marketplace. Since the market is driven by the forces of consumer spending, there are those who, through no fault of their own (they may be aged, young, infirm, or physically or mentally handicapped), may not have the wherewithal to participate in the economic system to any great extent. Others, however, perhaps because they are extremely lucky or because they have inherited wealth, not only have the ability to participate in the system, but they may also have the ability to direct the course of that system. Second, the unfettered marketplace does not and cannot handle spillover effects or what are known as "externalities." These are the third-party effects that may occur as a result of some action. Will a firm willingly compensate its neighbors for the pollutants it pours into a nearby lake? Will a truck driver willingly drive at 55 MPH and in the process reduce the highway accident rate? Liberal economists think not. These economists are therefore willing to have the government intervene in these and other, similar cases.

The liberal economists' role in macroeconomics is more readily apparent. Ever since the failure of free-market economics during the Great Depression of the 1930s, *Keynesianism* (still another label for liberal economics) has become widely known. In his 1935 book, *The General Theory of Employment, Interest, and Money*, Lord John Maynard Keynes laid the basic groundwork for this school of thought. Keynes argued that the history of freely operating market economies was marked by periods of recurring recessions, sometimes very deep recessions, which we call *depressions*. He maintained that government intervention through its fiscal policy—government tax and spending power—could eliminate or at least soften these sharp reductions in economic activity and, as a result, move the economy along a more stable growth path. Thus for the Keynesians, or liberal economists, one of the "extremely objectionable" aspects of a free-market economy is its inherent instability. Their call for active government participation is in sharp contrast to the policies of the free-market economists who argue that economic stability (growth, employment, and prices) can be achieved only if government intervenes less and not more.

Liberal economists are also far more concerned about the existence of imperfections in the marketplace than are their free-market counterparts. They reject the notion that imperfect competition is an acceptable substitute for competitive markets. These economists may agree that the imperfectly competitive firms can achieve some savings because of their large size and efficiency, but they assert that since there is little or no competition, the firms are not forced to pass these cost savings on to consumers. Thus liberal economists, who in some circles are labeled *antitrusters*, are willing to intervene in the market in two ways. In some cases they are prepared to allow some monopolies, such as public utilities, to exist, but they contend that these monopolies must be regulated by the government. In other cases they maintain that there is no justification for monopolies and that they are prepared to invoke the powers of antitrust legislation to break up existing monopolies or prevent the formation of new monopolies.

Unlike the free-market economist, the liberal economist does not believe that the free marketplace is the highest form of economic evolution. By definition, the liberal economist asserts that the highest form of economic evolution is a *mixed economy*—an economy where market forces are tempered by government intervention. These economists do not advocate extensive government planning or government ownership of productive resources, but they are also not willing to allow the market to operate on its own. They maintain that the immense power of the marketplace properly tempered with government intervention can improve the economy's equity and stability.

During the 1960s and up to the mid-1970s, liberal economics dominated economic policy in the United States. In the late 1970s, however, there was a reemergence of free-market economics, and during the 1980s, free-market economics dominated public policy decisions. A similar pattern prevailed in the United Kingdom. The recent changes in the Eastern European countries toward free-market economics reflect a desire, in part, for greater economic efficiency. But economic policy has a way of shifting in response to prevailing economic problems. To understand the full spectrum of policy choice, we must examine the ideas of mainstream critics and radical reform economists. These schools of thought are the subject of the next sections.

The Mainstream Critics

There are a number of economists who are vocal critics of the ideas of both free-market and liberal economics but who do not fall into the category of radical reformists. Some of these economic critics might be labeled as institutionalists, others as structuralists, and still others are post-Keynesians; they run the gamut from Thorstein Veblen (1857–1929) and his critique of conspicuous consumption to John Kenneth Galbraith (b. 1908) and his views on industrial structure. These economists find mainstream or traditional economics—free-market and liberal economics—to be an eloquent theory that does not conform to reality. Unfortunately, to date, the mainstream critics have not developed their own set of economic propositions or laws that they can offer as a substitute for traditional economics.

So what are the criticisms offered by these economists? One point of attack is the simplifying assumptions employed in traditional models. The critics maintain that the traditional models may explain how economic actors would behave if these actors behaved in a rational, self-interested manner and if these actors lived in a competitive world. However, the critics assert that consumers and business firms do not always act in a rational, self-interested fashion. Behavior is more complex. It is shaped by institutions and circumstances that are continuously changing. The critics also see the world in which we live as a dual-economy world. One part of that world is competitive. Another, larger, part of the world is dominated by a few firms that have the power to set prices.

Some of the mainstream critics have concentrated their efforts on the structure of corporations, particularly multinational corporations, as economic institutions. These economists, sometimes referred to as *structuralists*, examine the economic planning these large economic units undertake; the impact they have on the system; their influence on inflation, employment, income distribution, and efficiency; and the role they play in international affairs. The institutionalists recognize that large corporate entities engage in massive economic planning that affects the whole society, and they also analyze alternative forms of regional and economic planning undertaken by government.

One fairly cohesive group of mainstream critics are the *post-Keynesians*. They are post-Keynesians because they believe that their theories are closer to the spirit of Keynes than is the interpretation of Keynes that is used to support the position of the liberal economists. As some have suggested, the key aspect of Keynes, as far as the post-Keynesians are concerned, is his assertion that "expectations of the future are not necessarily certain." On a more practical level post-Keynesians assert, among other things, that the productivity of the economic system is not significantly affected by changes in income distribution, that the system can still be efficient without competitive markets, that conventional fiscal policies cannot control inflation, and that "incomes policies" are the means to an effective and equitable answer to the inflationary dilemma. (This characterization of the post-Keynesian is drawn from Alfred S. Eichner's introduction in *A Guide to Post-Keynesian Economics* [M. E. Sharpe, 1978].)

In spite of the lack of an integrated theory from the mainstream critics, it is useful to compare their ideas on our three criteria to those of the free-market economists and the liberal economists. On the basis of our first criterion, the mainstream critics differ dramatically. By rejecting the assumptions of rationality and self-interest, they maintain that whatever you set as your highest priority—be it efficiency, equity, or stability—you cannot achieve it using the abstract models of traditional economics. Indeed, their analysis indicates that the market as it exists in its concentrated form today leads to inefficiency, inequity, and inherent instability.

The second and third criteria further distinguish the mainstream critics from the other schools of economics. According to the mainstream critics, economics is in a constant state of evolution. At one time, perhaps when Adam Smith and his fellow classical economists were formulating their basic models, the economy could be legitimately characterized as competitive. At that moment, free-market economics reflected reality and therefore could explain that reality. Presently, functional competition rarely exists, and a new body of theorems and concepts must be developed to explain this reality. At some future date, another set of economic institutions will exist and still another body of theorems and concepts will be needed. Consequently, the mainstream critics do indeed attach great importance to the existence of imperfect competition and to the process of economic evolution. The mainstream critics know that new theories must be developed to explain today's reality of imperfect competition, and they know that the economy is always in a state of evolution. What they do not know with certainty is which direction future evolution will take our current reality.

Radical Reformist Economists
As we move further and further away from the economics of the free market, we encounter the *radical reformist economists* or the *Left*. These economists, who actually spring from several theoretical foundations, share a belief that the market and the capitalist system, no matter how well disciplined, is fatally flawed and doomed to eventual failure. Out of the ashes of this system, which is guided by the "invisible hand" of self-interest, will rise the "visible hand" of public interest. That is, the fundamental institutions of private ownership will slowly fade and be replaced by government ownership of productive resources.

This does not mean that all private ownership will cease to exist at some distant moment in time. Rather, many radical reformists maintain that it is the private ownership of the 1,000 largest firms that causes the basic problems for the capitalist economy. It is the operation of these highly concentrated economic entities for the benefit of a few that causes the basic problems, and it is the private ownership of these 1,000 firms that must eventually fade away. As a result, not all property must be owned collectively. Only the most radical of the Left would go that far.

As was the case with our other three broad clusters of economists, there is much diversity within this fourth cluster of economists. One group of economists within this cluster contains the radical political economists who often focus upon microeconomic issues. They are concerned with issues such as the abuses that may result from "administered prices"—prices that can be administered or set by a firm because of the firm's monopoly influence in the marketplace. Another identifiable subgroup is the *Marxists*. Their lineage can be traced to the nineteenth-century philosopher-economist Karl Marx (1818–1883). Ironically, Marx himself shares his economic roots with the free-market economists. Before writing what many consider his most impressive work, the three volumes of *Das Kapital*, Marx studied the work of the classical economists and incorporated a basic tenet of their works—David Ricardo's labor theory of value—into his own work. But unlike free-market economics, which Marx prophesied would fall of its own weight, Marx laid the foundation for *socialism*. In spite of the changes that have taken place in Eastern Europe, socialism, where some form of public ownership of the means of production is substituted for private ownership, is still more prevalent throughout the world than is capitalism. Thus, we in North America cannot afford to ignore this group of economists.

Note that socialism may take many forms. It varies from the democratic socialism of the United Kingdom and other Western European countries to the radical, largely unreformed socialism of China. The one common characteristic is public ownership of the means of production. However, the extent of this public ownership varies dramatically from one socialist country to another.

Although it may be difficult to classify the different subgroups of radical reformist economists, we can differentiate them from the other broad classifications of economists on the basis of our three criteria. In terms of the first criterion—the relative importance of economic efficiency, equity, and stabilization—they are clearly set apart from their nonradical counterparts. Not only do they set a much higher value on equity and stability when compared to the free-market economists (a posture they share with the liberal and mainstream critics), but they have also developed a set of economic models that attempts to ensure the attainment of equity and stability. The radical reformist economists assert that the economic efficiency of a market economy is based on exploitation, and therefore the market system is fundamentally flawed. These flaws, which result in unacceptable inequities and recurring bouts of economic instability, will eventually lead to the market's demise.

The radicals are concerned about the existence of imperfect competition. For them the current reality is an immense concentration of economic power, which is a far cry from Adam Smith's world of competitive markets. Today, in their view, the market economy operates to benefit a few at the expense of the masses. Firms with monopoly power control the economy. They administer prices. They are the invisible hand that guides the economy to their benefit.

The radicals' aversion to the market economy is so strong that they predict its demise as we know it. Indeed, if we look to the Marxist camp, they see capitalism as one step, a necessary step, in the evolution of economic systems. Capitalism is needed to raise the economy out of the chaos of a feudal society. But after capital has been accumulated and a modern economy is developed, the basic inequities and instabilities will bring the market economy to its knees and socialism will emerge. Socialism itself is not the end of the evolutionary process. Socialism will eventually give way to *communism*—where government is nonexistent and everyone works according to their abilities and receives according to their needs. Of course, not all radical reformist economists are Marxist. However, most radicals do share a desire for some form of socialism. Unlike their Marxist colleagues, most do not see socialism as evolving automatically, and they certainly do not see communism emerging at the end of an evolutionary process. Rather, these economists see a need to encourage explicitly the development of some form of socialism for North America. The socialism that results will then be considered the likely end of the evolutionary process.

What would these radical reformists say about the changes taking place in the former Soviet Union and other Eastern European countries? They would argue that these events do not mean the end of socialism; that the changes reflect the abuse of socialist practices and a despotic form of government. As these countries experiment with markets, they will encounter many problems that will lead them back to socialism, but a new, democratic socialism rather than the despotic socialism from which they have emerged.

Before we turn to the next section, we must warn you again to interpret these labels with extreme care. Our categories are not hard and fast. There is much grayness around the edges and little that is black and white in these classifications. This does not mean, however, that there is no value to these classifications. It is important to understand the philosophical background of the individual authors. This background does indeed color and shade their work. This can best be seen by examining several of the issues included in this volume.

However, before discussing a few of the issues, it is useful to repeat several of the themes developed in the preceding section. First, there is much disagreement among economists and others on economic problems. There is, however, rhyme and reason to this disagreement. In large measure, the disagreement stems from various ideologies or basic philosophies that these individuals may espouse. Indeed, the differences that exist between individual economists and groups of economists can be most sharply defined in terms of their respective views of efficiency, equity, and stability; on the relative merits of imperfect competition; and on the place of the market economy in the evolutionary process peculiar to economic systems.

Second, the identification of causes, effects, and cures for economic problems must be undertaken at the practical level. At this level sharp distinctions tend to disappear, and certain individuals may recommend actions that seem inconsistent with their ideology. Here the economist must sacrifice "ideological purity" for practical solutions. The science of economics must deal with real-world problems or it loses its meaning for most people.

THE ISSUES

It is not difficult to identify major problems in the American economy. Each month the news media discuss in detail the newly released statistics that reveal the success or failure of policies designed to reduce inflation and unemployment. It seems that every day some businessperson, some labor leader, some consumer advocate, or some public official releases a new proposal that will remedy pollution, improve the quality and the safety of products or the workplace, reduce unemployment and inflation, or halt and reverse the decay of our cities. Thus, the difficulty in developing this book was not in identifying real and important economic problems or in locating alternative views on those problems. Rather, the difficulty was one of selecting only 18 issues from what, at times, appears to be an endless list of both problems and views on those problems.

We have resolved this difficulty by attempting to provide a broad coverage of the conflicts that society faces. We have provided this generality in three different ways. First, the 18 issues are divided up into 8 micro-economic issues, 6 macroeconomic issues, and 4 issues dealing with international concerns. Second, within these sets of issues, the range of topics is broad. For example, within the macroeconomic set there are issues that represent basic disagreements among economists on specific policy topics, such as the desirability of reforming the current federal taxation of capital gains, as well as broader disagreements that reflect ideological differences, such as the effects of the economic policies under the Reagan administration. The third dimension concerns the ideologies of the views that are presented. The list of authors includes highly regarded academic economists, politicians, journalists, business leaders, and labor leaders. These individuals represent the far Right, the far Left, and many positions in between. Although ideology is sometimes tempered by practical considerations, the basic ideological positions remain apparent.

A summary of several of the issues may serve to indicate the extent of this generality. This discussion will also demonstrate the interplay that exists between basic philosophy and practical considerations in arriving at a real-world solution or position on an economic problem.

One of the macroeconomic issues is: *Is Workfare a Good Substitute for Welfare?* Free-market economists generally believe that the U.S. government has gone too far with its antipoverty programs, and they contend that these programs have become so attractive that people may choose not to work and instead stay at home and receive benefits available under several different welfare and income security programs. The solution to this "economic distortion of incentives" is apparent to the free-market economist: Make the welfare recipients work or prepare for work as a condition of their welfare payments. Thus, they would substitute workfare for welfare. In taking this position, the free-market economists stress individual self-interest. They maintain that the problem with our welfare system is that society has made not working so attractive that it is in the best interests of the poor to drop out and become dependent on those who are hardworking.

Liberal economists, on the other hand, argue that the free-market position oversimplifies the problem. All welfare recipients are not "welfare loafers." Many are children and too young to work. Others are aged and too old to work. Of those who remain, half find jobs and leave welfare after a brief stay in the program. Thus, for the liberal economist, the impact of workfare would be restricted to the 7 percent or so of all welfare recipients who are long-term users of welfare. In the liberal view, the question is whether or not these hard-core welfare recipients, who are often lacking in job skills and deficient academically, can best be motivated by short-term work experiences or comprehensive training programs. They find that the latter is far more expensive in absolute dollars but far more cost-effective in the long run.

Of course, both mainstream critics and radical reformist economists have also taken positions on this issue. The mainstream critics would probably side with the liberals but argue that it might be more appropriate to attack poverty through institutional change rather than through the current maze of antipoverty programs. While institutional changes are being made (such as improving the educational system and increasing labor mobility), it would be better to be too generous than not generous enough, they say. To the radical reformist, the whole question is an example of the inherent contradictions of a market economy. And in a class society, poverty programs are a means by which the dominant class can maintain its position. Radical reformists might even join conservatives in an effort to eliminate poverty programs. However, for the radical reformist, the motivation for opposing these programs is not greater efficiency but the desire to polarize the class struggle and bring the day of revolution ever closer.

Is Choice a Panacea for the Ills of Public Education? is one of eight microeconomic issues. Most Americans are aware of the problems with public education; they are bombarded with news stories of high school graduates who cannot read, of how American students rank last in mathematical and scientific knowledge in comparison with students from other industrialized nations, and of low Scholastic Aptitude Test scores. The question is what to do about the problem.

One alternative is to simply get the government out of the education business. This would be the solution offered by the far Right, by extreme free-market economists. They would argue that there is already a significant private sector that educates American youth, and this sector produces superior students. Moreover, the conservatives would argue that the gains from increased education are basically private—more education means a better job and greater income. Because the gains from education are private, education should be financed privately and not by government. In this fashion the consumers would demand quality education from the producers, and competition would force the producers into supplying quality education.

But this is an extreme position. Less extreme free-market economists and liberal economists believe that there are substantial externalities or spillover effects associated with education. An educated person is more likely to make better political decisions and less likely to engage in criminal activity or became dependent on the welfare system. Moreover, private financing of education is problematic. Unlike financing the purchase of a car or a house, the person consuming education is unable to earn income and pay back the loan while the product is being consumed; the educational loan can only be repaid after the education has been completed. And what if there is a default in loan payments? A car or a house can be repossessed, but what is to be repossessed when someone defaults on an educational loan? For these reasons, liberals and free-market economists believe in public education.

Given widespread support for governmentally funded education, the problem of improving educational outcomes remains. One alternative is to retain the current financing procedures and introduce internal reforms such as competency testing, increased spending, smaller class sizes, increased teacher requirements, decentralized administration, magnet schools, and so on. Another alternative, initially developed by free-market economists but increasingly accepted by liberals, is to introduce more competition among the educational producers, to create competition among schools in order to improve the quality of their product. This could be accomplished by providing students and their parents with a choice as to which schools they will attend. Students and parents would be issued vouchers, which the students and parents would present to the schools of their choice. Few students, of course, would choose to attend an "inferior school," so all schools would strive to produce the highest quality educational product possible. The vouchers would represent the dollar votes of educational consumers, and consumers would not cast their dollar votes for inferior products.

Of course, mainstream critics and radical reformists have their views on this issue as well. The mainstream critics might argue that the current problems in public education are a manifestation of larger social problems. Quality education requires parental involvement, but it also requires a stable home environment. Without changes in these areas, all efforts for education reform will fail. Radical reformist economists would argue that inferior public education and superior private education are the logical consequences of a capitalist economy. That is, only the privileged can afford private education, and by sending their children to private schools where they will obtain superior educations, the privileged parents will assure their children privileged positions in the future. Only a socialist educational reform will generate quality education for all.

One of the international issues deals with economic relations between Japan and the United States: *Is Japan a Threat to America's Economic and National Security?* Again, it is not difficult to document the currency of this issue. Each month, newspapers report the most recent data regarding the United States–Japan trade balance. We see ads for Japanese products in all the media, some even indicating that the Japanese products are made in the United States. News stories of Japan-bashing by Americans and America-bashing by Japanese are often on the front pages and the evening TV news. And, in early 1992, President Bush traveled to Japan in an attempt to get the Japanese to open their domestic markets to American goods.

It is not hard to summarize the views of free-market economists on United States–Japan economic relations. They believe that unrestricted free trade is the best policy; it will generate the greatest amount of well-being for the greatest number of people. So regardless of what the Japanese do in terms of their domestic markets, the United States should not protect American firms from Japanese competition. Such protection would prevent Americans from exercising their economic freedom, force them to pay higher prices for both domestic and foreign goods, and slow down the adjustment of American firms to higher-quality, lower-cost products. Japanese investment in the United States is also beneficial: It creates jobs and provides American workers with greater capital. Japanese protection only hurts Japan, forcing Japanese consumers to pay higher prices for goods. All of these arguments for free trade go back to classical economists Adam Smith and David Ricardo (1772–1823).

Although liberal economists are firm believers in free trade, accepting the concept of comparative advantage first formalized by Ricardo in the early nineteenth century, they are concerned that trade be fair as well as free. They believe that economic conditions can be altered by government action and, thus, comparative advantage can be manipulated by government intervention. Therefore, they feel actions by the American government to "level the playing field" are justified.

There is another difference between free-market and liberal economists in this area. Liberals support government programs designed to assist workers who are displaced by free trade. After all, the larger society gains from free trade and should be willing to use some of these gains to assist, in the interest of equity, those whose lives are disrupted by trade. Free-market economists worry that such assistance may delay the adjustment process and thereby promote inefficiency. This is the reason government activity under the trade assistance legislation was significantly reduced during the free-market Reagan administration.

What are the positions of the mainstream critics and radical reformist economists on this issue? Mainstream critics focus on industrial structure as shaped by an industrial policy. They believe that changes in the American economy, such as a preoccupation with finance rather than with production and an emphasis on the short run rather than on the long run, explain the decline in America's international economic position. They believe that in an era of increasing global integration, each country needs an industrial policy where government targets specific industries for special assistance. The radical reformists see the decline in America's international position as the logical consequence of a capitalist society. Other countries that stress mutual cooperation of government, business, and labor cannot help but outperform countries where segments of society are seen as adversaries. They would add that the United States' preoccupation with maintaining itself as the world's foremost military power has also contributed to America's international economic decline. Thus, because it is a cooperative society and because it has avoided unnecessary military expenditures, it is no surprise that Japan has attained such a lofty position in international economic affairs.

SUMMARY

It is clear that there is no shortage of economic problems. These problems demand solutions. At the same time there is no shortage of proposed solutions. In fact, the problem is often one of oversupply. The 18 issues included in this volume will acquaint you or, more accurately, reacquaint you with some of these problems. And, of course, there are at least two proposed solutions for each problem. Here we hope to provide new insights regarding the alternatives available and the differences and similarities of these alternative remedies.

If this introduction has served its purpose, you will be able to identify common elements in the proposed solutions to the different problems. For example, you will be able to identify the reliance on the forces of the market advocated by free-market economists as the remedy for several economic ills. This introduction should also help you understand why there are at least two proposed solutions for every economic problem: Each group of economists tends to interpret a problem from its own philosophical position and to advance a solution that is grounded in that same philosophical framework.

Our intention, of course, is not to connect persons to one philosophical position or another. We hope instead to generate discussion and promote understanding. To do this, readers must see not only a proposed solution, but they must also be aware of the foundation that supports that solution. With greater understanding, meaningful progress in addressing economic problems can be achieved.

PART 1

Microeconomic Issues

Our lives are profoundly affected by economic decisions made at the microeconomic level. These decisions are made on such diverse questions as those regarding profit motives of business firms, aid to farmers, requirements for national service, rent controls, and choice in public education, among others.

Are Profits the Only Business of
   Business?

Should American Farmers Be Forced to
   Face Market Competition?

Is National Service at Odds With
   American National Interest?

Are Women Paid Less than Men
   Because Their Working Conditions
   Are More Favorable?

Are Rent Controls the Cause of
   America's Homelessness?

Do Hostile Takeovers Harm Society?

Is Mass Transit the Answer to
   Improving U.S. Energy Efficiency?

Is Choice a Panacea for the Ills of
   Public Education?

ISSUE 1

Are Profits the Only Business of Business?

YES: Milton Friedman, from "The Social Responsibility of Business Is to Increase Its Profits," *The New York Times Magazine* (September 13, 1970)

NO: Christopher D. Stone, from "Corporate Accountability in Law and Morals," in Oliver F. Williams and John W. Houck, eds., *The Judeo-Christian Vision and the Modern Corporation* (University of Notre Dame Press, 1982)

ISSUE SUMMARY

YES: Free-market economist Milton Friedman contends that the sole responsibility of business is to increase its profits.
NO: Philosopher Christopher D. Stone insists that the time for corporate social responsibility has come and considerations other than profit making sometimes take precedence in a business.

Every economic society—whether it is a traditional society in Central Africa, a fossilized planned economy such as Cuba's, or a wealthy capitalist society such as those found in North America, Western Europe, or the Pacific Rim—must address the basic economic problem of resource allocation. These societies must determine *what* goods and services they can and will produce, *how* these goods and services will be produced, and *for whom* these goods and services will be produced.

The *what, how,* and *for whom* questions must be answered because of the problem of scarcity. Even if a given society were indescribably rich, it would still confront the problem of scarcity—in the case of a rich society, "relative scarcity." It might have all the resources it needs to produce all the goods and services it would ever want, but it could not produce all these things simultaneously. Thus, even a very rich society must set priorities and produce first those goods and services with the highest priority and postpone the production of those goods and services with lower priorities. If time is of the essence, this society would determine *how* these goods and services should be produced. And since this wealthy society cannot produce all it wants instantly, it must also determine *for whom* the first bundle of goods and services will be produced.

Few, if any, economic societies are indescribably rich. On the other hand, there are many examples of economic societies that face grinding deprivation daily. In these societies and in all the societies that fall between poverty and great affluence, the *what, how,* and *for whom* questions are immediately apparent. Somehow these questions must be answered.

In some societies, such as the Amish communities of North America, the answers to these questions are found in tradition: Sons and daughters follow in their parents' footsteps. Younger generations produce *what* older generations produced before them. The methods of production—the horsedrawn plow, the hand-held scythe, the use of natural fertilizers—remain unchanged; thus, the *how* question is answered in the same way that the *for whom* question is answered—by following historic patterns. In other societies, such as self-sustaining religious communities, there is a different pattern of responses to these questions. In these communities, the "elder" of the community determines *what* will be produced, *how* it will be produced, and *for whom* it will be produced. If there is a well-defined hierarchical system, it is similar to one of the former stereotypical command economies of Eastern Europe.

Although elements of tradition and command are found in the industrialized societies of Western Europe, North America, and Japan, the basic answers to the three questions of resource allocation in these countries are determined by profit. In these economic societies, *what* will be produced is determined by what will yield the greatest profit. Consumers, in their search for maximum satisfaction, will bid for those goods and services that they want most. This consumer action drives the prices of these goods and services up, which, in turn, increases producers' profits. The higher profits attract new firms into the industry and encourage existing firms to increase their output. Thus, profits are the mechanism that ensures consumers get what they want. Similarly, the profit-seeking behavior of business firms determines *how* the goods and services that consumers want will be produced. Since firms attempt to maximize their profits, they select those means of production that are economically most efficient. Lastly, the *for whom* question is also linked to profits. Wherever there is a shortage of goods and services, profits will be high. In the producers' attempts to increase their output, they must attract factors of production (land, labor, and capital) away from other economic activities. This bidding increases factor prices or factor incomes and ensures that these factors will be able to buy goods and services in the open marketplace.

Both Milton Friedman and Christopher D. Stone recognize the merits of a profit-driven economic system. They do not quarrel over the importance of profits. But they do quarrel over whether or not business firms have obligations beyond making profits. Friedman holds that the *only* responsibility of business is to make profits and that anyone who maintains otherwise is "preaching pure and unadulterated socialism." Stone, on the other hand, contends that there are occasions when a corporation should "select a course that voluntarily subordinates profit maximization to the realization of some other value that is not the organization's."

YES   Milton Friedman

THE SOCIAL RESPONSIBILITY OF BUSINESS IS TO INCREASE ITS PROFITS

When I hear businessmen speak eloquently about the "social responsibilities of business in a free-enterprise system," I am reminded of the wonderful line about the Frenchman who discovered at the age of 70 that he had been speaking prose all his life. The businessmen believe that they are defending free enterprise when they declaim that business is not concerned "merely" with profit but also with promoting desirable "social ends; that business has a social conscience" and takes seriously its responsibilities for providing employment, eliminating discrimination, avoiding pollution and whatever else may be the catchwords of the contemporary crop of reformers. In fact they are—or would be if they or anyone else took them seriously—preaching pure and unadulterated socialism. Businessmen who talk this way are unwitting puppets of the intellectual forces that have been undermining the basis of a free society these past decades.

The discussions of the "social responsibilities of business" are notable for their analytical looseness and lack of rigor. What does it mean to say that "business" has responsibilities? Only people can have responsibilities. A corporation is an artificial person and in this sense may have artificial responsibilities, but "business" as a whole cannot be said to have responsibilities, even in this vague sense. The first step toward clarity in examining the doctrine of the social responsibility of business is to ask precisely what it implies for whom.

Presumably, the individuals who are to be responsible are businessmen, which means individual proprietors or corporate executives. Most of the discussion of social responsibility is directed at corporations, so in what follows I shall mostly neglect the individual proprietor and speak of corporate executives.

In a free-enterprise, private-property system, a corporate executive is an employee of the owners of the business. He has direct responsibility to his employers. That responsibility is to conduct the business in accordance with their desires, which generally will be to make as much money as possible while conforming to the basic rules of the society, both those embodied in law and those embodied in ethical custom. Of course, in some cases his employers may have a different objective. A group of persons might establish a corporation for an eleemosynary purpose—for example, a hospital or a school. The manager of such a corporation will not have money profit as his objective but the rendering of certain services.

In either case, the key point is that, in his capacity as a corporate executive, the manager is the agent of the individuals who own the corporation or establish the eleemosynary institution, and his primary responsibility is to them.

Needless to say, this does not mean that it is easy to judge how well he is performing his task. But at least the criterion of performance is straightforward, and the persons among whom a voluntary contractual arrangement exists are clearly defined.

Of course, the corporate executive is also a person in his own right. As a person, he may have many other responsibilities that he recognizes or assumes voluntarily—to his family, his conscience, his feelings of charity, his church, his clubs, his city, his country. He may feel impelled by these responsibilities to devote part of his income to causes he regards as worthy, to refuse to work for particular corporations, even to leave his job, for example, to join his country's armed forces. If we wish, we may refer to some of these responsibilities as "social responsibilities." But in these respects he is acting as a principal, not an agent; he is spending his own money or time or energy, not the money of his employers or the time or energy he has contracted to devote to their purposes. If these are "social responsibilities," they are the social responsibilities of individuals, not of business.

What does it mean to say that the corporate executive has a "social responsibility" in his capacity as businessman? If this statement is not pure rhetoric, it must mean that he is to act in some way that is not in the interest of his employers. For example, that he is to refrain from increasing the price of the product in order to contribute to the social objective of preventing inflation, even though a price increase would be in the best interests of the corporation. Or that he is to make expenditures on reducing pollution beyond the amount that is in the best interests of the corporation or that is required by law in order to contribute to the social objective of improving the environment. Or that, at the expense of corporate profits, he is to hire "hard-core" unemployed instead of better-qualified available workmen to contribute to the social objective of reducing poverty.

In each of these cases, the corporate executive would be spending someone else's money for a general social interest. Insofar as his actions in accord with his "social responsibility" reduce returns to stockholders, he is spending their money. Insofar as his actions raise the price to customers, he is spending the customers' money. Insofar as his actions lower the wages of some employees, he is spending their money.

The stockholders or the customers or the employees could separately spend their own money on the particular action if they wished to do so. The executive is exercising a distinct "social responsibility," rather than serving as an agent of the stockholders or the customers or the employees, only if he spends the money in a different way than they would have spent it.

But if he does this, he is in effect imposing taxes, on the one hand, and deciding how the tax proceeds shall be spent, on the other.

This process raises political questions on two levels: principle and consequences. On the level of political principle, the imposition of taxes and the expenditure of tax proceeds are governmental functions. We have established elaborate constitutional, parliamentary and judicial provisions to control these functions, to assure that taxes are imposed so far as possible in accordance with the preferences and desires of the public—after all, "taxation without representation" was one of the battle cries of the American Revolution. We have a system of checks and balances to separate the legislative function of imposing taxes and enacting expenditures from the executive function of collecting taxes and administering expenditure programs and from the judicial function of mediating disputes and interpreting the law.

Here the businessman—self-selected or appointed directly or indirectly by stockholders—is to be simultaneously legislator, executive and jurist. He is to decide whom to tax by how much and for what purpose, and he is to spend the proceeds—all this guided only by general exhortations from on high to restrain inflation, improve the environment, fight poverty and so on and on.

The whole justification for permitting the corporate executive to be selected by the stockholders is that the executive is an agent serving the interests of his principal. This justification disappears when the corporate executive imposes taxes and spends the proceeds for "social" purposes. He becomes in effect a public employee, a civil servant, even though he remains in name an employee of a private enterprise. On grounds of political principle, it is intolerable that such civil servants—insofar as their actions in the name of social responsibility are real and not just window-dressing—should be selected as they are now. If they are to be civil servants, then they must be selected through a political process. If they are to impose taxes and make expenditures to foster "social" objectives, then political machinery must be set up to guide the assessment of taxes and to determine through a political process the objectives to be served.

This is the basic reason why the doctrine of "social responsibility" involves the acceptance of the socialist view that political mechanisms, not market mechanisms, are the appropriate way to determine the allocation of scarce resources to alternative uses.

On the grounds of consequences, can the corporate executive in fact discharge his alleged "social responsibilities"? On the one hand, suppose he could get away with spending the stockholders' or customers' or employees' money. How is he to know how to spend it? He is told that he must contribute to fighting inflation. How is he to know what action of his will contribute to that end? He is presumably an expert in running his company—in producing a product or selling it or financing it. But nothing about his selection makes him an expert on inflation. Will his holding down the price of his product reduce inflationary pressure? Or, by leaving more spending power in the hands of his customers, simply divert it elsewhere? Or, by forcing him to produce less because of the lower price, will it simply contribute to shortages? Even if he could answer these questions, how much cost is he justified in imposing on his stockholders, customers and employees for this social purpose? What is the appropriate share and what is the appropriate share of others?

And, whether he wants to or not, can he get away with spending his stockholders', customers' or employees' money? Will not the stockholders fire him? (Either the present ones or those who take over when his actions in the name of social responsibility have reduced the corporation's profits and the price of its stock.) His customers and his employees can desert him for other producers and employers less scrupulous in exercising their social responsibilities.

This facet of "social responsibility" doctrine is brought into sharp relief when the doctrine is used to justify wage restraint by trade unions. The conflict of interest is naked and clear when union officials are asked to subordinate the interest of their members to some more general social purpose. If the union officials try to enforce wage restraint, the consequence is likely to be wildcat strikes, rank-and-file revolts and the emergence of strong competitors for their jobs. We thus have the ironic phenomenon that union leaders—at least in the U.S.—have objected to Government interference with the market far more consistently and courageously than have business leaders.

The difficulty of exercising "social responsibility" illustrates, of course, the great virtue of private competitive enterprise—it forces people to be responsible for their own actions and makes it difficult for them to "exploit" other people for either selfish or unselfish purposes. They can do good—but only at their own expense.

Many a reader who has followed the argument this far may be tempted to remonstrate that it is all well and good to speak of government's having the responsibility to impose taxes and determine expenditures for such "social" purposes as controlling pollution or training the hard-core unemployed, but that the problems are too urgent to wait on the slow course of political processes, that the exercise of social responsibility by businessmen is a quicker and surer way to solve pressing current problems.

Aside from the question of fact—I share Adam Smith's skepticism about the benefits that can be expected from "those who affected to trade for the public good"—this argument must be rejected on grounds of principle. What it amounts to is an assertion that those who favor the taxes and expenditures in question have failed to persuade a majority of their fellow citizens to be of like mind and that they are seeking to attain by undemocratic procedures what they cannot attain by democratic procedures. In a free society, it is hard for "good" people to do "good," but that is a small price to pay for making it hard for "evil" people to do "evil," especially since one man's good is another's evil.

I have, for simplicity, concentrated on the special case of the corporate executive, except only for the brief digression on trade unions. But precisely the same argument applies to the newer phenomenon of calling upon stockholders to require corporations to exercise social responsibility (the recent G.M. crusade, for example). In most of these cases, what is in effect involved is some stockholders trying to get other stockholders (or customers or employees) to contribute against their will to "social" causes favored by the activists. Insofar as they succeed, they are again imposing taxes and spending the proceeds.

The situation of the individual proprietor is somewhat different. If he acts to reduce the returns of his enterprise in order to exercise his "social responsibility," he is spending his own money, not someone else's. If he wishes to spend his money on such purposes, that is his right, and I cannot see that there is any objection to his doing so. In the process, he, too, may impose costs on employees and customers. However, because he is far less likely than a large corporation or union to have monopolistic power, any such side effects will tend to be minor.

Of course, in practice the doctrine of social responsibility is frequently a cloak for actions that are justified on other grounds rather than a reason for those actions.

To illustrate, it may well be in the long-run interest of a corporation that is a major employer in a small community to devote resources to providing amenities to that community or to improving its government. That may make it easier to attract desirable employees, it may reduce the wage bill or lessen losses from pilferage and sabotage or have other worthwhile effects. Or it may be that, given the laws about the deductibility of corporate charitable contributions, the stockholders can contribute more to charities they favor by having the corporation make the gift than by doing it themselves, since they can in that way contribute an amount that would otherwise have been paid as corporate taxes.

In each of these—and many similar—cases, there is a strong temptation to rationalize these actions as an exercise of "social responsibility." In the present climate of opinion, with its widespread aversion to "capitalism," "profits," the "soulless corporation" and so on, this is one way for a corporation to generate goodwill as a by-product of expenditures that are entirely justified in its own self-interest.

It would be inconsistent of me to call on corporate executives to refrain from this hypocritical window-dressing because it harms the foundations of a free society. That would be to call on them to exercise a "social responsibility"! If our institutions, and the attitudes of the public make it in their self-interest to cloak their actions in this way, I cannot summon much indignation to denounce them. At the same time, I can express admiration for those individual proprietors or owners of closely held corporations or stockholders of more broadly held corporations who disdain such tactics as approaching fraud.

Whether blameworthy or not, the use of the cloak of social responsibility, and the nonsense spoken in its name by influential and prestigious businessmen, does clearly harm the foundations of a free society. I have been impressed time and again by the schizophrenic character of many businessmen. They are capable of being extremely far-sighted and clear-headed in matters that are internal to their businesses. They are incredibly short-sighted and muddle-headed in matters that are outside their businesses but affect the possible survival of business in general. This short-sightedness is strikingly exemplified in the calls from many businessmen for wage and price guidelines or controls or incomes policies. There is nothing that could do more in a brief period to destroy a market system and replace it by a centrally controlled system than effective governmental control of prices and wages.

The short-sightedness is also exemplified in speeches by businessmen on social responsibility. This may gain them kudos in the short run. But it helps to strengthen the already too prevalent view that the pursuit of profits is wicked and immoral and must be curbed and controlled by external forces. Once this view is adopted, the external forces that curb the market will not be the social consciences, however highly developed, of the pontificating executives; it will be the iron fist of Government bureaucrats. Here, as with price and wage controls, businessmen seem to me to reveal a suicidal impulse.

The political principle that underlies the market mechanism is unanimity. In an ideal free market resting on private property, no individual can coerce any other, all cooperation is voluntary, all parties to such cooperation benefit or they need not participate. There are no "social" values, no "social" responsibilities in any sense other than the shared values and responsibilities of individuals. Society is a collection of individuals and of the various groups they voluntarily form.

The political principle that underlies the political mechanism is conformity. The individual must serve a more general social interest—whether that be determined by a church or a dictator or a majority. The individual may have a vote and a say in what is to be done, but if he is overruled, he must conform. It is appropriate for some to require others to contribute to a general social purpose whether they wish to or not.

Unfortunately, unanimity is not always feasible. There are some respects in which conformity appears unavoidable, so I do not see how one can avoid the use of the political mechanism altogether.

But the doctrine of "social responsibility" taken seriously would extend the scope of the political mechanism to every human activity. It does not differ in philosophy from the most explicitly collectivist doctrine. It differs only by professing to believe that collectivist ends can be attained without collectivist means. That is why, in my book "Capitalism and Freedom," I have called it a "fundamentally subversive doctrine" in a free society, and have said that in such a society, "there is one and only one social responsibility of business—to use its resources and engage in activities designed to increase its profits so long as it stays within the rules of the game, which is to say, engages in open and free competition without deception or fraud."

NO

Christopher D. Stone

CORPORATE ACCOUNTABILITY IN LAW AND MORALS

During the past decade, along with a perceived growth in corporate power and the increased publicity given to corporate misconduct, there has been renewed interest in corporate social responsibility as an antidote. Indeed, to say that corporations should be socially responsible sounds at once so laudable and so limp that the notion has won broad support from both leaders within the corporate community and critics hammering from without. Corporate social responsibility is something we need, something whose "time has come"—but no one is being especially clear as to what it *is*. Exactly what are socially responsible corporations supposed to do, and why?

Certainly, in the space of these remarks, a complete and satisfactory set of answers is not forthcoming. But I hope to provide a few basic observations that are precise enough to steer the debate in a more productive direction. Specifically, I set out with an attempt to define the grounds under dispute: where do the proponents and opponents of corporate social responsibility agree, and where are they at odds? . . .

I. THE PROFITS POSITION VS. VOLUNTARISM

Some of the confusion in the corporate-social-responsibility literature begins with its choice of the term itself. To say that one is advocating "corporate social responsibility" is highly misleading, if it suggests that those who disagree favor corporations being irresponsible, in the sense of indifferent to the satisfaction of human wants. In truth, there probably exists, between the two camps—those who favor and those who oppose the talk about corporate social responsibility—some differences as to what each would regard as the ideal society. But I suspect that the differences between them are less significant than the common bonds. Both groups want to see a productive and sober use of society's resources. Neither wants to see people going around unfed, much less poisoned by toxic wastes. Hence, the basic dividing line is not over ends, but means. Those who demur to "corporate

From Christopher D. Stone, "Corporate Accountability in Law and Morals," in Oliver F. Williams and John W. Houck, eds., *The Judeo-Christian Vision and the Modern Corporation* (University of Notre Dame Press, 1982). Copyright © 1982 by University of Notre Dame Press. Reprinted by permission. Some notes omitted.

social responsibility" believe by and large, that corporations are most likely to satisfy human wants when they are seeking profits within the bounds of collectively agreed-upon constraints in the form of legal rules. By contrast, the "responsibility" advocates believe that the social welfare requires corporate managers to give some consideration to social-moral concerns that are not adequately captured in the profits-law signals.

In order not to "load" the issue in favor of the proponents, I will temporarily[1] drop the term "responsibility," and divide the contending camps into advocates of the *profits position*, and advocates of *voluntarism*. The issue can be put as follows: Is society generally better off if corporate managers decide among alternative courses of action on the basis of which choice promises to be most profitable? or should they, in certain defined circumstances, select a course that voluntarily subordinates profit maximization to the realization of some other value that is not the organization's? It is the first of these positions that I term the profits position; the second is what I shall call voluntarism. . . .

One reason why the distinction between the profits position and voluntarism is not more clearly drawn in the literature is that it is so often unclearly drawn in practice. In many situations in which the corporate managers, scanning the unknowable future, decide a concrete case, several alternatives will hold equal promise of yielding the most profit (or providing the corporation whatever else it may be seeking to maximize). Of course, it would be easy to argue that at least in these cases, in which the managers face an array of alternatives equally promising from the perspective of profits, they ought to select from the group that

choice which ranks best from some moral perspective. However, I do not want to be diverted by this set of cases (although it may possibly turn out to be a large and significant group), because to get at the fundamental issue, we have to postulate situations in which the conflict between the profits position and voluntarism appears clear-cut.

Making the conflict clear-cut is not easy, however, even in an illustration. Part of the problem stems from the fact that what is "morally" the right thing to do—considering the things the voluntarist wants the manager to account for—often comes out the same as "good business" considered simply from the vantage of profits. Consider, for example, a company that is considering "pulling up stakes" from the community that has been dependent upon it for many years, without giving warning, in order to head off community countermeasures. Obviously, the decision can be seen to raise considerations not only of ethics, but of profits, inasmuch as the proposed action has an adverse effect on profits—through loss of goodwill, jeopardization of government contracts, increase in wage costs necessary to retain employees in a firm with a "bad name," and so on. However, there is a firm conceptual distinction that we have to keep in mind. If the company looks to the unfavorable public reaction *as evidence of strongly held moral values*, and decides against the action *on those grounds*, we would be justified in labeling its decision voluntarist. If, on the other hand, it considers the unfavorable publicity only through the lens of, and to the extent of, *the impact on corporate profits*, to be weighed in the balance with the moving vans and all the other costs of the move out of town, then the company's decision would be animated not by voluntarism, but by the profits position, as we are employing the term.

Let us proceed to examine the theoretical foundation for each view: first, for the profits position, then—by way of rejoinder—for the voluntarist.

II. THE CASE FOR THE PROFITS POSITION

Voluntarism has broad appeal. For no one—perhaps the new breed of business executives coming out of the management schools, in particular—likes to believe that there is nothing to their job beyond making money. In fact, however, the case for the managers to set their sights on profits, and therefore benefit the entire society, has considerably broader appeal than most of the corporate responsibility advocates—both in and out of business—generally acknowledge. In fact, the case for the profits position has in its favor three arguments, all with—and this has to be emphasized—strong moral appeal. Each of these arguments would seem to place the burden of rebuttal on the voluntarists.

(1) *The Market Argument.* First, the voluntarists have to account for the presumptive capacity of the market both to produce and to allocate resources in a way that is morally superior to alternative social arrangements. In general, businesses make profits, or fail, in proportion to how adequately the goods and services they provide benefit society. This is not a presumption that is rebutted by showing—what I assume to be obvious to everyone—that the pursuit of profits leads to "excesses" that most of us oppose. For the issue that divides the advocates of the profits position from the voluntarists is one of selecting alternative *systems*. The profits defender may

respond that, whatever the failings of profits-oriented managerialism, voluntarism, established as a general principle of managerial orientation, would engender more "evil"—less social product, and less equitable distributions of what is produced. The managers, the way this point is ordinarily put, are trained to manage businesses. They are neither social accountants, nor politically accountable.

(2) *The Law "Corrections."* But the profits position need not stand or fall upon the much-vaunted, and often exaggerated virtues of "the market system" per se. Even the most diehard "market" advocate recognizes the need for occasional political action to keep certain abuses in check. If, under prevailing market conditions, a certain course of corporate conduct that society collectively disapproves of turns out to be profitable, society can "correct" the market signals through law. Consider, for example, a firm that finds it profitable—under pure market conditions—to dump its toxic wastes into the handiest marsh. If this state of affairs is widely disapproved of, society can make the firm civilly liable for all the damages its wastes cause. The conduct having been made that much less profitable by the prospects of damage suits, the company is induced to respond by installing pollution-abatement devices, or by redesigning its production processes so that the wastes are recycled. If, even in the face of this level of "correction," the pollution continues in an amount society deems "still too much," a second and even third level of "corrections"—in the form of punitive damages and criminal fines—can be superimposed on the civil damages.[2]

The point is that there is a politically legitimate response to undesired corporate conduct which does not involve uprooting the managers from their orientation to profits. If the course of conduct that the market makes profitable is the "wrong" one, the law is available to make the course of conduct less profitable, in proportion to society's aversion to it. In this manner, the corporate managers do not have to weigh independently the costs and values of different courses of conduct. ("Is *this* much pollution, at *these* costs, more valuable than *this* level of pharmaceutical production, at *these* costs?") That weighing process is left to society, through the agreed-upon, democratic decision procedures.

(3) *The Promissory-Agency Argument.* Third, the voluntarists have to account for the managers' obligation to their shareholders as an independent basis for the profits position. Here, the argument is not that social welfare, as such, obligates the managers to pursue profits, but that their principal obligations are to the shareholders, who are presumed to prefer profits. This argument is ordinarily garbed in the language of "agency," which is something of a misstatement, since in some technical legal sense, the directors are not the pure "agents" of the shareholders.[3] And certainly there is no express promise to maximize profits running from the managers to the shareholders. Indeed, shareholders do not typically buy their shares directly from the corporation, through the managers, at all; most shareholders have purchased their shares from prior stockholders through impersonal market transactions in which nothing is said but "buy" and "sell."

Nonetheless, a colorable, if not quite so rigorous, argument can be made to the same effect, based on an implied promise in the circumstances, fortified by rightful expectancies and reliance. The "top" managers of the corporation, the directors, are elected by the shareholders. The shareholders have come, through tradition, to expect the managers to resolve ambiguities on their behalf. These expectancies have even found sanction in the rules of fiduciary duties, which recognize the priority of the investors' claims. And, in purchasing their shares, the investors have, in anticipation of the superiority of their claims, paid more for their shares than they would have otherwise. Thus, while a strong, literal agency-promise basis of obligation is missing, a case remains that the shareholders have a moral right to expect the managers to give their interests preference.

In summary of the profits position, the voluntarist has a hard row to hoe. He must be prepared to identify circumstances in which the corporation ought to subordinate profit maximization to the advancement of some exogenous value in the face of (1) the presumptive capacity of market signals to express collective desires, (2) the presumptive capacity of society to "correct" for any defects in these market signals by providing appropriate liability rules, and (3) the not unreasonable preference that the managers, at the least, resolve any lingering ambiguities in favor of the investors.

III. THE COUNTERARGUMENTS OF THE VOLUNTARISTS

In my view, none of the arguments is adequate to displace the need for the corporation to take into account values exogenous to the corporation's "self-interest." Let me take up the third argument—the promissory/agency argument—first.

Even if we were prepared to infer from the circumstances that the managers made a constructive "promise" to the shareholders to give priority to their claims, the inference would hardly settle the issue. As a moral matter (which is what we are discussing here), the practice of making promises provides for the justifiable breaking of them in certain circumstances. It is sometimes morally justifiable to break promises in the furtherance of higher social and moral interests. Hence, promises—or the assumption of an agency role—can advance moral arguments, by way of creating prima facie cases in favor of conduct, but few of us believe that a promise or agency, per se, can put an end to moral discussion. Moreover, promises always have to be interpreted; we have to decide what a promise *means*, before we even reach the question of whether to *follow it*. Thus, even if managers were to make—as I observed they do not—an express promise to their shareholders to "maximize your profits," I am not persuaded that the ordinary investor would interpret it to mean "maximize *in every way you can possibly get away with*, even if that means polluting the environment, breaking the law if you will not get caught," etc. Nor if there *were* a promise that could be interpreted as such a commitment, would I lightly suppose there to be a moral argument that it must be kept.

In the last analysis, the strength of the profits position turns not on the promissory-agency claims, but on a combination of the first two arguments. Indeed, the issue over which the profits supporter and the voluntarist divide is one of the most fundamental in any society; the *ability* and *desirability* of law as a means of organizing human conduct. The profits position comes down to a strong—but I think overly strong—preference for law as the way to "correct,"

i.e., restrict the incidence of, profitable, but undesired behavior. The voluntarist wants to allow for, even to foster, alternative self-imposed constraints. It is largely because I, although a lawyer, harbor misgivings about our society's increasing reliance on law, that my own sympathies are divided.

Why might one harbor misgivings about law as a control device? First, as to the *abilities* of the law to transmit the desired signals to corporate managers, there are several serious drawbacks. There are, to begin with, the problems of what I call information gap and time lag. To illustrate, the first clues as to the existence of some corporate-connected hazards will often reach corporate managers before they reach, and can be acted upon by, the authoritative lawmaking bodies. For example, scientists in a company's laboratory are likely to suspect, and be able to evaluate, the dangers that some new product poses, long before governmental agencies get wind of them. In these circumstances, there would seem to be a strong case for the managers, at the least, to notify the appropriate agencies so as to set the lawmaking machinery in motion. Observe that such a moral obligation seems defensible whether or not the disclosure is the most profitable course for the managers to pursue, and even if the supplying of the data is not required by law. One can also imagine extending the argument to maintain not only that the managers should notify lawmakers, but that they should hold some particularly hazardous courses of action in abeyance until the legislative process has had a reasonable time to react. In other words, one might well take the basic presumption of the profits position—that anything profitable goes until the law says clearly "no"—and reverse it in some circumstances: one does not hazard some things (destruction of the ozone layer) unless and until the law clearly says "yes."

Moreover, it seems weak to argue that the corporation's obligations do not extend beyond *obeying* the law, when corporations are exerting so much influence on the laws that they are subject to. The voluntarist may be concerned to affect corporate behavior in the lawmaking process. The profits advocate is tempted to respond that the lawmaking context need present no exception to his general formula. After all, the participation of corporations in lawmaking can be made subject to its own laws—of lobbying, political contributions, and so on: let corporations maximize profits within *those laws*.

But this response has several defects. To begin with, it is somewhat circular, inasmuch as the political participation laws about corporate lobbying, and so on, are themselves subject to corporate influence. Moreover, even if the legislature were willing to enact tough restrictions on corporate political speech, it is not free to do so. Any legal constraints that touch on participation in the lawmaking process are themselves subject to superior constitutional restrictions, i.e., the First Amendment's guarantees of free speech, and the right to petition the government. As a consequence, even if we assume, for purposes of argument, that the law can provide a relatively acceptable response to abuses of commercial advertising for which First Amendment restrictions are less stringently applicable,[4] the law cannot—and ought not—be as restrictive when the corporation is engaged in political participation. When the corporation is acting as citizen, and not touting its products, we are committed to deal with it less through law, and

more through trust. In this context, the case can be made that the managers are committed, reciprocally, to react in kind: to exercise self-restraint that is in some measure *voluntary;* to bring into the legislative and administrative process their own grievances about "overregulation," and their own expertise—surely; but in doing so, to temper pure profit seeking with some measure of civic responsibility.

A further inadequacy of law (hence, a further toehold for voluntarism) is apparent when we shift from a consideration of features of lawmaking (above), to features of corporations as targets of the law. There are special reasons to doubt the adequacy of law when corporations are its target. Most obviously, some of the sanctions that society deems appropriate penalties for truly heinous wrongdoing, such as imprisonment and the death penalty, are simply unavailable when the corporation is the law's quarry. Other skepticism stems from the fact that the incentives of "the corporation"— which the law typically threatens—are distinct both from those of the managers, on the one hand, and the shareholders, on the other. The salaries of the managers are likely to be relatively unscathed by fines and damage awards that fall on the corporation.

The defect in law reliance vis-à-vis the shareholders is a consequence of limited liability. Suppose, for example, a company engaged in making toxic substances. The law's sanctions—the civil- and criminal-liability rules aimed at the corporation—may pose a threat to the corporate coffers of, say, $100 million, if the company recklessly skimps on safety measures with the result that communities are endangered. But if the catastrophe happens, and the penalties are invoked, the losses will be so severe that the company will fail. In this event, the shareholders—those who stand behind the firm—are, by virtue of limited liability, immune from personal judgment. Hence, in many of the most threatening situations, the law's threats are hollow: no one will have to pick up the tab.

Thus there is considerable reason to doubt that the law can provide a complete and reliable set of rules for constraining corporate misconduct. Something more is needed.

Not only is the profit position insensitive to the limits of the law as an *effective* constraint on corporate misconduct, it makes questionable assumptions about the *desirability* of law as a control device. That is, even if (contrary to the assumptions above) the legislators were adequately informed and competent, the legislative process was unaffected by corporate influence, the rules of limited liability were not in question, and so on, there would be lingering reasons to search for some other control techniques.

It must be kept in mind that there are a number of techniques by which social behavior is constrained; the law is only one of them, sometimes reinforcing, sometimes supplementing, other, less authoritative social constraints. If we turn to ordinary human conduct, for example, we find it continuously being given direction and hedged by customs, manners, mores, and so on. All these "looser" controls derive their source of authority not from the threat of the state's force, but through the internalized dynamics associated with feelings of shame, guilt, anxiety about the censure of others. Indeed, when it comes to ordinary mortals, these dynamics shoulder the largest brunt of social control: we rely on people acting *responsibly*. We would certainly think it odd for anyone to suggest that people ought to do whatever their id impulses tell them to do, within the bounds of what the law specifically condemns. The burden would seem to be on the profits advocate to tell us why it should be otherwise with corporations.

This, I think, is the central burden that the profits advocates have failed even to acknowledge. And it is not an easy burden to meet. . . .

It often appears, too, that the further the law goes in laying down precise "bright-line" standards of permissible and impermissible conduct, the more it may tempt people to press their behavior to the very bounds of what is allowed. Clear legal rules may induce more unwanted activity than no rules at all.[5] Indeed, we might say that the most serious "costs" of a law-ridden society involve the toll such reliance exacts from its citizens, measured in moral timbre. One thinks of the Confucians' objection to the codification of laws: "A litigious spirit awakes, invoking the letter of the law, and trusting that actions will not fall under its provisions.[6]

I cannot trace out how each of these infirmities may serve to shift some of our reliance on law to a reliance on morals and manners. But let me give an illustration to suggest some of the connections. Let us suppose that a majority of voters today would prefer that people do not smoke in public places. Yet, in recent referendums, the voters have consistently refused to ban smoking in public places by law. In my view, it would be a mistake to interpret these refusals to ban smoking as a vote in favor of letting anyone who wants to smoke do so whenever and wherever they want to. On the contrary, I suspect that what is being expressed is a preference *against* law, a decision to relegate the matter of smoking control to a complex social code of morals and manners. The minority who want to smoke are allowed to smoke so far as the law is concerned. But underneath, control is being relegated to a network of conventions. These include "mandates" that, before lighting up, the smoker look around to see if others are smoking; he is not to smoke if no one else is doing so; he is to make an inquiry of his neighbors to measure the intensity of feelings in the circumstances ("do you mind if I smoke?"); he is to adjust, flexibly, by finding a table as far away from nonsmokers as possible, or ideally situated, considering air circulation. Thus certain adjudicatory responsibilities fall, not on the judge, but on the maître d'.

In this context, more people may smoke, and more may be offended by smoke than otherwise. But notice the savings in enforcement costs and the quality of personal conduct and human interchange that are fostered. And might there not be some value in the fact that nonsmokers can feel that those who are resisting their impulses to smoke are doing so because they *care*, not because the law compels them?

In all events, if we look closely at the smoking example, and the pattern of control based on morals and manners, I think we will find that something is going on that is more complicated than what the term voluntarism suggests, i.e., something more than simply asking the smoker voluntarily to forgo his desire to smoke.

IV. RESPONSIBLE REFLECTION

I want now to argue that the flavor of this something extra *is* best captured by the term responsibility, which, while dropped earlier to avoid "loading" the issue, is therefore appropriate to rein-

troduce at this point. For when we begin to analyze what is going on, one can identify two separate, although related sets of techniques, both of which involve "responsibility" in different senses.

The first sense of responsibility—which I will call R_1—emphasizes following prescribed rules of conduct. It is in this sense that we judge someone "responsible" who follows the law, who abides by the rules—legal and moral—of his social office (as judge, prosecutor, or citizen). The second sense of responsibility—R_2—emphasizes cognitive process, reflection, how one goes about deciding, particularly when no special, clear-cut prescriptions of the R_1 sort are available. That the two senses of responsibility are separable is easy to demonstrate, inasmuch as the same act can, depending upon which sense one employs, be either "responsible" or "irresponsible." For example, a judge in Nazi Germany who carried out the orders of his superiors might be seen as "responsible" in sense R_1—in that he carried out the orders of his superiors, according to rules and the dictates of his office; and yet, we might say of him also that he was "irresponsible" in the sense—R_2—that he inadequately reflected as an autonomous, moral human being. . . .

Let us take, as an example that illustrates the misgivings of the profits supporters, a product safety case. Suppose that the managers of an automobile company are considering a design that will entail 3.4 fatalities from impact on crash per 100 million vehicle miles traveled (the current industry average). If they alter the designs slightly, incorporating a stronger, heavier frame at a cost of $500 per car, the projected fatalities would be reduced by approximately 10 percent, to 3 per 100 million vehicle miles. What guidance can responsible reflection, as I have described it, provide in these circumstances?

To begin with, a moral rule that required the managers, in essence, to put themselves in the place of the consumers would hardly be calculated to yield an unambiguous decision. If, as we are assuming, the decision to add the extra safety costs will reduce profits, there is already some rather good evidence that if the managers were in the consumers' place they would reject the marginal increases in safety at the marginal costs of providing it. True, this probability of what the consumers want does not settle the matter. Thinking about one's responsibilities sometimes produces paternalistic action—that is, sometimes we feel that we are morally obligated to do something in the interest of someone else in disregard of their own preferences, such as a parent or the state sometimes exercises on the behalf of a child. The argument might take the form that if the consumers *really knew,* as vividly and in the detail that our test data indicates— e.g., how much more solidly the proposed design resists impact—they would decide in its favor.

But this is hardly a strong reed to lean on, particularly since we recognize that, in a decision like this, the consumers are not the only other group whose place the managers ought responsibly "to stand in." There are many people other than the consumers who are variously and often conflictingly affected by the decision to strengthen or not to strengthen the car. For example, the increased weight of the car will reduce fuel efficiency. This will translate into an adverse impact not only on consumers; if the managers are to put themselves "in the place of" the society at large, they will have to think about the implications for increased dependency on oil, and for inflation. The new design would also contribute to inflation through increased demand for steel and labor, and consequent higher auto prices. Moreover, the additional coal and steel required to strengthen the cars will exact its toll in injuries among coal workers and steelworkers: how are the managers to feel if they put themselves in the places of these workers, balancing off the effect of increased wages, increased inflation, and increased injuries?

I think that this exercise is significant in reminding us that in many cases a "responsible" corporate decision, even one undertaken in the best of faith, is going to be indecisive, and the presumption for profits, when all is said and done, quite rightly remains. But the example is also, in its way, misleading. Much of what corporate responsibility advocates, such as myself, are seeking is not reducible to a binary decision such as whether to trade off $500 per car for 0.4 lives per 100 million miles traveled. What the responsibility advocates should be concentrating on is a *concern for safety,* and the willingness to design *an ongoing, internal corporate system* that advances safety concerns.

A corporation that consistently and fairly considers safety factors will undoubtedly come up with many possibilities of trade-offs that are, like the example employed above, in a range too ambiguous to overcome the profits presumption. But over time a company that sets up such a system may also discover the possibility of trade-offs that resist casuistry. For example, a company may come up with a lighter, safer, material that can save thousands of lives with virtually no increase in costs. To this, the profits defenders will respond that profit considerations alone will be enough to provide the incentives; "responsibility" is not required to institute such research since "safety sells." But such a response misses an important legal rub. Under present law, the very fact that a company undertakes to give thorough consideration to safety risks may operate to intensify corporate liability, should there be accidents, and encourage law suits seeking to exact criminal and punitive damages. Hence, it may not be *profitable* for a company to give full and responsible consideration to safety; but I would be prepared to argue that—profitable or no—a company should be obligated to press ahead in its safety research beyond the dictates of law-corrected market signals. This is particularly so when we consider that the company is the most efficient investigator of safety problems; it presumably can learn more about the problem and its solution, at less cost, than the rest of us.

Moreover, the auto-safety case we have just examined is not the only paradigm with which the responsibility advocate may be concerned. Many other cases seem to lie beyond the capacity of all but the most diehard profits defenders to complexify. In these situations, it is possible that "responsible" reflection will unearth several defensible decisions. But it is wrong to suppose that, once a multiplicity of defensible outcomes has been identified, we have no choice but to throw up our hands and revert to profits. Any one of the "responsible" outcomes may be clearly preferable to the outcome dictated by profits.

NOTES

1. Later in the text I will restore the term "responsibility" to the debate, but only after I have demonstrated the important sense that responsibility

captures, while terms like "voluntarism" and "altruism" do not.

2. I assume that most opponents of corporate social responsibility would agree that, once some form of conduct has been criminalized by the legislature, the managers ought not to engage in it, even if, though criminal, it remains profitable—either because conviction is unlikely, or because the profits to be made for lawbreaking exceed the penalties. David Engel has argued, however, that the presence of the criminal-liability rule ought not, in and of itself, preclude the corporation from performing the forbidden act, if doing so is profitable. He argues that there are only a few crimes so heinous as to be unacceptable under any circumstances; many fines are like business expenses. Where some form of criminal conduct is not absolutely clearly condemned by strong consensus in all cases, the managers would wrongly arrogate legislative power if they desist from a profitable course of lawbreaking. Suppose for example, a company that from some course of conduct will earn $12,000 and be fined $10,000; the $10,000 fine may represent a collective judgment that the social cost of the unlawful act is, say $2,000 (supposing that the legislature in setting the penalty of $10,000 assumed that the chances of getting caught were 1 in 5). Not to violate the law would be withholding goods or services the society values at $12,000 in exchange for avoiding a $2,000 cost, a course of conduct for which, Engel points out, there is no clear-cut consensus. Engel, "An Approach to Corporate Social Responsibility," *Stanford L. Rev.*, 32 (1979):1.

3. Most significantly, while a true principal is free to discharge his agent at will, the shareholders are subject to a complex body of constraints on recalling the directors from office, between terms of election, without "cause."

4. See *Virginia State Board of Pharmacy v. Virginia Citizens Consumer Council* 425 U.S. 748 (1976), holding that commercial advertising, while not as protected from interference as other forms of speech, is not wholly outside the protection of the First Amendment, either.

5. It is important to remember, however, that when the law gets involved in people's lives, especially where severe criminal penalties are involved, there are moral and constitutional reasons to provide clear rules in the service of "fair warning" and the restricting of governmental abuse.

6. The quote is attributed to Shu Shiang, criticizing the codification of the criminal law on mental cauldrons on the view that "since all crimes cannot be prevented" their Confucian ancestors had "set up the barrier of righteousness (*i*) . . . [and] treated . . . according to just usage (*li*)," quoted in J. Needham, *Science and Civilization in China*, 2 (Cambridge: Cambridge University Press, 1956), 521.

POSTSCRIPT

Are Profits the Only Business of Business?

Friedman dismisses the pleas of those who argue for socially responsible business action on the grounds that these individuals do not understand the role of the corporate executive in modern society. Friedman points out that the executives are responsible to the corporate owners, who expect these executives to do everything in their power to earn the owners a maximum return on their investment. If the corporate executives take a "socially responsible" action that reduces the return on the owners' investment, they have spent the owners' money. This, Friedman maintains, violates the very foundation of the American political-economic system: individual freedom. He believes that no individual should be deprived of his or her property without his or her permission. If the corporate executives wish to take socially responsible actions, they should use their own money; they should not prevent the owners from spending their money on whatever social actions they might wish to support.

Stone challenges Friedman's position directly. In Stone's view, corporations have a responsibility to consider the welfare of society even when there are no explicit laws governing their action. Laws are simply ineffective in controlling corporate conduct that is profitable but harmful to society at large. Stone does not believe that the special relationship that exists between shareholders and managers obligates these managers to maximize profits "in every way you can possibly get away with."

Perhaps no single topic is more fundamental to microeconomics than is the issue of profits. Many pages have been written in defense of profits, such as Milton and Rose Friedman's *Free to Choose: A Personal Statement* (Harcourt Brace Jovanovich, 1980). Other works have also added much to this discussion. A classic reference is Frank H. Knight's *Risk, Uncertainty, and Profits* (Kelly Press, 1921). Friedrich A. Hayek, the author of many journal articles and books, is a guru for many current free marketers. There are a number of other books and articles, however, that are highly critical of the Friedman-Knight-Hayek position, including Christopher D. Stone's *Where the Law Ends: Social Control of Corporate Behavior* (Harper & Row, 1975). Others who challenge the legitimacy of the notion that markets are morally free zones include Thomas Mulligan, "A Critique of Milton Friedman's Essay 'The Social Responsibility of Business Is to Increase Its Profits,' " *Journal of Business Ethics* (1986); Daniel M. Hausman, "Are Markets Morally Free Zones?" *Philosophy and Public Affairs* (Fall 1989); and Andrew Henley, "Economic Orthodoxy and the Free Market System: A Christian Critique," *International Journal of Social Economics* (vol. 14, no. 10, 1987).

ISSUE 2

Should American Farmers Be Forced to Face Market Competition?

YES: Dick Armey, from "Moscow on the Mississippi: America's Soviet-Style Farm Policy," *Policy Review* (Winter 1990)

NO: Andrew Larkin, from "Ethics, Economics, and Agricultural Policy: Considerations for the 1990 Farm Bill," *Journal of Economic Issues* (June 1990)

ISSUE SUMMARY

YES: Former economics professor and current congressman Dick Armey (R-Texas) asserts that government farm programs are costly, reduce productivity, decrease competitiveness, and only hurt those they are intended to help.

NO: Economics professor Andrew Larkin argues that lawmakers need to radically rethink U.S. farm policy so as to address the consequences of low farm prices and high farm costs that cause both farmers and the environment to suffer.

Agriculture, a highly competitive sector of the economy, is particularly susceptible to wide swings in profitability. When times are good, profits are very good, but when times are bad, profits are very bad. This vulnerability can be traced to two factors that are ultimately related to the nature of competitive markets. First, if market prices fall, small producers who are already operating on tight budgets because of debt obligations respond out of desperation by increasing supply. They do not bring less to the market; they bring more. However, these acts of desperation drive market prices down further. Second, although the majority of farmers have little or no control over the prices at which they sell their products, the goods and services they must buy from the nonagricultural community often come from firms that do have monopoly power. (The petrochemical industry, the farm implement industry, and the money markets are hardly "competitive" in a textbook sense.) Over time, the profits the farmers receive for their output are much lower than the prices they must pay for their inputs. The net result is that the farmers' relative income falls.

This phenomenon is exaggerated during periods of recession. Indeed, during the Great Depression of the 1930s, the disparity between farm income and nonfarm income became so great that the United States inaugurated its first farm price support program: the Agricultural Adjustment Act of 1933. This legislation, based on the concept of *parity* (the notion that the value of farm output be maintained relative to the value of nonfarm output), became the mainstay of U.S. agricultural policy in the 1930s, 1940s, and 1950s. In short, this policy was designed to protect the small family farm by reducing the supply of agricultural commodities that found their way to the marketplace. This reduced supply and increased agricultural prices, which increased incomes in the agricultural community.

During the 1960s and 1970s, agricultural policy was refocused. The opening of world markets and the presence of poor harvests in many parts of the world meant that the demand for U.S.–produced food and fiber were at all-time high levels. As a result, public policy shifted toward improving the operation of agricultural markets and reducing the cost of producing agricultural products, rather than supporting agricultural prices.

In the early 1980s, farmers were buffeted by a number of events that were largely beyond their control. First, the economy was gripped by "stagflation" (inflation that occurs while the economy is hardly growing or having a recession). The prices of inputs (nonagricultural products) that farmers had to buy skyrocketed, while at the same time the domestic demand for agricultural products slackened. Second, the monetary authority dramatically raised interest rates. In the agricultural sector—which is dependent upon loans to pay for its seed, fertilizer, and equipment—this represented a major financial blow. Third, the bubble burst on agricultural land speculations. In the face of a very deep recession, land prices leveled off and began to fall. Since farmers are land-intensive, the value of their major asset seemed to disappear before their eyes. Lastly, world demand for U.S.–produced food and fiber fell sharply. This was the result of a world recession, bumper crops throughout the world, and U.S. grain embargoes, which were imposed for political purposes. The net result was falling agricultural prices and incomes.

By the latter half of the 1980s the U.S. economy had not only survived the recession of 1981–82, but it also experienced the longest peacetime prosperity in its history. Unfortunately, this general prosperity was not enjoyed by most in the agricultural community. Federal agriculture subsidies rose to roughly $25 billion a year, yet in spite of this—or perhaps because of this—farmers, particularly small farmers, faced bankruptcy proceedings at rates unmatched since the Great Depression. Given the weak economy at the beginning of the 1990s, there seems to be no market relief in sight.

In the following selections, Dick Armey argues that the free operation of markets coupled with direct welfare payments to displaced farmers would solve the U.S. farm problem. Andrew Larkin asserts that lawmakers should look to "providing sufficient farm income, reducing socio-psychological stress, maintaining community, providing healthful nutrition, and preserving environmental quality" when they draft new legislation.

YES

Dick Armey

MOSCOW ON THE MISSISSIPPI: AMERICA'S SOVIET-STYLE FARM POLICY

Even as perestroika comes to the Communist world, our own federal farm programs remain as American monuments to the folly of central planning. Through subsidies, price supports, import barriers, and countless regulations, the Department of Agriculture continues to try to manage half of U.S. farming, with the predictable result of staggering waste and inefficiency of almost Soviet proportions. If we have reached the end of history with the vindication of the free economy, the USDA has not yet heard the word.

Fifty years ago, when the Roosevelt administration announced certain "temporary emergency measures," farm programs were highly controversial. Something about paying farmers *not* to farm, as many of the programs did, struck the public as ludicrous. Even Henry Wallace, the Agriculture Secretary who conceived the idea, remarked, "I hope we shall never have to resort to it again. To destroy a standing crop goes against the soundest instinct of human nature." The USDA has been resorting to it ever since.

Under the current farm law, passed in 1985, the Department of Agriculture has paid dairy farmers to kill 1.6 million cows and take five-year vacations from farming. It has enforced regulations that have led to the squandering of 3 billion oranges, 2 billion lemons, and hundreds of millions of pounds of nuts and raisins. It has rewarded crop farmers for leaving idle 61 million acres of farmland—an area equal to all the territory of Ohio and Indiana, and half of Illinois. For these dubious contributions to American competitiveness, the USDA has charged the taxpayers about $20 billion a year and forced consumers to pay $10 billion a year in higher food costs.

As James Bovard has recently written in *The Farm Fiasco*:

> Farm subsidies are the equivalent of giving every full-time subsidized farmer two new Mercedes Benz automobiles each year. Annual subsidies for each dairy cow in the United States exceed the per capita income for half the population of the world. With the $260 billion that the government and consumers have spent

on farm subsidies since 1980, Uncle Sam could have bought every farm, barn, and tractor in 33 states. The average American head of household worked almost one week a year in 1986 and 1987 simply to pay for welfare for fewer than a million farmers.

Farm programs are unrivaled for their sheet economic absurdity, and they are fertile ground for serious spending reductions. Sadly, however, they are being neglected by key policymakers—even as the new farm bill comes under consideration on Capitol Hill.

FIVE-YEAR PLANS

Our farm economy is governed by a series of five-year plans. (Surely Stalin would appreciate the irony.) The last five-year farm bill, which has cost over $100 billion to date, was signed by President Reagan in 1985. The next, which will guide farm spending through 1995, is now being considered by Congress.

Although the Reagan administration failed to terminate or privatize many deserving government programs, it at least restructured the major entitlements, saving billions of dollars in the long run. Cost controls were imposed on Medicare, the huge military and civil service pension programs were completely reorganized, and even Social Security benefits were trimmed in the reform of 1983. Virtually the only major program to escape is agriculture, which remains a stubborn pocket of resistance in the Reagan Revolution.

In fact, the cost of farm programs has exploded under the Republicans. As recently as 1980, farm price supports cost the taxpayers only about $3 billion. By 1986, they had skyrocketed to an unprecedented $25 billion, making farm pro-

grams the fastest growing part of the federal budget during the Reagan years, dwarfing the percentage increases of defense and health care. The farm sector was practically a free market economy when Jimmy Carter was president.

Today, farm programs are so generous and distort markets so severely that even the most self-reliant farmer has little choice but to sign up. In 1982, when farm programs were mushrooming, only one in five Indiana corn farmers signed up for federal benefits. David Rapp of *Congressional Quarterly* explains, "In Indiana, taking money from the federal government was a sign of poor farm management or, worse, socialistic political tendencies." By 1987, however, half the corn farmers in the state had joined the programs. Nationally, the amount of corn-growing land covered by federal programs jumped from 30 to 90 percent between 1982 and 1987. "It's almost to a point where it's mandatory for a farmer to be in the program," an Indiana banker says. . . .

PENNIES FROM WILLIE NELSON

. . . In 1985, farm programs had become a "cause" on a level with the Nuclear Freeze. Cissy Spacek and Jessica Lange testified before Congress to share the insights on agricultural policy they had gained while starring in Hollywood movies about farming. Country singer Willie Nelson held a Farm Aid concert, which collected a few million dollars for farmers above the $26 billion that Congress would soon be sending them. In the general hysteria of a "crisis on the farm," conservatives and liberals alike scrutinized the farm bill. But, as of this writing, the media has not yet discovered a new farm crisis to draw attention to the coming debate this year.

More important, the farm lobby is now using, with some effect, the breathtaking argument that farm programs are actually *contributing* to deficit reduction. They point out that this year's price support spending of $12 billion represents a decline from the $26 billion we spent in the record-shattering year of 1986 (which, of course, says more about spending in 1986 than it does about spending today).

When the 1981 farm bill came before Congress, the USDA said it would cost $12 billion over four years. It actually cost $60 billion. When the 1985 farm bill came to the floor, the USDA said it would cost $52 billion over five years. It has already cost more than $100 billion. Any recent reduction in farm spending is thus only a partial reduction of a spectacular cost overrun—a cost overrun larger than the gross national product of several countries. To fail to reform the USDA after such monumental prodigality would be comparable to making Deborah Gore Dean the new Secretary of HUD.

HOMEGROWN INDUSTRIAL POLICY

The farm lobby's most important advantage is that few people understand its programs. As one farmer told *Insight* magazine, "Sitting here on the farm and knowing the money being spent on farm programs, I think if people understood it more and knew they were paying that kind of price, there'd be an uprising." Even the eyes of otherwise well-informed policymakers glaze over at terms like "nonrecourse loans," "base acreage," and "deficiency payments." They tend to leave farm policy to the farm lobby

and legislators from farm states. While the Armed Services Committee has its Pat Schroeder and Ron Dellums, there are no fundamental critics of farm subsidies on the Agricultural Committees.

This is unfortunate. For all their apparent complexity, the general idea behind the biggest of the farm programs is simple. Basically, they work like this:

First, the government spends hundreds of millions of dollars to raise farm incomes by raising the prices of certain farm commodities. This has the effect of encouraging farmers to produce those commodities in large amounts, while encouraging customers (like those in our overseas export markets) to buy them in small amounts. Soon a massive surplus occurs. Then the government spends hundreds of millions of dollars to encourage farmers to stop producing them.

By analogy, suppose Congress decided that American cars should be sold for at least $15,000 apiece. Even though a Ford Escort might sell for half that on the open market, Congress might argue that making cars is expensive and the Great American Autoworker deserves to be adequately rewarded for his labors. So it passes a bill, and the government announces that, henceforth, no car will sell for a nickel less than that target price—even if the government has to buy them itself.

There is gaiety in Detroit. Suddenly, everyone wants to be in the car business. New factories open, old ones are expanded, some that were going to produce other things continue producing autos instead. Cars begin rolling off the assembly line by the thousands, then the tens of thousands.

But then something completely unexpected happens. A huge surplus of American cars mysteriously appears.

Foreign sales vanish, domestic sales drop. There aren't enough people willing to pay $15,000 for Ford Escorts. Baffled, government bureaucrats find themselves having to buy more and more. Soon government parking garages are overflowing. For a time, the crisis is eased when the government gives some of the extra cars to Zimbabwe under the "Drive for Peace" program. Others are given to poor people and students through the welfare system. But these measures are inadequate.

Eventually, the government hits upon a solution. Stop guaranteeing a $15,000 sticker price for cars? Not at all. Instead, the government decides to pay Detroit to shut down its factories (at which point there is gaiety in Tokyo).

THE OPEC SCHOOL OF FARMING

The largest farm programs apply to wheat, corn, rice, cotton, and a few other crops. The prices on these commodities are artificially supported by various government policies. For example, the government may make a loan to farmers, based on a loan rate set by Congress. If the farmer can sell his crop for more than the loan amount, he does so, and returns the government's money. But if he cannot, he can keep the loan money and give the government his crop instead. In effect, the farmer is guaranteed that he can sell his crop at the government's price. The problem is that Congress sets that price above market level.

This leads to massive surpluses. At that point, the government buys the surplus and tries to distribute it through the welfare system, foreign aid, or other programs, and begins paying farmers not to farm in a frantic effort to reduce production. The government manages farms like a man trying to drive a car by putting his feet on the accelerator and the brake at the same time.

Other farm programs hike prices and cut production in other ways. Under the dairy program, local dairy cooperatives are allowed to form government-protected monopolies. Because there is no competition, people have no choice but to buy milk at high prices—which is a good arrangement for the big cooperatives, but a bad arrangement for parents who buy milk for their children. The resulting dairy surpluses have been reduced by the government's paying dairy farmers to slaughter or export their cows and leave dairy farming for five years. (Can anyone imagine the government paying automakers to destroy *or export* their machines? And then not to work for five years?)

Similar rules, called marketing orders, allow a few large California orange growers to decide how many California oranges may be released to the market. By forcing that state's orange growers to withhold as much as two-thirds of their crops (and watch them rot), the large producers can set the price for the rest of their fruits at a high level. If a small producer defies the large growers and tries to sell his oranges at a lower price, he is prosecuted by the federal government. This is great for Sunkist, bad for everyone else. One grower merely tried to give away his oranges to a church helping the needy, and the USDA threatened to sue him for it. In effect, the government is the enforcer of a cartel—a miniature OPEC for oranges.

DEPORTING OUR FARMLAND

"Supply control" policies—paying farmers not to farm—epitomize the attitude, prevalent throughout the USDA and the Agriculture Committees in Congress, that farm productivity is a problem rather than a national asset. In the 1985 Farm Bill and in other legislation, Congress has given the USDA a number of weapons to use against farmers who are too productive. The Acreage Reduction Program is typical. A farmer is told that if he wants to receive federal farm benefits, he must first agree to take a percentage of his land out of production. It is not uncommon for a wheat farmer, for instance, to be told to leave a quarter of his land idle.

There is also a "paid land diversion" program, in which a farmer simply receives a check from the government for idling acres; a conservation program, in which he is paid to take erosion-prone land out of production (as if he cannot himself see the wisdom in preserving his land); and a new "0/92" program in which he can get up to 92 percent of his federal benefits if he agrees not to plant anything at all.

Like any central planning effort, whether in the Soviet Union or the American Corn Belt, all supply-control policies are riddled with irrationalities and unintended consequences. Even though the USDA has one bureaucrat for every six full-time farmers, fine-tuning the farm economy is a difficult task.

While the set-asides are supposed to be good for farmers, they inadvertently devastate the rural businesses that depend on farming, and end up hurting almost as many people as they are intended to help. Just as a government policy that would pay automakers not to make cars would hurt the glass, steel, and rubber industries, paying farmers not to farm hurts everyone from the fertilizer companies to the tractor dealers. According to the USDA's own figures,

payments to farmers to idle acreage cost the economy 300,000 potential jobs and $4 billion in lost sales for the "farm input" industry in 1987.

Then there is unfair competition. Under the Dairy Termination program, the government's final solution to the "problem" of milk productivity, dairy farmers were paid to slaughter their cows and take five-year vacations. It apparently never occurred to the USDA or Congress that this might have an effect on the ranchers who raise beef cattle. It did. When the government announced that it was going to have a million dairy cows killed, everyone realized that the market would soon be inundated with tons of additional meat. The market instantly collapsed, and cattlemen lost $25 million in the first week alone.

The government typically behaves as if its many different policies were conceived by different groups of people who never talk to each other. At the same time one part of the government is spending billions of dollars to encourage farmers to take their land out of production, another is spending billions more (and wasting precious water resources) to irrigate new farmland in the Southwest. While the government is paying some dairy farmers to take a vacation from farming for five years, it is giving cheap loans to others farmers to expand their operations. Our farm programs are at war with themselves.

For all their contradictions and unintended consequences, however, supply controls ultimately represent a calculated government effort to lower the productivity of one of our largest industries. Telling farmers to idle their land is like telling factory managers to operate their plants far below full capacity. It is tremendously inefficient, and the consequences are predictable. While U.S. farmers are being directed by the government to take their land out of production, farmers in Canada, Australia, Argentina, and Europe have been eagerly planting. As the USDA has paid U.S. farmers to idle 61 million acres, foreigners have planted 70 million new acres since 1980. In effect, the USDA deported our farmland.

The problem at the root of farm programs is this: While a sound economy should produce an abundance of goods that can then be sold at a low price, our farm programs are designed to create a scarcity of goods that can then be sold at a high price. Having a "surplus" of corn does not mean that farmers produce too much corn, only that they produce more corn than can be sold at the government-inflated price. Farm productivity is good, so long as the market is permitted to function. If the government did not artificially inflate the price of corn and wheat, efficient U.S. farmers could plant fencerow to fencerow and dominate global markets. If high production then forced the price of corn and wheat very low—which wouldn't be the worst thing that could happen in a hungry world—then some farmers would switch to growing crops that people need more. And some farmers might even leave farming.

LATTER-DAY LUDDITES

This last possibility—that even a single farmer might quit farming—haunts some farm legislators. The guiding spirit of much of our farm policy seems to be a desire to freeze the farm economy in time—to stop all change, prevent all in-novations, scorn all efficiencies—out of a fear that somebody in the farming business might have to switch jobs. In 1985, the House Agriculture Committee even voted to outlaw an automatic egg-breaking machine, "The Egg King," because it would hurt egg producers who package powdered eggs for the armed services cafeterias. More recently, a milk producers' lobby opposed the use of a hormone that would vastly increase the production of milk. As we move into the competitive 1990s, one of America's largest industries is being run by latter-day Luddites.

Many believe that farming is a uniquely uncertain business because of the weather. Without some government cushions in the form of price supports and other programs, no farmer according to this argument could survive the vagaries of the farm marketplace.

But how would the farmer fare without farm programs? Contrary to popular misconception, almost half of U.S. farmers grow crops that receive no federal price supports. Anything from meat to vegetables to specialty crops are produced by farmers operating in a free or nearly free economy. The bankruptcy rate of those farmers has actually been lower than the bankruptcy rate of farmers "benefiting" from federal programs. If potatoes can be grown without federal help, corn can as well.

The fluctuations in the market caused by the USDA's inept attempts at central planning have caused the modern farmer more grief than Mother Nature ever has. Any cattleman who was nearly bankrupted when the USDA and Congress had a whim to pay for the slaughter of a million cows can tell us much about the vagaries of the marketplace.

In a number of ways, federal programs hurt the farmers they are intended to benefit. For example, federal crop subsidies raise the value of farmland, which is good for the landowners, but almost half of American farmers rent their own land. When the government raises the value of the land, their rents rise.

The Farm Credit System provides cheap, subsidized loans to farmers who are uncreditworthy and cannot receive loans elsewhere. This means that farmers who saved their money and managed their farms wisely have to compete against those who have been bailed out by the government. It also means that inept farmers are encouraged by the government to stay in farming longer than many of them should. Rather than move to town after a few bad years, the cheap federal money encourages them to stay on the farm until they have lost everything. Then the government forecloses on them.

The family farm might flourish in the absence of farm programs. The current subsidy system compels farmers to concentrate on maximizing their yields rather than on minimizing their costs. This gives an advantage to large, heavily mechanized farms over smaller, family operations. Wealthy farmers can afford the huge combines that allow them to outproduce small farmers and even buy them out. Without price supports, however, the advantage would shift to small operations with low production costs and free labor—the family farm. As Dennis Avery, an analyst with the Hudson Institute, has written: "Federal farm programs have led to an overcapitalization of agriculture with less actual employment that what it would otherwise have." Contrary to the fears of the Agriculture Committees, without farm programs, we might have *more* farmers than we do today.

WORLD CHAMPION LOG ROLLERS

The farm lobby cannot prevail through its numbers alone. According to Bernal Green and Thomas Carlin, two economists with the USDA, while no one expects farming to be a dominant industry in large metropolitan areas, "it's surprising to find that farming isn't all that important to most of the nation's rural counties either." They estimate that only 46 of the 435 congressional districts are farm oriented.

Like the labor unions, however, farm groups have used political organizing skill to amplify their power far beyond their numbers. First, differences between the various groups are minimized. Although the dairy farmers have different interests than do the sugar producers, for example, they tend to support each other's claims before Congress. They are champion logrollers. David Nagle, a Democrat from Iowa, took the floor last fall and referred quite explicitly to a deal farm state legislators had cut with the maritime unions. In return for congressmen from farm states supporting "cargo preference requirements" (sort of a "ship-American" rule), the maritime interests agreed to support the farm programs. As Nagle explained it:

> Had we been forced to rely on our own farm state votes, none of those [agriculture] programs would have been enacted. Our numbers are small and getting smaller. So—back in 1985—we farm state members sat down with other groups facing the same problem and reached an agreement on the proper scope of the cargo preference requirements.

Nevertheless, the strength of the farm bloc may be overrated. As recently as 1980 the farm economy was relatively free of intrusive farm programs. The dairy program could have been terminated in 1985 had it not been for the general "farm crisis" hysteria that year. The House voted to abolish both the sugar and honey programs in 1981 (although they still survived).

AN AGENDA FOR PERESTROIKA

As we continue the farm debate this spring, there are several initiatives that should be considered in Congress. While major reforms are unlikely without the active involvement of the administration, public discussion of many points could cause the farm lobby some healthy discomfiture and cast farm programs in their proper light. The policies we consider should:

• **Shift from price supports to welfare for farmers.** If the goal of our farm programs is to help needy farmers, we should do so directly with welfare payments rather than with the complex and costly system of price supports. Agricultural economist Clifton B. Luttrell estimates that such a welfare policy would cost $4 billion a year at most, far less than the $12 billion the USDA is now spending.

• **Repeal all marketing orders.** The semi-feudal regulations that prohibit free Americans from selling oranges in California without the approval of Sunkist are perhaps the most offensive element of our farm programs in principle. Current law prohibits the Office of Management and Budget from even studying them. Marketing orders should be repealed.

• **Terminate the dairy program.** This is the program in which farmers were paid to kill their cows and take five-year vacations from farming so that parents can pay higher prices for milk at the grocery store. It should not exist.

• **Stop paying farmers not to farm.** The average man on the street does not want the USDA to pay farmers not to farm. It is an affront to common sense, an insult to farmers, and an attack on American competitiveness. An amendment should be attached to this year's farm bill repealing the USDA's authority to reward farmers for idling their land.

When I was an economics professor, I liked to tell my students about Armey's Axiom No. 1: "The market is rational; the government is dumb." Farm programs are replete with examples that validate that principle. In the stench of billions of rotting oranges, the spectacle of a million slaughtered cows, and the stillness of 61 million acres of idled farmland, one can discern the fundamental truth: The free market works and central planning does not.

NO

Andrew Larkin

ETHICS, ECONOMICS, AND AGRICULTURAL POLICY: CONSIDERATIONS FOR THE 1990 FARM BILL

> When the market place is made the main idea, it diminishes other values, leads to a degrading of personal independence, social bonds, virtue, and patriotism—for those qualities cannot thrive in an unbridled culture of acquisition, which the mentality of market maximization leads to. . . . When pushed to the extreme as we have pushed it, that market mentality becomes seriously destabilizing to rural communities. It produces a perpetually crisis-ridden farm economy. Worse, it embitters people because it cannot deliver what it says it will: a general contentment and happiness.
>
> —Donald Worster[1]

This article attempts to bridge several disciplines, especially ethics, ecology, politics, and economics, in an effort to improve the agricultural sector of the economy and the rural sector of society. Because of the numerous and important consequences of economic decisions and government economic policy, it is not surprising that economists would be called upon to include ethical standards in their investigations and activities. Many other professions and areas of inquiry in the human, social, and environmental disciplines have developed ethical components. Recent examples include medical ethics and bioethics. Colleges now offer courses in business and journalistic ethics: law students are required to take courses in legal ethics. Social workers and anthropologists are also expected to take into consideration ethical concerns. All do so because of the consequences of their actions, and the consequences of economic decisions are no less important.

The particular theme of this article is that because of the importance of economic policies, the economics (and other) profession(s) should provide ethical perspectives on the agricultural policy of the United States; reliance

From Andrew Larkin, "Ethics, Economics, and Agricultural Policy: Considerations for the 1990 Farm Bill," *Journal of Economic Issues*, vol. 24, no. 2 (June 1990). Copyright © 1990 by the Association for Evolutionary Economics. Reprinted by permission.

on the *laissez faire* of the past is no longer feasible. To counteract arguments against ethical considerations, the article briefly investigates the controversy about positive and normative science and introduces the instrumentalist perspective. But the main purpose here is to provide an overview of combined ethical and institutionalist considerations for farm policy. This task will be divided into two segments: (1) rural equity and livelihood and (2) rural environmental quality.

INSTRUMENTALISM AND THE POSITIVE-NORMATIVE DICHOTOMY

A major obstacle to incorporating an ethical perspective in economics is the positive-normative dichotomy, which claims that genuine science is strictly separate from considerations of values. The concern is that values will bias scientific investigation, resulting in incorrect and detrimental outcomes. That concern is genuine with regard to narrow personal attitudes, but it is shortsighted with regard to broader social values. Even the most positivistic of economists must acknowledge their affirmation and incorporation of such values as efficiency, individual choice, competition, and balance.[2]

Much has already been written by evolutionary economists and instrumental philosophers (such as John Dewey and C. E. Ayres) on the topic of values and the positive-normative dichotomy. Some of the major tenets of instrumentalism are (1) fact and value are not separate, but are intricately interrelated; (2) judgment is by consequences, with science and technology determining the value of the consequences; and (3) the divisions among the sciences are misleading: science is a community activity.

John Dewey's writings are especially useful for clarifying notions of fact and value. For Dewey, science is value-laden and values are empirical and scientific topics. It is empirically accurate to assert that human behavior is influenced and controlled by considerations of good and bad and right and wrong.[3] . . . In short, economics cannot be concerned about means without being concerned about ends.[4] In particular, economic policy cannot be concerned about the one without being concerned about the other.

For the instrumentalist, the divisions among scientific disciplines are also mistaken and misleading. Instead, social inquiry should be a seamless whole that encompasses politics and economics, sociology and ecology, values, ethics, and morality, to name a few. That any of these might exist separately would preclude instrumental outcomes and effective policy. In effect, then, economics is valuation, as C. E. Ayres wrote.[5] Throughout its history, economics has been concerned with questions of morality—both ethical questions, such as how people relate to each other in important matters, and political questions, such as the nature of the good society. But as the neoclassical branch of the discipline has risen in power, its spokespersons have asserted that values should be excluded from economic inquiry, meanwhile seemingly ignoring their own values, such as efficiency and choice. Instrumentalists, though, do not let those positivist assertions impede attempts to incorporate every instrumental value into the discipline, and not just a few.

The claims of this article, then, are twofold: (1) there are overriding values for economics, not just efficiency, competition, and choice, but others, such as freedom, justice, equity, livelihood, community, nutrition, health, environmental quality, and sustainability[6] and (2) these values are equally important and compelling. This article makes no claim that any one (or more) of these values is paramount. However, because high levels of efficiency, output, and productivity have been attained by agriculture in the United States, and because other factors are more critical at this time, this article emphasizes the environmental and the livelihood aspects of farming—that is, providing sufficient farm income, reducing socio-psychological stress, maintaining community, providing healthful nutrition, and preserving environmental quality. It is the position of this article that not just efficiency but the latter values as well should be included in agricultural policy and in the research agenda of institutionalist economists.

For the instrumentalist, the ultimate concern of economic inquiry is solving socioeconomic problems in accord with instrumental values. Problems that are systemic in nature, such as those in the rural sector, require system-wide correction, which is available through responsible government action. The primary instrument for government amelioration of agricultural problems in the United States is farm policy legislation. Because problems in the agricultural and rural sectors are not the result of individual mistakes or low productivity but of systemwide attitudes and practices, correction must originate with government policy and must provide incentives, preferably positive, for people to conform to instrumental values. Instrumental values must be applied to agricultural policy in order to move food production "from what is to what ought to be."[7]

FARM POLICY CONSIDERATIONS: RURAL EQUITY

Since the origins of farm policy legislation in the 1930s, the federal government has attempted in numerous ways to increase the income of farm families. Assuring adequate income for farm families makes special moral sense now in light of comparable worth, that is, the remuneration of work according to its importance, difficulty, danger, and so on. In order to raise farm incomes, various devices have been suggested or attempted to raise agricultural prices either by increasing demand or by decreasing farm supplies. However, neither demand measures nor supply controls are completely adequate for correcting the unacceptable inequity of farming.

Among the demand measures available are (1) various means of providing purchasing power to those unable to purchase farm products, (2) expanding farm markets into foreign countries, and (3) developing new uses for farm products. Programs such as food stamps, WIC, and school breakfasts and lunches should be maintained for the sake of their beneficiaries, but it would be better to institute comprehensive policies to improve the livelihoods of low-income people so that they would not need governmental assistance. Providing low cost or free food to other countries risks undermining those countries' agricultural sectors and can only be used with caution. Demand for agricultural products could be increased by converting farm products to alcohol and selling the alcohol as a fuel; however, the income from alcohol fuel is more likely to accrue to fuel producers than to farmers. Still, government policy should include subsidies or tax incentives for alcohol fuel, at least for the sake of reduced vehicular pollution.

Measures to control agricultural supplies are not effective in raising prices because reducing supply does not increase farm prices when those farm prices are well above "market equilibrium." Farm supplies would have to be reduced so low as to verge on shortage in order to cause farm price increases, and those prices would be well below the minimum needed to sustain farm families. Under the usual conditions of more than adequate supplies, farm prices are mostly determined by corporate administered pricing. For the sake of overall social welfare, farm product prices should continue to be stabilized at low levels for consumers, while farm costs (machines, chemicals, borrowed funds, and so on) should also be kept low by legislating price controls to enable farm families to achieve adequate net incomes. Controls will not be easily enacted or enforced, but that is not an instrumental argument against such controls.

For the sake both of farm families and rural communities, it is necessary to stabilize and raise net farm income to arrest the decline in the number of farm families. If rural communities are preserved, the farm bill also becomes an urban welfare bill by reducing migration into urban areas and by rendering less necessary the construction of new urban infrastructure and the expansion of urban services. In order to maintain rural communities, government subsidies must be distributed more toward the smaller family farms, and must not be awarded to absentee corporate owners. Subsidies have been among the rewards of large-scale farming and absentee ownership at the expense of both family farming and rural communities. Tax structures, too,

should begin to redress the imbalance of benefits to large farms over small.[8] Finally, for the benefit of improved farm incomes, farm policy should also discourage reliance on expensive inputs, such as petrochemicals and large machines, in order to reduce farm costs as well as to reduce agricultural impact on the biophysical environment.

This is not to claim that stabilizing net farm income at a more equitable level will resolve all rural problems, nor that reducing the migration from farms will solve all the problems of rural communities. A farm policy act should also encourage local product diversification. In the upper midwest, for example, this might mean more fruit and vegetable crops, which would have the additional benefit of reducing the community's reliance on chemically contaminated imports. In addition, farm and rural policy should encourage other forms of rural development, such as food processing, health and educational facilities, resorts and tourism, light manufacturing, and other imaginative and useful activities.

An important consideration in farm policy is the need to make available healthful, nutritious food. The overall nutritional quality of foods is being lessened, mostly in the processing phases, while harmful contaminants are being added to the typical diet.[9] Problems that are attributable to the farm sector itself, such as pesticides applied to produce, result at least in part from the desire of farmers to maximize net farm income. For the sake of the general social welfare, national farm policy should assert the responsibility of all economic components of the food chain to increase, rather than decrease, the nutrition and wholesomeness of food. Agricultural policy should support and encourage the rising popularity of organic farming in order to reduce the chemical contamination of food and the environment as well as to reduce the costs of agriculture, enabling more families to farm.

FARM POLICY CONSIDERATIONS: ENVIRONMENTAL QUALITY

Farm policy must also contain many new provisions for restoring and protecting the biophysical environment, especially because topsoil erosion and contamination threaten to reduce food production. Contour farming may not have to be mandated, but funds should be made available to assist in the construction of terraces, greenways, and ponds. The few remaining wetlands need to be preserved, and efforts made to restore drained wetlands as well. Arid and semi-arid lands also need protection. At this time, with surplus production, it is appropriate to remove fragile land from agricultural use, but to do so will require government funding. The excess use of pesticides and heavy machinery can be discouraged by reducing the tax and subsidy incentives that accrue to larger farms. Stabilizing net farm income is a first step in enabling farmers to afford environmentally benign practices. But farmers have practiced environmental neglect for so long that it has become habitual, requiring legislation against harmful practices.

The land ethic introduced by Aldo Leopold should be adopted and applied.[10] Leopold is important for clarifying our ideas about our relationships with the biophysical environment. He observed that ethics originate in the tendency of people and groups to evolve modes of cooperation or symbioses: "All ethics so far evolved rest upon a single premise: that the individual is a member of a community of interdependent parts. . . . The land ethic simply enlarges the boundaries of the community to include soils, waters, plants, and animals."[11] Leopold's argument was that ethical consciousness has developed through a series of stages, beginning with relations among people, proceeding through relations between the person and society, but not yet arriving at the third stage, relations between people and the land.

The purpose of a land ethic is to affirm the right of natural components of the biophysical environment to exist in their natural state. One way to do that is to give natural objects legal standing—that is, to recognize them in courts of law, which would require prior legislation. Rights have already been extended to other non-human objects such as corporations and municipalities. According to Kristin Shrader-Frechette, an environmental philosopher, rights of natural objects would mean that legal actions could be instituted on their behalf, injuries to them could be recognized, and natural objects could serve as beneficiaries when damages are proved and relief is provided.[12] Both Leopold and Shrader-Frechette realize that conservation of these components of nature are essential for the survival of human life, but they also recognize rights of natural objects for their own sakes.

Especially important at this time is the conservation of topsoil, which, in the United States, is being eroded faster than it is naturally rejuvenated. Also important is the protection of ground and surface waters from petrochemical contaminants, eroded topsoil, feedlot runoffs, and so on. Wildlife habitat must also be preserved and restored, for the sake of animals and plants and as wilderness with varied functions. In short, ecosystems themselves have rights to existence.

Animal rights are also worthy of consideration at this time.[13] Although the animal rights movement now involves only a small portion of society, it is strong and can be expected to become more influential in the future. (It has effectively discouraged Raïssa Gorbachev from wearing a fur coat while visiting the United States.) Many people already observe animal rights by not inflicting unnecessary pain on animals, but the movement urges more than that. It has opposed, for example, certain types of trapping and the use of animals for testing cosmetics. Some have become concerned about the confinement of livestock, such as cattle, pigs, and poultry, in small pens and overcrowded buildings. A new farm bill should begin to address such concerns in order to ease the transition, perhaps by providing financial incentives to end unnecessary practices.

CONCLUDING COMMENTS

This article has been based on the premise that income stress and obsolete attitudes in the rural sector have resulted in inequitable impacts on farm families and rural communities and in damage to the biophysical environment. Low net farm income is not attributable to low productivity (U.S. farmers are among the most productive in human history), but is systemic, caused by low farm prices and high farm costs. It is the conclusion of this article that corrective measures must be introduced through an effective farm policy act. It is also a conclusion of this article that more extensive research into the ethical impacts of farm policy should be conducted. Specifically, the next farm bill should include a provision that government-sponsored agricultural research must devote 2 to 5 percent of the funding to research into the ethical implications of agricultural policy. From now on, agricultural policy should be designed not only to increase the efficiency and productivity of agriculture, but also to improve rural lives, rural communities, consumer diets, and the impact on the biophysical environment.

NOTES

1. Donald Worster, "Good Farming and the Public Good" in *Meeting the Expectations of the Land: Essays in Sustainable Agriculture and Stewardship*, ed. Wes Jackson, Wendell Berry, and Bruce Colman (San Francisco: North Point Press, 1984), p. 35.

2. See Marc R. Tool, "The Social Value Theory of Neoclassical Orthodoxy: A Review and Critique" and "The Competitive Model as Value Premise" in his *Essays in Social Value Theory: A Neoinstitutionalist Contribution* (Armonk, N.Y.: M. E. Sharpe, 1986), pp. 87–125.

3. John Dewey, *Theory of Valuation* (Chicago: University of Chicago Press, 1939), pp. 3 and 58.

4. Further insights about instrumental value theory can be found in recent writings by Marc R. Tool and Steven R. Hickerson. See Marc R. Tool, "A Social Value Theory in Neo-Institutional Economics" in his *Essays in Social Value Theory: A Neoinstitutionalist Contribution*, pp. 33–54 and Steven R. Hickerson, "Instrumental Valuation: The Normative Compass of Institutional Economics," *Journal of Economic Issues* 21 (September 1987): 1117–43.

5. C. E. Ayres, *The Theory of Economic Progress: A Study of the Fundamentals of Economic Development and Cultural Change*, 2d ed. (New York: Schocken Books, 1962), p. 85.

6. See Jerry L. Petr, "The Nature and Necessity of the Mixed Economy," *Journal of Economic Issues* 21 (December 1987): 1445–67.

7. Marc R. Tool, "The Neoinstitutionalist Perspective in Political Economy" in his *Essays in Social Value Theory: A Neoinstitutionalist Contribution* (Armonk, N.Y.: M. E. Sharpe, 1986), p. 9.

8. Carol D. Petersen, William Shear, and Charles L. Vehorn, "Cash Accounting Rules for Farmers: Differential Benefits and Federal Costs," *Journal of Economic Issues* 21 (June 1987): 639–47.

9. See Louis J. Junker, "Nutrition and Economy: Some Observations on Diet and Disease in the American Food Power System," *Review of Institutional Thought* 2 (December 1982): 27–58.

10. Aldo Leopold, *A Sand County Almanac* (New York: Ballantine Books, 1966 [1949], esp. pp. 237–64.

11. Ibid., p. 239.

12. K. S. Shrader-Frechette, "Ethics and the Rights of Natural Objects" in her book, *Environmental Ethics* (Pacific Grove, Calif.: The Boxwood Press, 1981), pp. 82–83 and 89–99.

13. See, for example, Peter Singer, "Animal Liberation" in K. S. Shrader-Frechette, *Environmental Ethics* (Pacific Grove, Calif.: The Boxwood Press, 1981), pp. 103–12.

POSTSCRIPT

Should American Farmers Be Forced to Face Market Competition?

This issue provides a stark comparison of the policy prescriptions of a free-market economist and an institutionalist. For the former, future policy should witness a disengagement of government from the agricultural marketplace. Farmers should be forced to compete. The strong, efficient farms will survive and the weak, inefficient farms will be driven out of the market. The farms that remain can then provide low-cost agricultural products to the market. The farmers who are weeded out can be provided direct welfare payments that are paid for by eliminating farm supports.

Larkin rejects the premise upon which Armey builds his case: the notion that economic efficiency considerations should drive U.S. farm policy. Larkin argues that economics and economic policy are not value free. Indeed, he maintains that focusing upon efficiency is itself a value decision.

The side you take partially depends upon the faith you place in markets. If the United States is to reap the benefits of competition, it should be able to do so in the agricultural sector of the economy. This sector, above all other sectors of the vast U.S. economy, best characterizes a competitive marketplace. There is competition among large numbers, the products produced by farmers are generally homogeneous, and there is a reasonable degree of freedom for entry and exit. Yet economists who are sympathetic with Larkin remind us that as small farmers are forced to leave the industry, the average size of a farm must increase. They also note that there is a growing number of farms that are vertically integrated. These corporate agribusinesses provide their own seed and fertilizers, process their agricultural products, and market them by brand names. The presence of these agribusinesses creates differentiated products and raises entry and exit costs.

Whether you place a greater or a lesser significance on the changes that have occurred in the farming community in the past may also help to determine which side you support. Your library is filled with books and articles that discuss both sides. To trace the progress made by the 1990 farm bill and later proposed agricultural legislations, look for articles written by David S. Cloud in the *Congressional Quarterly Weekly Report*. Two articles that support Larkin's concerns are Harold F. Breimyer, "New Farm Law Saves More Dollars But Less Soil," *Challenge* (May/June 1991), and Barbara A. Meister, "Analysis of Federal Farm Policy Using Social Fabric Matrix," *Journal of Economic Issues* (March 1990). Two articles that share Armey's perspective are Doug Bandow, "America's Permanent Dependent Class," *Policy Review* (Spring 1987), and James Bovard, "Lost in the American Agricultural Swamp," *Economic Affairs* (December/January 1990–91).

ISSUE 3

Is National Service at Odds With American National Interest?

YES: Doug Bandow, from "National Service: Unnecessary and Un-American," *Orbis: A Journal of World Affairs* (Summer 1990)

NO: Charles Moskos, from "Rebuttal: Necessary and American," *Orbis: A Journal of World Affairs* (Summer 1990)

ISSUE SUMMARY

YES: Doug Bandow, a former special assistant to President Reagan, argues that the Nunn-McCurdy proposal on national service represents an objectionable intrusion of the state into the affairs of individual members of society—an intrusion that will weaken our future military preparedness.
NO: Professor of sociology Charles Moskos, who advises the conservative-leaning Democratic Leadership Conference, characterizes this proposal as "bold legislation" and "a GI Bill without the GI."

In the spring of 1989, eight separate national service bills were introduced before Congress by such legislators as Senator Claiborne Pell (D-Rhode Island), Senator Barbara A. Milkulski (D-Maryland), Representative Morris K. Udall (D-Arizona), Representative Leon E. Panetta (D-California), Senator Edward M. Kennedy (D-Massachusetts), and Senator Dale Bumpers (D-Arkansas). Of these bills, none was more important than the Citizenship and National Service Act that was introduced by Senator Sam Nunn (D-Georgia) and Representative David McCurdy (D-Oklahoma) and whose merits are debated in this issue.

All of these proposals, to a greater or lesser extent, are patterned after the immensely popular "GI Bill" that was made available to veterans of World War II. (GI is an informal term used to describe a member or former member of the military—particularly enlisted members. It came into general usage during World War II and originally was an abbreviation for galvanized iron, but it was also taken as an abbreviation for government issue.) Members of the military who served during the war were given the opportunity to attend colleges, universities, or other training facilities after they were discharged from service. They were provided a tuition grant plus a living allowance. This program generated tens of thousands of first-generation college graduates, and the United States has reaped benefits from the human capital created by this public policy.

The Nunn-McCurdy Plan, like the GI Bill, would provide vouchers that could be used to offset the expenses of a college education. This plan, however, broadens the coverage in several ways. In addition to using the vouchers to cover the cost of a college education, the vouchers could be used as a down payment on a home. Secondly, participants could earn their vouchers in military service or in civilian service. That is, a participant would be required to engage in one or two years of full-time civilian service or two years active plus six years reserve service in the military. While in national service, the participant would earn a nominal income of $100 per week, which would include health insurance.

For fiscal year 1989, 6 million students in the United States received federal aid totaling approximately $9 billion. The Nunn-McCurdy bill directly challenges the premise of the existing system of educational grants and subsidized loans that are currently in place. This system is designed to provide equal access for all citizens to postsecondary educational opportunities with a minimum number of restrictions or conditions. The new system would explicitly tell high school graduates that if they want a college education paid for by society, then they have to serve society. After a five-year phase-in period, education grants-in-aid would be conditional on national service.

The Bush administration took steps in the direction of implementing a program of national service by creating the White House Office on National Service, which was given the responsibility of initiating a program called Youth Engaged in Service to America.

The bills introduced in Congress and presidential initiatives are signals that national priorities may be changing. But should they? Should the federal government tie government financial support for higher education to national service? It appears that policymakers in the executive and congressional branches of government support this as a wise decision. However, others, including many in the education community, even if they support the positive aims and good intentions of this legislation, are concerned that the proposed legislation will undermine the national commitment to equal educational opportunities.

In the following selections, Doug Bandow and Charles Moskos discuss the problems and strengths of national service legislation. In assessing the merits or lack thereof of national service for young people, you might also want to see if you can relate what you may have already learned in your economics course about the operations of the labor market and about human capital theory to this debate.

YES

Doug Bandow

NATIONAL SERVICE: UNNECESSARY AND UN-AMERICAN

The U.S. government inaugurated an All-Volunteer Force (AVF) in 1973, despite the skepticism of the Pentagon and many in Congress. After almost two decades, it has proven its success by providing an above average group of young Americans to fill the military's ranks. In fact, despite some problems in the late 1970s, the AVF is now delivering a higher quality force than ever was acquired through conscription. . . .

CRITICISMS OF THE ALL-VOLUNTEER FORCE

Though the idea of freedom has attenuated greatly in America over the past 150 years, a majority of Americans probably still associate national service only with military service. Consequently, military service remains a key selling point of national service proposals, and criticism of the AVF therefore remains a leading basis for proposing national service.

Typically, four charges are levelled against the AVF: that the annual cohort of volunteers is not large enough; not smart enough; not representative of America; and not idealistic. Let us consider each argument in turn.

Not enough volunteers. The first criticism says that the AVF cannot withstand the coming of the "baby bust" generation. Since 1979, the pool of eighteen-year-olds has been shrinking and it will continue to do so until 1992. Moreover, the number of eighteen- to twenty-four-year-olds will decline throughout the 1990s. The DLC [Democratic Leadership Council] and its allies believe that these demographic changes present the United States with a crisis requiring dramatic action.

Demographics, though, are not decisive. The eighteen-year-old cohort peaked in 1979; yet that was the last year the services failed to meet their objectives. By the end of the 1980s, the Pentagon had endured more than two-thirds of the total expected population drop (which will end in 1992), all the while meeting its goals and increasing the quality of its recruits. As for the shrinking eighteen- to twenty-four-year-old pool, the Pentagon estimates

From Doug Bandow, "National Service: Unnecessary and Un-American," *Orbis: A Journal of World Affairs* (Summer 1990). Copyright © 1990 by The Foreign Policy Research Institute. Reprinted by permission. Notes omitted.

that there will be more than 7.3 million males eligible to serve in 1996, of whom the Pentagon will need to recruit only 5 percent.

Moreover, these estimates, made barely three years ago, are now out of date. Events in the Soviet Union and Eastern Europe are almost certain to reduce sharply the size of the military. In November 1989, the services drafted plans to cut overall manpower levels by 250,000, more than one-tenth of the force. The army, the most personnel-intensive service, proposed dropping three of eighteen active-duty divisions and reducing the number of reserve divisions from ten to nine. The result would be to slash 135,000 of 769,000 active duty soldiers, roughly 18 percent of its force. Only two months later, in January 1990, Defense Secretary Richard Cheney announced that the Pentagon expected to dismantle not four but five of its twenty-eight active and reserve army divisions.

Not smart enough. The AVF, it is said, does not attract enough qualified volunteers to handle the military's increasingly complex weapons. This charge is hard to sustain. Reviewing everything from family background to educational aspirations to SAT scores suggests that the military is attracting high-quality recruits. In fact, the Pentagon's performance has been superlative. In FY 1989, 92 percent of its recruits were high school graduates, compared to 75 percent of the general youth population. While only 69 percent of civilian youth score in the top three (of five) categories of the Armed Forces Qualification Test (AFQT), 94 percent of new enlistees did so last year. Furthermore, the military has maintained these excellent results throughout the 1980s despite a lengthy economic recovery.

That current recruits are smarter than average has led some hawks to conclude that there is no security justification for national service. As Representative G.V. "Sonny" Montgomery (Democrat of Mississippi) testified before his colleagues in early 1989: "We're in great shape and should not tamper with the effective tools we've given the military."

Not sufficiently representative. The DLC complains in its book on national service that "Americans should be concerned that our armed forces today are not representative of society as a whole," that the poor and minorities are carrying a disproportionate share of the burden of defense. Specifically, what they mean is that not enough white, middle-class youths are serving. The DLC argues that minorities comprise roughly 38 percent of army personnel and 30 percent of all servicemen, compared to just 14 percent of the civilian labor force. The DLC believes that "an unrepresentative army undermines the civic ethic of equal sacrifice."

Obviously, few if any critics of AVF are concerned about unrepresentativeness as such. Few of them are troubled that women make up well under half of America's forces. No one has decried the absence of a proportionate number of handicapped people, nor the services' failure to incorporate a socially typical number of those who score in the lowest category of the AFQT. And, frankly, there would probably be little criticism from national-service advocates were whites overrepresented.

The critics' selectivity points to a conceptual problem: their notion that all civic roles should be shared equally. Wealthy people tend to pay more in taxes. Construction workers are overwhelmingly male. The Irish, for many years, bore a disproportionate "burden" of New York City's policing duties. And nonurban residents are overrepresented in the military. Should all such roles be shared equally? As long as rich and poor, black and white, men and women, ethnic groups, and regional groups face different situations in life, they are likely to assume certain social roles disproportionately. To think that it should be otherwise is simply to advocate an equality of result that is alien to America.

Anyway, the DLC overstates its case, once again. First, it uses overall Pentagon figures. Minorities reenlist in higher numbers than whites, something that would not be affected by national service. Second, civilian labor force statistics are incorrectly cited. Bruce Chapman of the Hudson Institute points out that when the DLC compares figures for minority eighteen- to twenty-one-year-olds, it uses 26.9 percent for the military and 17.8 percent for the civilian population. Yet the latter figure does not include Hispanics, who comprise 9.5 percent of the relevant population. Thus, although blacks are overrepresented in the military, (during FY 1989, 22 percent of new recruits were black, compared to 14 percent of the corresponding youth population), Hispanics, Asians, and other minority groups are underrepresented. As a result, the overall percentage of minorities in the military roughly matches their percentage in the population as a whole.

As for rich whites serving: They always have and always will, although trying to measure their participation is difficult. Using zip codes and average family incomes, a 1977 Rand Corporation report, conducted during a relatively difficult recruiting period, found that while 1.06 percent of all sixteen- to twenty-one-year-olds came from families in the top 1 percent of income, 0.34 percent of those joining the military did. Moreover, while 5.13 percent of all sixteen- to twenty-one-year-olds came from families in the 95 to 99 percentiles of income, 2.67 of those joining the military did. Thus, as one might expect, the wealthy are somewhat less likely to serve; but still many do join. The Rand report concluded that "military service apparently continues to be viewed as an alternative employment option for a very broad cross section of American society, from the wealthiest to the poorest."

Not idealistic. Proponents of mandatory service hold that the AVF has, in [Charles] Moskos's words, moved "from citizen soldier to economic man," placing an undue emphasis on marketplace values. That is, the AVF has fostered an "it's just a job" mentality. Moskos goes so far as to argue that "the most far-reaching consequence of the AVF is that it ultimately reduces recruiting an armed forces to a form of consumerism, even hedonism, which is hardly a basis for the kind of commitment required in a military organization."

Moskos's critique deserves to be taken seriously. Although military surveys consistently find that many servicemen joined to serve and to fulfill a sense of duty, much of the armed services' recruiting certainly seems pitched to the casual job hunter—learn a skill, earn some money, travel the world. That said, however, even Moskos acknowledges that many of the changes we see in the military are tied to social trends. In other words, no job ought to be "just a job," but any job can be "just a job." It depends on the individual and the value he places on his performance as a worker. Thus, a particularly serious problem of "ticket-punch-ing" exists among some military officers, who of course would be unaffected by national service.

No doubt, the military would be stronger if it better emphasized its institutional uniqueness and its history as a high calling. But this seems contrary to Moskos's proposal of flooding the field with "young people who serve short terms in the military at less than market wages." Anyway, in the late 1980s, there has been an upsurge of idealism and activism on the part of the young without a new federal program. Those trends are likely to affect military recruiting; moreover, the down-sizing of the force will allow the military to choose a larger portion of enlistees who take duty seriously.

In sum, critics of the AVF have failed to make a convincing case. Nonetheless, national service advocates continue to believe that the military has a problem, and that their new national service program is the answer.

NATIONAL SERVICE PROPOSALS

Nearly a dozen different pieces of legislation concerning national service are now circulating in Washington. Some mirror the president's [Bush] "Thousand Points of Light" initiative, and would simply hand out federal money to promote volunteerism. Others encourage part-time civilian service along the lines of the National Guard, providing financial assistance in return for weekend civilian service. The Citizen Corps program advocated by [Senator Sam] Nunn [Democrat of Georgia], Representative David McCurdy (Democrat of Oklahoma), Moskos, and the DLC, seems to be the only attempt to employ national service in a way that would significantly affect the military.

The Citizen Corps program would create a Corporation for National Service to implement a civilian service program administered through state and local councils. (Military service would be handled by the Pentagon.) Federal financial aid for education would be conditioned on one or two years of service; and completion of the program would be rewarded with a voucher usable for education or a home purchase. In this way, national service advocates say, their program would bring in more recruits and more upper-income white recruits.

Moreover, Moskos predicts that "a citizen soldier option would dramatically lower per capita manpower costs" in two ways. It would attract college-bound youths with lower attrition rates than today's recruits; and the program would pay "citizen soldiers," serving only two years, less than "professional soldiers."

But Moskos and his allies may well be wrong on all counts. National service is likely to raise costs and hurt the services.

First, despite the DLC's desire to employ inexpensive, semivolunteer "citizen soldiers," use of an education/housing voucher would result in higher net annual benefits for the two-year enlistees than for longer-term enlistees. As Walter Oi of the University of Rochester points out, the tax-free voucher could easily be "cashed out" through home buy-backs, with the result that a national service participant would end up with pay "63 percent higher than that paid to a regular enlisted man or woman." Instead of appealing to middle- and upper-class youths on the basis of something other than money, national service would in this way encourage enlistments from all income levels precisely because of the material incentives offered. (Moskos's version of the voucher, which could not be used to purchase a home, would be less subject to abuse.)

Second, with a plethora of two-year enlistment terms, training and turnover expenses would be much greater. In its official response to the Nunn-McCurdy national service proposal, the Defense Department warned:

> Because of the large influx of 2-year enlistments, the training base (and associated costs) would have to expand markedly. In addition, unit training work loads, personnel turbulence, and attrition experienced in active and Reserve operational units would all increase. Minimum overseas tour lengths would need to be cut, sharply increasing permanent change of station costs. The combined effect of these factors would drive sharp accession and end strength increases, disrupt unit cohesion, weaken esprit and morale, reduce individual proficiency and compromise unit readiness.

Third, the advantages of the two-year plan would induce many career-minded recruits to take the "citizen" option, further upsetting the balance between short- and long-term enlistments. Pay and benefits for professionals would probably have to rise to encourage reenlistment and to maintain an adequate career force. All told, the research firm Syllogistics estimates, costs could rise between $1.1 billion and $9.2 billion annually. (See Table 1.)

Clearly, the impact of the plan on professionals is critical. The DLC appears to view a more experienced force as a detriment, citing as a possible source of savings the "reduction in the number of soldiers in higher pay grades." But not only is that saving illusory, an older force (in addition to being more effective) can actually offer significant savings through efficiency. In fact, a decade ago, man-

Table 1

Military-Related Costs of National Service FY 1985 Career Mix

Element	Estimated Cost Increases (Millions of Dollars)	
	Trained Man-year Method*	Productivity-weighted Man-year Method**
Savings from Cutting Regular Army Pay	(8316)	(8316)
Tax Loss from Cutting Regular Army Pay	433	433
Citizen Corps Pay (Net Taxes)	5320	9314
Reenlistment Bonuses	382	382
G.I Bill	(1629)	(1629)
Citizen Corps Educational Voucher	4605	8063
Additional Training	341	983
Total	1136	9230

*Trained man-year method merely preserves a force with equal years of training.
**Productivity weighting recognizes that an additional year of training is often worth more than an earlier year of training.
Source: Syllogistics, Inc., "The Effects of National Service on Military Personnel Programs," September 1988, pp. 6–19.

power experts Martin Binkin and Irene Kyriakopoulos urged the Pentagon to "take steps to improve retention among certain experienced personnel, thereby reducing the demands for new volunteers and for the resources now devoted to maintaining a relatively large pool of nonproductive employees. These steps not only would allow the nation to field more effective armed forces but could save money as well."

Fourth, one needs to keep in mind that potential savings from the personnel costs of new recruits are always going to be small, simply because most personnel spending goes for careerists, civilians, and retirees. When the DLC's book, *Citizenship and National Service*, compares personnel costs in 1964 and 1986 and blames the rise on the termination of conscription, something is clearly wrong. Barely one-tenth of personnel costs is now attributable to soldiers serving in their first two years (the ones who replaced draftees). Any added expense from increasing their pay is more than offset by eliminating the costs of conscription, lowered turnover, and lowered reenlistment incentives. (The rise was in fact due largely to increased costs associated with career soldiers, civilians, and retirees.)

Fifth, the military is today the one large-scale government service program that provides educational benefits; national service is therefore likely to draw people away from the military rather than encourage them to enlist. Thomas Byrne of the (private) Association of the U.S. Army complains, "We don't want high-caliber people who might otherwise join the Army off planting trees instead." It makes no sense to create a federal civilian service program to compete with the armed services for young men.

If the decision is made to use education aid to increase the number of young people enlisting in the military, there is a much simpler method. The government need only adopt the principle of "earned benefits" advocated by national service proponents—but apply it more selectively. That is, federal educational aid could still be conditioned on service, but on military service alone. No service, no aid. Such an approach would implement the sensible philosophical point advanced by Nunn and his colleagues, that educational subsidies are not an entitle-

ment, and would also avoid creating a civilian program to compete with the military.

Lastly, what would national service do for a volunteer military thought to emphasize a "just-a-job" attitude? Moskos has observed that "we must encourage a general attitude, a cast of mind, an outlook." And that is true—in the military and in every other line of work. But many of today's servicemen already serve for less than a civilian market wage. Naval personnel who work long hours on aircraft carriers handling multimillion-dollar aircraft make no more than supermarket clerks. They—like many doctors, lawyers, journalists, teachers, entrepreneurs, and other citizens—have chosen their profession for reasons of personal fulfillment.

Would national service pull in more patriots in place of time-servers? No, an educational voucher would tend to attract people who want to go to college. Indeed, because "citizen soldiers" would get greater benefits under the voucher system than career soldiers, the scheme could create an entire class of recruits who joined solely because of the material rewards and who looked forward only to getting out and using their vouchers.

THE MORAL ARGUMENT

If national service has so little to commend it, why does the specter haunt us still? It seems likely that most of those who advocate national service are driven by something more than practical considerations. Like Edward Bellamy and William James, they appear to possess an intense dislike of America's individualist, bourgeois political culture.

Former representative Paul McCloskey, who introduced a mandatory national service program in 1979, observed that "the privilege of being an American justifies a duty to serve the country a year or two in one's youth." This implies that the government is the grantor, rather than the protector, of rights—fundamentally misconstruing the American view of the relationship between the individual and the state. It is a privilege to be an American only because it is a stroke of luck to live in a society that respects individual rights more than most other societies. But the rights of a free man are not a benefit or privilege bestowed by the government. The contrary views— that the status of freedom is a gift from the king, or the state, or society, and therefore something for which one must pay homage—reflects the view of feudalism, of fascism, and of socialism.

Of course, free individuals should defend themselves and their communities. But in a free society this decision must be a personal moral choice, not a legal duty imposed from above. Individuals operating within the informal social and community networks that surround them should be the ones to decide how best to fulfill their social obligations. As Daniel Webster asked: "Who will show me any constitutional injunction, which makes it the duty of the American people to surrender everything valuable in life, and even life itself . . . whenever the purposes of an ambitious and mischievous government may require it?"

Today, most advocates of national service say that their schemes are voluntary. But many of these advocates openly admit that they prefer national service to be involuntary. And in a sense, they are right. For if national service is in fact a duty owed to the country, why should it not be enforced, just as contractual obligations are enforced? Indeed, it must be

enforced, since those who most need to learn to obey will not volunteer. Once this logic of "duty" takes hold, Washington will not long foot the huge bill for a "public service" army it can employ on the cheap.

Moreover, why stop the process at national service? Charles Moskos wants young people to act as prison guards, teachers, and in a host of other roles. Why not conscript them? William James wanted to draft men to do everything from wash windows to serve on fishing fleets in December. That may be going a bit far, but surely defense of the local community is not much less compelling than defense of the country. Why not conscript people for a "home guard" in the police and fire departments? Why not compel them to participate in neighborhood watch associations? This would bring in mature adults, otherwise not so easily lured from home and career. And if this sounds absurd, remember the DLC argument that "in a democracy . . . citizenship requires not just sharing burdens, but sharing them equally."

In the end, the DLC gets one part right, asserting that "No obligation is more fundamental to citizenship than that of preserving our free institutions." Just so, and the conclusion is obvious: no obligation is more fundamental than opposing national service.

NO

Charles Moskos

REBUTTAL: NECESSARY AND AMERICAN

Doug Bandow has done a great service by highlighting key issues in the current debate on national service. He focuses on the national service proposal introduced by Senator Sam Nunn, Representative Dave McCurdy, and other congressional Democrats. This bold legislation, shaped by the Democratic Leadership Council's study, *Citizenship and National Service*,[1] would establish a voluntary national service program aimed primarily at young people between the ages of eighteen and twenty six.

By presenting a program of national service embracing both military and civilian dimensions, the DLC study broke new ground. The military side would include two tracks: one a new lower-paid "citizen-soldier" track, offering short enlistments coupled with generous post-service educational benefits, the other a professional soldier track—basically the system as it presently exists. The civilian side would consist of an entirely new youth service, which would focus on conservation work and social services, and which would be administered mainly through state governments, local agencies, and voluntary associations.

The linchpin of the proposal lies in its extension to civilian service of the GI Bill established after World War II. The basic principle of that original GI Bill was to provide education or job training in return for military service. Under one DLC proposal, young people who perform one or two years of service, either military or civilian, would become the main recipients of federal student aid. This moves away from the present program under which the government gives $9 billion each year in loan subsidies and grants to college students without asking anything in return—in effect, a GI Bill without the GI. By linking service to student aid, the DLC proposal incurred the wrath of the higher education establishment and its paleo-liberal allies on Capitol Hill.

Libertarians take issue with national service for different reasons, of course. As well articulated by Bandow, these concerns center around three core contentions: (1) A national service plan will hurt (or at least will not

From Charles Moskos, "Rebuttal: Necessary and American," *Orbis: A Journal of World Affairs* (Summer 1990). Copyright © 1990 by The Foreign Policy Research Institute. Reprinted by permission.

significantly improve) the all-volunteer force (AVF); (2) The nonmilitary roles envisioned by national service plans are unneeded, or better met in other ways; (3) The concept of national service is un-American.

NATIONAL SERVICE AND THE AVF

Critics of the marketplace AVF (and I am one) focus their arguments on the army, the largest of the services, the one that formerly relied most on draftees, and the bellwether of the AVF. Of the many practical criticisms that have been lodged against AVF, Bandow presents rebuttals to four of the commonest: its poor quality; its unrepresentativeness; its high costs; and its difficulties in hiring and firing people.

Not smart enough. When it comes to the relation between quality and length of service, Bandow echoes an article of faith held by the Office of the Secretary of Defense (OSD)—that longer enlistments are nearly always preferable to shorter ones. But this dogma does not stand up to scrutiny. The effectiveness of soldiers is based on ability and training, not on time in a grade. Every study of combat soldiers supports this conclusion.[2] Army data show that two-year soldiers, compared with longer enlistees, are twice as likely to score in the upper aptitude categories and much less likely to be removed from the army for disciplinary causes. The army command structure is quite happy with its two-year enlistees. Why does Bandow want to change a winning formula?

Also, Bandow's use of accession figures to demonstrate the quality of the enlisted force is misleading. Rather than focusing on recruits alone, one ought to look at the total enlisted membership brought into the army under AVF. And here the picture is different. Even in the late 1980s, the best years in AVF history, the percentage of the army's enlisted personnel in the top two mental categories was lower than the percentage of the total population in those categories. The reason for this is that today's noncommissioned officers (NCOs) entered the army in the late 1970s, when the quality of recruits was at rock bottom. Thus, we now have a situation where the aptitude scores of privates are much higher than those of their sergeants. For example, 5 percent of recruits fall into the lowest test level compared with 26 percent of staff sergeants.

Not sufficiently representative. To argue, as does the 1977 Rand report Bandow cites, that the military was "viewed as an alternative employment option . . . from the wealthiest to the poorest" is laughable. In 1977, one-third of all army entrants were black and close to half of the white males were high school dropouts. To see this as a representative army takes some leap of imagination. Surely, Bandow recognizes that the representativeness issue does not center on creating a mirror of the civilian population (i.e., proportionate numbers of handicapped, mentally ill, and so forth). It centers, rather, on unrepresentativeness that affects the fighting capabilities of the armed forces. Is there any level of unrepresentativeness that would disturb Bandow?

Costs. When calculating the costs of a national service plan, Bandow displays a faulty comprehension of military manpower, for he ignores the concept of a Total Force—reserves as well as active forces. When reserve components are included in military manpower analysis, savings occur in training costs even with short-term enlistments, if these are tied to reserve obligations. This is precisely what the DLC proposal stated. Indeed, in 1989, Army Chief of Staff Carl E. Vuono supported an enlistment option of two years in the active force, two years in the ready reserve, and two years in the stand-by reserve. That military manpower trends, for both budgetary and strategic reasons, are moving toward greater reliance on reserve components makes the case for the citizen-soldier component of the DLC proposal all the more timely.

In support of his contention that long-term enlistments are less expensive than short-term enlistments, Bandow also perpetuates another OSD myth—that the AVF has proven less expensive than conscription. . . . [A] look at dollar figures (given in constant 1990 values) shows the real changes in military personnel costs since the advent of the AVF. In 1964, the last year of the peacetime draft, average personnel costs for each active-duty soldier were $22,500; this compares with $35,600 in 1990. The contrast in total manpower costs is enormous. The total bill in 1964 for the active-duty force was $55.1 billion, in 1990 it came to $73.9 billion. In other words, even though there are a half million fewer soldiers on active duty, the AVF costs $18 billion more! Nor does this include the extra $10 billion a year now paid to civilians or the skyrocketing retirement costs. Whatever arguments there are against the draft, cost savings is not one of them.[3]

Hiring and firing. The contention that the DLC proposal and the Nunn-McCurdy bill would hurt military recruitment by drawing young people into civilian work is foolishness. To require service from college youth who now receive federal education benefits without a service requirement can only create an unparalleled reservoir of potential military recruits. The Syllogistics study cited by Bandow, which suggested that a national service plan might require higher pay to bring in military recruits, never addressed the specifics of the Nunn-McCurdy bill and is irrelevant to the discussion at hand. A 1989 study by Juri Toomepuu, of the United States Army Recruiting Command, concludes that the Nunn-McCurdy bill would be an unprecedented boon for recruitment.[4] To this date, Toomepuu's analyses have never been publicly rebutted by anyone, including Doug Bandow, and indeed efforts to repress the study were partially successful: the study was not publicly available until reporters acquired copies through the Freedom of Information Act—too late to have an impact on the Nunn-McCurdy bill in Congress.

Obviously, as Bandow rightly points out, we now face a new environment for military manpower. As we enter the post-cold war era, the immediate issue is one of "downsizing," rather than recruitment. But here again AVF has created problems. Reductions would be demoralizing for the military under any scenario, but a career-heavy force makes them immeasurably worse. The AVF is smaller today, compared to what it would have been with a draft, entirely owing to the paucity of lower-ranking enlisted members and junior officers. In effect, the AVF emptied the military of privates and lieutenants—and this is now making necessary draconian reductions of the career force. Of the army's proposed 200,000-man reduction, 80,000 will be through "involuntary retirement."[5] Of course, there was nothing inevitable about having an AVF top-heavy with career soldiers. But this was the path favored by OSD with its resistance to the concept of the citizen-soldier.

Finally, let it be said, Bandow is quite right to note the current success of AVF recruitment. But he fails to mention that the OSD fought the two major recruitment initiatives of the 1980s—the army's two-year enlistment and GI Bill educational benefits.

NATIONAL SERVICE AND CIVILIAN NEEDS

The practical argument for national service is that it can be a means of providing services that the government cannot afford and in which the private sector finds no profit. For example, the most pressing social problem in the United States may be that citizens over the age of eighty-five constitute the fastest growing segment of the population. Already 1.4 million people live in nursing homes; as many as one-third of these people could live at home if someone helped them get outside the house and ran errands for them. In Germany, such services to the elderly are performed by young men in lieu of serving as draftees in the military, and the system operates successfully. Studies show that each youth server in the German system performs labor with a net worth of more than $21,000 a year.[6]

Such youths in short-term service are an effective and humane way to meet the needs of an aging population. If a young person were attracted to such service under the provisions of the DLC proposal, would Bandow oppose it? Does he favor the present system of federal student aid, which requires no payback of service? Youth servers would also be less expensive than the market or conventional bureaucracy in meeting the needs of the elderly. Or can Bandow think of better and cheaper ways to meet such needs?

There is another consideration. With the cutback in military manpower, a major and honorable avenue for deprived youth to escape a dead-end existence is being cut off. A national service program would be a way to recapitulate the military's record in salvaging impoverished youths through new forms of civilian youth corps.

Proponents of national service must always answer a simple question. Is national service more likely to achieve its purpose, and at less cost, than some other means? If the answer is no, then I will categorically state that national service is not appropriate. If it is yes, will Doug Bandow support national service?

NATIONAL SERVICE AND AMERICAN IDEALS

Only a simplistic reading of American history could ignore recurring connections between citizen duties and rights—the militia system of the colonial and early republican era, the "common defense" and "general welfare" provisions of the Constitution, the mandatory public schools of the Northwest Ordinances, the twentieth-century drafts in both peace and war, the military training requirements of the land grant colleges, the CCC of the New Deal, the alternative service provisions for conscientious objectors, the GI Bill, the Peace Corps and VISTA, the Solomon Amendment requiring draft registration for federal student aid, and the more than twenty local and state youth corps in the contemporary period. The history of the United States shows that notions of civic obligation periodically expand and contract—and that the solutions of one period are as American as those of another.

For example, scholars consistently stress the crucial role of the militia in the War of Independence.[7] But because of his unalloyed opposition to the citizen soldier, Bandow seems not to appreciate this or the strong militia tradition that followed. From the origins of the American nation onward, the ideal of the citizen soldier has coexisted with the need for the professional soldier; although the proper balance of these two has been a perennial dilemma. George Washington favored a small regular army *and* a militia of male citizens. Today, Title 10 of the U.S. Code reiterates the tenet that every physically sound and mentally fit male between eighteen and forty-five years of age is part of the unorganized militia of the United States.

Perhaps most telling, though, is Bandow's perception of the DLC proposal as a stalking horse for a full-scale mandatory program. This is a serious point. But the transition from the comprehensive but nonmandatory system of the Nunn-McCurdy bill to a compulsory program would be a momentous step—one that would require widespread support. Such support would exist only if the comprehensive program were widely viewed as a great success. It seems perverse to argue against a voluntary national service program on the grounds that it might prove too successfull.

Political theorists as well as ordinary citizens are showing a growing appreciation of citizens' obligations and the importance of shared values. For example, four out of five Americans favor a volunteer youth corps at the federal level. And support even for mandatory service is high, with 55 percent favoring such a program for young men and 44 percent for young women.[8] This new interest in the duties of citizens results from the inadequacies of Marxism, with its materialistic analysis and collectivist prescriptions, and the inadequacies of libertarianism, which offers a similar materialist analysis but with an insistent stress on the individual.

We may be on the verge of a break-out from those "left versus right" mind-sets. Advocacy of national service is the political center reasserting itself. In this sense, national service is quintessentially American.

NOTES

1. Democratic Leadership Council (DLC), *Citizenship and National Service* (Washington, D.C.: Democratic Leadership Council, 1988). Will Marshall, president of the Progressive Policy Institute, was the primary author of this study. By way of full disclosure: both the DLC proposal and the Nunn-McCurdy legislation incorporated ideas from my book, *A Call to Civic Service* (New York: The Free Press, 1988).

2. "Soldier Performance Research Project," a report issued by the U.S. Army Training and Doctrine Command, August 31, 1989. For a summary of the literature, see Juri Toomepuu, *Soldier Capability—Army Combat Effectiveness*, vol. 1, Main Report (Ft. Benjamin Harrison, Ind.: U.S. Army Support Center, April 1981).

3. Although studies sponsored by the Department of Defense consistently find that a draft would cost more than the volunteer force, studies done outside conclude—with equal consistency—that a draft would result in budgetary savings of over $7 billion annually. For one example of the latter, see the General Accounting Office, *Military Draft: Potential Impacts and Other Issues* (Washington, D.C.: Government Printing Office, March 1988).

4. Juri Toomepuu, *Effects of a National Service Program on Army Recruiting* (Fort Sheridan, Ill.: U.S. Army Recruiting Command, February 1989).

5. *The Washington Post*, May 14, 1990.

6. Juergen Kuhlmann, "National Service Policy and Programs: The Case of West Germany," in Donald J. Eberly and Michael W. Sherraden, eds., *The Moral Equivalent of War?* (Westport, Conn.: Greenwood Press, 1990).

7. For example, John Shy, *A People Numerous and Armed* (New York: Oxford University Press, 1976); Charles Royster, *A Revolutionary People at War* (New York: The Free Press, 1984).

8. Gallup Poll, January 24, 1988.

POSTSCRIPT

Is National Service at Odds With American National Interest?

In this debate, two conservatives battle over the advisability of dramatically altering how tuition support is provided for needy college-bound youths without unduly disturbing the supply of talented young men and women that is needed to maintain military preparedness. Currently, these two public policies are uncoordinated even though they draw their "recruits" from the same age cohort.

Moskos argues that those who enter both the military and institutions of higher learning will benefit by the introduction of "national service." In Moskos's view, this program provides a unique opportunity to join together and to underscore the *duties and the rights* of America's youth; this is "quintessentially American."

Obviously Bandow does not share this view. Although he, too, is concerned with the rights and the obligations of young Americans, he fears that this voluntary program will evolve into a mandatory national service. In this case, government would be seen as the "grantor, rather than the protector of rights." In Bandow's opinion, this would fundamentally misconstrue "the American view of the relationship between the individual and the state."

Much has been written and will continue to be written about national service as Congress continues to address this issue. One source of further information is a volume prepared by the Democratic Leadership Council (DLC), a group of Democrats who are attempting to attract the political right back to their party. See their monograph *Citizenship and National Service: A Blueprint for Civic Enterprise* (May 1988). A second group to contact for information is the National Service Secretariat, a Washington, D.C.–based group that sponsors the Coalition for National Service. Since 1986, this nonprofit organization has acted as a clearinghouse for information; additionally they sponsored the Wingspread Conference in July 1988, which articulated an action agenda for the 1990s. See *National Service: An Action Agenda for the 1990s* (The National Service Secretariat, 1988). Other sources are the written statements prepared by those who have testified before the Committee on Education and Labor concerning the topic "Citizenship and National Service." These hearings were held during the spring of 1989. Coverage has appeared in the *Chronicle of Higher Education* (March 15, 1989), the *Wall Street Journal* (October 16, 1989), and, on a continuing basis, in *Experiential Education*, a publication of the National Society for Internships and Experiential Education. One other source might be of value: Charles Moskos's *A Call to Civic Service—National Service for Country and Community* (Free Press, 1988).

In response to new legislative efforts introduced in Congress in January 1990 that called for a national service corps, Janet Lieberman, a spokesperson for the U.S. Student Association, declared that the measures are a "step backward for student aid." The U.S. Student Association argues that measures to provide college students who volunteer for national service with vouchers for education expenses or the purchase of a first home discriminate against lower-income students. They charge that low-income students should be guaranteed access to college, and they feel that the provision linking national service to student aid might discourage such students from attending college.

ISSUE 4

Are Women Paid Less Than Men Because Their Working Conditions Are More Favorable?

YES: Randall K. Filer, from "Occupational Segregation, Compensating Differentials, and Comparable Worth," in Robert T. Michael et al., eds., *Pay Equity: Empirical Inquiries* (National Academy Press, 1989)

NO: Jerry A. Jacobs and Ronnie J. Steinberg, from "Compensating Differentials and the Male-Female Wage Gap: Evidence from the New York State Comparable Worth Study," *Social Forces* (December 1990)

ISSUE SUMMARY

YES: Associate professor of economics Randall K. Filer maintains that comparable worth policies are unnecessary since wage differentials simply reflect differences in workers' preferences for jobs with varying degrees of pleasantness.
NO: Associate professors of sociology Jerry A. Jacobs and Ronnie J. Steinberg argue that empirical evidence proves that wage differentials cannot be explained by worker employment choices.

The term *comparable worth* may be relatively new, but the problem that it is intended to address has plagued the U.S. economy for many years: Women are and have been paid less than men for work activities that have *comparable* characteristics. As Randall K. Filer notes, "Median weekly earnings of full-time female workers over age 16 have risen from 61 percent of those for men in 1978 to 71 percent of male earnings in the second quarter of 1987." Although this marks a clear and considerable improvement in the economic well-being of women wage earners over this 10-year period, and a remarkable improvement over the differentials in wages that existed as recently as 25 years ago, there still exists an apparent 30 percent penalty for being female in the labor markets.

This is not a problem that has been ignored by public policymakers. In 1917 the federal government created the War Labor Board in part to handle charges of sex discrimination in the war industries. The board ordered that the wages of women should equal the wages paid to men when the services rendered were equal. During World War II the War Labor Board again attempted to establish the basic concept of equal pay for equal work. This time the board was less successful. A few corporations, notably Westinghouse and General Electric, persisted in setting different wages for men and women doing equal work.

Although lobbying efforts for federal legislation that would guarantee equal pay for equal work continued throughout the 1940s and 1950s, this right was not established by Congress until 1963, when the Equal Pay Act was passed. The following year, Congress took yet another step toward closing the wage gap by enacting Title VII of the Civil Rights Act, which broadly prohibited employment discrimination based upon race, color, national origin, religion, or sex. The net result of these two major legislative initiatives was to establish clearly the right of women to "equal pay for substantially equal work."

Yet more than 25 years after these laws were passed, large wage differentials between men and women still exist. Although the laws have eliminated most of the blatant forms of wage discrimination that existed where women and men doing the same jobs were paid at different rates, the laws have done little to address the wage discrepancies that continue to exist between pay for work traditionally considered to be "women's work" and pay for "men's" jobs.

Proponents of comparable worth argue that on the basis of objective criteria—job skill requirements, job responsibilities, education, training, and experience levels needed—many low-paying jobs that by tradition have been held by women are as demanding as some high-paying jobs that have been predominately held by men. These proponents go on to argue that the only way to correct these wage differences is to objectively judge each job classification and correct for any sex-biased differences that are uncovered.

In 1981, the Supreme Court issued a decision in *Washington County v. Gunther* that appears to make it possible to bring comparable worth cases to the courts. Additionally, two-thirds of the states have introduced or are attempting to introduce comparable worth legislation, while six states have implemented explicit forms of comparable worth programs for their public employees. Lastly, a number of trade unions are bringing this issue to the bargaining table.

Some comparable worth policies have caused concern among many free-market economists. This is the case for Randall K. Filer. He argues that if poorly conceived policies are put in place, they can only "lead to distortions in resource allocation and the creation of inefficiencies." Other researchers, such as Jerry A. Jacobs and Ronnie J. Steinberg, find that the wage differentials found in the marketplace reflect the relative economic and political power that male workers have as compared to female workers.

YES
Randall K. Filer

OCCUPATIONAL SEGREGATION, COMPENSATING DIFFERENTIALS, AND COMPARABLE WORTH

In surveying the relative positions of men and women in the labor market, two facts stand out. First, wage differences between the two sexes are substantial. Second, differences in occupational structure are significant; men and women are concentrated in different occupations and heavily female occupations tend to be lower paying. Recent years have seen substantial shifts in both of these factors. Median weekly earnings of full-time female workers over age 16 have risen from 61 percent of those for men in 1978 to 71 percent of male earnings in the second quarter of 1987. Thus, in the past 10 years approximately 25 percent of the difference in male and female earnings has been eliminated. At the same time, although there are methodological difficulties in measuring changes in the degree of occupational sex segregation over time, numerous recent studies have documented that the degree of sex segregation in occupations has declined since at least 1970 (and probably since 1960).[1] . . .

Despite these improvements in the relative economic position of women over the past few years, significant differences in occupational distributions and earnings between the sexes persist. There are important policy implications to be derived from an understanding of why these differences exist. To the extent that they arise from unequal opportunities caused by unfair hiring or promotional practices, the economy has failed to make appropriate use of human resources and has created inefficiencies. In this case there is justification for intervention to facilitate greater sex equality in the labor market. On the other hand, to the extent that sex differences in occupational structure and earnings arise from differences in individual productivity or choices, despite equal labor market opportunity, interventions to change either employment or earnings patterns would lead to distortions in resource allocation and the creation of inefficiencies.

POSSIBLE CAUSES OF SEX DIFFERENCES

The observed pattern of the genders being concentrated in different occupations, coupled with lower average wages in the occupations that are heavily female, is consistent with a number of possible explanations that have been proposed by economists. Those explanations provide the framework for the analysis in this paper.

Differences in Productivity

It may be that one gender has lower average levels of productivity and has concentrated in occupations in which it has a comparative advantage. Primary among the factors that may contribute to differences in productivity between typical men and women is past work experience. Previous research has established that between one-quarter and one-half of the gender gap in wages may be due to differences in the extent of previous employment (Corcoran, 1979; Mincer and Ofek, 1982; Mincer and Polachek, 1978; Sandell and Shapiro, 1978).

Physical differences may also contribute to differing occupational comparative advantages and overall productivity. In one setting, Hoffmann and Hoffman (1987) found that upper body strength and lifting requirements limited women's bidding on and accepting "male" jobs even though they were actively encouraged to do so by their employer. Similarly, several authors (e.g., Daymont and Andrisani, 1984; Filer, 1983; Greenfield et al., 1980) have observed that women and men in the labor market have substantially different personality patterns with respect to such characteristics as empathy and aggression, which may lead to different job choices and, consequently, different reward structures.[2]

Differences in Utility Functions

Men and women may make rational choices in the job market based on differences in utility functions that create differing preferences for certain types of work and other duties. For example, some evidence indicates that women attach greater importance to various forms of attractive working conditions and that men place relatively greater emphasis on incomes (Forgionne and Peters, 1982; Harvey, 1986; Murray and Atkinson, 1981). Such a difference in preferences, coupled with the fact that the market forces employers to pay compensating differentials to those workers who fill jobs with relatively unattractive working conditions, will, even given equal productivity, result in women being concentrated in lower paying but otherwise more attractive jobs. Evidence presented in Filer (1985) suggests that such compensating differentials may be responsible for up to one-quarter of earnings differences between men and women.

Much of the literature regarding differences between men and women in labor market preferences starts with the fact that there are differences in home duties. Filer (1985) reports that jobs typically held by women are those from which it is easier to take time off for personal reasons and are typically located closer to their homes.[3] Others (O'Neill, 1983, 1985; Waite and Berryman, 1985) have pointed out that female-dominated jobs require less overtime, are less likely to have rotating shifts, and are more likely to be part time. All of these findings are consistent with women assuming responsibility for child rearing.

Perhaps the most frequently advanced reason why differing home responsibilities might lead to occupational segregation comes from the fact that women tend to have more discontinuous work histories. This should lead them to choose jobs that require little firm-specific human capital and in which there is relatively little atrophy of skills when not in use. . . .

Employers may respond to a greater propensity of women to leave the labor force by investing less in training women and being less likely to promote women (see Lazear and Rosen, 1989). Such theories of "statistical discrimination" rest on the inability of employers to distinguish between those women who will remain on the job and those who will leave. They do not, however, explain why women, who presumably know whether they intend to leave their employer to assume responsibilities at home, do not negotiate contingent claims contracts insuring employers against lost investments. Finally, Becker (1985) provides a theoretical rationale for why differing home duties will result in men providing greater levels of effort on the job.

Discrimination

If lower wages for one group are not the result of lower productivity and are not fully compensated by nonwage aspects of the job, the labor market is not in equilibrium and members of the group receiving lower wages should move into higher wage occupations. The absence of such equilibrating movement (and thus a stability over time in the extent of occupational sex segregation) would suggest that women have been involuntarily denied access to certain occupations (see Bergmann, 1974; Blau, 1984; Madden, 1975; Stevenson, 1984). Obviously, such conscious denial of access to occupations, whether through the actions of employers, other workers, customers, or legislative action, would create occupational segregation.[4] This could explain lower wages for women through one of two mechanisms. "Crowding" of women into a limited number of jobs could artificially increase supply and depress wages (see Bergmann, 1974; Johnson and Solon, 1984). Alternatively, employers may consciously take the sex composition of jobs into account when setting pay levels (see England et al., 1982; Treiman and Hartmann, 1981).

If discriminatory differences in occupational structures are not being eliminated by labor market mobility, some structural barrier must be preventing such movement. This would suggest two possible courses of action. Either the barrier(s) to mobility may be removed so that rational mobility decisions on the part of workers will create equality of compensation, or the occupational distribution may be taken as fixed and an attempt made to raise wages in jobs heavily filled by women.[5]

It is the latter policy that has come to be known as "comparable worth." Advocates of comparable worth call for pay to be administratively set so that differences in wages (or full compensation, including the value of fringe benefits) not based on differences in productive skills, effort, responsibility, and working conditions are eliminated. An excellent review of the development and implementation of the concept of comparable worth is presented in Weiler (1986).

ANALYTIC FRAMEWORK

This paper investigates the extent to which there exist differences in the wages paid in various occupations that are not related to levels of effort and responsibility, working conditions, or the productive characteristics of incumbents in them, but which are related to the sex composition of the occupation. Much recent work has applied a similar procedure to micro-level data, regressing individual wages on personal characteristics and the percentage of women in an individual's occupation.[6] Studies such as England (1982, 1985), England et al. (1986), Ferber and Lowry (1976), Jusenius (1977), and Stevenson (1975) have found a negative relationship between the proportion of female workers in an occupation and its average wage.

Other studies (Aldrich and Buchele, 1986; England et al., 1982; Fuchs, 1971; Treiman et al., 1984) have used occupations as the unit of analysis, regressing average wages in an occupation (either separately for men and women or combined) on a set of explanatory variables as well as the occupation's sex composition. These studies have been handicapped by their ability to include, at most, a small subset of the factors encompassed in an occupation's "effort, responsibility, working conditions and productive requirements." . . .

RESULTS

The first column in Table 1 reports the estimated impact on the wages in a job if it were to move from 0 percent female to 100 percent female as estimated from a combined sample of men and women. Columns two and three show results for men and women separately. Differences between them and column one represent the extent to which women's lower wages *within* occupations bias the gender effect when it is estimated using a combined sample. To calculate the impact of gender composition on wage differentials, one must calculate the change in wages that would occur if each occupation exactly mirrored the proportion female in the work force. Forty-two percent of the workers in the 5 percent census sample were women. The average man was in a job that was 23 percent female and the average woman was in a job that was 68 percent female.

Adding Demographic and Personal Characteristics

The first row of Table 1 shows the estimated effect of a job's being 100 percent female on the wages of full-time workers in that job if no other characteristics of either the worker or the job are taken into account. The most standard adjustment is to recognize that men and women do not, on average, bring the same levels of productive attributes to the labor market. Census data provide a limited set of personal and demographic characteristics that may capture these productivity differences and can be included in the regression. Among them are racial group, marital and citizenship status, education, and crude measures of the type of employer. In addition, estimated actual work experience . . . was included in this specification. Results from this estimation are reported in the second row of Table 1. Increased femaleness of an occupation still implies significantly lower wages after controlling for these characteristics. Moving from being 100 percent male to being entirely female would, according to these estimates, bring a reduction of $1.92 an hour in average wages for women and $1.38 an hour for men. The relationship is significant for both sexes, although, unlike results found by other researchers, it appears to be stronger for women than for men.

Table 1

Estimated Coefficients of Gender Composition on Wages, All Full-Time, Full-Year Workers

	Estimated Coefficient[a] (Standard Error)		
Equation Specification	Men and Women Combined	Women Only	Men Only
Gender composition only	−4.41	−1.73	−2.32
	(.38)	(.25)	(.42)
Gender composition and	−3.30	−1.92	−1.38
demographic variables	(.30)	(.19)	(.32)
Gender composition, demographic	−3.13	−1.59	−1.29
variables, and union coverage	(.30)	(.19)	(.32)
Gender composition, demographic	−1.70	0.30	0.31
variables, union coverage,	(.31)	(.24)	(.32)
effort, responsibility, and			
working conditions (maximum R²)			
Gender composition, demographic	−1.35	−0.55	0.18
variables, union coverage,	(.50)	(.37)	(.53)
effort, responsibility, and			
working conditions (all variables)			

[a]The estimated impact of an occupation shifting from entirely male to entirely female composition. Multiply by the difference in the femaleness of the job held by the typical woman and that held by the typical man to obtain the estimated gender contribution to the gross wage differential.

It is often asserted that one reason women earn less than men is their lower participation in unions that obtain higher than competitive wages. The third row of Table 1 reports estimated gender coefficients for an equation including personal characteristics and the proportion of the occupation covered by a collective bargaining agreement. There is some support for the hypothesis that lack of female participation in unions contributes to the estimated gender impact on wages. When unionization is added, the gender impact in the female equation falls by almost 20 percent.

Due to space considerations, coefficients on other variables are not reported in full.[7] In general, however, they are as expected. Education effects are some-what stronger than found in micro-level studies. An additional year of schooling is estimated to result in between 51 and 76 cents an hour in additional earnings. Estimated union effects are consistent with those from micro-level studies. The estimated benefits to joining unions are substantially greater for women than for men. This raises the question of why women's unionization rates have traditionally been lower then men's. The answer may lie in discrimination within unions, higher costs to women in joining unions, or the fact that women must amortize organizational costs over shorter expected periods of job tenure.

No relationship was found between the imputed average level of experience of women in an occupation and its wages. For men, a positive relationship was found. . . . Results regarding the impact of the ethnic composition of an occupation on its wages will be discussed below.

Adding the Full Set of "Comparable Worth" Factors

Even after the addition of census demographic characteristics, the effect of the proportion female in an occupation on its average wages remains substantial. We can turn now to the extent to which this is a statistical bias resulting from the omission of significant characteristics that are correlated with the proportion female in an occupation but which advocates of comparable worth recognize as compensable in their own right, such as a job's working conditions and levels of effort and responsibility.

The results of two versions of the "complete" comparable worth specification are presented. The fourth row of Table 1 contains estimates of the gender impact from an equation constrained to include the variables discussed in the previous section plus the job characteristics that maximized the adjusted R^2 of the linear hedonic wage equation for men and women combined (since there were slight differences in the set that was entered for the sexes separately).[8] [R^2 refers to the percentage of the variation in the wage rate that is explained by the independent variables in the equation.— Eds.] The reader is cautioned, however, that where there are several measures relating to any comparable worth factor, patterns of multicollinearity make interpretation of any one coefficient impossible. It is only the effect of the full set taken jointly that has meaning. What is of interest here is not the coefficients in and of themselves (for a discussion of

their meaning see Filer, 1987), but rather the impact that their inclusion has on estimates of the effect of gender composition on wages in an occupation. Finally, the last row of Table 1 reports the result when all 225 job characteristics were entered into the wage equation.

The impact of adjusting for compensable job characteristics is striking. Once compensating differentials for a job's effort, responsibility, fringe benefits, and working conditions are taken into account there *is no significant relationship between an occupation's gender composition and its wages* for either men or women. What appears to be an effect in the combined equation results from lower wages for women within each occupation, which, to the extent that they represent other than legitimate compensation practices, can be addressed by equal employment laws but which are immune to comparable worth adjustments.

Some of the results for other variables in this equation are worthy of note. For a more thorough analysis, the reader is referred to Filer (1987). The pattern of the census variables remains the same. There is an approximately 25 percent reduction in the estimated impact of education on wages, although this coefficient is still highly significant. Examining comparable worth concepts such as effort and responsibility is complicated by the fact that there are several related and highly intercorrelated measures of each. When taken as a group (say by assuming a change of one standard deviation in each), the results suggest that occupations requiring more effort or responsibility, exposure to worse working conditions, or longer commutes pay higher wages for both men and women; while those with higher levels of fringe benefits, more interaction with other people, or employment in smaller establishments can pay lower average wages.[9] . . .

Changes in Sex Composition

To what extent are mobility patterns of women consistent with a labor market moving toward an equilibrium resulting in equality of wages? Women can be expected to enter those jobs for which pay is greatest for women, no matter what the extent of any discriminatory pay gap in that occupation.

Women can also be expected, all else being equal, to enter those jobs for which there is the least degree of penalty for being female. The size of such a potential gap can be estimated by comparing the actual earnings of women in an occupation with the earnings they would be predicted to have if they were rewarded in the same manner as men (the sum of the average levels of independent variables for women times the coefficients for men). If these predicted earnings are equal to their actual earnings, women in the occupation are being exactly compensated for their productive attributes, effort, responsibility, and working conditions faced. If predicted earnings exceed actual earnings, women are being undercompensated in that occupation (i.e., there is a discriminatory gap). The greater the gap, the greater should be the incentive for women to move out of that occupation and into ones in which they do not face such a disadvantage. Finally, if predicted earnings are lower than actual earnings, the incentive goes in the opposite direction, the discriminatory gap favors women, and women should desire to enter the occupation.

Thus, if occupational mobility is serving to equalize wages between men and women, a positive relationship between actual wages paid to women in an occu-

pation and the movement of women into that occupation should be found as well as a negative relationship between the gap between predicted and actual wages and the rate of growth of female employment. Both of these results are seen. The correlation between the percentage of increase in the proportion of workers in an occupation who were women before 1970 and 1980 and its average wage in 1980 was .24, a result that is statistically significant at a better than .0001 confidence level. . . . Thus, it would appear that movements of women in the 1970s were in directions consistent with improving their labor market status. One can only speculate that the greater shifts of the current decade will be seen to have furthered this tendency when the 1990 census becomes available.

SUMMARY AND CONCLUSIONS

The results of this analysis should serve to give pause before the United States rushes to adopt the complex legal remedy of comparable worth to deal with a perception of gender effects on wages. Although the methodology has limitations, it provides a framework designed to capture far more gender effects than could be removed by the comparable worth laws advocated in the United States. Yet, even in this most favorable case, the results provide no evidence that once legitimate influences on wages (e.g., an occupation's effort, responsibility, fringe benefits, and working conditions) are taken into account there remains any detectable effect of its sex composition on the wages of either men or women in that occupation.

To the extent that such effects have been claimed from other studies, they may be due to an inability to include more than a limited array of job characteristics. When the characteristics included more fully capture the nature of the job rather than being limited by either data availability or the researcher's prior beliefs, the labor market appears to reward job attributes and worker productivity and not the race or sex of the worker.

NOTES

1. The methodological difficulties arise from changes over time in the categories into which occupations are classified (England, 1981).

2. It should be noted that nothing has been said about how these personality differences may have arisen. Some maintain that they are innately linked to biological differences between the sexes; others believe they are the result of childhood conditioning. The reality is probably some combination of these and other sources.

3. Such locational differences contribute to wage differentials because commuting time is a negative characteristic that must be compensated for and because, by restricting the opportunity set from which a job may be chosen, individuals who desire to work close to home limit their ability to seek out their highest productivity and highest paying match. Occupational segregation will result from the fact that workers who desire employment close to home will only be available to those industries that are well suited to decentralized production in residential areas. Firms requiring large work forces (therefore having to draw workers from a wide geographic area) or not able to locate in residential neighborhoods (due to the need to be in a central place or because of production externalities) will tend to have a disproportionate share of male workers. To the extent that such firms are (as would appear likely) better paying establishments, this segregation will also contribute to wage differentials.

4. It is an unanswered question to what extent observed patterns of occupational segregation result from impositions from outside the labor market. An obvious example is the law preventing women from serving in combat specialties in the armed forces. Until very recently, many states had protective legislation that limited the exposure of women to hazardous working conditions and restricted the schedules and number of hours women could work.

It has been very difficult to develop models of how denial of access can be stable over time and not create incentives for nondiscriminatory em-

ployers (including women themselves) to employ women in the previously denied occupations. Indeed, most models of discriminatory actions on the part of employers lead to firm segregation rather than occupational segregation, a result consistent with the finding of Bielby and Baron (1984) that segregation among firms is generally greater than that across occupations.

5. These policies are, to a certain extent, mutually exclusive. If policies are enacted to raise wages in women's occupations to a level commensurate with their productivity and working conditions, this reduces the incentive for women to move into jobs previously held by men.

6. See Polachek (1987) for an explanation of why this procedure is unable to distinguish adequately between human capital and occupational sex segregation explanations for sexual differences in earnings.

7. They are available from the author.

8. As an alternative method of data reduction, factor analysis was tried on the full set of raw variables. Even when rotated in several alternative ways, however, a large number of factors were required to capture even a moderate portion of the complexity in the data. Given the pattern of loadings on the factors, it proved difficult to assign any meaningful interpretation to them. An attempt was then made to group the variables on an ad hoc basis into 25 distinct sets based on what they apparently measured and then extract factors only within each set. Results from this experiment were highly ungratifying, and the resulting factors were of little use in explaining average wages in occupations. Thus, the decision was reached to retain variables in their raw form and reduce the number of variables used through a stepwise procedure.

9. Fringe benefits are one of the clearest cases for which compensating differentials theory suggests that wages will adjust to job characteristics. For example, a job that provides health coverage can attract workers at a lower wage than one that does not provide health benefits since workers will not have to pay for them out of pocket. Although one might alternatively add fringe benefits to wages to obtain a measure of full compensation, there are difficulties with this approach. Since fringe benefits are typically offered as a take-it-or-leave-it package, there can be no assumption that any given worker values them at their full cost to the employer (e.g., consider the value of maternity leave to a single man). Thus, the value of a fringe benefit package to employees is best established not by accounting costs but rather by the wage reductions workers are willing to accept in order to obtain the package.

NO

Jerry A. Jacobs and
Ronnie J. Steinberg

COMPENSATING DIFFERENTIALS AND THE MALE-FEMALE WAGE GAP: EVIDENCE FROM THE NEW YORK STATE COMPARABLE WORTH STUDY

Though the sex gap in wages has declined somewhat in recent years, it remains substantial. In 1986, the earnings of women working full time were 64% of those of comparably employed men. Measured human-capital characteristics explain only a small proportion of this difference. One prominent line of inquiry attempting to explain gender-based earnings inequality has focused on the concentration of women in relatively low-paying occupations. Approximately one-fifth of the sex gap in wages has been associated with sex segregation of occupations, and, when industrial segregation is also considered, the proportion of the wage gap resulting from sex segregation increases to 36%. Thus the low wages associated with female-dominated occupations are not primarily the result of sex differences in measurable human-capital traits. Jacobs has further proposed that sex segregation is not simply the result of early-life socialization but rather a consequence of a life-long system of social control that channels and rechannels women into female-dominated fields.

Since human-capital and socialization explanations have proven insufficient in explaining occupational segregation, research interest has been increasingly directed to the role of organizational personnel policies and practices. The comparable worth movement has made such a shift in its focus on compensation practices in its attempt to elevate the relative pay of female-dominated occupations by correcting for the undervaluation of "women's work."

Though most researchers have accepted as a given that women's work is more poorly paid than men's in jobs requiring similar education and experience, Randall Filer's prominent article in the National Research

Council's *Pay Equity: Empirical Inquiries* (1989) maintains that female-dominated occupations in fact are not underpaid. He frames his argument in terms of the economic "compensating differentials" hypothesis, suggesting that women work in "lower paying but otherwise more attractive jobs" and concluding that the wage gap can be accounted for by the wage premium paid to men because of undesirable working conditions in their jobs. The implication is that the wage gap that flows from sex segregation is the legitimate result of job differences. Filer holds that sex segregation of occupations is largely voluntary because of differences in "tastes" regarding the importance of working conditions. Wages between female- and male-dominated occupations differ because women choose to take a larger proportion of their total compensation package in nonpecuniary amenities, whereas men opt for a larger proportion of their benefits in wages.

If correct, the conclusion that women's work is not undervalued would be significant, not only for our understanding of the processes of sex segregation but also for our assessment of policy efforts such as comparable worth. Filer is well aware of the policy relevance of his findings. "The results," he cautions, "should serve to give pause before the United States rushes to adopt . . . comparable worth to deal with a perception of gender effects on wages."

In this article we examine Filer's argument directly by testing the proposition that differences in undesirable features of work between male- and female-dominated occupations account for the sex gap in wages. We argue that the compensating differentials argument is flawed both empirically and conceptually. We first review studies that offer compensat-

ing differentials as an explanation of the gender gap in wages and then examine in detail the compensation associated with a wide array of working conditions found in New York State government employment. Specifically, we test whether male-dominated jobs are characterized by more unfavorable working conditions than female-dominated jobs and whether these differences translate into wage differentials that account for the gender gap in wages. In addition, we compile pertinent data on this thesis from a number of comparable worth studies.

We conclude by suggesting that our results are consistent with a power-based perspective on intraorganizational wage-setting. We hold that the ability of workers to obtain compensating differentials depends on the politics of the workplace—that workers receive extra compensation for working in unfavorable or dangerous conditions only when they are powerful enough to insert this claim directly into their labor contract.

This article contributes to related research literature and policy discussions in several respects. First, it adds to the small body of research on the possible contribution of working conditions to the gender gap in wages. It also broadens one's understanding of the role of working conditions in wage determination by examining a wide set of job attributes in a unique data set drawn from the New York State Comparable Pay Study.

Further, the evidence presented contributes to the general question of the role of preferences as an explanation for occupational sex segregation. The compensating differentials hypothesis is the economists' version of the view that women bring different goals and values with them into the labor market. Sociologists and social psychologists have also argued that socialization results in such work-oriented differences in traits, although Jacobs has found that such differences do not account for the persistence of occupational segregation. An examination of the impact of job characteristics on wages will shed light on whether women's preferences are responsible for their lower pay. Finally, this analysis will contribute to a vigorous, ongoing policy debate regarding the legitimacy and significance of comparable worth as a strategy for decreasing the sex gap in wages.

COMPENSATING DIFFERENTIALS

The idea that workers receive extra compensation for toiling under unfavorable conditions originated with Adam Smith. In *Wealth of Nations*, Smith's first postulate concerning wage variation is that "the wages of labor vary with the ease or hardship, the cleanliness or dirtiness, the honourableness or dishonourableness of the employment." Smith held that workers doing physically onerous or dirty jobs receive extra compensation for their troubles, whereas those employed in the "honourable professions are 'under-recompensed.' " Simply stated, he reasoned that an undesirable feature of a job reduces the supply of individuals interested in that job and that anything that reduces the supply of workers increases the wage employers must pay to fill that position.

Contemporary economists refer to this phenomenon as a "compensating differential" whereby an observed difference in the wages between two jobs may represent monetary compensation for a countervailing differential in working conditions. This reasoning would hold, for example, that garbage collectors are likely to be paid more than bus drivers. . . . This

wage premium is paid because the former position is less pleasant and consequently requires an added wage incentive to induce prospective employees to pursue this line of work. The assumption is that the "utility" of the higher wage to the marginal worker is just sufficient to compensate for the unpleasantness (and associated "disutility") of the less desirable job. While high-income positions may have better working conditions than low-income ones, among jobs with similar entry requirements, higher wages should be observed in jobs with less desirable working conditions. Though most often discussed by economists, the compensating differentials logic is consistent with the logic of the functional theory of stratification.

Can the compensating differentials hypothesis predict which specific job characteristics will be positively rewarded and which negatively? The preferences of the "marginal" worker are considered crucial in determining which working conditions will be associated with a wage premium. Since no one knows who the marginal worker is or what his or her preferences are, in principle it is impossible to predict which job characteristics will be positively or negatively valued. As Robert Smith notes in his review of recent literature on compensating differentials, "Given the variety of human preferences, it is doubtful that [job] characteristics . . . can be claimed, a priori, to be disagreeable at the margin."

Nonetheless, the operationalization of undesirable working conditions has largely rested on plausible assertions relying on face validity. In their reviews of ten articles, all focusing on exclusively male samples, both Brown and Smith cite a common list of job conditions economists have isolated as undesirable. These are work requiring heavy physical labor; work involving noise, temperature extremes, dirt, or hazardous materials; repetitious work; fast-paced work; work involving low autonomy; stressful work; job insecurity; work with machines; and work involving risk of injury or death. The implicit assumption is that most workers prefer secure jobs that are clean and safe and do not involve extreme noise and temperature, and in which there is sufficient autonomy to regulate the pace of one's work. In practice, most empirical research selects a subset of these job characteristics, asserts their undesirability, and leaves it up to the reader to judge the reasonableness of such an evaluation.

Empirical evidence on the compensating differentials hypothesis remains mixed despite its illustrious pedigree. In his review of compensating differentials literature, Robert Smith concludes that, except for jobs that involve risk of injury or death, working conditions such as those involving heavy physical labor, low autonomy, or a fast pace often produce negative wage effects instead of the positive ones predicted by the compensating differentials hypothesis. Brown also reports that the literature contains an "uncomfortable number" of exceptions to the predictions of this hypothesis. Nevertheless, the logic of compensating differentials has recently been employed as an explanation for the difference in pay between male- and female-dominated jobs.

COMPENSATING DIFFERENTIALS AND THE WAGE GAP

Randall Filer has advanced the most serious empirical effort to demonstrate the importance of working conditions in ex-
plaining the sex gap in wages. Filer asserts that both men and women assess the undesirable features of jobs uniformly but act differently in making job choices, with men attaching more importance to wages and benefits and women to "interpersonal and other non-wage aspects of the job." He further maintains that women are paid less because they work in more pleasant jobs. In his words,

> Once compensating differentials for a job's effort, responsibility, fringe benefits, and working conditions are taken into account, there is no significant relationship between an occupation's gender composition and its wages for either men or women.

Filer is not especially concerned with specifying which job characteristics are undesirable *a priori*. Instead, he states, "No preconceived notions of whether these characteristics are 'good' or 'bad' are required. The data will tell us how the marginal worker evaluates them." In other words, if a job characteristic is positively compensated, it must be undesirable. Thus Filer's identification of job characteristics that require a wage premium is decidedly *post hoc*.

Filer's 1985 article analyzes a national sample of men and women from the 1977 Quality of Employment Survey [QES] to estimate the effects of 28 different job characteristics, controlling for individual variation in education and experience. Based on a sample of 250 women and 350 men employed in jobs that pay hourly wages, he finds that women generally report more favorable working conditions than men. Further, Filer concludes that, depending on the equation, between 31% and 65% of the gender gap in wages is attributable to differences in job characteristics.

However, closer scrutiny reveals that Filer's estimate of the wage gap attributable to working conditions is based on little statistically reliable evidence. Because of his small sample size, few of the coefficients for job attribute variables Filer reports are statistically significant, raising questions about whether a given job characteristic can be viewed as a basis for compensation. Specifically, only 7 of the 28 coefficients for working conditions are statistically significant for men, and a mere 4 for women. Further, in our reanalysis of the QES data, the introduction of a simple control for occupation substantially reduces the number of coefficients that remain significant and in the direction predicted by the compensating differentials hypothesis. Yet, for purposes of decomposing the sex gap in wages, Filer treats all of these coefficients as if they were meaningful and precise. Since the decomposition of the wage gap sums up the effects of a large number of statistically insignificant coefficients associated with particular job attributes, we consider the analysis suspect. . . .

Finally, we are skeptical about the impact of compensating differentials on the wage gap because evidence suggests that compensation typically offered for working conditions constitutes a small fraction of workers' wages. Aldrich and Buchele note, for example, that skills are typically fourteen times as important as working conditions in the job evaluation systems they examined.

Nevertheless, the conclusion that female-dominated jobs are not underpaid once associated working conditions are taken into account strikes at the heart of the justification for comparable worth. Because this argument is receiving considerable play in policy circles and among economists, a careful examination of the compensating differentials hypothesis is warranted.

COMPENSATING DIFFERENTIALS: A TEST

For the compensating differentials logic to account for the wage gap between men and women, three things must be true. First, male-dominated positions must feature less desirable working conditions than female-dominated jobs. A fair test of this premise would involve measuring a wide array of job characteristics found in both male- and female-dominated jobs. While certain undesirable working conditions are concentrated in male-dominated jobs, occupations dominated by women may have their own set of undesirable working conditions. Previous research on compensating differentials has focused almost exclusively on undesirable working conditions typically found in male-dominated jobs.

Second, jobs must receive a wage premium for such undesirable employment conditions. After controls for entry requirements such as education are introduced, undesirable working conditions should have a positive association with wages. If there were no wage bonus for undesirable working conditions, the presence of such conditions in male-dominated occupations would not be able to account for the male-female pay gap.

Third, the sex gap in earnings attributable to working conditions must be shown to account for a substantial portion of the difference in pay between male- and female-dominated jobs. In other words, one must show statistically that little or no sex composition effect persists once working-conditions measures are controlled.

... [T]he data from the New York State Comparable Pay Study, which include more variegated measures of job attributes than any survey data of which we are aware, constitute an excellent testing ground for assessing the compensating differentials model. ...

RESULTS

Distribution of Job Attributes by Sex-Type of Job

Our first test of the compensating differentials hypothesis assesses whether white male-dominated jobs are characterized by more undesirable working conditions than female-dominated jobs. ...

If we based our test simply on the working-conditions summary index, we would find that male-dominated jobs have somewhat more undesirable attributes than those dominated by women. This result is not surprising—we note ... the connection of this index to conventional measures of hazards historically associated with male-dominated blue-collar jobs. However, when we disaggregate this measure, we find that female-dominated jobs are more likely to be noisy and to involve cleaning others' dirt, whereas jobs dominated by men are likelier to involve working in hot or cold conditions, exposure to fumes, risk of injury, and strenuous physical activity.

Yet, as expected, other undesirable characteristics are concentrated in female-dominated positions, which are more likely to involve working with difficult clients and sick or dying patients as well as less autonomy and more repetition. Male-dominated jobs, on the other hand, are likelier to involve communication with the public and (slightly) more stress.

The productivity-related job content of male- and female-dominated jobs also vary. White male-dominated jobs involve such desirable features as managerial, supervisory, and fiscal responsibilities. Because these are productivity-related job attributes rather than working conditions *per se*, we do not consider these measures tests of the compensating differentials thesis.

Thus the first premise of the compensating differentials explanation of women's low wages receives mixed support at best. On the basis of some 25,000 employee reports on job content and conditions associated with 1,605 different jobs held by approximately 170,000 workers, we find that in New York State female-dominated jobs involve somewhat *different* (and not necessarily fewer) undesirable working conditions than jobs dominated by men. Since we don't know how seriously employees view each of these items, this analysis by itself is not definitive. But these data do suggest that male-dominated jobs do not have a monopoly on undesirable working conditions. Yet, as Barry discovered, compensation may be made for undesirable working conditions in male-dominated jobs though it may not be in jobs dominated by women. We now examine how each of these working-conditions items relates to wage structure.

Job Attributes and Wages

A second test of the compensating differentials argument examines whether additional wages are paid for jobs that involve undesirable working conditions. In other words, for the compensating differentials thesis to be an accurate predictor of wage premiums, undesirable job attributes would have to be associated with premiums, net of other compensable job attributes such as experience and educational requirements and managerial and supervisory responsibility. . . .

Of the 14 job-characteristic measures considered, the signs of 10 are contrary to the prediction of the compensating differentials model. Only 4 of the measures have the expected positive effect on wages for undesirable working conditions: stress, fumes, handling sick patients, and unexpected problems. Of these, only handling sick patients is statistically significant.

In the analysis restricted to statistically significant variables, we find that jobs that involve working in hot, cold, or noisy conditions, cleaning others' dirt, engaging in strenuous physical activity, and even risking injury—the most direct measure of on-the-job hazard—are each associated with lower wages than are other jobs. Incumbents in jobs with these attributes earn less than those in other jobs with similar educational, writing, and experience requirements, and at similar levels of time, effort and supervisory responsibility. Repetitive work and being told what to do are also negatively compensated. For only one job measure—dealing with sick or dying patients—is there evidence of positive compensation associated with an undesirable job characteristic. Ironically, since this attribute is found disproportionately in female-dominated jobs, it cannot explain the gap between men's and women's wages. To do so, other positively compensated attributes would have to be concentrated in male-dominated occupations.

We next test for interaction effects between sex composition of the job and undesirable working conditions to determine whether the latter might be compensated for in either male- or female-dominated jobs but not across-the-board. . . . In general, the sign of each of the working-conditions measures is the same for both male- and female-dominated jobs: traits that are negatively valued for male-dominated jobs are also negatively valued for female-dominated jobs. The exceptions run counter to what would be predicted by the compensating differentials explanation of the gender gap. Male-dominated jobs seem to be more heavily penalized than jobs dominated by women for undesirable working conditions that are strenuous jobs. Indeed, we find that in New York State employees in white male-dominated jobs are actually negatively compensated for the two job conditions that have conventionally been most associated with the compensating differentials argument: risk of injury and work involving strenuous physical activity. Similarly, female-dominated jobs are more heavily penalized for repetitive work, an attribute more prevalent in these jobs.

As a final test, we repeat this analysis for the jobs included in each of the three collective bargaining units. In New York State government employment, each of the bargaining units represents a "natural" break in job groupings. One union, for example, represents clerical, operational, and nonprofessional institutional service jobs; a second bargains for entry-level positions requiring a bachelor's degree and/or the so-called women's professions; a third unit represents nonunionized managerial and professional employees. We carried out this analysis because we suspected that, while compensating differentials might not account for wage differences between a heavy equipment operator and an assistant commissioner of the Office of General Services, they might explain wage differences between nonexempt male-

NO Jacobs and Steinberg / 73

and female-dominated jobs in which the differences in wages are less extreme.

The results indicate that, with one interesting exception, compensating differentials do not explain these differences. Within each bargaining unit, most undesirable working conditions are associated with lower wages, controlling for all other job attributes. The exception is that, among the lowest-tier jobs, which include craft and construction workers, risk of injury becomes positively associated with wages. This is worth highlighting, since it foreshadows our discussion of the complexities of assuming that compensating differentials, as opposed to political manipulation, are the basis for wage-setting practices.

Explaining the Sex Gap in Wages

The third test of the compensating differentials explanation determines whether the difference in pay between women and men can be accounted for by the wage effects of undesirable working conditions. We find that the explanation fails to meet this test as well: net of all factors examined, the proportion of women in a job continues to depress the wage associated with it. Therefore, even when these content and context factors are taken into account, the greater the presence of women in a job, the lower the salary accorded it. The percent minority does not remain statistically significant once job-content controls and other job characteristics are included in the analysis. But a detailed test of whether the race gap in wages is accounted for by the compensating differentials thesis is beyond the scope of this article.

First we note that working conditions explain only a small proportion of the

variance in wages in New York State. Productivity-related variables account for 86% of the variation in salary grades, and adding working conditions to the analysis adds only 3% to the explained variance. This suggests that working conditions are unlikely to account for the substantial sex gap in wages in this employment system. Our findings are consistent with those of Aldrich and Buchele, indicating the small weight accorded to working conditions relative to skills in existing job-evaluation systems. We summarize the practical significance of our results by considering the results of three hypotheticals which indicate how much impact working conditions has on the sex gap in wages.

What would happen to wages for female-dominated jobs if the sex bias in wage-setting were removed? Specifically, how much change would we observe in wages associated with female-dominated jobs if the negative effect of sex composition of occupations were removed? Note that this is the sex composition effect that remains after both productivity and working-conditions measures are controlled. . . . In this model, a 100% change in the percent female with a job reduces its associated wage by 2.56 salary grades. Since the average female-dominated job is held by 85% women, removing this presumably discriminatory effect would increase the wages for female-dominated jobs by 2.18 salary grades, or 18% of its base pay. The ratio of wages for female-dominated jobs to white male-dominated jobs would increase from 61.5% to 72.3%. Thus using this equation as the basis for a comparable worth remedy would result in a 27.9% reduction in the gap between the wages for male- and female-dominated jobs.

Second, what would be the effect on wages for female-dominated jobs if these jobs were characterized by the same working conditions as male-dominated ones? We hold the education, experience, and responsibility measures for female-dominated jobs constant and substitute men's means for the working-conditions variables in calculating the salary grade of female-dominated jobs. This substitution results in a *reduction* in wages for these jobs from an average salary grade of 12.12 to 11.87, or 60.4% of the salary of white male-dominated jobs. If women in the New York State Civil Service worked in conditions more like those in which men do, their wages would *decline* slightly, since working conditions generally have negative effects on wages: since men have somewhat higher levels of these negatively valued job attributes, substituting their levels for women's reduces women's remuneration relative to men's.

Third, what would be the effect of eliminating the negative effect of working conditions on wages of both men and women? On the face of it, it makes no sense for employees to lose money for performing unpleasant tasks or tolerating undesirable conditions. If we removed the negative effect of all working conditions, what would be the effect on the wages of female-dominated jobs relative to those of white male-dominated jobs?

. . . We find that the average salary grade of female-dominated jobs increases substantially from 12.12 to 17.35. At the same time, the average salary grade of white male-dominated jobs rises from 19.66 to 23.63. While the absolute increase is similar, it constitutes a larger fraction of women's wages. Thus we find that the wages of both women and men would increase as a result of such a program but that women's wages would increase more than men's. The ratio of the salary grade of female-dominated jobs to white male-dominated jobs would increase from 61.6% to 73.4%. Most of this change, it should be noted, is caused by the removal of the sex composition of jobs: only a slight positive increment results from the "zeroing out" of negatively valued working conditions.

Even though incumbents in some female-dominated jobs receive a relative salary advantage because they deal with sick and injured patients, their salaries are deflated because of their tendency to clean up after others and to work in noisy settings. Repetition and being told what to do also contribute to a reduction in their wages. In New York State government employment, therefore, removing the negative impact of the range of undesirable working conditions found in jobs would slightly improve women's wages relative to men. Once again, these results are inconsistent with the predictions of a compensating differentials approach to the sex gap in wages, since that approach predicts wage bonuses and not wage penalties for working in undesirable conditions.

Corroborating evidence was culled from a number of state and local comparable worth studies, all of which have explicit measures of working conditions as well as productivity-related job-content measures. Though these studies, which are often methodologically sophisticated and professionally conducted, have not found their way into the research literature and were not constructed to test the compensating differentials thesis, they do constitute direct evidence of the effect of working conditions on wages. Each study measures job content differently and each controls for different variables. . . .

These studies generally find that undesirable working conditions *negatively* related to wages after appropriate controls are introduced. Only 6 of the 22 working conditions coefficients . . . are in the positive direction predicted by the compensating differentials thesis. In 3 of the studies, the results are entirely inconsistent with compensating differentials. Moreover, the evidence indicates that, while productivity-related and other job characteristics account for some of the gender gap in wages, female-dominated positions remain undervalued even after these effects are removed.

DISCUSSION

The three basic tests of the compensating differentials argument fail to receive support in this analysis. The results are directly at odds with the compensating differentials explanation of the gender gap in wages. Male-dominated positions do not have a monopoly on undesirable working conditions. There are countless undesirable features of work, and many of these are concentrated in female-dominated jobs. Further, in general, neither men nor women are positively compensated for working in unpleasant or unsafe conditions. The majority of the measures of undesirable working conditions have a negative effect on wages, net of education, experience, responsibility, and other productivity-related job attributes. We did find that trade and construction workers receive some additional compensation for risk of injury on the job relative to those in the same bargaining unit, and that health workers receive additional compensation for working with sick or injured patients. As we will elaborate below, we view these exceptions to be grounded in particular

political circumstances rather than an indication of some general economic imperative requiring the compensation of workers in undesirable settings. As a rule, undesirable working conditions have been penalized in the compensation policy of the New York State government. Finally, a significant negative gender coefficient remains in all the equations estimated. Thus, even after all the factors considered are taken into account (factors that explain 90% of the variance in wages), women's work remains significantly undervalued. Each of the links in the compensating differentials chain fails to receive support in our analysis. Putting women in jobs with the same working conditions as men would not reduce the sex gap in wages, while eliminating the perverse effects of working conditions on wages would benefit women slightly more than men.

We have even deeper problems with the compensating differentials approach. We believe that the general pattern of wage penalties associated with undesirable working conditions, as well as the occasional wage premium, can be explained by a model of wage determination that begins not with preferences but with an analysis of the politics of wage determination in a firm or an organization. The ability of specific groups of employees to obtain additional compensation for working in undesirable conditions depends on their ability to legitimate a claim of entitlement and their power to insert this claim into their organization's compensation policy. Once a claim has been inserted into the compensation practices of enough employers in a local labor market and not found to be economically deleterious, it becomes institutionalized into most wage structures in that local labor market. . . .

Recent experience with comparable worth initiatives is especially instructive in that they reveal the way political arrangements affect efforts to reform the wage structure. Steinberg shows that in New York State one of the motives for undertaking a comparable worth study was to satisfy a long-standing union demand that clerical jobs be reclassified upward. During the New York study, decisions about the definition of female-dominated jobs and jobs held by a disproportionate number of minorities, the nondiscriminatory pay standard, and job-content factors and factor weights were the subject of lengthy and often heated negotiations between management, labor, and the feminist proponents conducting the study. The poststudy implementation of wage adjustments was filled with political manipulation and conflict, which included unilateral managerial reworking of the statistical analysis to minimize equity adjustments and threats to one union of wage cuts in the male-dominated jobs it represented.

In Oregon, Acker found that managers and unions were able to reproduce class and gender hierarchy in the wage structure even during an initiative whose goal was a substantial reduction in such inequalities. After more than four years of intense conflict among labor, management, and feminists, only feminists fell short of their goals for modifying the wage structure. The general power resources and specific access to decision making available to labor and management was simply not open to feminists.

We maintain that workers' efforts to receive supplemental compensation for working in undesirable conditions generally involves a process of conflict in a context of unequal power similar to what is being observed in comparable worth initiatives. Workers are not without power, however, and one source of power not often discussed in the literature is the legitimation of employee demands by recourse to an argument that carries compelling face validity. Risk, noise, and other negative job attributes can be translated into wages most often when workers are powerful enough to introduce such issues into discussions regarding wages, often through unions or other workplace pressure groups, and when there is a basis for constructing a plausible and effective rationale.

This process at the organizational level parallels the one that occurs in the political arena when employees demand that the state intervene in the setting of the terms and conditions of their employment contract. Given a commitment to laissez-faire, the state would only intervene in circumstances regarded as "extraordinary," where the legal assumption of bargaining equality was visibly violated. During the Progressive Era, for example, labor standards legislation specifying working hours or prohibiting nightwork was extended to women, minors, and males who succeeded in arguing that they worked in physically dangerous conditions. Thus men who worked in underground mines obtained statutory rights to an 8-hour day, whereas men who worked in bakeries were denied such rights because their jobs were not viewed as dangerous. Even women's rights were limited by the industry or occupation in which they worked: it took decades of vigorous political action by women to extend the right to a 48-hour work week from manufacturing to retail sales. The labor standard laws extended to women were the result of a conscious strategy by groups such as the National Consumers League, collaborating with unions, to use the ideology of women's biological inferiority as a power resource to extend to them rights legally denied men. In general, the inclusion of particular types of work under the umbrella of protection was the result of the political success of these unions in defining specific types of work as deserving this designation, as workers failed to achieve a universal entitlement to protection.

Thus a political or what might be called "negotiated" model of wage determination does not assume that undesirable working conditions automatically translate into wages, even if there is a shortage in the supply of workers. In the case of labor shortage, a number of outcomes is possible. Employers might raise wages to attract a larger pool of workers, in which case a number of other categories of workers may also obtain wage increases on grounds of equity or by attempting to show that they are also in great demand. Alternatively, the tasks involved might be redefined to minimize or alleviate the shortage. In a large bureaucratic setting with an elaborate division of labor, those with power have been known to reorganize their work to have tasks that are viewed as "dirty" or "routine" handled by others. A labor shortage might present itself as an opportunity to a group endeavoring such a strategy. We suggest that power arrangements will affect the conditions of work, its content, and its assessment for purposes of compensation. Indeed, from the perspective of the sociology of work, undesirable working conditions may be a sign of lack of power, indicating that the job is unlikely to receive high wages.

Future research needs to develop specific independent measures of power that can be employed to empirically explain wage patterns that cannot be explained by the imperatives of economic efficiency and utility maximization underlying the compensating differentials perspective. Comparable worth efforts may be a strategic vantage point for such case studies because the political struggles over comparable worth raise questions regarding what makes a job "deserving" of additional compensation. Study of such initiatives can also inform us of the conditions under which employees will actually obtain wage increases once they are viewed as underpaid.

Authors are listed alphabetically and share authorship equally. An earlier draft of this article was presented at the American Sociological Association Meetings, Atlanta, August 1988. The research assistance of Tahmina Ferdousi is greatly appreciated. We thank Paula England, Lois Haignere, David Karen, Janice Madden, Patricia Roos, Leo Rigsby, and Helen Remick for their comments and suggestions.

POSTSCRIPT

Are Women Paid Less Than Men Because Their Working Conditions Are More Favorable?

This issue allows us to examine how labor markets work. It provides us an opportunity to test our understanding of economic theory and to observe how researchers test hypotheses. Because of the sophisticated statistical/ econometrics techniques employed in these two essays, we might miss the basic economic argument that takes place here. That would be unfortunate, since the wage differentials that currently exist in the labor market may be imposing a substantial financial burden on female workers. If the differentials are justifiable, then the comparable worth legislation that is currently in place creates a windfall gain to some female workers, an economic distortion in the labor markets, and an unnecessary burden on taxpayers.

Filer provides evidence to support this latter set of conclusions. His research suggests that women are attracted to occupations that have more "pleasant" job characteristics than those jobs that are dominated by men. Since the female-dominated occupations are more pleasant, their compensation is lower than the less pleasant but more highly paid male-dominated occupations.

Jacobs and Steinberg reject this conclusion. Their research implies that women simply do not have sufficient *power* to demand and receive the compensation that they are entitled to in a workplace that is dominated by male workers. They conclude that compensating differentials depend on the politics of the workplace. If workers are relatively strong, they can negotiate extra compensation for tolerating dangerous or unpleasant working conditions. If they are weak, which historically has been the case for women, they suffer the consequences of lower wages.

Much has been written about the advisability and inadvisability of comparable worth. An excellent introduction to this topic by an advocate of comparable worth is in Helen Reinick, ed., *Comparable Worth and Wage Discrimination* (Temple University Press, 1984). The opposition's arguments are well argued in E. Robert Levernash, ed., *Comparable Worth: Issues and Alternatives* (Equal Employment Advisory Council, 1980). An extremely readable and informative set of congressional hearings is found in *Hearings before the Subcommittees on Human Resources, Civil Service, and Compensation and Employee Benefits, Committee on Post Office and Civil Service, Pay Equity: Equal Pay for Work of Comparable Worth,* 97th Congress, 2d session (1982).

Finally we should note that you can follow the Filer–Jacobs/Steinberg debate in the professional literature. Filer provides a final "Comment" in the December 1990 issue of *Social Forces.* His work in turn is critiqued by James P. Smith in an essay entitled "Commentary," which can be found in Robert T. Michael, Heidi Hartman, and Bridget O'Farrell, eds., *Pay Equity: Empirical Inquiries,* (National Academy Press, 1989).

ISSUE 5

Are Rent Controls the Cause of America's Homelessness?

YES: William Tucker, from "How Housing Regulations Cause Homelessness," *The Public Interest* (Winter 1991)

NO: Richard P. Appelbaum, Michael Dolny, Peter Dreier, and John I. Gilderbloom, from "Scapegoating Rent Control: Masking the Causes of Homelessness," *Journal of the American Planning Association* (Spring 1991)

ISSUE SUMMARY

YES: Journalist William Tucker analyzes the problem of homelessness across the United States and suggests that rent controls and homelessness are correlated.

NO: Sociologist Richard P. Appelbaum and his research associates submit that Tucker's statistical analysis is flawed and that he ignores the real causes of homelessness: poverty, the lack of affordable housing, and inadequate support services for those who suffer from mental illness and alcoholism.

Most principles of economics textbooks spend some time discussing rent controls and how they distort the operation of the market system. Most use rent controls as an example of a price ceiling, which is a legal maximum on the price that may be charged for a commodity. The objective of rent control is, of course, to protect the consumer from high rents. However, supply and demand analysis suggests that, as a result of rent controls, an excess in the quantity demanded for rental housing occurs. This in turn forces landlords to ration the limited supply of rental units on some nonprice basis (personal habits, family size, and length of residence in the community, for example). With the imposition of rent controls, the market is not allowed to reach its equilibrium level, and a "net loss" to society is assumed to result as consumers are forced to pay a high price for the relatively small quantity that suppliers of housing units make available to the market.

Some textbooks go beyond discussing the efficiency implications of these market interferences and examine the historical experiences of New York City, Boston, Los Angeles, San Francisco, Washington, D.C., and other U.S. cities that have experimented with rent controls. These textbooks generally assume that purely competitive market conditions, which are necessary to utilize a supply and demand analysis, are or would be present in these housing markets if there were no rent controls. They conclude that these well-meaning governmental interventions in housing markets have left those in search of affordable housing worse off than if the market were allowed to operate on its own. They allege that renters hold on to apartments because rents are low, while at the same time these low rents discourage landlords from maintaining, upgrading, and/or investing in new units. Thus there are simply fewer housing units on the market.

It is only in recent years, however, that homelessness has been linked to the imposition of rent controls. This connection can be directly traced to the research findings of William Tucker.

In the early 1980s, under pressure from groups charged with the responsibility to provide social services to the homeless, the Reagan administration began to count the number of homeless persons. In 1984, the U.S. Department of Housing and Urban Development issued a study entitled "Report to the Secretary on the Homeless and Emergency Shelters," which estimated that the national homeless population was somewhere between 250,000 and 350,000 persons. (This study forms the statistical foundation for the Tucker selection in this debate.) This estimate and the Reagan administration's hands-off policy to deal with this problem came under intense attack. Groups such as the Coalition for the Homeless in New York and the Committee for Creative Non-Violence in Washington, D.C., estimated that this population was in reality between 2 and 3 million persons in 1984.

Who are these people who find themselves homeless? (*Homeless* refers to an individual who regularly has no place to sleep and must seek refuge in a shelter or remain on the streets after nightfall.) Besides the mentally ill who have not found adequate community care following deinstitutionalization and the drug and alcohol addicts, there are: low-income families who have been evicted for nonpayment of rent; the unemployed; those who have lost their benefits from federal or state welfare or unemployment programs; battered women; and individuals and families that have been displaced by condominium conversions, gentrification, and urban renewal.

It seems reasonable to ask, why has the market not responded by providing "affordable housing" for these people? If we are to believe Tucker, it is because of rent controls. Prospective landlords do not believe that they can earn a financial return sufficient to compensate them for the risk that they must bear. Richard P. Appelbaum and his research team reject Tucker's analysis and his conclusion, largely on the basis of a systematic statistical critique of the Tucker study.

YES
William Tucker

HOW HOUSING REGULATIONS CAUSE HOMELESSNESS

The problem of homelessness in the 1980s has puzzled liberals and conservatives alike. Both have tended to fit the problem into their preconceived
views, without looking at what is new and different about the phenomenon.

For liberals, the issue has been fairly straightforward. Homelessness, they
say, stems from a lack of government effort and compassion. Reacting
almost reflexively, liberals have blamed homelessness on federal spending
cuts and the heartlessness of the Reagan administration. The most commonly cited figure is that budget authorizations for the Department of
Housing and Urban Development (HUD) were cut 75 percent in the Reagan
years, from $32 billion in 1981 to $8 billion in 1988. Everything else is
presumably self-explanatory. This compelling logic has even been repeated
in the *Wall Street Journal*.

Conservatives, on the other hand, have taken two approaches. Either they
deny the problem's existence or they assert that homelessness is almost
always the result of personal pathologies. On the first count, it has often
been argued (as in Martin Morse Wooster's June 1987 *Reason* article, "The
Homeless: An Adman's Dream") that homelessness is really no worse than
it ever was, but that the problem has been exaggerated to justify increases in
government spending. On the other, conservatives have also argued that
most of the homeless are insane, alcoholics, or drug addicts, and that their
personal failings make it impossible for them to find housing, even when it
is available.

UNPERSUASIVE EXPLANATIONS

But these arguments, whether liberal or conservative, do not really hold up
under close scrutiny.

The most obviously flawed explanation lies in the figures that seem to
indicate a massive federal cutback in housing assistance. There has been no

such cutback. Federal low-income housing assistance actually *increased* from $5.7 billion in 1980 to $13.8 billion in 1988. The number of households receiving low-income housing assistance also rose, going from 3.1 million to 4.2 million during the same period.

The commonly cited "cutback" from $32 billion to $8 billion is the figure for HUD's future authorizations. This figure has nothing to do with actual housing assistance, however, since it only indicates the amount of money that Congress authorized HUD to spend in the future. These authorizations often run forty years in advance—and much of the money is never spent anyway.

The reason for this cutback has been the changeover from a program centered around public-housing construction to one centered around housing vouchers. When Congress authorizes a unit of new public housing, it must include all future mortgage payments, running decades ahead. In authorizing a housing voucher, Congress pledges money for only five years—the lifetime of the voucher.

In addition, vouchers provide the same housing at only half the price. A unit of public housing costs the federal government $8,000 a year, while a voucher costs only $4,000. Thus, twice as many people can be reached with the same amount of money. This is why HUD has been able to extend housing aid to more low-income people without an equivalent increase in spending.

But if the liberal argument about "spending cuts" is based largely on a misunderstanding of the budgetary process, the conservative argument that homelessness has not really increased at all seems equally ill-founded.

There were indeed homeless people long before 1980, and their numbers have always been difficult to count. But it is hard to ignore the almost unanimous reports from shelter providers (many of them old-line conservative church groups) that the problem has been getting steadily worse since 1980. The anecdotal evidence is also abundant. Anyone who has walked the streets of New York or Washington over the last decade knows that there are more beggars sitting on the sidewalks and sleeping on park benches than there were ten years ago.

Although many of the homeless are obviously alcoholics, drug addicts, and people who are clinically insane, large numbers appear only to be down on their luck. The most widely accepted statistical breakdown was first proposed in a 1988 Urban Institute paper: "Feeding the Homeless: Does the Prepared Meals Provision Help?" According to authors Martha Burt and Barbara Cohen, one-third of the homeless can be categorized as released mental patients, one-third as alcoholics and drug abusers, and one-third as people who are homeless for purely economic reasons.

Thus the component of homeless people who are not affected by personal pathologies is large. It should also be noted that being a chronic alcoholic or drug addict does not condemn a person to living in the streets. Even "winos" or "stumblebums" were able to find minimal housing in the past.

And so paradoxes remain. How can we have such a large homeless population at a time when rental vacancy rates are near postwar highs? How can there be plenty of housing but not enough "affordable housing"? In short, how can there be scarcity in the housing market when so much housing is still available?

VARIATIONS AMONG HOUSING MARKETS

These paradoxes can be resolved when we recognize that the housing market is not a national market but is instead the sum of many regional and local markets. Rental vacancy rates probably serve as the best measure of the availability of affordable housing, since most poor people rent. These rates vary widely from city to city. During the 1980s, rental vacancy rates in Dallas and Houston were rarely below 12 percent—a figure that is about twice what is considered a normal vacancy rate. At the same time, housing has been absurdly scarce in other cities. New York has not had vacancy rates over 3 percent since 1972. San Francisco had normal vacancy rates during the 1970s, but they plunged to 2 percent during the 1980s, where they remain today.

Since the poor tend to be limited in their mobility, vacancy rates significantly affect their ability to find housing. Although southern and southwestern cities claim to receive a regular seasonal migration of homeless people during the winter months, there is little evidence that people are moving from city to city to find housing. Other factors, like work opportunities, proximity to family members, and sheer inertia, seem to dominate people's choice of locale.

What should be far more mobile is the capital that builds housing and has created such a superabundance in specific cities. If it is difficult to find tenants for new apartments in Dallas and Phoenix, why don't builders shift to Boston or San Francisco, where housing is desperately needed?

Once we start asking this question, the impediments in the housing market suddenly become visible. It is obviously not equally easy to build housing in all cities. In particular, the local regulatory climate has a tremendous impact on the housing supply. Dallas and Houston are free-wheeling, market-oriented cities with little or no zoning regulation and negligible antigrowth sentiment. They have been able to keep abreast of housing demand even as their populations grew rapidly. Boston and San Francisco, on the other hand, have highly regulated housing markets. Both are surrounded by tight rings of exclusionary suburbs, where zoning and growth-control sentiment make new construction extremely difficult. In addition, both have adopted rent control as a way of "solving" local housing shortages. As a result, both have extremely high housing prices and extremely tight rental markets. The median home price in each approaches $200,000, while in Dallas and Phoenix the median price is below the national median of $88,000.

Thus it makes little sense to talk about a national housing market's effect on homelessness. Local markets vary widely, and municipal regulation seems to be the deciding factor.

This is what has misled both liberals and conservatives. Conservatives look at the national superabundance of housing and conclude that local problems do not exist. Liberals look at local shortages and conclude that there is a national housing problem. In fact, housing shortages are a local problem created by local regulation, which is the work of local municipal governments.

It is not surprising, then, to find that homelessness varies widely from city to city, with local housing policies once again the decisive factor. These conclusions are supported by research that I conducted in 1988: I calculated comparative rates of per-capita homelessness for various cities, using the homelessness figures for the largest thirty-five cities investigated in the 1984 *Report to the Secretary of Housing and Urban Development on the Homeless and Emergency Shelters*. I also added fifteen other large cities that were not included in the initial HUD survey. I then subjected the comparative rates of homelessness to regression analysis, in order to look for possible associations with other factors.

Among the independent variables that I considered were the local unemployment rate, the poverty rate, city size, the availability of public housing, the median rent, annual mean temperature, annual rainfall, the size of the minority population, population growth over the past fifteen years, the rental vacancy rate, the presence or absence of rent control, and the median home price in the metropolitan area surrounding each city.

Of all these variables, only four showed a significant correlation: the median home price, the rental vacancy rate, the presence of rent control, and the size of the minority population. The first three formed an overlapping cluster, with the median home price being the strongest predictor (accounting for around 42 percent of the variation, with a chance of error of less than .001 percent). The size of the minority population added about another 10 percent. The total predictive value for both factors was 51 percent, with a margin of error below .00001 percent.

When combined on a single graph (see [graph]), the figures for the forty cities for which all of the relevant data are available show a strong trendline for median home prices; the cities with rent control are predominantly clustered in the top right-hand quadrant. Of the four major cities with minority populations of more than 60 percent, the two with rent control (Newark and Washington) are right on the trendline, while the two without it (Miami and Detroit) are the sole "outliers"—cities whose rates of homelessness do not seem to correspond with their positions in correlation with median home prices.

Altogether, these data suggest that housing variables are a better indicator of homelessness than are the traditional measures of unemployment, poverty, and the relative size of a city's public housing stock. High median home prices are usually found in cities with strict zoning ordinances and a strong no-growth effort. Cities with a tight ring of exclusionary suburbs (such as Boston, New York, Washington, San Francisco, and Los Angeles) have high home prices. Strangely enough, most have also adopted rent control.

At the same time, rent control is closely correlated with low rental vacancy rates. Every city in the country with rent control (except Los Angeles) has a vacancy rate below 4 percent, while the average for cities without rent control is over 8 percent.

When viewed historically, these low vacancy rates are obviously the result of rent control rather than its cause. When most of these cities adopted rent control in the 1970s, all had vacancy rates around the norm of 6 percent. Rather than being spurred by low vacancies, the rent-control ordinances that swept the East and West Coasts during the 1970s were advertised as a response to inflation. The housing shortages came later. (New York, on the other hand, has had rent control since 1943, when it was imposed as part of World War II price

Homelessness in Forty American Cities, Correlated with Rent Control, Size of Minority Population, and Median Home Price

(R = .649   P < .0001)

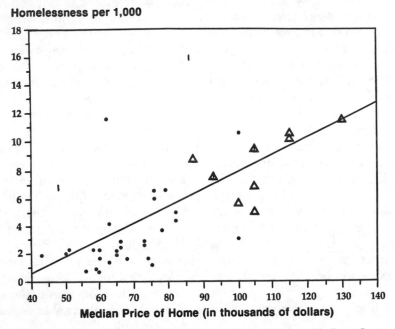

Homelessness per 1,000

Median Price of Home (in thousands of dollars)

ı Cities with Minority Populations > 60 percent   △ Cities with Rent Control

• All Other Cities

controls. Vacancy rates stood at 10 percent in 1940, but have never been above 5 percent since the war ended; they have been below 3 percent since the late 1960s.)

Given these facts, the most plausible explanation of the relation of homelessness to high median home prices, low rental vacancies, and the presence of rent control seems to be what might be called "intense housing regulation." Many cities, such as San Francisco, Berkeley, and Santa Monica, have adopted rent control as part of municipal efforts to slow growth and stop development. These efforts are often aimed against new housing construction, particularly of apartments and rentals.

Since most communities that adopt no-growth ordinances usually like to think of themselves as liberal-minded, they do not like to admit to limiting housing opportunities for low-income people. So they try to compensate by imposing rent control, which they claim "protects" tenants from rising rents.

But of course rent control makes things only worse, by causing vacancy rates to decline and apartments to become much harder to find. The words of Assa Lindbeck, the Swedish socialist (and now chairman of the Nobel Prize Committee for Economics) can hardly be improved upon:

The effects of rent control have in fact been exactly what can be predicted from the simplest type of supply-and-demand analysis—"housing shortage" (excess demand for housing), black markets, privileges for those who happen to have a contract for a rent-controlled apartment, nepotism in the distribution of the available apartments, difficulties in getting apartments for families with children, and, in many places, deterioration of the housing stock. In fact, next to bombing, rent control seems in many cases to be the most efficient technique so far known for destroying cities.

ATTACKS ON GROWTH AND SRO's

Perhaps the best place to see this syndrome at work is in the San Francisco area, which has some of the country's most intense and innovative housing regulation and is also generally considered to be the center of some of the nation's worst homelessness.

It may be hard to believe, but housing prices in California in 1970 were no higher than the national average—even though the state experienced astonishing population growth during the 1950s and 1960s. It was not until the wave of environmental regulation and no-growth sentiment emerged in the 1970s that housing prices began to climb. Throughout California, the increase in home prices has consistently outpaced the national average over the last two decades. By 1988, the median price for a home stood at $158,000 there, in contrast to the nationwide figure of $88,000. In the highly regulated San Francisco Bay area, the median was $178,000, more than twice the national median.

California also experienced a wave of rent-control ordinances in the 1970s. Berkeley adopted rent control in 1971, shortly after imposing a "neighborhood preservation ordinance" that all but prohibited new development. The ordinance was eventually overturned in the California courts in 1975. Then in 1978, Howard Jarvis made an ill-fated promise that Proposition 13 would lower rents by reducing property taxes. When rent reductions failed to materialize, angry tenants in more than a dozen cities retaliated by adopting rent control.

As a result, housing in highly regulated metropolitan regions around San Francisco, San Jose, and Los Angeles has become very scarce. At the same time, homelessness has become a pronounced problem. Santa Monica, which imposed rent control in 1979 as part of an intense antidevelopment campaign, has become the homelessness capital of the West Coast.

Once growth control, tight zoning, and rent control are in place, even middle-class people may have trouble finding housing. A municipality in effect becomes a closed community, open only to its current residents (who either experience remarkable run-ups in the value of their homes or live at rents far below market) and people with strong inside connections. Mark Kann's 1986 book *Middle Class Radicalism in Santa Monica*, which generally praised the city's housing policies, speaks of a "woman who tried to get a Santa Monica apartment for more than a year without success[;] . . . she broke into the city, finally, by marrying someone who already had an apartment there."

No-growth ordinances and rent control have not, of course, been embraced everywhere; but city administrations have often produced comparable results through intense housing-code enforcement, designed to drive "undesirable" housing (and the people who live in it) out of their jurisdictions.

In *New Homeless and Old: Community and the Skid Row Hotel*, Charles Hoch and Robert Slayton have traced the disappearance of the single-room occupancy (SRO) and "cubicle" hotels that once provided cheap housing to thousands of marginal tenants in downtown Chicago. Over 8,000 of these hotel rooms—still available to Chicago's low-income transients in 1963—have disappeared, leaving barely 2,000 today. These lost accommodations were all supplied by the private market. Although remarkably inexpensive (often costing only $2 a night), these rooms offered residents exactly what they wanted—security and privacy. Most of the hotels had elaborate security systems, with desk clerks screening visitors and protecting residents from unwanted ones. In addition, the cheap hotels were usually convenient to stores and public transportation, allowing low-income residents with few family connections to lead frugal but relatively dignified lives.

What happened to these old SRO hotels? Almost without exception, they became the target of urban-renewal efforts and municipal campaigns to "clean up downtown." Intense building-code enforcement and outright condemnation drove most of them out of business. Strict zoning ordinances have since made it virtually impossible to build replacements. Hoch and Slayton conclude:

> We do not believe that the demise of Skid Row and the SRO hotels was the inevitable result of market forces, or that Skid Row residents embodied peculiar social and psychological characteristics that produced deviant and pathological social behavior. . . . [Instead,] this loss was the result of decades of antagonism from civic and business leaders, legitimated from the 1950s on by social scientists, and incorporated into dramatic

change-oriented programs like urban renewal.

Nor have these policies abated today. Despite the hue and cry over the loss of SRO hotels, their replacement is still generally forbidden by zoning ordinances. In Los Angeles, there is a movement afoot to close down SRO hotels—even those subsidized by the city government—because they are not built to withstand earthquakes. Peter Smith, president of the New York City Partnership for the Homeless, comments: "It's essentially illegal for private developers to build SRO hotels in New York anymore."

RESTRICTING DEVELOPMENT

What is causing homelessness, then, is the familiar phenomenon of government regulation. This regulation tends to escape the attention of the public and the enthusiasts of deregulation, because it is done at the local rather than the state or national level.

The truth is that cities and towns do not always welcome new development. At bottom, even the most enthusiastic advocates of progress would often prefer to see their own neighborhoods remain just as they are. People will usually settle for higher-priced housing, because it raises the value of their own homes; but few want tenements, rentals, or other forms of "low-income" housing.

Through regulation, most cities and towns hold a tight rein on their housing markets. Suburbs are particularly exclusionary, zoning out everything but high-priced single-family homes (which require large lot sizes), and prohibiting the rental of rooms or apartments. Cities themselves, although sometimes offering rhetorical welcomes, often play the same exclusionary games.

An example can be seen in Takoma Park, Maryland, a nineteenth-century "streetcar suburb" of Washington, D.C., which until recently had a long history of tolerant housing policies. Takoma Park is a hodgepodge of two-, three-, and four-family homes within easy commuting distance of Washington. During World War II, homeowners rented attics and spare bedrooms to wartime officials who could not find housing in Washington. This tradition continued after the war, when many returning GI's sought housing while attending nearby Columbia Union College. Many homeowners permanently converted their homes to two- and three-family units.

During the 1970s, however, a group of homeowners living in a recently constructed, more suburban part of the city asked Montgomery County to enforce a sixty-year-old zoning ordinance that prohibited rentals in single-family zones. (Zoning is controlled by county governments in Maryland.) After a long dispute, the city council adopted a compromise in 1978, which permitted anyone who was renting before 1954 to continue to do so for another ten years. In 1988 the reprieve expired, however, and evictions began. More than six hundred tenants were forced to leave their homes.

THE APPEAL OF UTOPIANISM

It is important to realize that housing regulations are to blame for a lot of homelessness. But at the same time, we must acknowledge the impulses that make people want to intervene in the housing marketplace.

About a year ago, I spent a few days in San Francisco's Market Street district, a notorious skid row. Although not particularly dangerous, the surroundings were decidedly unpleasant. Weather-beaten young men, each of whom seemed to have his entire worldly belongings wrapped in a sleeping bag, lounged along the sidewalks. Ragged holdovers from the sixties perched on public monuments, performing drunken imitations of rock singers. Veterans of motorcycle gangs weaved past timid pedestrians, carrying on garrulous arguments with their equally disheveled girlfriends. Along the side streets, tattoo parlors jostled with cheap cafeterias, pornography shops, and the inevitable flophouse hotels.

It is easy enough to imagine some ambitious politician surveying the scene and deciding that it was time to "clean up Market Street." Such campaigns have occurred all over the country and have inevitably produced the disjuncture that we now find between the supply of housing and the price that poor people can afford to pay for it.

Yet distasteful as it may seem, skid rows play a crucial role in providing the poor and near-poor with cheap housing. Not everyone can live in suburban subdivisions or high-rise condominiums. To provide for everyone, we also need rooms for rent, fleabag hotels, tenements, trailer parks—and the "slumlords" who often run them. Although usually imagined to be rich and powerful, these bottom-rung entrepreneurs almost always turn out to be only slightly more affluent than the people for whom they are providing housing.

In the utopian dreams of regulators and "housing activists," such landlords are always eliminated. They are inevitably replaced by the federal government and the "non-profits," orchestrated by the city planners and visionary architects who would "tear down the slums" and replace them with "model tenements" and the "garden cities of tomorrow."

It is not wrong to have such visions. But let us do things in stages. Let us build the new housing *first*—and only then tear down the old "substandard" housing that is no longer needed. If we let the best become the enemy of the good—or even the barely adequate—the homeless will have nothing more substantial to live in than the dreams of the housing visionaries themselves.

NO

Richard P. Appelbaum,
Michael Dolny, Peter Dreier,
and John I. Gilderbloom

SCAPEGOATING RENT CONTROL: MASKING THE CAUSES OF HOMELESSNESS

The U.S. Congress has recently considered legislation that would withhold federal housing funds from the numerous locales that have adopted rent control. Such legislation is supported by HUD [Department of Housing and Urban Development] Secretary Jack Kemp, who strongly believes that rent control is partly responsible for discouraging badly needed investment in rental housing. Sixteen states currently have laws that restrict the ability of localities to enact rent control, while another 29 have been targeted for such laws by the National Apartment Owners' Association and the National Multi-Housing Council. While the belief that rent control has adverse consequences for housing markets has long been advanced by housing economists, a new claim has recently emerged in support of anti-rent control legislation: the assertion that rent control should be dismantled because it is the chief underlying cause of homelessness. The evidence for this claim can be traced to a single study by journalist William Tucker (1987a, 1987b, 1989a, 1989b). Since homelessness is such a visible national issue, local rent regulations—affecting millions of tenants nationwide—are more vulnerable to federal anti–rent-control legislation than at any time in the recent past. . . .

Despite the widespread attention it has received, Tucker's research is seriously flawed. The link between rent control and homelessness it purports to demonstrate does not withstand serious scrutiny. Given the political context in which the research appears, the following critique of Tucker's thesis is doubly important. Unchallenged, Tucker's work represents a serious threat to local rent control by linking it with a national problem of high concern. Pointing the finger at rent control can only divert attention from a serious effort to uncover and address the actual causes of homelessness.

From Richard P. Appelbaum, Michael Dolny, Peter Dreier, and John I. Gilderbloom, "Scapegoating Rent Control: Masking the Causes of Homelessness," *Journal of the American Planning Association*, vol. 57, no. 2 (Spring 1991). Copyright © 1991 by The American Planning Association. Reprinted by permission. Notes and references omitted.

The growth of homelessness during the 1980s is not linked with the efforts by a handful of local governments to regulate skyrocketing rents. Homelessness is directly related to the overall level of poverty, to the availability of affordable housing, and to the accessibility of support services for people suffering from mental illness or alcoholism. It is no accident that the number of homeless Americans increased dramatically during the 1980s. The past decade has witnessed growing poverty, especially among the "working poor"; a decline in low-rent housing, including sharp cuts in federal low-income housing assistance; and a failure to adequately serve the deinstitutionalized mentally ill. As a result, since the early 1980s the homeless population has increased between 20 and 25 percent a year, according to the U.S. Conference of Mayors annual surveys (1989, 2). Moreover, the profile of the homeless population includes a growing number of families with young children, as well as individuals with jobs (U.S. Conference of Mayors 1989).

This assessment of the underlying causes of America's homeless problem would seem to suggest fairly straightforward remedies directed at increasing the wages of America's working poor, expanding the supply of affordable housing, and providing residential and social support programs for the nation's mentally ill. A comprehensive examination of the evidence gives no support to the claim that rent control is the root cause of homelessness in the United States. . . .

THE EFFECT OF RENT CONTROL ON INVESTMENT IN RENTAL HOUSING

Two hundred cities and counties currently have some form of rent regulation. This group includes over 100 communities in New Jersey, as well as cities and counties in Massachusetts, New York, Virginia, Maryland, Alaska, Connecticut, and California. Most of these ordinances were first enacted in the early 1970s. Approximately 10 percent of the nation's rental housing stock is estimated to be covered by some form of rent control (Baar 1983). Current rent control measures can be categorized as *moderate*, in comparison with the more *restrictive* rent control that was in effect in New York City during the immediate postwar period.

Moderate rent controls permit rent increases sufficient for the landlord to maintain an adequate return on investment, while protecting tenants against rent gouging. All ordinances currently in effect are moderate in nature. Such controls typically peg annual rent increases to increases in the landlords' costs, and exempt newly constructed rental units from controls altogether. They also often require adequate maintenance as a condition for annual rent adjustments: tenants in buildings that are inadequately maintained can appeal their rent increases. Some rent control laws permit vacated units to be temporarily decontrolled so that rents can be raised to market levels for incoming tenants, after which they are recontrolled. Moderate rent controls thus contain a number of provisions explicitly designed to encourage both construction of new rental housing and maintenance of existing units.

In a few highly inflationary California housing markets, some controls are coupled with an additional provision: they exclude increased mortgage costs from the formulas relating landlords' costs and allowable rent increases. This provision is designed to discourage speculation in rental housing. Under such an exclusion, a landlord who has incurred increased capital costs (either through recent purchase or through refinancing to obtain equity capital) cannot pass the higher financing costs through to tenants in the form of rent increases.

In sum, current rent controls contain provisions that are intended to guarantee the landlord a fair and reasonable rate of return on investment, while protecting the interests of tenants by preserving affordable housing. Maintenance is strongly encouraged; newly built units are not controlled at all.

Nonetheless, critics continue to argue that rent control discourages investment in rental housing. According to Tucker (1987a, 1987b, 1989a), for example, localities that enact rent control rob landlords of their rightful returns. So deprived, landlords cut costs. Maintenance suffers; buildings are abandoned. Badly needed new units are never constructed. Although rents may be lowered in the short run, the argument goes, housing scarcity eventually results. Scarcity, in turn, causes homelessness. In posh areas like Santa Monica, Cambridge, or the Upper West Side of Manhattan, yuppies squeeze out low income tenants in the fight for scarce apartments. In blighted areas like the South Bronx, buildings are abandoned, and eventually razed by arsonists or government bulldozers. Either way, says Tucker, the poor are relegated to the streets and shelters.

This analysis is not original to Tucker; on the contrary, it is shared by a number of housing economists as well as many people in the real estate community. For example, ten years ago a national survey of economists found virtually unanimous agreement that "a ceiling on rents reduces the quantity and quality of hous-

ing available" (Kearl et al. 1979). These conclusions are not based on empirical studies, but on theoretical assumptions about how housing markets are supposed to operate. The real estate lobby has been highly effective in communicating this analysis to its members and the media. Major news organizations, including the *Wall Street Journal* and *Forbes* magazine, have editorialized against rent controls (Gilderbloom 1983).

Numerous empirical studies have been conducted on the effects of moderate rent control on rental housing investment; none support the views just described. A comprehensive review . . . finds that such controls have not caused a decline in construction, capital improvements, maintenance, abandonment, or demolition of controlled units relative to noncontrolled ones. This is because of the nonrestrictive nature of moderate controls, which, as we have seen, guarantee landlords a fair and reasonable rate of return. Rent controls eliminate extreme rent increases, particularly in highly inflationary markets, but they do not eliminate the profits necessary to encourage investment in private rental housing (Gilderbloom 1984, 1986; Heffley and Santerre 1985; Mollenkopf and Pynoos 1973; Daugherbaugh 1975; Vitaliano 1983). In particular, the vacancy decontrol-recontrol provision in some localities results in significantly higher average rents than those that would occur in the absence of such a provision (Gilderbloom and Keating 1982; Hartman 1984; Clark and Heskin 1982; Rydell 1981; Los Angeles Rent Stabilization Division 1985). While moderate rent control is successful in eliminating exorbitant rent increases, its impact on redistributing income from landlords to tenants clearly depends on the degree to which market conditions would otherwise have led to rent increases that greatly exceed the allowable rent levels.

RENT CONTROL AND HOMELESSNESS: TUCKER'S ANALYSIS

Tucker's study is the first to look at the impact of rent control on homelessness. In order to support his argument that rent control produces homelessness by discouraging investment and thereby creating housing scarcity, Tucker sought to show that cities with rent control had lower vacancy rates and greater homelessness than cities without rent control.

For his primary data set, Tucker relied on the single comparative study of homelessness that had been done at the time of his study—the HUD survey of homelessness in 60 metropolitan areas (1984). HUD had conducted a random sample of 20 cities in each of three size strata (50,000–250,000; 250,000–1,000,000; and over, 1,000,000). For each city, HUD telephoned people they labeled "knowledgeable informants" and asked for their estimates of the homeless street population in their areas. (Shelter estimates were more accurately obtained from information provided by shelter operators.) The various estimates for each locale were then combined into an average figure that was weighted to reflect the presumed reliability of the different sources. Tucker took the HUD estimates for the 40 metropolitan areas in the two largest strata. He then computed a homeless rate for each city by dividing HUD's estimate of the total number of homeless by the population of the core city for each metropolitan area.

Tucker did not rely exclusively on HUD's random sample of places; rather, he modified the HUD sample in several ways. First, he dropped six cities from among HUD's 40 metropolitan areas over 250,000 in population: Dayton, Davenport, Colorado Springs, Scranton, Raleigh, and Baton Rouge. These six places were reportedly eliminated because of "the great difficulty in determining local vacancy rates" (Tucker 1989a, 5, n. 4). For unexplained reasons, Tucker then added to his list one of HUD's smallest (under 250,000) metropolitan areas—Lincoln, Nebraska. He also mistakenly classified Hartford as a city with rent control. Finally, he added 15 additional cities "to include some notable HUD omissions" (1987a, 1); he does not explain how these cities were selected out of thousands of possible places across the United States. Since these cities were not a part of HUD's original study, Tucker developed his own homeless estimates by making telephone calls to unspecified informants in each city. This misguided sampling methodology yielded a final list of 50 places for his analysis.

Once he had obtained his list of places, Tucker identified factors that might be important determinants of homelessness. He originally chose rates of poverty, unemployment, public housing availability, and rental housing vacancy; total population; mean annual temperature; and the presence (or absence) of rent control. Two additional variables—population growth rate and mean annual rainfall—are employed in a recent study (1989a) but apparently not in the original studies (1987a, 1987b); nonetheless, the appendix in the recent study reports only the seven original variables. High rates of poverty and unemployment are indicative of an economically marginal population, and therefore should be associated with greater homelessness. Public housing availability, on the other hand, provides one form of protection against homelessness, and so should be associated with lower rates. Low vacancy rates indicate scarcity in the private rental housing market, and—according to Tucker—should be associated with both rent control and homelessness. Larger, faster-growing places may well attract the unemployed with the lure of jobs, thereby contributing to homelessness in such cities. Finally, locales with warm temperatures and low rainfalls have an obvious appeal to the homeless.

Having selected these key variables, Tucker employed them in two- and three-variable regression equations predicting homelessness. While his results vary somewhat among his various reports, he generally found that the only variables that made any substantial difference in the rate of homelessness were the local vacancy rate and rent control—and that the latter statistically accounts for much of the impact of the former. In fact, Tucker found that rent control by itself explains fully 27 percent of the difference in homelessness among cities; when combined with mean temperature, it accounts for 31 percent. According to these findings, homeless people are attracted to cities with hospitable climates; when such places have rent control, increased housing scarcity is assumed to result, and—with it—greater homelessness.

In evaluating Tucker's findings, it is important to bear in mind that he classified only 9 of the 50 cities as having any form of rent control at all. Since all of the cities had homeless problems to varying degrees, it is obvious that rent control cannot be the principal cause of homelessness, as Tucker contends. Miami, with the highest rate of homelessness in the cities under study, does not currently have rent control. Nor does St. Louis,

which ranks second. Nor does Worcester, which ranks fourth. The fact that three out of four places with the most severe homeless problems lack rent control would seem to provide a prima facie case for rejecting Tucker's claim out of hand.

The first major difficulty in Tucker's study lies with his use of HUD's measure of homelessness (1984) as his key variable. According to two congressional hearings that examined HUD's methods in detail, that measure was highly unreliable. HUD relied on what it called "knowledgeable informants"—police departments, social service agencies, shelter staffs—who simply *guessed* at the numbers of homeless people in the 60 areas HUD reviewed. There was no actual count of the number of homeless in the streets, park benches, abandoned cars, and elsewhere—and certainly no estimate of the "invisible" homeless temporarily living in overcrowded apartments with friends or relatives. Although the guesses were mainly for downtown neighborhoods, HUD acted as if they applied to much larger metropolitan areas—Rand McNally marketing areas (RMAs), areas with four or five times as many people. This method, not surprisingly, produced very low rates of homelessness for the metropolitan areas HUD studied, since they guaranteed that homeless people outside the downtown areas would be excluded from the study. Tucker's principal variable, therefore, substantially undercounts the homeless.

The second major problem results from the questionable procedures by which Tucker arrived at his 50 cities, which—as will be demonstrated in the next section of this article—skew his results towards his foregone conclusions. As noted above, he began with HUD's random sample of 40 medium and large metropolitan areas, added one smaller HUD metropolitan area, selectively eliminated six places, and then added 15 others of his own choosing. Since only five of HUD's cities were among the more than 200 places with rent control, Tucker made certain that three rent-controlled cities were included among those he added. But sampling problems are compounded by the fact that the three rent-controlled cities he added are already presumably included in HUD's homeless estimates: Newark and Yonkers are part of the New York City metropolitan area, while Santa Monica is part of Los Angeles.

Tucker's third major error is his failure to consider the possibility that high rents might themselves be a chief cause of homelessness, while at the same time causing tenants to demand rent control. In other words, his reported correlation between rent control and homelessness might be an artifact of the association of both with high rents. He nowhere looks at the possible causal effect of rent on homelessness. . . .

WHY DO WE HAVE A HOMELESSNESS PROBLEM?

The United States now faces the worst housing crisis since the Great Depression. The underlying problem is a widening gap between what Americans can afford to pay and what it costs to build and operate housing. In this situation, the poor are the most vulnerable to joining the ranks of those without a home.

The number of poor Americans, now about 33 million people, is growing, and the poor are getting poorer (Center on Budget and Policy Priorities 1988, 1; Children's Defense Fund 1989, 16–26, 100–106, 115; U.S. Joint Economic Committee of Congress 1988, ch. VII). The largest increase is among the "working poor"— people who earn their poverty on the job because of low wages. Among the "welfare poor"—primarily single mothers and their children—Aid to Families with Dependent Children (AFDC) and other benefits have declined far below the poverty level. These are people who are only one rent increase, hospital stay, or layoff from becoming homeless. In fact, a recent report by the U.S. Conference of Mayors (1989, 2) found that almost one-quarter of the homeless *work*, but simply have wages too low to afford permanent housing.

The plight of the poor is worsened by the steadily rising housing costs that have plagued the economy throughout the past decade (see U.S. Comptroller General 1979 for an early announcement of the housing crisis). On one hand, rising homeownership costs have forced many would-be first-time buyers into the status of reluctant long-term renters, greatly increasing pressures on the rental housing market. Homeownership rates have been declining steadily since 1980, particularly among first-time homebuyers. Among households where the head was under 25, for example, ownership has declined from 23.4 percent to 15.1 percent of all households, a drop of 36 percent; for those headed by someone aged 25 to 34, the decline has been from 51.4 percent to 45.1 percent, or 12 percent (Apgar 1988, 24). In 1973, it took 23 percent of the median income of a young family with children to carry a new mortgage on an average-priced house. Today, it takes over half of a young family's income (Children's Defense Fund 1988, 57).

On the other hand, renters confront chronic production shortages and rising rents. Between 1970 and 1983 rents tripled, while renters' income only doubled. As a result the average rent-income ratio grew from roughly one-quarter to one-third; the proportion of tenants paying 25 percent or more income into rent increased from one-third to one-half. By 1985, close to one out of every four renters paid over half of their income for housing costs. Eleven million families now pay over one-third of income on rent; 5 million pay over half.

The problem is especially acute for the poor, who are now competing with the middle class for scarce apartments. It is estimated that by 1985 there was a national shortage of some 3.3 million affordable units for households earning under $5,000—an increase of more than 80 percent since 1978 (Leonard et al. 1989, 9). Among the nation's nearly 7 million poor renter households, 45 percent spent more than 70 percent of their income on housing in 1985; 65 percent paid more than half; while 85 percent—some 5.8 million households—paid more than the 30 percent officially regarded as "affordable" under current federal standards. The median tenant household paid almost two-thirds of its income on rent (Leonard et al. 1989, 1–2). The typical young single parent pays 81 percent of her meager income just to keep a roof over her children's heads (Children's Defense Fund 1988, 59).

Despite the severity of these problems, less than one-third of poor households receive any kind of housing subsidy (Leonard et al. 1989, 27; U.S. Congressional Budget Office 1988, 3). This housing subsidy level is the lowest of any industrial nation in the world. Some 6 to 7 million low-income renter families receive no housing assistance whatsoever, and are therefore completely at the mercy of housing markets that place them im-

mediately at risk of being homeless. And, while the number of poor families has risen during the 1980s, the number of low-rent private apartments has plummeted as a result of rising rents, urban redevelopment activities, condo conversions, and arson. Between 1974 and 1985, the number of privately owned, unsubsidized apartments renting for less than $300 (measured in 1988 dollars) fell by one-third, a loss of nearly 3 million units (Apgar et al. 1989, 4). The swelling waiting lists of even the most deteriorated subsidized housing projects are telling evidence of the desperation of the poor looking for affordable homes.

The already existing shortages of affordable private housing were worsened considerably by the short-sighted actions of the Reagan administration. The 1986 Tax Reform Act, for example, removed many of the tax benefits that previously made it profitable for the private sector to rent housing to poorer families. It is estimated that the loss of tax shelters for housing will eventually reduce the value of income property by 20 percent, forcing compensating rent increases of 25 percent by the early 1990s. The National Association of Home Builders predicted that rental housing construction would decline by half as a direct result (Furlong 1986, 16); an MIT market simulation predicted an eventual loss of 1.4 million units (Apgar et al. 1985, 1).

The Reagan administration's budget cutbacks virtually eviscerated publicly owned and subsidized housing, all but eliminating the already small federal commitment to providing housing for the poor. Not only were safety net programs cut in general, but housing was selected to bear the brunt of budgetary retrenchment. Between 1981 and 1989 federal expenditures for subsidized housing declined by four-fifths, from $32 billion to $6 billion. Total federal housing starts declined from 183,000 in 1980 to 20,000 in 1989 (Low Income Housing Information Service 1989). The administration even proposed to sell off 100,000 units of public housing, an effort that was stymied largely because public housing tenants were too poor to afford their units. A number of specific programs, including several directed at the needs of the homeless, were "zeroed out" in the 1989 budget. It should be pointed out that, as severe as these measures may appear, President Reagan's proposed cuts were still deeper: philosophically committed to ending federal involvement in housing altogether, he was prevented from doing so only by the lobbying efforts of low-income housing advocates before a Democrat-controlled Congress. A single statistic tells the story in unambiguous terms. When President Reagan came to office in 1981, the federal government spent seven dollars on defense for every dollar on housing. When he left office in 1989, the ratio of dollars spent was 46 to one.

In sum, declining incomes at the bottom have converged with rising housing costs to produce a potentially explosive situation, which unwise short-term federal policies have served to worsen. Rent control plays no role in this unfolding tragedy. According to one estimate (Clay 1987, i), by 2003 "the gap between the total low-rent housing supply (subsidized and unsubsidized) and households needing such housing is expected to grow to 7.8 million units," representing an affordable housing loss for nearly 19 million people. This figure represents the probable constituency of the homeless, as the United States moves into the twenty-first century.

On its own, rent control can't solve the housing crisis. It is merely one tool available to local governments for confronting skyrocketing rents and a shortage of affordable housing. Tucker's study does not demonstrate what it sets out to do, and so cannot be used to justify a scapegoating of rent control for the mounting tragedy of homelessness.

AUTHOR'S NOTE

We would like to thank Jon Lorence and William Bielby for giving us special assistance in the analysis of this data. Carrie Donald, Gary Dworkin, Neal King, and Bob Nideffer also provided important technical assistance. Special thanks go to Kevin Quinn and the staff of the Economic Policy Institute, who published an earlier version as a briefing paper. Authors are listed in alphabetical order.

POSTSCRIPT

Are Rent Controls the Cause of America's Homelessness?

This is a debate where the protagonists defend their positions with reasoned arguments and statistical evidence. But note, the provision of statistical evidence can itself be subject to challenge. Your task here is to bring critical questions to bear on the statistics used as you untangle the conflicting claims made in these two essays. Which essay provides the most reasonable set of assumptions? Which analysis employs data that are least subject to question? Which set of conclusions is justifiable?

These are not easy questions to answer. Yet if we do not attempt to systematically examine the assumptions, data, economic theories, and conclusions of empirical studies such as those of Tucker and Appelbaum et al., we would simply allow our uninformed preconceptions to determine which argument we would accept as the foundation for the public policy we endorse. If we lean toward the conservative, free-market camp, we might be inclined to accept unquestioningly Tucker's analysis, since it suggests that government interferences in the market rent controls cause the social problem of homelessness. If, on the other hand, we find ourselves sympathetic toward the liberal, institutional, or even the radical view of economics, we would tend to accept without question the Appelbaum et al. work, since they suggest that the interference-free market fails to provide affordable housing to the large majority of individuals and families who find themselves homeless. By now we hope we have convinced you that a knee-jerk reaction is never correct. That means that, on occasion, we must reject the arguments of some researchers, even if we want to believe them.

To help you make this determination, we suggest that you look at other published work in this area. In the anti–rent control camp you will find noted housing authority Anthony Downs, *Residential Rent Controls: An Evaluation* (Urban Land Institute, 1988). You will also find other works published by Tucker, since his work provides the empirical foundation for the anti–rent control camp. See, for example, *The Excluded Americans: Homelessness and Housing Policies* (Regnery Gateway, 1990) and *The Source of America's Housing Problem: Look in Your Own Back Yard*, Policy Analysis Series, no. 127 (Cato Institute, February 6, 1990). On the other side we suggest that you read some of the other work published by Appelbaum and Gilderbloom. Among other contributions to this literature, Appelbaum has published *Rent Controls: Facts, Not Fiction* (California State Senate Rules Committee, 1990). Gilderbloom has also written widely in this area, including "Towards A Sociology of Rent," *Social Problems* (vol. 34, no. 3, 1987).

ISSUE 6

Do Hostile Takeovers Harm Society?

YES: Lisa Newton, from "The Hostile Takeover: An Opposition View," in Tom L. Beauchamp and Norman E. Bowie, eds., *Ethical Theory and Business,* 3rd ed. (Prentice Hall, 1988)

NO: Robert Almeder and David Carey, from "In Defense of Sharks: Moral Issues in Hostile Liquidating Takeovers," *Journal of Business Ethics* (July 1991)

ISSUE SUMMARY

YES: Professor of philosophy Lisa Newton warns that hostile corporate takeovers are *"not* business as usual"; rather, they are an "assault with a deadly weapon."

NO: Philosophers Robert Almeder and David Carey charge that Newton's arguments are "seriously flawed," and that it is the use of "shark repellents" that is immoral.

The wave of mergers and acquisitions in the 1980s raises many questions. What laws and court decisions control acquisitions and mergers? What is the difference between the current merger movement and the mergers and acquisitions that took place before the 1980s? And finally, do friendly mergers and acquisitions have the same economic consequences as unfriendly, or hostile, takeovers?

The answers to these questions are found in part in U.S. economic history. Mergers and acquisitions have appeared in four waves. Just before the turn of this century, the first great merger movement dominated the economy. The whiskey trust, the sugar trust, the cottonseed oil trust, and the Standard Oil trust were attempts to pull together small and larger firms into new business organizations that could act collectively to reduce supply and increase price. Since Congress concluded that these new business organizations could inflict abuses upon society, which was in direct conflict with the tenets of a free-market economy, Congress passed its first antitrust legislation, the Sherman Antitrust Act of 1890.

But this act did not slow the approach of the second wave of mergers and acquisitions that appeared shortly after World War I. This wave had many of the same characteristics as the first wave. Business combinations were generally in the form of horizontal mergers (mergers of firms at the same stage of production within one industry, such as merging two steel manufacturers). At the same time, however, two new forms of mergers and acquisitions began to appear: vertical mergers (mergers of firms at different stages of production within one industry, such as merging a firm that manufactures shoes with another firm that is a retail shoe chain) and conglomerate mergers (mergers between a firm in one industry and a firm in a totally different industry, such as the merger of an oil company with a department store chain). In the face of this second wave of mergers and acquisitions, Congress attempted to strengthen the Sherman Act by passing the Clayton Antitrust Act of 1914.

The third wave of mergers and acquisitions took place from 1948 to 1979. The Federal Trade Commission (FTC)—the federal agency that is responsible for assuring competitive markets in the United States—estimates that of the more than 2,000 large mergers in manufacturing and mining that occurred in this period, three-fourths of these mergers and acquisitions were conglomerate mergers.

Lastly, and of immediate importance for this issue, is the fourth wave of takeovers, mostly hostile, that began to appear in the 1980s. In the case of a hostile takeover, the acquiring firm is able to complete the merger without the aid or cooperation of the firm to be acquired, and it usually does so by buying a controlling quantity of the to-be-acquired firm's publicly held stock. Since the threat of a hostile takeover constitutes a direct challenge to the management of the acquired firm, management is forced into evasive action. In extreme cases, this results in the payment of greenmail—buying back the stock from the corporate raider at inflated prices. Thus, corporate raiders such as Rupert Murdock, the Bass brothers, and T. Boone Pickens have made huge speculative gains by merely *starting* to acquire the stock of an unsuspecting firm.

In self-defense, firms have pushed their state legislatures for laws that would protect them from unfriendly advances. Currently, 21 states restrict unfriendly takeovers, and more states are likely to follow since the Supreme Court has upheld, in the *Arvin* case (1987), the right of states to regulate takeovers. On April 21, 1987, in a six to three vote, justices from both the conservative and the liberal sides of the Court joined retiring justice Lewis F. Powell, Jr., in his majority opinion that state action in this area was not a burdensome infringement on interstate commerce.

In her attempt to justify existing state statutes and to support the imposition of new laws that would protect corporations from hostile takeovers, Lisa Newton raises two interrelated questions. First she asks whether or not these takeovers "serve the public interest." Then she asks whether or not corporations have some basic right to exist that is violated by a hostile takeover. Robert Almeder and David Carey challenge the logic of Newton's arguments. They conclude that hostile takeovers are morally defensible. Indeed, they are offended by legislation that constrains corporate takeover activity. For them, it is these constraints that are immoral.

YES

Lisa Newton

THE HOSTILE TAKEOVER:
AN OPPOSITION VIEW

RIGHTS AND CONSEQUENCES

Given the nature and prestige of the players, we might be tempted to think that the *hostile takeover* is just one more game businessmen play. But the business literature on the subject sounds atypically harsh notes, describing this activity in the unbusinesslike language of threat and attacks, followed by occasionally desperate and increasingly sophisticated defenses—the junk-bond bust-up takeover versus the Pac-Man, Poison Pill, Crown Jewel Option defenses ranged against the two-tier tender offer and finally the launching of the golden parachutes.

In this colorful literature, the most noticeable feature of a corporate takeover is its terrible human cost. *Fortune* magazine entitled a 1984 article, "Help! My Company Has Just Been Taken Over," and began the article with the story of the suicide of a corporate executive precipitated by his termination following a takeover. "There are more mergers than ever these days," the author warns, "and their human toll is higher than ever too."[1] A more recent *New York Times* article, entitled "'People Trauma' in Mergers," documents the anxiety and feelings of betrayal experienced by employees—increasingly, down to the hourly level—when the prospect of takeover looms into view. Trust is broken, loyalty ebbs, and, if none of the above is of any interest to managers, productivity plummets.[2] The fact that these alarms come from publications inside the business world is significant; outsiders might be expected to see human effects more clearly than the economic realities that underlie the takeover activity, yet here are the insiders suddenly concluding that the realities of profit may actually be less important than the injuries to the people caught up in it against their will. The hostile corporate takeover is simply *not* business as usual. It is assault with a deadly weapon; and the question seems to be, how can it be right?

Let us backtrack for the moment. A practice requires moral scrutiny if it regularly derogates from human dignity, causes human pain, or with no apparent reason treats one class of human beings less well than another. Any practice that regularly throws people out of work does at least the first two of those (work being possibly the largest factor in self-worth and the major instrument to creature satisfactions), and unless we find the raider's urgent need for self-aggrandizement as a worthy reason for dismembering working units, it probably does the third also. To be sure, all manner of evil things can happen to people in non-takeover situations; part of the fun of being alive is the risk, and part of being in business is knowing that your livelihood may depend on the next quarter's earnings. But as a general moral principle, if I, by my voluntary act and for my own profit, increase the riskiness of your life, no matter how high the base risk and no matter how small the increment by which I raise it for you, then I owe you an explanation. The hostile takeover regularly disemploys at least some people who would not have been unemployed absent the takeover; that makes it, by the above, a proper candidate for moral scrutiny, without presumption one way or another on the results of the scrutiny.

A further problem, if it is a problem, is that a takeover deliberately destroys something—a company, corporation, an instance of human association. In the other cases, it can be said that the association itself "decided" to do something to make itself better, or more efficient. But when it is taken over, it does nothing—it is killed, and the atmosphere of the threat of death hangs over the entire proceeding, from the raider's first phone call to the final resolution (usually the acquisition of the company by some party other than the raider). Does it make any difference that a company is

destroyed? Is that an evil over and above all the other disruptions that takeovers occasion? Or is it, strictly speaking, meaningless, beyond the sufferings of the individuals?

We have, in short, two very separate and distinct questions. First, does the hostile corporate takeover serve some ordinary and necessary role in the economy? Whatever the present injuries, is the practice justified in the long run as improving the economic condition of the greatest number? That very pragmatic question is accompanied by a second, metaphysical one: Is the corporation the type of thing whose demise could or should be regretted? Could it have some right to live, to persevere in existence—a right appropriately exercised in management's series of "defenses"? Ordinarily we assume that only individual human beings have dignity, worth, or rights (beyond the uninteresting legal "rights" bestowed on the corporation to permit it to conduct business). But that assumption fits poorly with the fact that people will willingly die for their associations when they will not willingly sacrifice their lives for personal interests; that fact needs further examination before we dismiss the association as a merely instrumental good. We will pursue, then, two separate and logically independent lines of inquiry: First, on straightforward utilitarian reasoning, does the business practice that we know as the *hostile takeover* serve the public interest by performing some useful role in the economy, or are there good utilitarian reasons for limiting or prohibiting it? Second, does the corporation have some right to exist that is violated by any business practice that ends its existence without the consent of its present governors? Along the line of the first inquiry, we will argue, first, that the hostile takeover is damaging to the economy (and the people in it) in the short and middle run and, second, that this practice is a deadly symptom of a long-term process in our relation to material goods, a loss of "ownership," which ought to be noted and, as far as possible, reversed. On the line of the second inquiry, we will argue that "the association," usually the political association, has been invested with dignity since Aristotle's day, and that its right to self-defense is firmly grounded in individual rights of undisputed worth. Therefore the corporation, acting through its present management, has the right and (sometimes) the duty to defend itself when its existence is threatened, apart from any arguments about immediate effects on the wealth of individuals.

RESPONSIBLE OWNERSHIP PROFITS

Takeovers are generally defended on the utilitarian grounds that they are in the public interest. The "takeover" is simply capital flowing from one sector of the economy to a more profitable one, in this instance, to buy up the stock of a company the value of whose assets is significantly greater than the value of its outstanding stock. Where stock is undervalued, an inefficiency exists in the economy; whether through management ineptness or other market conditions, the return on the shareholder's investment is not as high as it could be. It would be maximized by selling off the assets and distributing the proceeds among the owners; but then, by the above, it is management's duty to do that. The takeover merely does the job that the managers were supposed to do, and the prospect of a takeover, should the stock become undervalued, is

an excellent incentive to management to keep the shareholders' interest in mind.

Moreover, defenses against takeovers often involve managers in apparent conflicts of interest. They are protecting their jobs rather than meeting their fiduciary obligations to stockholders. Theory in this instance concurs with current case law; there should be no regulation of takeovers beyond (not very rigorous) anti-trust scrutiny, and defensive moves on the part of management are morally and probably legally illegitimate. To be sure, people get hurt in takeovers, but the shareholders profit, and control of the corporation belongs by statute to them. Against these considerations, what arguments can be raised that unregulated takeover activity is harmful, wrong, contrary to the public interest, and ought to be stopped by new legislation?

The best approach to a response may be to peel an onion: All of the evils seem to be related, differing primarily in the level of analysis suited to elicit them. Beginning with the surface, then, we may note the simple disruption caused by hostile takeover activity: The raider's announcement that a certain percentage of shares of a company have been purchased, more to follow, immediately puts the company in play in a deadly game from which it will not emerge intact. Productive activity, at least at the upper levels of the target (where salaries are highest), stops. Blitzkrieg raider tactics are met with poison pills, sales of crown jewels and other defenses—often of questionable legality. Orderly planning disappears. Employees, terrified for their jobs, spend their days in speculation and the search for another job.[3] Other bidders emerge from the Midwest, from abroad, from next door. Nobody sleeps. All the players hire lawyers, financiers, banks, and start paying them incredible amounts of money. (In the takeover of Revlon by Pantry Pride in the fall of 1985, the investment bankers' share alone came to over $100 million, legal fees to over $10 million, and the negotiated "golden parachutes" to $40 million. Added up, the costs of the take-over—not one penny of which went to shareholders—came to close to 9 percent of the $1.83 billion deal.)[4] However the game ends, people are exhausted, betrayed, out of work, and demoralized. The huge debt incurred by the acquiring company, secured by the assets of the target (by the infamous *junk bonds*), requires the immediate dismemberment of the company for financial survival (more on this later), and financial health, under those circumstances, is out of the question. And all this to what end?

"Hostile takeovers create no new wealth," Andrew Sigler pointed out to the House Committee on Energy and Commerce, "They merely shift ownership, and replace equity with large amounts of debt." He continues:

More and more companies are being pushed—either in self-defense against the raiders or by the raiders once they achieve control—into unhealthy recapitalizations that run contrary to the concepts of sound management I have learned over thirty years. This type of leveraging exposes companies to inordinate risks in the event of recession, unanticipated reverses, or significant increases in interest rates. . . . Generation after generation of American managers have believed that there *must* be a solid equity basis for an enterprise to be successful in the long term. This long-term equity base absorbs—in exchange for the expectation of higher returns—the perils of depression, product failure,

strikes, and all the other dangers that characterize business in a free economy. That healthy conservatism is now being replaced by a new game in which the object is to see how far that equity base can be squeezed down by layers of debt. And too much of this debt is carrying interest rates far in excess of those a prudent manager can possibly be comfortable with.[5]

At a second level, then, the takeover has two deleterious effects on the management of corporations: First, when the takeover materializes, equity is inevitably transformed into debt, leaving the company terribly vulnerable to foreseeable reverses; second, anticipating takeover attempts, management may well be tempted to aim for short-term profits and engage in aggressive accounting practices to show higher current earnings. These practices may weaken the company and deceive long-term investors, but they will be reflected in a higher stock price and thus one more resistant to attack.[6] As Peter Drucker put it, "Fear of the raider and his unfriendly takeover bid is increasingly distorting business judgment and decisions. In company after company the first question is no longer: Is this decision best for the business? But, will it encourage or discourage the raider?"[7] Fear of the raider may encourage the managers of a company to put up their own money as well as to incur debts well beyond prudence, to take the company privately in a "leveraged buyout." All the same risks, including bankruptcy in the event of any reversal, attend the buyout as attend the takeover.[8] Nor is it clear that the damaging effects of these maneuvers are limited to the domestic scene: As Harold Williams (chairman of the Securities and

Exchange Commission during the Carter administration) points out,

> The pursuit of constantly higher earnings can compel managers to avoid needed writedowns, capital programs, research projects, and other bets on the long term. The competitiveness of U.S. corporations has already been impaired by the failure to make long-term commitments. To compound the problem because of fears of takeovers is a gift to foreign competitors that we cannot afford.[9]

The alarms, confusions, and pains first noted as the result of hostile takeover activity, are then compounded by what seems to be very imprudent business practice. But imprudent for whom? Do the target shareholders, at least, get some profit from the takeover—and if they do, does that not justify it? Michael Jensen, one of a new breed of scholar known as the "shark defenders," argues that they do and that does. He dismisses worries about shareholders' welfare as "folklore," and insists that "science" shows otherwise.[10] His evidence for this claim is interesting:

> More than a dozen studies have painstakingly gathered evidence on the stock price effect of successful takeovers. . . . According to these studies, companies involved in takeovers experience abnormal increases in their stock prices for approximately one month surrounding the initial announcement of the takeover. . . . The evidence shows that target company shareholders gain 30% from tender offers and 20% from mergers.[11]

But isn't the raider's effect pure artifice? Let his initiative be withdrawn—because of government opposition, or because he has agreed to purchase no more stock for whatever reason—and the same studies show that the stock immediately reverts to its previous value.[12] So it was not, really, that the company's stock was too low. It was rather that the flurry of activity, leading to speculation that the stock might be purchased at an enormous premium, fueled the price rise all by itself. Or could it be that certain professional investors find out about the raid before the public does, buy the target's stock at the lowest point, sending it up before the announcement, wait for the announcement, ride the stock to the top, then sell off before the defense moves, government action, or "targeted repurchase" . . . stop the takeover bid and send the stock back down to its true market value? As Jensen's figures confirm,[13] that value is often a bit *lower* than the starting value of the stock; after all those payouts we are dealing with a much poorer company. Nothing but evil, for all concerned except professional fund managers and investment bankers, seems to come of this takeover activity.

Hence, at the first level there is disruption and tens of millions of dollars' worth of unproductive expense; at the second level there is very dubious business practice. At a third, there is the betrayal of the stakeholders. Current laws, as discussed earlier, force the directors of the target company to consider only shareholder rights and interests, to the probable disadvantage of the other stakeholders: employees, retirees, creditors, host communities, customers, and suppliers. But each of these has helped to build the company to its present state, relying on the company's character and credit-worthiness; the employees and retirees, especially, have worked in expectation of future benefits that may depend in part on the good faith of management, good faith that can hardly be presumed in a raider.[14] The mid-career, upper middle-level managers are especially vulnerable to redundancy and the least likely to be able to transfer their acquired skills and knowledge elsewhere.

Some elimination of positions resulting from duplication is inevitable in any merger, of course, hostile or otherwise, and when carried out under normal conditions succeeds at least in making the company more efficient, even if the cost to the individual is very high. But only some of the people-cutting in these extravagant takeovers stems from real redundancy. Companies are paying such high takeover prices that they have to engage in deep cost-cutting immediately, even to the elimination of personnel crucial to continued operations. The "efficiency" achieved may not serve the company well in the long run, but the raider's calculations rarely run very long. As a consequence, middle-management employees (who are, on the whole, not stupid, and read the same business publications as we do) seem to have taken all this into account and reoriented their work lives accordingly:

> Management turnover at all levels is on the rise and employee loyalty is at a low, according to consultants, executive recruiters and the companies themselves. And there is growing evidence, they say, that merger mania is an important reason for both problems, spreading fear about layoffs and dissatisfaction with other changes in the corporate environment. These problems, in turn, promise to make it harder for companies to realize the anticipated efficiencies that many of them pointed to in justifying their acquisitions. . . . Critics of the takeover binge maintain that the short shrift given to 'people issues' . . . [is] one reason why perhaps half to two-thirds of mergers and acquisitions ultimately fail.[15]

Do we owe anything to people who have worked for a company and who may actually love the company and may be devastated by its dismemberment or transformation? At present, our law does not recognize, or even have any language to describe, the rights possessed by those who have contributed to the growth of an association, have participated in it and loved it, and now see it threatened. The fact that such rights are by no means absolute does not mean they are not there. Classical political theory has the vocabulary to discuss them, under the rubric of the "just war"; discussion of the implications of that doctrine for the hostile takeover issue will occupy the final section of this paper. Rights or no rights, and prudential considerations (as discussed earlier) aside, the condition of the stakeholders ought not, in charity, to be ignored; yet our institutions make no provision for them. Here we have, in the center of the most civilized sector of the civilized world, an open wound, a gap of institutional protection most needed by those who have worked hardest, which we struggle to paper over with the "unemployment benefits" fashioned for different people in different circumstances. Law and business practice seem to require a callousness toward human need and human desert that is incompatible with our notions of justice.

Inevitable disruption, mandated imprudence and legally required injustice are the first three levels of palpable wrong in the hostile takeover phenomenon. It may be that the fourth layer, the last under consideration in this section, has more worrisome implications than all of the above. The thesis is simple: At primary risk in all of this is our concept of ownership. For all of human history, we have been able to trust property owners (individuals or groups) to take care of their property, because it was in their interest to do so, and outside of military and government property, that was how the property of the world was cared for. With the corporate takeover, that may no longer be the case for the kind of property that looms so large in Western economies, the publicly held corporation. And this development is very alarming.

To begin with the concepts: Ordinarily we use the concepts of *ownership* and *property* interchangeably; even etymologically, they are indistinguishable. But the concept does have two distinct aspects: the primary aspect of a legally protected complex of rights and duties obtaining between the owner and other *persons* and the less prominent aspect of a diffuse set of nonlegal duties, or imperatives, incumbent upon the owner to take care of the *owned thing*, itself. This duty of care has a history of its own; the duty to the thing, analogous to the duty of *stewardship* when the property of others is in question, attaches naturally to the legal owner.

Ownership has the longest history of any concept still extant in the West, certainly longer than its ultimate derivative, *personhood*. Aristotle assumed that the union of man and property, along with the union of man and woman, lay at the foundation of the household and hence of all society. Ownership is presupposed, and discussed, throughout the earliest books of the Bible. The list of *what* was owned was very short: animals, people (slaves), land, tools, buildings, and personal effects. Except for the last item, all were essential to survival, and all required care. The duty arises from that fact.

Whether ownership is single or shared, the duty corresponds to personal interest. If I own a sheep, it is very much in my interest, and incumbent upon me, to take care of the beast and see that it thrives. If you and I together own a sheep, the same interest applies to both of us, the same imperative follows, and we shall divide up the responsibilities of caring for it. If you and I and 998 others own it, enormous practical difficulties attend that care. But however small my interest in that sheep, it is still in my interest that the animal should thrive. Similarly, partial ownership in a whole herd of sheep, or a farm, or a factory, or a business that owns several factories, does not necessitate a change in the notion of *ownership*.

Liquidation consumes something that is owned, or turns it into money that can be spent on consumption. The easiest way to liquidate a sheep is to eat it. The way to liquidate most owned things is to sell them. Then you no longer own the thing, and your responsibilities terminate; but so, of course, does all future good you might have gotten of the thing. Part of the cultural evolution of ownership has been the elaboration of a tension between retention and liquidation, saving and spending, with the moral weight of the most successful cultures on the side of thrift and preservation. The business system probably depends as much on Ben Franklin's "A penny saved is a penny earned" as it does on Adam Smith's "invisible hand." The foreseen result of the hand, we may remember, was to increase the wealth, the assets, of a nation. For the herdsman it is self-evident that if you slaughter or sell all your sheep, you will starve in the next year; for Smith, it was equally self-evident that it is in a businessman's interest, whatever business he may be in, to save his money and invest it in clearing more land, breeding more beasts, or building more plants, to make more money in the future. Hence the cleared land, the herds, and the factories—the assets of the nation—increase without limit, and all persons, no matter how they participate in the economy, in fact share in this increased wealth. Presupposed is the willingness of all players in the free enterprise game to acquire things that need care if they are to yield profit, hence to render that care, and to accept that responsibility, over the long run. Should that willingness disappear, and the population suddenly show a preference for liquidation, all bets are off for the wealth of the nation.

And the problem is, of course, that the developments of ownership made possible in the last century create excess tendencies toward liquidation. If several thousand of us jointly own several thousand shares of stock, we may in theory bear the traditional responsibilities of owners for those companies, but we shall surely not *feel* them. And if we purchased those shares not for the sake of investing in the companies, but for the sake of having money available to us at some future time (say, in a pension fund), we will have acquired them for a purpose that is directly contrary to our concerns as owners. We will be involved in a conflict of interest and obligation with ourselves: On the one hand, we should be protecting and nurturing the company(s) we (partially) own, plowing profit back into improvements in plant on occasion, even if that means no profit this year; on the other, if it seems we could get more money if the company were liquidated and the proceeds shared around, we should work toward that

end. Suppose that we several thousand owners hire a fund manager to make sure our pension fund provides us with as much pension as possible. That manager, hired with those instructions, is not an owner, and has *no* responsibility toward the companies. On the contrary, his entire obligation is to us and the increase of our money. Where liquidation serves that purpose, it is his job to bring it about. Ownership, for such a manager, is no more than present legal title to property, a way station between sums of money, and its whole moral framework has become totally irrelevant. To complete the picture, let only the tax structure subsidize that liquidation in cases of takeover:

> Accounting procedures and tax laws . . . shift much of the cost of acquisitions to taxpayers through the deductibility of interest payments and the revaluation of assets in ways that reduce taxes. . . . I suspect that many of the acquisitions that proved profitable for acquirers did so largely because of tax benefits and the proceeds from busting up the target company. If liquidation is subsidized by the tax system, are we getting more liquidations than good business would dictate?[16]

The answer is probably yes.

Institutional investors—those gargantuan funds—now own up to 70 percent of the stock of the publicly owned corporations. It must be unprecedented in human history that majority ownership of such entities lies with "owners" whose interests may be best served by the destruction of the object owned. In the case of companies that own large holdings of natural resources, forests, or oil reserves, it is usually the case that the assets sold separately will yield more than the companies' stock. (As Minow and Sawyier grimly put it, under current practices such companies "are worth more dead than alive.")[17] Any company, in fact, that regularly works for the long term (funding research and development, for example), can be profitably liquidated: Whatever those raiders may be, they do not need to be geniuses to figure out which companies to attack. The only limits on the process of liquidation of the country's assets by the managers hired by those investors, or by the raiders that cater to their own interests, might be the success of new and inventive defenses.

The evils of the takeover market, then, go to the philosophical base of our market system, striking at the root of moral habits evolved over 2500 years. The corporate raiders have yet to make their first widget, grow their first carrot, or deliver their first lunch. *All* they do is turn money into money, cantilevering the profit off the shell of responsible ownership. No doubt capital is more productively lodged in some places than others, but it follows from no known economic theory that it is more beneficial to the world when lodged in T. Boone Pickens's bank account than when lodged wherever it was before he got it. Possibly it will end up facilitating some industrial projects—he has no intention of keeping it in a mattress, after all—but only in those that promise quick profits. We need not look to him to revitalize our smokestack industries and make them competitive on the world markets. The whole productive capacity of the American economy seems at the mercy of moneymen on the rampage, with all productive companies under threat of being taken over, taken apart, and eradicated. Surely this condition cannot be healthy or good.

In sum: This section has tried to provide a series of pragmatic arguments that the present rash of corporate takeover activity is harmful to the stakeholders, to the economy, and to the general public, from all of which it would follow that regulation is justified. In the next section we attempt to provide a defense for the proposition that a corporation has a real right to exist, hence to resist takeover. . . .

CONCLUSION

We have argued that as a matter of right, and as a matter of utility, the takeover game should be ended. Capital is not unlimited; in a country rapidly losing out to foreign competition in part because of outdated plant, and declining in its quality of urban life in part because of obsolete and crumbling infrastructure, there are plenty of worthwhile uses for capital. Law that turns the attentions of the restless rich away from cannibalizing productive corporations, toward investing in the undercapitalized areas of the economy, would be a great public service.[18]

NOTES

1. Myron Magnet, "Help! My Company Has Just Been Taken Over," *Fortune*, July 9, 1984, pp. 44–51. See also Joel Lang, "Aftermath of a Merger," *Northeast Magazine*, April 21, 1985, pp. 10–17.
2. Steven Prokesch, " 'People Trauma' in Mergers," *New York Times*, November 19, 1985.
3. *Ibid.*
4. *Wall Street Journal*, November 8, 1985.
5. Testimony of Andrew C. Sigler, Chairman and Chief Executive Officer of Champion International Corporation, representing the Business Roundtable, before hearings of the Subcommittee on Telecommunications, Consumer Protection and Finance of the House Committee on Energy and Commerce, Thursday, May 23, 1985.
6. Some of these considerations I owe to conversations and correspondence with S. Bruce Smart, Jr.
7. Drucker, *Wall Street Journal*, January 5, 1983.
8. Leslie Wayne, "Buyouts Altering Face of Corporate America," *New York Times*, November 23, 1985.

9. Harold M. Williams, "It's Time for a Takeover Moratorium," *Fortune*, July 22, 1985, pp. 133–136.

10. Michael Jensen, "Takeovers: Folklore and Science," *Harvard Business Review* 62 (November-December 1984): 109–121.

11. P. 112. The footnote on the studies cites, for a summary of these studies, Michael C. Jensen and Richard S. Ruback, "The Market for Corporate Control: The Scientific Evidence," *Journal of Financial Economics* (April 1983). The studies are cited individually in the same footnote; *ibid.*, p. 120.

12. *Ibid.*, p. 116.

13. *Ibid.*

14. Another point owed to conversations and correspondence with S. Bruce Smart, Jr.

15. Prokesch, " 'People Trauma' in Mergers."

16. Williams, "It's Time for a Takeover Moratorium," pp. 133–136.

17. Newton Minow and David Sawyier, "The Free Market Blather Behind Takeovers" Op-ed, *The New York Times*, December 10, 1985.

18. In developing the ideas for this paper, I have profited enormously from conversations with Lucy Katz, Philip O'Connell, Stuart Richardson, Mark Shanley, Andrew Sigler, S. Bruce Smart, Jr., and C. Roger Williams.

NO

Robert Almeder and David Carey

IN DEFENSE OF SHARKS: MORAL ISSUES IN HOSTILE LIQUIDATING TAKEOVERS

In this essay we will examine the major arguments attacking the practice of hostile buyouts initiated solely for the purpose of liquidation. This practice occurs only when management is unable or unwilling to close a significant gap between the market value of the company's shares and the breakup value of the company. Accordingly, these buyouts are usually "hostile" to the intentions of the current management. The "corporate raider" (sometimes more affectionately described by management as "the shark"), after buying a significant percentage of the company's shares, then offers to buy the shares from the other shareholders at a price considerably higher than current market value, buys the company, and makes a profit by selling off the underlying assets of the company. The raider may, or may not, take on a great deal of expensive debt in order to succeed in buying the target company. Such debt-based takeovers are called "leveraged," and takeovers can be more or less "highly leveraged" or not leveraged at all—as would occur if the raider proposed to buy the company with cash. If the proposed hostile offer is leveraged (and especially if it is leveraged) the raider typically seeks to eliminate the debt with the sale of the underlying assets and then pocket the difference.

The raider's practice is unlike the practice of a hostile takeover of one company by another where the primary purpose is not so much to liquidate the assets for a quick profit, but rather to increase marketshare or shareholder value for the buying company which may, or may not, involve liquidating assets of the purchased company. . . . Similarly, the practice we are discussing in this essay is to be distinguished from "friendly" buyouts or takeovers invited by management.

But the practice of the corporate raider is quite a different story. Various corporate managers, employee groups, politicians and philosophers have argued strenuously against the practice, and the first question is whether

From Robert Almeder and David Carey, "In Defense of Sharks: Moral Issues in Hostile Liquidating Takeovers," *Journal of Business Ethics*, vol. 10 (July 1991), pp. 471–480, 482–484. Copyright © 1991 by D. Reidel Publishing Co., Dordrecht, Holland, and Boston, U.S.A. Reprinted by permission of Kluwer Academic Publishers. Some notes omitted.

those arguments justify eliminating or constraining the practice legislatively or otherwise. After reviewing both the proposed arguments against the practice and the proposed legislation seeking to prevent it, we shall argue negatively that such arguments are unsound, and positively that there are good rule-utilitarian grounds for allowing the practice. (Whether this is more of an indictment of rule-utilitarianism than a defense of hostile takeovers, of course, is beyond the scope of this essay.) [Rule-utilitarianism postulates that any action that creates more harm than good should be prohibited.—Eds.]. . . .

ARGUMENTS AGAINST THE SHARK

We find, distilled from the general rhetoric on the issue, three arguments against the practice of the hostile liquidating buyout. The first two apply even when the proposed buyout is not highly leveraged and all three apply when the buyout is highly leveraged.

The Argument from Human Cost

As Lisa Newton has argued, any business practice that causes massive employee firing, with all its attendant trauma and suffering, when the company is both profitable and the employees not demonstrably incompetent, requires a justification. Moreover, for Newton, the long-term human costs involved certainly cannot be justified in terms of the self-aggrandizement of a few. The pleasure and limited good of a few in making a large profit cannot be justified by the overwhelming human suffering typically involved when a large company is liquidated. In describing the hostile corporate takeover as a form of assault with a deadly weapon, she says:

A practice requires moral scrutiny if it regularly derogates from human dignity, causes human pain, or with no apparent reason treats one class of human beings less well than another. Any practice that regularly throws people out of work has at least the first two of those . . . and unless we find the raider's urgent need for self-aggrandizement as a worthy reason for dismembering working units, it probably does the third also (p. 501).

She goes on to note that such takeovers are usually defended on a rule-utilitarian basis with the claim that, however painful in the short run, such takeovers are in the public interest because they increase the long-term efficiency of the market and enhance shareholder return. However, Newton (and many others along with her) reject this reason by appealing to people, such as Andrew Sigler, who have argued that as reasons go, the rule-utilitarian defense of the practice is unacceptable even on its own terms because such practices in no way produce real wealth. Rather, as a rule, they cause great pain and destroy wealth by creating great debt. In testimony before the house Committee on Energy and Commerce, Sigler said:

Hostile takeovers create no new wealth . . . they merely shift ownership, and replace equity with large amounts of debt. . . . More and more companies are being pushed . . . either in self-defense against the raiders or by the raiders once they achieve control—into unhealthy recapitalizations that run contrary to the concepts of sound management I have learned over thirty years. This type of leveraging exposes companies to inordinate risks in the event of recession, unanticipated reverses, or significant increases in interest rates. . . . Generation after generation of American managers have believed that there must be a solid equity base for an enterprise to be successful in the long term. This long-term equity base absorbs—in exchange for the expectation of higher returns—the perils of depression, product failure, strikes, and all the other dangers that characterize business in a free economy. That healthy conservatism is now being replaced by a new game in which the object is to see how far that equity base can be squeezed down by layers of debt. And too much of this debt is carrying interest rates far in excess of those a prudent manager can possibly be comfortable with.

And a number of others have agreed with Sigler that the practice generally, as a rule, erodes equity necessary for long-term survival and promotes heavy debt by forcing the corporation in the presence of the raider's threat to defend itself by taking on the sort of debt that undermines real productivity. Appealing to these considerations, Newton rejects the utilitarian defense that the practice is in the general interest, and hence she finds no countervailing social benefit to compensate for the human suffering typically caused by the practice. There is a large number of people who will agree with her reasoning.

The Argument from the Destruction of Wealth

According to this second argument, the hostile liquidating buyout, whether leveraged or not, is unacceptable, quite independently of the human cost and trauma involved. The reasoning here is that even if there were no such suffering attending the practice, it would still be against the public interest because, as a general rule, even the threat of a hostile buyout destroys wealth by undermining competitiveness at home and abroad. If

so, such a business practice should be stopped for being contrary to the general well-being of society. (Hence, this too may be construed as a rule-utilitarian argument.) In support of this particular argument, Harold Williams, after noting that fear of the raider forces management to seek ever higher earnings at all costs, says:

> The pursuit of constantly higher earnings can compel managers to avoid needed writedowns, capital programs, research projects, and other bets on the long term. The competitiveness of U.S. corporations has already been impaired by the failure to make long-term commitments. To compound the problem because of fears of takeovers is a gift to foreign competitors that we cannot afford.

This point was made in Andrew Sigler's testimony cited above. So, whether leveraged or not, even the threat of a liquidating hostile takeover engenders corporate behavior that, as a rule, undermines long-term corporate productivity and hence, by implication, destroys wealth in the long run rather than creates it. Accordingly, even if in the short-term we could find mechanisms guaranteeing that all displaced employees could be rehired nearby with roughly the same salary and working conditions, the practice would still be against the long-term common good for these reasons. And all this is doubly true if the hostile buyout is heavily leveraged. . . .

Incidentally, proponents of this argument need not, and generally do not, deny that sharks and raiders spend their ill-gotten profits and hence redistribute these profits back into the economy. Their point is that as long as raiders make their money in this way, it is not at all conducive to the kind of capital for-

mation necessary for the long-term production of wealth and general prosperity.
Financiers, investment bankers, attor-
neys and stock brokers are integral to a
service economy, but service economies
without a strong basis in productive
manufacturing, or in companies that are
generally capital intensive in the name of
competitiveness, will wither on the vine.

The Argument from the Death of Ownership

Lisa Newton has offered a third argument to the effect that allowing the hostile liquidating buyout will as a rule tend
to militate against the right to private
property and the right to ownership. In
her view, in addition to being a practice
unconscionably inhumane and destruc-
tive of the common good (because de-
structive of long-term general wealth),
the liquidating hostile buyout is, as a
rule, an assault on the right of ownership. As we shall see, this argument too
is rule-utilitarian in perspective.

Her argument begins with the premise
that *ownership*, as a social institution essential for the survival of society, imposes a fundamental moral duty on the
owner to take care of the thing owned.
The duty arises from the fact that without such care the wealth necessary for
survival is imperiled. Whether ownership is single or shared, the duty corresponds to personal interest. In explicating
this premise, she says:

> If I own a sheep, it is very much in my
> interest and incumbent upon me to take
> care of the beast and see that it thrives. If
> you and I together own a sheep, the
> same interest applies to both of us, the
> same imperative follows, and we shall
> divide up the responsibilities of caring
> for it. If you and I and 998 others own it,
> enormous practical difficulties attend
> that care. But however small my interest

> in that sheep, it is still in my interest that
> the animal should thrive. Similarly, par-
> tial ownership in a whole herd of sheep,
> or a farm or a factory, or a business that
> owns several factories, does not necessi-
> tate a change in the notion of ownership
> (p. 506).

The next premise in the argument is that
liquidation of property turns property
into money that can be spent on consumption, but with liquidation all future
good one might have gotten from the
property disappears (p. 507). Hence, so
the argument concludes, the tendency to
liquidation goes strongly against the
duty of owners to take care of property
in the interest of producing long-term
wealth necessary for social good and
survival. She adds that the moral weight
of the most successful cultures is not on
liquidation, but rather on the side of
thrift and preservation. In spelling out
this argument, she says:

> *Liquidation* consumes something that is
> owned, or turns it into money that can
> be spent on consumption. The easiest
> way to liquidate the sheep is to eat it.
> The way to liquidate most owned things
> is to sell them. Then you no longer own
> the thing, and your responsibilities ter-
> minate; but so, of course, does all future
> good you might have gotten of the
> thing. Part of the cultural evolution of
> ownership has been the elaboration of a
> tension between retention and liquida-
> tion, saving and spending, with the
> moral weight of the most successful cul-
> tures on the side of thrift and preser-
> vation. The business system probably
> depends as much on Ben Franklin's "a
> penny saved is a penny earned" as it
> does on Adam Smith's "invisible hand."
> The foreseen result of the *hand*, we may
> remember, was to increase the wealth,
> the assets, of a nation. For the herdsman
> it's evident that if you slaughter or sell
> all your sheep, you will starve in the

next year; for Smith it was equally self-evident that it is in a businessman's interest, whatever business he may be in, to save his money and invest in clearing more land, breeding more beasts or building more plants, to make more money in the future. Hence the cleared land, the herds and the factories—the assets of the nation—increase without limit, and all persons, no matter how they participate in the economy, in fact share in this increased wealth. Presupposed is the willingness of all players in the free enterprise game to acquire things that need care if they are to yield profit, hence to render that care, and to accept that responsibility, over the long run. Should that willingness disappear, and the population suddenly show a preference for liquidation, all bets are off for the wealth of the nation.

And the problem is, of course, that the developments of ownership made possible in the last century create excess tendencies toward liquidation (p. 506).

As an example of such excess tendencies toward liquidation, she notes that institutional investors own up to 70% of all publicly owned corporations and their only contractual obligation is to profit-taking for the sake of having money available at some future date. They recognize no responsibilities to preserve companies for future growth (p. 507). Moreover, accounting procedures and tax laws shift the cost of hostile acquisitions and liquidations to taxpayers by allowing the raider to take tax deductions for interest payments and to re-evaluate assets so as to reduce his taxes. In summing up her position, she concludes:

> The evils of the takeover market, then, go to the philosophical base of our market system, striking at the root of moral habits evolved over 2500 years. The corporate raiders have yet to make their first widget, grow their first carrot, or deliver their first lunch. *All* they do is turn money into money, cantilevering the profit off the shell of responsible ownership. No doubt capital is more productively lodged in some places than in others, but it follows from no known economic theory that it is more beneficial to the world when lodged in T. Boone Pickens's bank account than when lodged wherever it was before he got it. Possibly, it will end up in facilitating some industrial projects—he has no intention of keeping it in a mattress, after all—but only in those that promise quick profits. We need not look to him to revitalize our smokestack industries and make them competitive on the world markets. The whole productive capacity of the American economy seems at the mercy of moneymen on the rampage, with all productive companies under threat of being taken over, taken apart, and eradicated. Surely, this condition cannot be healthy or good (p. 507).

From this argument she concludes that regulation favoring the elimination of such takeover practices is certainly in order. We know of no other available arguments seeking to justify such regulation. Before examining the above arguments, however, it may be useful to summarize proposed federal legislation seeking to constrain such takeover practices.

PROPOSED REGULATION

Because of the frequency of the sorts of arguments offered above, and because of the public outcry against the activities of corporate raiders, and managements threatened by them, Congressmen Edward Markey (D. Mass.) and John Dingell (D. Michigan) introduced *The Tender Offer Reform Act of 1987* in a stated effort "to curb abuses in the takeover process."

In fact, the point of the legislation has put strong constraints on hostile liquidating takeovers on the part of corporate raiders, or corporate managers who would use the same tactics to take a company private. The key provisions of the bill are:

Restrictions on availability of greenmail payments. Often raiders take a position in a company not to buy it out, but simply to coerce management into buying the raider's shares at a very elevated price (thereby persuading the raider to drop the offer). To prevent this practice, which increases corporate debt and undermines real growth and competition, the bill provides that a company would be prohibited from purchasing its securities "at a price above the average market price of the securities during the thirty preceding trading days from any person who has held more than three percent of its shares for less than two years. Greenmail would be permitted only if a majority of the shareholders approve, or if the company makes an equal offer to all other shareholders."

Controls on golden parachutes. Frequently, management has, on the occasion of a hostile offer, voted itself hefty compensation packages in the event of an actual takeover. If the package is sufficiently attractive, there is little desire on the part of management to resist the offer, thereby assisting the liquidation process, and increasing debt by raiding corporate assets. To curb this abuse the bill provides that "hefty compensation packages for corporate officers or directors, awarded in the event of a change in corporate control, could not be established *during* the tender offer." Mackey has also noted that recent amendments to the tax code also discourage golden parachutes by increasing the tax imposed upon them. Similarly, under the bill, a corporation cannot "establish or implement, during the proxy or tender offer time period, without shareholder approval, poison pills, tin parachutes, or lock-ups" (p. 20).

Closing the ten day window. To prevent the raider from taking too big a position in the company before making the offer (thereby undermining the attractiveness of greenmail both as a motive and as a successful practice), the bill requires that "anyone who acquires more than 5% of a company must announce the acquisition publicly, and, within twenty-four hours, repeat the filing on the SEC [Securities and Exchange Commission] and to each exchange on which the company is traded. The acquirer is then precluded from acquiring additional securities of the same class for two business days after the offer. . . ." Also these filing requirements would extend "to groups acting in concert, such as teams of raiders, bankers and others" (p. 20). And tender offers would need to remain open for at least 60 calendar days, rather than the present 20 business days (p. 20).

Prohibition of market sweeps. In order to further reduce the likelihood of raider success, the bill specifies that there be a "thirty day cooling off period" during which, if one makes a tender offer and terminates it, he is "precluded from acquiring securities of the class he tendered for thirty days, except by a new tender offer." This section also prohibits "creeping tender offers." That is, "if one acquires 10% of a company, and if he wants to acquire more, he must do so by tender offer" (p. 21).

Executive summary. For reasons that seem obvious, the bill also requires of the person or group making the offer a concise statement of the price, terms, and key conditions of the offer, including financing arrangements. And finally:

Easier access to proxy material. The bill provides to holders of three per cent of a company's shares, or more than 500,000 of the corporation's voting securities—whichever is higher—free and easy publication in corporate proxy solicitations for the purpose of nominating candidates for election to the board of directors.

There can be little doubt that the passage of such a bill would make it more difficult for raiders to be successful in either liquidating companies or profiting by greenmail. It would also prevent management from being unduly sympathetic to the raider as a result of instituting their own golden parachutes. But certainly the legislation does not propose to eliminate the practice, but merely to curb obvious abuses. The question is whether the reasoning behind this proposed legislation justifies such a measure, or whether legislation based upon such reasoning constitutes in some measure a well-intentioned but nonetheless immoral legislative assault on the right to private property. . . .

ARGUMENTS FAVORING
THE SHARK

In response to the three arguments cited earlier against the practice of hostile liquidating buyouts, the corporate raider will be able to offer the following replies in defense of the practice of hostile liquidating buyouts.

Responses to the Arguments from Human Cost and the Destruction of Wealth

The raider is by no means blind to the human costs and pain involved in liquidating a profitable company in order to sell off the underlying assets. But his position is that of a rule-utilitarian according to whom only those acts are wrong (and ought to be prohibited) which, *as a rule or as a practice*, tend to promote more harm than good in the long run for all those affected by the practice. Acts which have just the opposite effect, i.e., those which *as a rule* tend to promote more good than harm in the long run are morally obligatory; and those which cannot be shown to do either are permissible rather than obligatory or prohibited. Given this general moral position, the raider need only reply to the argument from human cost by asserting that he may pursue a practice until someone shows that, as a matter of fact, the practice as a rule tends *in the long run* to promote more suffering than benefit, all things considered. In situations of real uncertainty or invincible ignorance, raiders may bet that their activities have long-term net social benefits. That is, the raider can defend the practice as permissible on the grounds that nobody has *shown*, rather than simply asserted, that the practice will in all likelihood lead to more harm than good in the long run. If he is right in this last claim then the raider will have responded adequately to both the argument from human cost and also to the argument from the destruction of wealth. In so doing he will have established the *permissibility* of the practice rather than the stronger and more difficult thesis that the practice *should be encouraged* because it tends to promote more good than harm in the long run for all those affected. . . .

That the hostile liquidating buyout need not inevitably, or even be more likely to, destroy wealth can be established in the following way. Suppose, for the sake of argument, that we allowed "sharks" to buy and liquidate every publicly owned company whose breakup value was sufficiently higher than the market value of its shares to generate an above average return on capital for the breakup. The argument against such a practice, as we saw above, is that the practice will, as a rule, tend to be against the public interest because it will render impossible the kind of capital formation and asset base necessary for long-term productivity and competitive success in world markets. This latter argument *assumes* that, as a general rule, open market economies will need, in order to create and maintain the sort of wealth consistent with long-term social stability, publicly held companies whose asset base allows the kinds of efficiencies of scale that only truly successful competitive companies have. In other words, the creation and maintenance of social wealth will require an economy with at least a large number of publicly owned companies whose breakup value will sufficiently exceed the market share value to make them attractive as targets for hostile liquidating buyouts. But where is the evidence for such an assumption?

Does it not seem equally plausible to assume that if all such companies were liquidated, the wealth thereby acquired would then be concentrated in privately held companies (or companies 51% private) producing the efficiencies of scale that are necessary for maintaining and creating public wealth? Stated differently, why not assume, for the sake of argument, that if we eliminated all such publicly owned companies, it would just as likely lead not to a destruction of public wealth but rather to a change in the way such public wealth is held? Does this not seem equally plausible?

Take the steel industry, for example. Suppose we liquidate all major publicly owned steel producers in the interest of enhancing shareholder value by liquidating the underlying assets of the company. What would then happen? According to the main argument against such a practice, we would as a rule lose wealth and jobs to those large competitive companies with the sort of asset or capital base we have just destroyed. They would control ever larger shares of the market, and the real profit would leave the nation. As a matter of fact, however, it would seem as natural to expect that the price of steel, in the absence of domestic competition, would rise to that point where there was a suitable incentive to form privately held, or largely privately held, companies managed on a more efficient basis. This seems as natural to expect as any other scenario because of the plausibility behind the claim that large companies often become inefficient as long as they are not confronted with competition. Indeed, while the current breakup value of the steel operation at USX, for example, is worth considerably more than its corresponding value reflected in the share value, there has been an ever increasing number of smaller and largely private steel companies (such as Weirton Steel and Birmingham Steel) making a substantial profit and whose share value is very close to their breakup value. In short, we have good reason to think the main argument against the practice of "the shark" is unsound because, first and foremost, it is by no means obvious that if we allow the practice to liquidate all companies whose breakup value is considerably more than their share value, we will (either necessarily or in all likelihood) thereby decrease sooner or later public wealth rather than shift the way in which wealth is owned from largely public corporations. So, it is by no means clear that the practice will inevitably, or even likely, produce the economic Armageddon some managers have suggested. In itself, this conclusion seems sufficient to block any argument for outlawing the practice based upon the so-called long-term tendency of the practice to promote social harm by destroying public wealth.

There is a second argument, moreover, to the effect that the practice should be encouraged. . . . This second argument asserts, as we saw above, that in the long run the practice will not only destroy public wealth, it will create more wealth. Typically, in the face of such a claim, those opposed to the practice tend to grant that the profits made by the liquidation of such companies flow to other parts of the economy, but, as Lisa Newton has said, only insofar as those parts produce a quick profit and never into those parts that require large underlying assets rendering the breakup value of a company considerably higher than its market share value. Here again, however, we can easily imagine T. Boone Pickens, for example, deciding to enter the oil drilling business if the price of crude got high enough as a result of a significant loss of competition resulting from hostile liquidating buyouts. The higher the price of crude, the quicker he could depreciate the cost of the underlying assets, thereby bringing the shares to their full value quickly. And if the company he establishes is private (or only

49% public) he would need to compete efficiently, or sooner or later lose his market share and profits to those who could raise capital and run a more efficient company. In short, as long as there is reason to think that liquidating buyouts will promote more general market efficiency even though it may be in terms of private or largely private ownership. Thus, while various managers have often claimed that the creation of long-term wealth requires a kind of efficiency that necessitates a considerable gap between the breakup value of core industries and their share value, there is good reason to think that this claim is false. Rather, there is more reason to think that what is required in the interest of efficiency and the creation of long-term public wealth, is that there be no interesting gap between breakup value and share value. This is the stronger argument favoring the promotion of the practice rather than the regulation of it. . . .

Of course, those opposed to the liquidating hostile buyout will be quick to urge, in response to the above arguments, that nobody has shown, rather than simply asserted, that the practice will in fact create more wealth in the long run.[1] As Lawrence Summers has noted:

> There is, in my view, almost no evidence, other than the dubious evidence of the stock market, that takeover premia actually reflect improved economic efficiency as a result of acquisition.

The shark's response to this is twofold.

In the first place, as we noted above, even if the point were well-taken, nobody needs to show as much in order to be justified in preventing regulation of the practice. Those who would outlaw the practice need to show that, as matter of fact, the practice *will* produce a net balance of general public harm over good *in the long run*. And that has not been shown. Newton's argument itself presupposes the social benefit of private ownership. Accordingly, the right to private ownership, and its free exercise, while *prima facie* and subordinate to the common good, should not be compromised except by rules constraining those practices which are shown on the whole to do long-term, and not merely short-term, net social harm. Society has other less objectionable options to alleviate the short-term pain incurred by the practice in question.

In the second place, Professor Summers notwithstanding, it seems fair to say that there is an argument from standard economic theory that the practice *will* indeed tend in the long run to produce the general public good. Craig Lehman, for example, has offered in his essay "Takeovers and Takeover Defenses: Some Utilities of the Free Market" a core argument favoring the practice as a mechanism that enhances capital allocation which is a necessary condition for an open market to run efficiently and, in the long run, produce the general good that justifies open-market economies as more conducive to real productivity and the creation of wealth than constrained market economies. In Lehman's view, rather than *destroy* large assets, the hostile liquidating buyout promotes efficient capital re-allocation for a more efficient use of assets. On his argument, it is the primary responsibility of management to promote shareholder value and long-term public wealth by eliminating inefficiencies and waste; and when management fails in that responsibility the market can, and must, force

reallocation of assets to eliminate those sorts of inefficiencies. Doing so *promotes*, rather than *undermines* the general welfare. He says:

> If the market is to respond efficiently to increasing demands for some products and decreasing demand for others—and capitalism's defenders claim that this is one of the system's major virtues—then capital must be free to flow in and out of various sectors of the economy.
>
> This can happen in a variety of ways. Suppose, for instance, that widgets are the product of the future, but that right now there is only one widget manufacturer. The new megatrend has not yet arrived. So, right now the stock of Widget Corporation (which represents ownership of widget-producing assets and a flow of future earnings from widget sales) may well be selling for less than it is worth, according to various theories of securities valuation. As the boom in widgets becomes more visible and finally arrives, however, the price of Widget Corporation stock will be bid up, and eventually it will become high enough that some investors will prefer to put up capital for new widget-producing facilities (or alternative technologies), rather than paying for the stream of earnings from the current facilities. Thus the realization of asset values is the first step in a larger process that eventually leads to a greater supply of the products consumers desire, at a price constrained by competitive pressures. This is one of the basic and fundamental utilities of a capitalistic system.

One way in which takeovers are part of this picture is that they can *speed* the process of asset value realization and capital flow. If individual investors who see the value of owning widget-producing assets start buying up the stock of Widget Corporation, it may be several years before the stock is fully priced and there is an economic incentive to bankroll new widget facilities. (Common advice to asset-oriented investors is to be very patient.) But if Behemoth Corporation or Octopus Investors Group devour all the stock of Widget Corporation in one gulp, there is no pure play left in widgets; those who want to make a killing in this area will have to put their capital into new facilities. Takeovers can thus *accelerate* the process of asset-value realization and capital flow. In any case, however, capital flow is capital flow whether it comes from the treasury of a large, established corporation or the investments of individuals.

He goes on to note that in the light of the above, many oil company takeovers, in addition to many takeovers in other industries (where assets are more valuable unbundled than conglomerated) are to be seen simply as manifestations of the open market trying to reallocate capital efficiently. Lehman claims that while current managements may think bigger is better, capital markets have in effect been demanding that organizations with inefficient divisions grow smaller and devote resources only to operations in which they can achieve an acceptable return on investment. . . .

In short, the basic point behind this argument is that efficiency in market activities serves the long-term general public good, companies whose breakup asset value *suitably* exceeds the share value, are not acting efficiently, and the hostile liquidating takeover is a predictable and good mechanism for imposing efficiency and promoting the long-term general good. We submit that this general argument, without involving a long-term study of the effects of the practice, tips the scale in favor of the view that the practice tends to promote more long-term good than evil for society at large. . . .

Response to the Argument from the Destruction of Ownership

Finally, if everything we have just said is true, then far from destroying ownership, the hostile liquidating buyout not only does not destroy long-term wealth, it would tend to create it; and failure to support such buyouts as market mechanisms for long-term efficiency will likely promote the sort of inefficiency that will guarantee a loss of wealth and with it, ownership. This is not to say, of course, that the efficiency promoted by such a mechanism may not change the ways in which ownership is exercised. We may, as we saw above, see more corporations with less than 50% public ownership; but, barring monopolistic activities, if such companies become inefficient in having more breakup value than what is reflected in share value, we can expect the market to allocate capital in a way that provides real competition. But none of this implies the death of ownership in any interesting way.

Moreover, Newton's version of the argument from destruction of ownership too closely associates liquidation with consumption. To liquidate assets is often simply to convert them to a more socially useful form; it may merely reallocate wealth rather than diminish it. To this extent, her argument fails. . . .

CONCLUSION

The general conclusion to be drawn here is that it is difficult to establish that there is something particularly immoral about the general practice of liquidating hostile buyouts. This is not to say that we would not be justified in outlawing for good reasons the practice in special circumstances. In those cases, however, one would need to show that an overriding public interest was at stake and that there would be too much of a predictable long-term loss of social wealth to allow the practice. In the absence of such a demonstration, the practice would be morally permissible, and legally pro-scribing the practice in the absence of such a demonstration seems a highly dubious policy for a nation committed to the basic right to private property.

Naturally, those most opposed to the practice are concerned about the short-term human pain inevitably caused by the practice. For them, the rule-util-itarian defense of the practice may well constitute a reason for abandoning rule-utilitarianism. If so, what we are dealing with is the question of whether one should be acting out of interest for the long-term good of society even when it means the possible sacrifice of one's own long-term interest because one's own long-term interest often does not coin-cide with that of society's. Perhaps only the most saintly among us could act on that basis, and the rest of us might wonder why, or even how, such a person could be so motivated. At any rate, it seems clear what the rule-utilitarian po-sition requires of public policy on the issue.

NOTE

1. For example, Kohlberg Kravis Roberts and Company (KKR) conducted a study in which it argued that LBOs had five beneficial conse-quences, namely, increased employment, higher research-and-development spending, higher tax yield for the government, continued strong capital spending, and strengthening of companies against recession. Criticising the study, William Long and David Ravenscraft came to the conclusion that in fact LBOs, among other things, reduced employ-ment, decreased research and development spend-ing, and decreased capital spending. See Ricks, T.: 1989, 'Two Scholars Blast KKR Buy-Out Study that Reached Pro-Takeover Conclusions,' *Wall Street Journal*, May 10, p. A2; and Ricks, T.: 1989, 'KKR

says Critics of its Buy-Out Study Misconstrue—but They Don't Buy That,' *Wall Street Journal*, May 22, p. A2.

The problem with this whole discussion is that it is hard to believe that the long-term benefits of the practice could be assessed in terms of a study conducted only three years after a company is bought out. KKR would have been well-advised to argue the case solely on the basis of the well-known fact that open-market economies sooner or later (but not necessarily in three years) reward the kinds of efficiencies typically promoted by the efficient flow of capital stimulated by liquidating LBOs and that, at any rate, until somebody could show that the long-term interests are not served by this process, the right of shareholders to sell at a price they think fit is a basic inalienable human right. The methodology of both parties to this argument is questionable because it seems unduly arbitrary to argue for the long-term economic ef-fects of a practice on the basis of the effects precipi-tated by the practice over a three-year period. Why not a twenty-year study?

POSTSCRIPT

Do Hostile Takeovers Harm Society?

This issue provides an opportunity for you to examine the trade-off between short-run costs and the long-run benefits of hostile takeovers. The question comes down to this: Do hostile takeovers, which are undertaken for the explicit purpose of liquidation, provide long-run benefits that exceed the short-run costs? Almeder and Carey believe that the benefits do exceed costs, while Newton defends the opposite viewpoint.

Newton's position is clear: Hostile takeovers are "damaging to the economy (and the people in it)." For her, no matter what the alleged long-run benefits may be, they do not outweigh the costs that are incurred in the "short and middle run." She goes on to argue that, just as an individual has a right to self-defense, a corporation, acting through its present management, has the same right and perhaps even an obligation to defend itself against those who would purchase it only to dismember and destroy it.

Almeder and Carey, however, take exception to Newton's logic. Their defense of the "shark" is intimately tied to the "right to private ownership, and its free exercise." If this right is guaranteed, society can reap the long-run benefits of market efficiency. That is, in the long run a hostile liquidation buyout will allow capital to be reallocated to its most productive use, rather than locking it into a suboptimal use. Thus, for Almeder and Carey, T. Boone Pickens, Rupert Murdock, the Bass brothers, and others like them are not "villains," they are necessary economic actors who are vital to the future success of the American economic system.

Many professional and popular publications contain articles on hostile takeovers. Charles R. Knoeber's essay entitled "Golden Parachutes, Shark Repellents, and Hostile Tender Offers," which appeared in the March 1986 issue of the *American Economic Review*, presents an excellent summary of the professional literature for those who are more technically minded. A number of other quasi-professional publications can also provide you with essays about hostile takeovers, particularly after the Ivan Boesky insider trading scandal made national headlines. For articles that are generally sympathetic to mergers and acquisitions—the Almeder/Carey position—see *Dunn's Business Monthly, Business Week, Forbes,* and *Fortune.* An alternative view is offered in an emotional article by Paul O. Gaddis, "Taken Over, Turned Out," *Harvard Business Review* (July/August 1987). In this article, Gaddis provides a firsthand account of what happens when a company is taken over in a hostile environment. Andrew C. Sigler provides another firsthand account of a hostile takeover. (Both Newton and Almeder/Carey refer to Sigler's case: See Testimony of Andrew C. Sigler Before the Subcommittee on Telecommunications, Consumer Protection, and Finance, Committee on Energy and Commerce, U.S. House [May 23, 1985].)

ISSUE 7

Is Mass Transit the Answer to Improving U.S. Energy Efficiency?

YES: Peter W. G. Newman and Jeffrey R. Kenworthy, from "Gasoline Consumption and Cities: A Comparison of U.S. Cities With a Global Survey," *Journal of the American Planning Association* (Winter 1989)

NO: Peter Gordon and Harry W. Richardson, from "Gasoline Consumption and Cities: A Reply," *Journal of the American Planning Association* (Summer 1989)

ISSUE SUMMARY

YES: Environmental scientists Peter W. G. Newman and Jeffrey R. Kenworthy conclude that land use and transportation priorities are more important than price, income, and vehicle efficiency in the determination of urban gasoline consumption patterns.
NO: Urban economists Peter Gordon and Harry W. Richardson allege that Newman and Kenworthy "ignore a mountain of research that contradicts their view" and draw very troubling conclusions.

North American has long been blessed with cheap energy. The abundant natural resources found on this continent—vast stands of trees, swift-moving rivers, enormous quantities of coal, and what appeared to be endless supplies of natural gas and oil—were supplemented by the importation of inexpensive oil from other parts of the world, particularly the Middle East. From the time of the Industrial Revolution all the way up to the early 1970s, cheap energy was readily available. During the two world wars and some of the more major flare-ups in the Middle East, concerns arose about the continuing supply of cheap energy, but by and large, the United States was confident it was energy independent.

Any time the price of an item remains low for long periods of time, there is a tendency to increase the usage of that item. Oil is no exception. It was substituted for other sources of energy. Industries were designed to depend upon it. Homes and cars consume it lavishly. In short, until the early 1970s, there was no incentive to either conserve energy or to develop renewable sources of energy. As a consequence, energy consumption, particularly of oil, increased at a rapid rate during the post–World War II period.

During this same period, the price paid for the oil purchased from the Organization of Petroleum Exporting Countries (OPEC) remained remarkably stable. (The price rarely rose above $2.00 a barrel.) Thus OPEC was faced with a declining level of income, as its import prices increased over time and its export prices stayed constant. Since these countries were forced to forfeit larger and larger quantities of oil to obtain a given quantity of imports, it is understandable that they attempted to force the world price of oil upwards.

And force the price of oil upwards they did! In 1973 and in 1978, OPEC sharply increased the price of oil. Shock waves were felt around the world as oil prices rose from $2.00 a barrel to peak levels that exceeded $40.00 a barrel. As a result, home heating costs skyrocketed. Fertilizers and other petrochemical products found their prices doubling, tripling, and then doubling again. Of course, gasoline prices were impacted. Prices rose from 35 cents for a gallon of gasoline to $1.75, where they were frozen below the equilibrium level, which was estimated to be well in excess of $2.00 a gallon.

There were consequences: Long lines appeared at service stations, voters called on Congress to impose strict mileage standards on automakers, and generous tax credits were offered to individuals who would insulate their homes and places of business. Sales of large gas-guzzling cars plummeted, while imports of small economy cars began to climb upwards. The end result was that in the United States, reliance on foreign oil fell to record lows—a mere 36 percent of the total oil consumed in the United States.

However, as the OPEC cartel weakened, prices of gasoline fell, and the energy crisis seemed to fade into the past. America's love affair with big automobiles began to warm again. More and more bigger cars crowded the highways, particularly in arteries in and around our cities. It did not take long before the consequences became apparent. Foreign oil dependency has risen to the 50 percent level, and environmental concerns have become a more urgent subject for television and radio talk shows and policymakers.

Why does the United States consume more gasoline per capita than countries in Europe, Australia, and Asia? Is it because urban centers have been poorly planned? Because the benefits of mass transportation systems have been ignored? These presumptions are rigorously debated in the pages that follow.

YES

Peter W. G. Newman and
Jeffrey R. Kenworthy

GASOLINE CONSUMPTION AND CITIES:
A COMPARISON OF U.S. CITIES WITH
A GLOBAL SURVEY

Assessments of United States oil dependence suggest that the widening gap between consumption and production is a cause for concern, given the U.S. government's deficit and potential political vulnerability in the 1990s (Abelson 1986; U.S. Department of Energy 1980). Conserving oil has been strongly advocated for other environmental, economic, and social reasons as well (Clark and Munn 1986; Energy Policy Project 1974). Policies to reduce oil consumption in the United States have successfully concentrated on stationary uses (e.g., industry and home heating) and improving vehicle fuel efficiency rather than on reducing the need for motor vehicle use. Studies rarely focus on cities, and those that do generally suggest only minimal energy savings would result from greater use of transit and land use changes (La Belle and Moses 1982; Sharpe 1982; Small 1980). Such studies tend to have a limited data base, as urban energy statistics are generally not available. Since cities are being built in patterns that last for 30 to 50 years, the implications for transportation energy use should at the very least be better understood. As Beaumont and Keys (1982) state, "[T]here has been insufficient examination of what an energy efficient urban form is actually composed of and how such a state can be reached given the present arrangements."

This article summarizes a study funded by the Australian government (Newman and Kenworthy 1988a) to evaluate physical planning policies for conserving transportation energy in urban areas by comparing how motor gasoline is used in 32 cities around the world. The data on ten United States cities are extracted and analyzed before they are compared with data from the global sample.

The scope of the broader study, involving the collection of data from 32 principal cities in North America, Australia, Europe, and Asia on land use, automobile use, transit, and other transportation factors like parking facilities and road length, has provided an important data set on cities covering 1960, 1970, and 1980. It can be used to examine a range of urban issues besides gasoline use—e.g., air pollution (directly related to gasoline use) and road accidents (directly related to auto use). Although this article does not include an examination of all of these issues, it does suggest that reducing gasoline use through physical planning will achieve other important gains related to the impact of the automobile on cities. . . .

THE UNITED STATES SAMPLE

The per capita gasoline consumption in U.S. cities (Table 1) varies by some 40 percent between the newer and more automobile-oriented cities like Houston and the older cities like New York. **[We have not included most of the tables that were part of the original Newman and Kenworthy article. They are technical in nature and the authors summarize the content of the tables in the body of their article.—Eds.]** This pattern can be compared to factors typically considered in economic analyses, such as income, gasoline price, and car ownership. . . . This article concentrates on the urban structure parameters, and therefore its focus, as illustrated in Tables 1 and 3, is on the physical planning parameters that were expected to have some role in the relative dependence of a city on automotive gasoline.

Land Use Planning Parameters
The size of a city could be expected to have an influence on transportation patterns. However, in this sample the correlation of gasoline use with size—both

population size and urban area—are weakly significant but negative; smaller cities appear to have higher, not lower, automobile travel, which is the reverse of what one would expect. This correlation suggests that, at least in this sample of relatively large cities, size is less important than other physical planning parameters.

Population and job density are key land use parameters. Together they show how intensively a city uses its land. Studies have shown that, the more intensive the land use, the shorter the distances of travel, the greater the viability of transit (more people per stop and hence better service), the greater the amount of walking and biking, the higher the occupancy of vehicles and, overall, the less need for a car (Newman and Kenworthy 1980, 1985; Hillman and Whalley 1979, 1983). The relative intensity of land use in the ten U.S. cities is clearly correlated with gasoline use overall and in the inner and outer areas. The strongest relationship is with the population density in the inner area; in fact, the largest variations in land use in these U.S. cities are between the inner areas of places like Houston and Phoenix, which contain around 8 people per acre and 10 jobs per acre compared with New York, which contains more than 40 people per acre and 20 jobs per acre. The overall intensity of activity in New York and Chicago is around double that of Houston and Phoenix. The outer areas of all U.S. cities, including New York, have uniformly low densities (although with some gradation); on average the inner areas are four to five times as dense as the outer areas.[1]

These patterns suggest that the urban structure within a city is fundamental to its gasoline consumption. Some data within particular cities confirmed this. Table 2 shows that the New York tristate region gasoline use is 335 gallons per person. However, for the inner city residents (city of New York), this amount reduces to around 153 gallons per person and, for the 1.4 million inhabitants of Manhattan, gasoline use drops to an extraordinary 90 gallons per person. The link to density is clear. In Denver the 240,000 exurban residents who live at very low density on the fringe of the city consume some 1,043 gallons per capita, 12 times the Manhattan consumption.

The strength of the city center can also affect transportation patterns—the more jobs in the city center the more viable generally is transit, which has its justification in large numbers of people all going to one place (Thomson 1977). The data in Table 1 support this idea with significant correlations between gasoline use and both the number and the proportion of jobs in the city center. They also support the hypothesis by Thomson that a city center cannot grow much beyond 120,000 jobs based around automobile access. The patterns of transit use are given in Table 3 and are examined further on in this article.

The other land use parameters explored in this study are the proportion of the population living in the inner city and the average journey-to-work trip length. The latter factor is related to the density and size of the city. The inner city proportion parameter gives an idea of how much of that city is in the pre-World War II form, prior to the assumption of large-scale automobile use, i.e., where densities are higher and land use is mixed residential/commercial/industrial (Duxbury et al. 1988; Witherspoon 1976; Van der Ryn and Calthorpe 1986). Table 1 shows that there is a significant

negative correlation of gasoline use with the proportion of population living in the inner city. The overall metropolitan journey-to-work trip length does not reveal any significant relationship to gasoline use. However, this parameter becomes more meaningful when we examine the perspective of other types of cities in different parts of the world.

Transportation Planning Factors

The use of transit, walking, and biking are related not only to the intensity and siting of urban activity but also to the extent to which a city provides for its automobile and its nonautomobile modes. Table 3 brings out these patterns clearly. The usage of nonautomobile modes (both transit and walking or biking) is strongly correlated with gasoline use, particularly in the journey-to-work modal split data, which highlight the variation from the Houston-Phoenix-Detroit type of city, which has more than 93-percent car use, down to New York, which has only 64-percent car use. This pattern is even more evident within New York, where private car use for work trips drops to 31 percent for inner city residents and to 12 percent for Manhattan (New York County) residents.

Traffic speeds in the New York inner city average 16 miles per hour and in Manhattan 10 miles per hour, coinciding with the very low per capita gasoline consumption of the residents given previously. This pattern of lower gasoline use per capita in areas with lower average traffic speeds is confirmed by the overall pattern in Table 2 and does not support studies (and the view of most traffic authorities) that suggest there will be fuel savings when average speeds are increased due to better vehicle efficiency (Newman and Kenworthy 1984). Rather,

Table 2

Gasoline Use and Urban Density in New York by Region (1980)

Area	Gasoline use (gallons/ capita)	Urban density (persons/ acre)
Outer area	454	5.3
Whole urban area (Tristate metro area)	335	8.1
Inner area (City of New York)	153	43.3
Central city (New York County— mainly Manhattan)	90	101.6

this pattern confirms the picture being developed here that urban structure is a more fundamental determinant of gasoline use than is vehicle efficiency. We elaborate on this point in the discussion of the larger sample of cities.

Average speed data highlight the relative position of road and parking infrastructure. The availability of roads and central city parking follows the pattern of gasoline consumption with highly significant positive correlations. The average speed data also highlight the importance of a separated rail transportation alternative. These data show clearly that buses are much slower than the overall traffic speed but that trains mostly can compete with the automobile for time savings. These speed data do not take account of time lost getting to and from bus stops, rail stations, or car parks.

The Low-Consumption City
A stylized picture emerges of a low transportation-energy city with a dense form, a strong center, and intensively utilized suburbs (especially the inner area) that provide the backbone for a significantly better transit system and

more walking and biking. The outer areas of U.S. cities appear to be quite similar in density (and car use) to those cities with strong inner areas and transit (e.g., New York and Chicago), which are able to extend their commuter trains to outer suburbs, so that at least some journeys are less demanding of an automobile.

There are, of course, many problems in suggesting that one city should become more like another. Nonetheless, the data suggest that there is a theoretical potential for fuel savings of some 20 to 30 percent in cities like Houston and Phoenix, if they were to become something more like Boston or Washington in urban structure. This would require a modest increase in the intensity of urban activity and the provision of a basic rail transit system. With more extreme changes in land use, such as increasing the density of population and jobs to the level of the inner areas of New York, much higher fuel savings would seem likely. Such savings would be considerably higher than the few percentage points generally predicted for transit and land use changes (Small 1980; Sharpe 1982). It appears from this study that the effects of land use and transit are more strongly interconnected than expected and that substituting car trips by transit results in more than just improved technological efficiency. Rather, it fosters a total change in transportation patterns, including an increase in walking and biking, and shorter distances for all modes, including car trips.

THE GLOBAL SAMPLE

The relationships between gasoline use in cities and land use/transportation factors can be further developed by expanding the comparison to a sample of major cities around the world. In order to summarize the data for the global sample, we placed the cities in regional groups. In this global comparison the range of gasoline use extends much further than in the United States sample. The average U.S. city uses nearly double the per capita gasoline consumed by Australian cities, a little less than double the gas used in Toronto, four times the gas consumed in the average European city, and ten times the average of the gas used in the three "westernized" Asian cities. We included Moscow in the sample to show an example of a city where there are almost no private cars (only 2 percent of the city go to work in a car) and hence where there is virtually no gasoline use; however, because Moscow is so fundamentally different from other cities, and because other data on Moscow are limited, it has been excluded from most of the analysis.

Economic Factors

The immediate response to any such comparisons across nations is to try to find variables like gasoline price, income, and relative vehicle efficiency that can help explain the large differences. There are significant correlations between gasoline use and price (–.7704), income per capita (0.7994), and vehicle fuel efficiency (–0.8830).[2] Therefore, we will examine these variables to see how important they are before pursuing urban structure and the other factors discussed in the previous section.

Many econometric analyses have been conducted to determine the way price and income relate to gasoline. These analyses have been used here to calculate how much more gasoline would have been consumed if the other cities had had U.S. gasoline prices, incomes, and vehicle efficiencies. The adjusted values using short-term (2 years) and long-term (20 years) elasticities are given in Table 4.[3] It could be argued that the long-term adjusted gasoline values overstate the effect of the economic variables (as separate from urban structure variables), for after 20 years urban structure would have adjusted to minimize travel to some degree. However, they do provide an upper bound. The discrepancy between actual U.S. gas use and adjusted gas use by other cities in Table 6 suggests that the price, income, and vehicle efficiency variables leave unexplained a large part of the difference between U.S. cities and others. On average the economic factors cannot account for 63 percent of the gasoline use in the short term and 47 percent in the long term. For Australian cities only 25 percent is left unexplained, but in Asian cities it is nearly 80 percent. We would suggest that urban structure, directly under the control of physical planners, is central to explaining the patterns in gasoline use and automobile dependence.

One of the key features drawn out by the economic adjustment data is the place of Toronto, which resembles a European city in its fuel use. Toronto is a less car-dependent city than are U.S. and Australian cities (6,118 passenger miles per capita by car in Toronto compared with 7,768 passenger miles in the U.S. and 6,634 passenger miles in Australia), but its vehicle fuel efficiency and gasoline price were lower than in the U.S. in 1980. The reasons for Toronto's low car usage are examined below.

The role of the economic variables will be addressed further on in this article. At this point we will look at the importance in the global sample of the physical planning factors that were found partially to explain U.S. city gasoline variations.

Land Use Planning Factors

The intensity of urban activity (Table 5) measured by the density of population and density of jobs is strongly correlated with gasoline use in both inner and outer areas. Australian cities resemble U.S. cities in their density patterns. Toronto, on the other hand, has a strong inner area similar to that of the five U.S. cities with the lowest gas consumption, but its outer area is more compact in population and jobs by nearly three times on average. Thus, Toronto has land use characteristics tending more towards those of a European city. From observation, a key difference between Toronto and U.S. cities seems to be the strong subcenters developed in the suburbs around transit stations. Cervero (1986) confirms this in his detailed assessment of how Toronto and other Canadian cities use transit to guide urban development. European cities on average have four times the intensity of urban activity overall compared with U.S. cities, their inner cities being nearly double and their outer areas nearly four times that found in the United States. Asian cities are even more extreme, their urban land being more than ten times as intensively utilized. Hong Kong appears to be the highest-density city in the world, with an overall population density of just under 120 people per acre, and a density of over 400 people per acre in its inner area.

Figure 1 shows the link between gasoline use and population density. The most obvious feature of this curve is the exponential relationship. The same shape is found when the gasoline data are adjusted for the price, income, and vehicle efficiency factors. The relationship suggests a strong increase in gasoline consumption where population density is under 12 people per acre. This relationship is conceptually quite possible, as low density appears to have a multiplicative effect, not only ensuring longer distances for all kinds of travel but making all nonautomobile modes virtually impossible, since many people live too far from a transit line and walking and biking become impossible.

The central city strength pattern is less obvious than the density relationship. There is a significant negative correlation between gasoline consumption and the proportion of jobs in the city center, but not for the absolute number of jobs. However, the differences in central city land use are not as marked in the total sample as are the differences in land use throughout the rest of the city. This suggests that the overall density is more important for travel characteristics than is the centralization factor.

There is probably another reason for the less clear effect of central city strength on gasoline use as measured by jobs. U.S., Australian, European, and Asian cities all concentrate jobs in city centers, in some cases to a similar extent. For example, Houston, with 174,000 jobs in the center and Hamburg with 187,000 are very similar. However, these two cities are vastly different in their modes of access to the city center and parking; Houston is almost totally automobile-oriented, with ample parking, and Hamburg is extremely rail-oriented, with limited parking. Many such comparisons can be drawn from our detailed data. They suggest that it is largely the transportation policies applied to central cities that determine whether or not a significantly centralized work force is going to have a positive or negative effect on gasoline use. We have not evaluated the role and importance of strong subcenters within the urban area in these

Figure 1

Gasoline Use Per Capita Versus Population Density (1980)

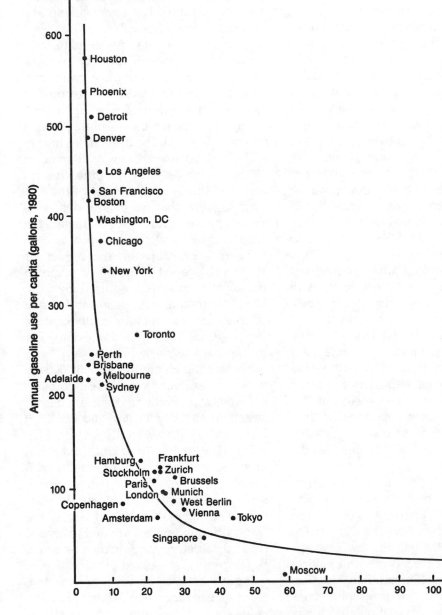

data. However such an evaluation could be a valuable exercise, as subcenters could be the means for more intensive outer area land use.

The proportion of population living in the inner city is also significantly correlated with gasoline use in the global sample. This correlation highlights again the importance of this inner city type of land use where travel distances are shorter. Unlike the U.S. sample, the global sample shows a significant positive correlation of journey-to-work trip lengths with gasoline use. Distances in European cities are generally 40 percent shorter than in the North American and Australian cities, which have sprawled extensively through construction of post World War II outer suburban housing. In Asian cities average journey distances are half those in European cities. This feature helps to explain the high proportion of walking trips in these cities.

Transportation Planning Factors
Table 6 shows the same strong relationships as seen with U.S. cities between gasoline use and both the use of transit (especially rail) and the amount of provision for the automobile.

Australian cities with land use similar to that of U.S. cities have a higher usage of transit, although they have a similarly high provision of roads and parking spaces. The significant difference in gasoline use between Australian and U.S. cities may well be explained by this difference in transit, which is perhaps due to a higher provision of service (an average of 35.0 vehicle miles per capita in Australia compared with 18.6 vehicle miles in the U.S.).

Toronto has a much stronger transit system (50.4 vehicle miles of service per capita) than do U.S. or Australian cities,

a feature consistent with its denser land use; its provision for automobiles is also much less than that in U.S. and Australian cities. The diversity of its transit systems, which include commuter rail, subway, modern trams on-street and new LRTs on separated tracks, electric trolleys, and diesel buses (as well as comprehensive cycle ways), provides a powerful comparison to nearby Detroit, which has an almost complete commitment to the automobile. The per capita gasoline consumption in Detroit is double that in Toronto; transit use is 0.8 percent of total passenger miles in Detroit, compared with 16.7 percent in Toronto. However, the difference in gasoline consumption in Detroit and Toronto cannot be explained simply by the difference in transit use. For example, if all of Toronto's transit users transferred to car the per capita use of gasoline would increase by 53 gallons, making Toronto's usage still 184 gallons per capita lower than that of Detroit. The Toronto transit system is part of an overall more energy-efficient city, despite Toronto having lower gasoline prices in 1980 and less fuel-efficient vehicles than the U.S. Indeed, Toronto is one of the few cities in the world with well-developed policies for transportation energy conservation based on land use strategies (Municipality of Metropolitan Toronto 1984).

European cities show even greater efficiency; 25 percent of all passenger travel is by transit and only 44 percent use a car for the journey to work. The importance of walking or biking in these more compact cities is highlighted by the fact that 21 percent use these modes for their work trip. In Amsterdam the proportion rises to 28 percent and in Copenhagen to 32 percent. The provision of roads and central city parking is expectably much less generous than in U.S. and Australian cities.

Asian cities again show the most extreme pattern, with nearly two-thirds of their total transportation passenger miles on transit. The car is only a minor (15 percent) factor in work journeys, coming after walking and biking (25 percent). In the modern city of Tokyo there are one sixth of the central-area parking spaces per 1,000 jobs and nearly a quarter of the roads that are in U.S. cities: only 16 percent use a car to go to work.

The average traffic speed is strongly correlated with gasoline use per capita and is positive, not negative, as predicted by those who study only the effects of congestion on individual vehicles. This tradeoff between fuel-efficient traffic and fuel-efficient cities is confirmed at a local level by the data on regions of New York (Table 2). The tradeoff was examined in a detailed analysis by suburb in the Australian city of Perth. Here we found that, in central areas, vehicles were 19 percent less efficient than average but that residents in these accessible, although congested, areas used 22 percent less fuel. In outer areas, on the other hand, vehicles were 12 percent more efficient than the urban average but residents had to drive so much more that they used 29 percent more fuel overall (Newman and Kenworthy 1988b).

The data in Table 6 also show that a rail-based transit system can compete with the automobile and that in Europe and Asia train speeds are generally faster than the average traffic speed. Bus travel is universally slower than 15 mph and cannot be considered competitive with car travel. The much slower speeds of the streetcar do not diminish their importance in European cities, as streetcars play an important role in short local trips linking in to major train stations that again lower car use (Vuchic 1985). Central area pedestrianization, which is so extensive and so popular as a means of revitalizing central areas of European cities, is made possible by the strong transit operations in these cities based primarily around trams and trains (Vuchic 1981).

These clear relationships between gasoline use and a range of physical planning and transportation variables confirm the model of a gasoline-conserving urban structure developed earlier with the ten U.S. cities. In this model the city is compact, with a strong city center, combined with a commitment to transit (especially rail) and other nonautomobile modes, and to restraint in the provision of automobile infrastructure. Further clarification of the relationships would help. However, the relationships already established begin to suggest a number of policy areas in which cities like those in the U.S. (and Australia) could respond to the challenge of using less gasoline, as well as to the other benefits that flow from a less automobile-oriented city.

POLICY IMPLICATIONS

Policy studies on gasoline use derive mainly from simulation studies or econometric models. Simulation studies that have examined urban land use or transit changes have generally suggested that only minimal savings would be possible. For example, Small (1980) suggests that an energy-induced land use control that resulted in densities of 15 units per acre, compared with the current U.S. average of 5 units per acre would reduce automobile usage for work trips by only 1.4 percent after 6 years. Sharpe (1982) suggests energy savings of only 11 percent if urban density in Melbourne is tripled. None of the assessments in these studies suggest that simulations and policy studies concerning the effect of density on transport will need to consider the much more extensive pattern of changes occurring from increased urban activity and lowered automobile dependence, since, in their joint effect, these changes appear to lead to much higher potential gasoline savings. In particular, as Figure 1 shows, there is an exponential relationship between gasoline use and density, suggesting that major fuel savings are possible as cities move from the 4 to 6 people per acre to the 12 to 14 people per acre range.

Economic Versus Physical Planning Factors

Econometric models are based on correlations of variables considered to be the key determinants of gasoline use. Gasoline models have nearly all been based on national data and all show that price, income, and vehicle efficiency are sufficient to explain their data. The problem with using econometric models to attempt to explain variations in urban gasoline consumption is that these models are assuming urban spatial variations, and modal split patterns can be accounted for solely by gasoline price and income variations. On a national basis this is broadly the case, as rural driving will mainly be determined by these variables and in general there is a correlation between wealth and urban space, i.e., money tends to buy space. However, there are many important variations in this pattern, due to:

• Constraints in urban sites, such as New York;

• Social and cultural factors, such as those in European cities, where frequently money buys location, not space (and a central location is often preferred);[4] and

• Such factors as a good transit system, which concentrates land use and provides a real alternative to the automobile because it saves time.

Omitting these factors means that policy developed from econometric models will have limited application to transportation in cities. This would explain why in the sample of U.S. cities there is no significant correlation between gasoline consumption and income or between vehicle ownership and income, and why there was the same lack of correlation in a previous study of Australian cities (Newman and Kenworthy 1980).

These factors are extremely important where policy is concerned. The econometric models suggest that there is little that can be done to reduce gasoline consumption other than taxing gasoline and vehicles or legislating for better vehicle fuel efficiency. This study, on the other hand, suggests that there are a variety of policies with potential to save fuel. They include:

• Increasing urban density;
• Strengthening the city center;
• Extending the proportion of city that has inner-area land use;
• Providing a good transit option; and
• Restraining the provision of automobile infrastructure.

These parameters are in the direct control of physical planners. In the remainder of this article we discuss the two main physical planning policy areas that appear to follow from the data analysis: reurbanization and reorientation of transportation priorities.

Figure 2

Reurbanization as a Fourth Phase in Urban Development

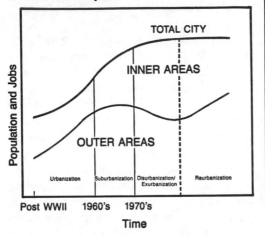

Post WWII   1960's   1970's

Time

Reurbanization

Increasing the intensity of urban activity within the present urban area rather than continuing to push into green-field rural areas has come to be called reurbanization. It follows the pattern of urban trends outlined in Figure 2. In the reurbanization process population and jobs once again begin to grow in inner areas and outer areas concentrate development and begin to take on more of the intensity and mixed character of the old inner areas. . . .

Reurbanization is discussed mainly in Europe and is only minimally considered for its fuel savings; the principal motivations usually are its economic and social benefits—a vital and attractive central and inner city and better utilization of the existing urban infrastructure (v.d. Berg et al. 1982; Klaassen, Bourdrez, and Volmuller 1981). In addition, reurbanization is considered to help diminish vehicle emissions that contribute to acid rain and smog. Despite the suburbanization processes of the postwar period,

most European cities have not deconcentrated as rapidly as have cities in the United States (the densities in this study reflect this difference). Likewise, European cities do not face the same inner and central city crises (Heinritz and Lichtenberger 1986). Nevertheless, there is an ongoing effort to reurbanize. Many case studies outline evidence of successful reurbanization in Europe (Tanghe, Vlaeminck, and Berghoef 1984; v.d. Berg, Klaassen, and v.d. Meer 1983).

The same trend to redevelop, restore, reuse, and more intensively develop urban land is evident in U.S. cities, but the trend is in its infancy. Brian Berry (1985) calls U.S. reurbanization efforts "islands of renewal in seas of decay." Nevertheless, the potential for the reurbanization of U.S. cities is clear; in fact, this study's comparison of U.S. cities with other global cities shows the potential to be quite considerable. Recent data show that the deconcentration of people and jobs from U.S. cities has reached the slowest rate since the 1920s (Macauley 1985) and that the return of younger people to the city is becoming demographically evident (Dynarski 1986). These studies suggest that the return to the city will probably proceed due to factors such as lifestyle preference rather than economics. However, other studies are now showing that trends in technology (towards more office and service-oriented employment) and demography (towards fewer households with children) are aiding the process (v.d. Ryn and Calthorpe 1986).

Working against a revival of the inner city are the problems of the concentrated racial and poorer communities that are in the majority in most U.S. inner cities (Peterson 1986). These communities have expressed fear of gentrification by upper middle class whites taking over cheap inner city housing (Purnick 1986; Celis 1986). The solution, at least in theory, would appear to be to reurbanize through building additional inner city housing. The value of reducing infrastructure needs on the urban fringe is obvious. A policy generating creative ways of building more central and inner city housing and forging new and more integrated communities appears to be crucial to a variety of concerns besides gasoline conservation.

San Francisco and Portland have made recent advances in reurbanization through creating new housing and jobs in their central cities. San Francisco has had a long tradition of central city living, with a 1980 population of almost 34,500 in a central business district (CBD) of 946 acres, compared with Phoenix, Houston, Denver, Detroit, Perth, Adelaide, Los Angeles, and Brisbane, which have an average of just over 5,000 people in a CBD area of 924 acres. The density of jobs has not suffered, as San Francisco had 273,000 jobs in 1980 compared with 96,000 on average for the other eight cities. San Francisco is now building its Mission Bay project on 300 acres of waterfront land adjacent to downtown; it will house over 15,000 people and will have millions of square feet for office, research and development, and retail activity.

Portland, Oregon, is an example of a smaller U.S. city beginning to reverse its previous land use patterns through the redevelopment of a former freeway reserve in the Banfield corridor with a light rail line and thousands of new homes from the city center to a new subcenter at the end of the line. Twenty percent of all new homes in the eastern county are expected to be within walk-ing distance of the new transit system. This example represents not only a commitment to reurbanization but also a reorientation of transportation priorities (Edner and Arrington 1985).

Reorientation of Transportation Priorities

Although land use provides the framework for a city's transportation system, the actual patterns that emerge can of course be altered to some degree by the priority given to various modes. Many European cities are as compact as Amsterdam and Copenhagen, but these two are noted for strong commitments to bicyclists and pedestrians. Vienna's priorities were summed up by its mayor when he states that "unlimited individual mobility . . . is an illusion," that "the future belongs to the means of public transportation," and that the need for public transportation will be "a driving force of city renewal" (Gratz 1981). Australian cities show a greater commitment to transit than do most U.S. cities with comparable land use. Within the U.S. the urban structure of cities such as Los Angeles and Detroit could support much more transit use, but these cities have obviously directed their priorities in the past to automobiles. For example, Detroit has an inner area population density that approaches that of Toronto, yet it provides only one fifth of the transit service per person.

A reorientation of transportation priorities in U.S. cities would include elements of the following policies:

Upgraded and extended transit. The technology and management structures for high-cost or low-cost separated-way transit systems have been adequately demonstrated in U.S. cities and elsewhere, with both positive and negative assessments (Vuchic 1981; Small 1985; Hall and Hass-Klau 1985). However, such systems—especially new light rail options—are increasing in popularity as a means of coping with high- and medium-capacity transportation requirements. To make transit a more fundamental part of the U.S. city will require a major commitment of planning and capital not unlike the commitment that has been more recently shown in highway building. The full benefits of such transit systems will be realized only when land use is allowed and encouraged to concentrate around transit stations, as has occurred around Washington's Metro (Metropolitan Washington Council of Governments 1983). Transit authorities can also help to pay for their systems by entrepreneurial activity on their land, such as development above and around stations.

The sheer inadequacy of totally automobile-dominated transportation is evident in the fact that many West Coast cities like San Diego, Los Angeles, San Jose, Sacramento, and Portland, after years of growing car use, have recognized the need for rail systems. Even Houston has now opted for a rail system. Such changes will play only a minor part in the short-term future of these cities, but they signal the beginning of an effort to build a less auto-dependent, fuel-hungry city.

Increased pedestrianization and bicyclization. The cheapest and most fuel-efficient transportation modes rarely achieve much priority in an automobile-oriented society. But, where land use is sufficiently concentrated, the opportunities for more walking and biking can be greatly encouraged by improvement of facilities. This task can include enhancing separation through establishing pathways and bike lanes and, particularly, through pedestrianizing central cities. Planning for linkages between transit and these facilities is particularly important, as such linkages provide low-cost flexibility to an inflexible transit route, thus increasing the door-to-door competitiveness of transit (Bowden, Campbell, and Newman 1980). The other low-cost method is the European "Woonerf" treatment of high density residential streets, which allows complete car access, but, by careful landscaping and provision of angle parking, narrows and winds streets to give greater priority to pedestrians and bicyclists (van Vliet 1983).

Planned congestion. "Woonerf" is also labeled planned congestion, as it involves placing a limit on private vehicle movement and adjusting priorities to give advantage to other transportation modes. It also involves the acceptance of limits on the provision of parking (as recently announced in Chicago) and the level of road availability; it shifts the orientation from road construction to traffic system management (Organization for Economic Cooperation and Development 1973, 1978). Planned congestion should reduce environmental impact from large highways in urban areas. It does require accepting lower average traffic speeds and favoring accessibility over mobility. That these techniques are likely to save gasoline is strongly indicated by the data in this study. But, as with reurbanization, there are many other sides to this policy.

Many observers will say that a policy accepting congestion denies fundamental rights. Others have suggested that far from being an economic disincentive, "automobile restraint" can be a tool to improve a city's "viability as a business centre" (Small 1985); that a less car-dependent transportation system is far more equitable, especially for the young (Schaeffer and Sclar 1975); and that cities limiting auto use provide the opportunity for a more convivial, community-oriented urban society (Illich 1973). At the least, we can say that the transition to a lower gasoline-using city need not be painful if the perceived problems from congestion are consistently being offset by real gains in access through new transit systems and new, more centrally located housing.

CONCLUSION

This study suggests that physical planning agencies have a major contribution to make in the conservation of transportation energy in cities. Policies that relate to prices, income, and vehicle efficiency as generated by econometricians undoubtedly have their role, but without direction in land use and commitment of transportation resources to nonautomobile modes, these policies will not be sufficient. The data in this study suggest that there is a large potential for conserving gasoline in U.S. cities by shifting to land use and transportation patterns that are evident in other cities. The more precise data that are now available through this study provide perspective for physical planners in establishing achievable goals. The policies of reurbanization and reorientation of transportation priorities outlined here should reduce gasoline use, and may also provide economic, social, and environmental benefits. Indeed, one could argue that reducing dependence on gasoline and the automobile in general is a significant element in the present thrust for "the return of the livable city" in the United States (McNulty et al. 1986).

AUTHORS' NOTE

Dr Newman was a visiting scholar at Resources For the Future, Washington, D.C., when this paper was first written. Thanks to Joel Darmstadter, Philip Abelson, and Lester Brown for comments on the text and to Sue Levinson and Sue Flay for typing. The Australian government's National Energy Research Development and Demonstration Council provided financial support for this project.

NOTES

1. Los Angeles is a little higher in its outer area density, probably because of the definition of the city that was used. Los Angeles is defined as the Los Angeles/Long Beach SMSA (L.A. County), which is not the full functional urban region embracing a number of other smaller SMSAs. This definition had to be used because of the difficulties in compiling such an array of data across so many separate administrative areas. Were the true urban region to be used, as is the case in the Tristate area of New York, then outer area densities could be expected to be lower, although not by much.

2. Data sources were: price—United Nations (1981) (data for Sweden, Singapore, Hong Kong, and Moscow were obtained directly from the cities); income—Summers, Heston (1984); vehicle efficiency—Chandler (1985), Energy and Environmental Analysis Inc. (1982), U.S. Department of Transportation (1985b), Transport Canada (1984).

3. The calculation method is described in the footnote to Table 4. Elasticities are derived from Pindyck (1979); Dahl (1982); Archibald and Gillingham (1981); and Wheaton (1982).

4. The hypothesis that it is primarily an Anglo-Saxon tradition to value rural "garden suburb" environments rather than compact urban environments is pursued by authors like A. D. King (on U.K. cities) and M. White and L. White and S. Grabow (on U.S. cities) and is reviewed in P. W. G. Newman and T. L. F. Hogan (1981).

NO

Peter Gordon and
Harry W. Richardson

GASOLINE CONSUMPTION
AND CITIES: A REPLY

In their article "Gasoline Consumption and Cities," which appeared in the Winter 1989 issue of the *Journal* (55, 1: 24–37), Peter W. G. Newman and Jeffrey R. Kenworthy, NK for short, compare gasoline consumption per capita across cities and countries. They find that average consumption in U.S. cities is approximately twice as high as in Australian cities and Toronto, four times higher than in European cities, and ten times higher than in three "westernized" Asian cities. Moreover, they report that gas consumption per capita within ten large U.S. cities varies by up to 40 percent. They argue that these differences cannot be explained by price, income, and vehicle efficiency variables, but mainly reflect land use patterns and the transportation system. On the basis of these observations, they implicitly set up a policy objective of minimizing gasoline consumption, and recommend a twin strategy of "reurbanization" (i.e., a return to more compact and more monocentric urban land use patterns) and investment in urban rail transit.

This reply will argue that NK's analysis is faulty, that the problems are wrongly diagnosed, and that their policy and planning prescriptions are inappropriate and infeasible. We will focus on five key issues, namely:

1. The wisdom of fuel use minimization in the context of efficient resource allocation;
2. The validity of global comparisons;
3. The impact of urban structure on travel;
4. The potential for rail transit and modal choice; and
5. The debate on the land impact of transit development.

Most of our examples are drawn from the United States, partly because we know the territory, and partly because United States cities occupy most of NK's attention and suffer most from their lack of understanding.

IS FUEL USE MINIMIZATION EFFICIENT?

The pursuit of a single objective, such as minimizing gasoline consumption, makes no sense. As Lowry (1988) points out, " '[E]fficiency' does not imply rearranging our lives to minimize transport costs. Rather it implies a search for a suitable balance between transport costs (including the travelers' time) and the costs of compatibly configured land uses." More generally, all resources are scarce, and efficiency requires that resources be allocated among competing uses according to the criterion of maximizing social welfare. This requires a price system—the relative prices of which reflect the relative values that consumers attach to the full array of goods and services—not administrative fiat. Even in the energy crisis of the 1970s the preoccupation with minimizing energy use was inappropriate. The gasoline lines of those times resulted from substituting administrative allocations for market adjustments (Chapman 1980). Since then, new oil reserves have been discovered and technological alternatives to a gasoline-powered automobile are closer (although the relative price of gasoline currently gives no stimulus to this search).

Even if policy makers wished to be very conservative or to use national security concerns as a rationale for reducing gasoline consumption, a fuel tax would be much simpler, faster, more effective, and cheaper than rearranging metropolitan areas and/or major investments in transit. Even applying NK's own criterion, the substitution of rail for automobiles does not achieve energy efficiency. Subways consume fuel, especially during construction. At their current levels of utilization, all the post-World War II subways in the United States waste fuel (Congressional Budget Office 1977). The idea of planners turning our lives upside down in pursuit of a singleminded goal is as horrible as it is alien. NK's world is the Kafkaesque nightmare that Hayek (1945) always dreaded, a world in which consumers have no voice, relative prices have no role, and planners are tyrants.

GLOBAL COMPARISONS: ARE THEY VALID?

The value of using international comparisons of gasoline consumption per capita as a rationale for policy intervention is open to dispute. The attempt to justify such comparisons by adjusting the raw data for differences in prices, incomes, and vehicle efficiency (NK, Table 4) is not convincing, because applying some kind of average estimate of elasticities derived from U.S. data to other countries ignores the fact that elasticities vary widely with different price ranges, different patterns of consumer behavior, and different sets of relative prices. Moreover, finding that a significant proportion of intercountry differences (up to 79 percent in Asian cities) is not explained by these factors does not help the comparative approach as NK believe.

To suggest that the unexplained differentials are explained by urban structure and the presence of transit is merely an assertion; variations in lifestyles and travel behavior may be as important. In any event, even if urban structure and transit were the key factors, there would be no policy implications because the case for converting an existing dispersed metropolitan settlement pattern and building a new rail system cannot be based on the prior existence of a compact city with a sunk-cost transit system long in place somewhere else in the world. Cities are not made of Lego, and 1990s transit capital costs are not those of the 1890s.

If international comparisons are to be used, a more appropriate focal point might have been the international experience with rail transit (Gordon and Willson, 1985; World Bank 1986). Declining transit use and high costs per passenger mile are common phenomena. The World Bank reports that, in 18 metro-, light-, and suburban rail systems, the ratio of operating revenue to costs varied between 0.16 and 0.53 (0.16 and 0.33 for the U.S. examples), with the sole exceptions of Hong Kong (0.87) and Nagoya (1.16 for the suburban rail system, not its metro) (World Bank 1986). But this is not the story NK want to hear.

THE IMPACT OF URBAN STRUCTURE ON TRAVEL

Changes in the spatial structure of cities reflect the interaction of transportation, labor, land, and housing markets. The suburbanization of the labor force was stimulated by lifestyle choices and the increased range and mobility offered by automobiles and highways. Labor supply attracts economic activity and has pulled jobs to the suburbs. NK should have examined the data more closely. By 1980 only 7.5 percent of jobs in the largest U.S. urbanized areas remained in the central business district (CBD). Commuting times in the five "gas-guzzling" cities are shorter (by 19 to 33 percent) than in either the transit champion, New York, or the runner-up, Chicago (U.S. Department of Transportation 1985). The co-location of firms and households at decentralized locations has reduced, not lengthened, commuting times and distances. Decentralization reduces pressures

on the CBD, relieves congestion, and avoids "gridlock." Pisarski (1987) shows that, nationwide, most commuting is now suburb-to-suburb. Analysis from the 1977 and 1983–84 Nationwide Personal Transportation Study shows that there is no relationship between city size and trip lengths, times, or speeds; moreover, average commuting speeds did not decline (Gordon, Kumar, and Richardson 1988a).

NK are preoccupied with work trips, whereas the most striking change in U.S. travel behavior is the boom in non-work trips associated with social phenomena, such as an aging population, smaller households, and higher levels of service consumption (Gordon, Kumar, and Richardson 1988b). This growth in non-work trips was primarily for "family and personal" and "social and recreational" purposes, which are consistent with higher levels of welfare. Moreover, because more numerous and shorter trips were associated with a *decline* in vehicle miles traveled, they did not imply more gas consumption. However, non-work trip growth has been facilitated by decentralized lifestyles and automobiles. The intervention advocated by NK—planning for stronger downtowns and limiting suburbanization—would be the problem, not the solution. Moreover, to the extent that rail transit is used, it accelerates rather than reverses suburbanization (Capozza 1973). NK refer to a return to the city movement as if it were a strong nationwide phenomenon rather than sporadic gentrification in a small selective list of cities.

THE POTENTIAL FOR RAIL TRANSIT AND MODAL CHOICE

NK make a strong pitch for rail transit, relying on a spurious travel time comparison: "[B]uses are much slower than the overall traffic speed but . . . trains mostly can compete with the automobile for time savings." Although NK refer to out-of-vehicle time in the subsequent sentence, they choose to ignore it. This misses the whole point. As noted by Webber (1976), "[T]he time spent inside vehicles is judged to be far less onerous than the time spent walking, waiting, and transferring, by a factor of up to three or four times. For commuters waiting on platforms, the factor may be as high as ten times! . . . It is the door-to-door, no-wait, no-transfer features of the automobile that, by eliminating access time, make private cars so attractive to commuters—not its top speed."[1] The closer a mode is to sharing automobile characteristics, as do many of the paratransit modes (jitneys, airport shuttles, vanpools, etc.), the better its prospects.

The case for rail is very weak. Consider the capital costs alone. Los Angeles has plans to spend $43.7 billion on new transit investments, plus $2.96 billion for annual operations and maintenance; under this investment and budgeting, each work trip would cost $14.75 *if* the target ridership of 19 percent of total trips could be attained. Because revenues leave shortfalls of 72 percent on capital account and 55 percent on current account (Southern California Association of Governments 1988), the tax bite would be about $250 on each man, woman, and child in the five-county region. To create the same number of route-miles of rail transit as in Tokyo would cost Los Angeles $250 billion, and would merely serve its core because its urbanized area is twice as large as Tokyo's. In any event, for all its transit dependence Tokyo has one of the longest mean commuting times and the

most cramped living spaces in the developed world.

Rail transit requires 20,000 passengers per hour to compete with other modes; this implies high residential and workplace densities. But the population densities of U.S. urbanized areas fell by 30 percent between 1960 and 1980, and even central city densities fell (Lowry 1988). Does this decline suggest that "reurbanization" would work? U.S. metropolitan planners have neither the will nor the capacity. There is no case for reinforcing weak-headed analysis with heavy-handed implementation. NK suggest that Houston and Phoenix should be more like Boston or Washington, D.C., ignoring the fact that the former have stronger growth, more investment, faster commuting, and less congestion. The last thing they need is "a basic rail transit system." NK refer to recognition of "the need for rail transit" and the "sheer inadequacy of totally automobile-dominated transportation" in West Cost cities without a mention of the influence of the Urban Mass Transit Administration subsidies program in distorting the decisions of local planners and policy makers (Kain 1988).

NK also make a plea for the cheapest and most fuel-efficient transportation modes, walking and biking. Are they recommending the Beijingization of U.S. cities to reinforce their Maoist planning methods? They argue for limits on automobile use, trying to cripple the more efficient mode, but via the adoption of direct controls rather than road congestion pricing. They claim that pain and loss of rights will be offset by more equity, a stronger sense of community, and "real gains in access through new transit systems and new, more centrally located housing." But in the United States most poor households need cars, walkers in many locations are more concerned with safety than a sense of community, new transit systems are too expensive and too inconvenient, and developers exploit the availability of central city housing subsidies to build high-income housing.

LAND VALUE IMPACTS OF TRANSIT DEVELOPMENT

Because of the high costs of conventional rail, NK embrace light rail, the mode with the most dismal prospects (Kain 1988) and suggest development around stations as a mechanism to make light rail pay, citing the Washington, D.C., Metro as an example (Metropolitan Washington Council of Governments 1983). They seem to be unaware of the dearth of public-private development success stories. No credible studies of land value/use effects of rail transit investments in U.S. cities make the case for significant direct impacts. This is not surprising. Modest ridership implies modest secondary impacts. Unscrambling the effects of transit from other concurrent influences on development is very difficult analytically, perhaps impossible. Knight (1980) is one of the most widely cited studies: "On the basis of the available evidence we cannot clearly establish a causal relationship between rail transit and changes in land use and development patterns. At best, such changes would seem to occur only in the presence of other favorable factors" (Knight 1980). Boyce (1979) similarly concluded, "On balance, however, development impacts are more of a long-term phenomenon. Existing development is unlikely to be affected except in unusual situations. The timing of development may be affected slightly by transit investments, but in general land development tends

to proceed independently of new rail transit system construction."

San Francisco's Bay Area Rapid Transit (BART) is a test case in the United States, and it is difficult to explain NK's neglect of Webber's (1976) seminal BART analysis, except by noting that it contradicts their case. Webber observes: "The planners fully expected that increased accessibility at train stations would make the surrounding areas attractive to business firms and apartment dwellers, following the model of earlier commuter railroads in the East. In turn, clusters of offices, shops, and high density housing around the stations would visibly restructure the region, stemming the drift towards low-density dispersion and urban sprawl. . . . [T]here is . . . little evidence to corroborate those forecasts and hopes" (Webber 1976). Moreover, Webber notes, "rising values in one location will be about equally matched by declines elsewhere, rather as levels in an air mattress rise and fall as one section or another is squeezed or released" (Webber 1979). Furthermore, "rather than deterring suburban sprawl, BART may instead be encouraging it" (Webber 1979).

Since 1976, probably not coincidentally, downtown San Francisco has suffered from relative decline, and Los Angeles has pulled far ahead of San Francisco as a corporate headquarters hub. As for suburban impacts, Giuliano (1986) concluded that growth "in non-BART zones is greater than in BART zones. The most rapid growth in BART zones has occurred in the outermost zones, but growth in suburban non-BART zones has been even greater." BART has also suffered from major financial problems, especially recently (Demoro 1987). This is particularly significant because, among western cities, San Francisco has been considered to have the best prospects for rail transit, while Los Angeles has been seen as having the poorest prospects (Hilton 1968).

Giuliano (1986) writes that the "evidence provided by impact studies indicates that rail systems have had little influence on urban structure. The most significant impacts have occurred in Toronto, Canada, where stringent land use controls have been employed to direct land use changes. In the United States, these controls do not exist, and there is frequently a lack of local support for increases in development density." Research on Philadelphia's 20-year-old Lindenwold commuter-rail line shows that "it has had no discernible effect on the downtown area and that it had a small one-time positive effect on property values elsewhere along the route (Altschuler 1981) and that not much impact is observable except where development is supported by other forces" (Meyer and Gomez-Ibanez 1981). NK's lone example is the Washington, D.C., Metro; but in the past 20 years the District of Columbia's population has declined, while that of the suburbs has increased, suburban job growth has been triple the rate of growth in the central city, and the most rapid increase in commuting has been via automobile and from suburb to suburb (Baker 1983).

CONCLUSION

NK have written a very troubling paper. Their distortions are not innocent, because the uninformed may use them as ammunition to support expensive plans for central city revitalization and rail transit projects or stringent land use controls in a futile attempt to enforce urban compactness. Planners can, and perhaps should, take normative positions, but

they ought to be able to agree, more or less, about the facts. NK have ignored a mountain of research that contradicts their views, quoting only Small (1980) and Sharpe (1982) on the other side of their argument. How could they overlook Webber's (1976) trenchant analysis of BART, Pickrell's (1985) destruction of Pushkarev and Zupan's (1980) arguments for rail transit, or the other researchers quoted in this paper? More important, how do they justify their arrogance in prescribing policy implications primarily aimed at the United States, given their revealed ignorance of metropolitan transit experiences in this country and total misunderstanding of the changes in U.S. metropolitan spatial structure?

Fortunately, the United States remains a free society where consumers and group interests retain sufficient power and influence to restrain draconian means of intervention. American planners are, for the most part, fully aware of this fact, and attempt to work with the flow rather than fight against it. Even the Soviet Union, Eastern Europe, and the People's Republic of China are becoming increasingly aware of the virtues of consumer sovereignty and market adjustments. Perhaps Newman and Kenworthy would be well advised to seek out another planet, preferably unpopulated, where they can build their compact cities from scratch with solar-powered transit.

NOTE

1. Amusingly, a recent newspaper report (Flinn 1989) presents comments from transit chiefs about their own commuting habits in one of America's most compact cities with a newer subway system. All five drive to work! They don't use public transportation for the same reasons that ordinary commuters choose to drive: transit is inconvenient (not close enough to their homes) or too slow, they need their car during the day, they use the car as an office, and the car is cheap to operate. Yet they all insist that public transit is the answer—for other people.

POSTSCRIPT

Is Mass Transit the Answer to Improving U.S. Energy Efficiency?

The unvarnished reality is that the United States has more cars per capita as compared to other developed countries. Cars in the United States are less fuel efficient and are driven two or three times more miles than cars in Europe, Australia, or Japan. If this consumption pattern is harmful to the environment and a threat to the world's depletable supply of fossil fuels, we must ask ourselves why this pattern exists and whether or not public policy should intervene.

This issue has allowed you to grapple with these questions. It is based on a study conducted by Newman and Kenworthy for the Australian government entitled *Automobile Dependence in Cities: Urban Land Use, Transport and Energy in Principal Cities of North America, Europe, Asia and Australia* (Gower Press, 1988). This study concluded that gasoline prices, personal income, and vehicle efficiency can only partially explain the high gasoline consumption levels found in the United States. They attribute this high consumption level to poor land use planning and underdeveloped mass transportation systems in most U.S. cities.

Gordon and Richardson, on the other hand, argue that these policy prescriptions represent a "draconian intervention" into the marketplace. They allege that Newman and Kenworthy have distorted the facts and falsely create a need to "revitalize" central cities, invest in "rail transit" projects, and impose "stringent land use controls." For Gordon and Richardson, these are not "innocent" mistakes; rather they represent the pipe dreams of urban planners who "would be well advised to seek out another planet" to try out their ideas.

Given that the majority of the 200 billion gallons of fuel consumed each year in the United States is for vehicles operated in and around cities, mass transit schemes appear to be an attractive alternative. We invite you, however, to examine some of the counterevidence provided by Gordon and Richardson. A few articles they suggest are: M. Webber, "The BART Experiences: What Have We Learned?" *The Public Interest* (vol. 45, 1976), pp. 79–103, and D. H. Pickrell, "The Cost of Constructing Mass Rail Transit Systems," *Transportation Research Record* (vol. 1006, 1985), pp. 48–55. These and other literature cited by Gordon and Richardson should provide some balance to Newman and Kenworthy's Australian governmental study previously cited.

ISSUE 8

Is Choice a Panacea for the Ills of Public Education?

YES: John E. Chubb and Terry M. Moe, from "America's Public Schools: Choice *Is* a Panacea," *The Brookings Review* (Summer 1990)

NO: Bill Honig, from "Why Privatizing Public Education Is a Bad Idea," *The Brookings Review* (Winter 1990/1991)

ISSUE SUMMARY

YES: Political scientists John E. Chubb and Terry M. Moe believe that the United States must free public schools from "political and bureaucratic control" and instead rely upon "markets and parental choice" in the quest for quality education.

NO: Public school superintendent Bill Honig replies that privatizing public schools through a system of choice is both unnecessary, given the school reforms of the 1980s, and dangerous, in light of the expected market consequences.

Before we embark upon a discussion of the benefits and costs of privatizing public schools, we should recognize that the provision of education, whether it is elementary, secondary, or higher education, can be undertaken by either the private sector or the public sector. That is, education can be marketed. If the United States wanted an unfettered market to operate in the education industry, it could. Without public education, however, those individuals who could afford education and wanted it would purchase it from private vendors; but those who wanted it but could not afford it would be excluded from the classroom.

It is only in recent years that a large percentage of the population has reaped the benefits of education. In 1940, about 14 percent of the adult population had less than six years of formal education. Now all but 2.4 percent have at least six years of schooling. Since 1940, the number of adults with four or more years of high school has grown from less than 25 percent of those 25 years or older to more than 76 percent, and those with four or more years of college has grown from 1 in 20 to more than 1 in 5.

The consequences of this educational attainment are far-reaching. Not only are individuals better off—there is a high positive correlation between education and income—but society is better off. That is, there are externalities or spillover effects associated with the consumption of education. Individuals who are educated are more likely to make better political decisions. Those who are educated and earn higher incomes are less likely to engage in criminal activity or become dependent on welfare. As the average level of education increases in a community, economic productivity is enhanced, and this in turn results in a higher rate of economic growth. Even if these third-party effects were not present, the public sector probably would continue to underwrite the cost of education. Educational opportunity is too closely bound up with American notions of equal opportunity to be ignored by lawmakers.

This does not mean, however, that the provision of public education has come without a cost. Quite the contrary, public education has been massively expensive. In 1987, state and local governments spent approximately $226.7 billion on education, while the federal government spent an additional $14 billion. This represents more than 5 percent of U.S. gross national product. These dollar expenditures are only part of the cost, however. Public schools, at least at the elementary and secondary level, exert a significant monopoly influence in the education marketplace.

Some argue that this public monopoly stifles creativity and has led to inferior education. These individuals cite the large number of school dropouts and the decline in Scholastic Aptitude Test (SAT) scores as evidence of the flagging effectiveness of the public school system. (They note that SAT scores drifted downward from the mid-1960s to the early 1980s. For the past 10 years they have remained in the lower ranges of the 25-year experience with this examination.)

During the 1980s corrective steps were taken by many state governments: Spending was increased, standards were raised, rigorous testing was introduced, and teacher certification and training requirements were augmented. Whether these actions are sufficient or whether there is a need to introduce market competitors into the education system is debated in the pages that follow. The ultimate resolution of this clash of educational philosophies could dramatically reshape schools.

YES

John E. Chubb and
Terry M. Moe

AMERICA'S PUBLIC SCHOOLS: CHOICE *IS* A PANACEA

For America's public schools, the last decade has been the worst of times and the best of times. Never before have the public schools been subjected to such savage criticism for failing to meet the nation's educational needs—yet never before have governments been so aggressively dedicated to studying the schools' problems and finding the resources for solving them.

The signs of poor performance were there for all to see during the 1970s. Test scores headed downward year after year. Large numbers of teenagers continued to drop out of school. Drugs and violence poisoned the learning environment. In math and science, two areas crucial to the nation's success in the world economy, American students fell far behind their counterparts in virtually every other industrialized country. Something was clearly wrong.

During the 1980s a growing sense of crisis fueled a powerful movement for educational change, and the nation's political institutions responded with aggressive reforms. State after state increased spending on schools, imposed tougher requirements, introduced more rigorous testing, and strengthened teacher certification and training. And, as the decade came to an end, creative experiments of various forms—from school-based management to magnet schools—were being launched around the nation.

We think these reforms are destined to fail. They simply do not get to the root of the problem. The fundamental causes of poor academic performance are not to be found in the schools, but rather in the institutions by which the schools have traditionally been governed. Reformers fail by automatically relying on these institutions to solve the problem—when the institutions are the problem.

The key to better schools, therefore, is institutional reform. What we propose is a new system of public education that eliminates most political and bureaucratic control over the schools and relies instead on indirect control through markets and parental choice. These new institutions naturally function to promote and nurture the kinds of effective schools that reformers have wanted all along.

SCHOOLS AND INSTITUTIONS

Three basic questions lie at the heart of our analysis. What is the relationship between school organization and student achievement? What are the conditions that promote or inhibit desirable forms of organization? And how are these conditions affected by their institutional settings?

Our perspective on school organization and student achievement is in agreement with the most basic claims and findings of the "effective schools" literature, which served as the analytical base of the education reform movement throughout the 1980s. We believe, as most others do, that how much students learn is not determined simply by their aptitude or family background—although, as we show, these are certainly influential—but also by how effectively schools are organized. By our estimates, the typical high school student tends to learn considerably more, comparable to at least an extra year's worth of study, when he or she attends a high school that is effectively organized rather than one that is not.

Generally speaking, effective schools—be they public or private—have the kinds of organizational characteristics that the mainstream literature would lead one to expect: strong leadership, clear and ambitious goals, strong academic programs, teacher professionalism, shared influence, and staff harmony, among other things. These are best understood as integral parts of a coherent syndrome of organization. When this syndrome is viewed as a functioning whole, moreover, it seems to capture the essential features of what

people normally mean by a team—principals and teachers working together, cooperatively and informally, in pursuit of a common mission.

How do these kinds of schools develop and take root? Here again, our own perspective dovetails with a central theme of educational analysis and criticism: the dysfunctions of bureaucracy, the value of autonomy, and the inherent tension between the two in American public education. Bureaucracy vitiates the most basic requirements of effective organization. It imposes goals, structures, and requirements that tell principals and teachers what to do and how to do it—denying them not only the discretion they need to exercise their expertise and professional judgment but also the flexibility they need to develop and operate as teams. The key to effective education rests with unleashing the productive potential already present in the schools and their personnel. It rests with granting them the autonomy to do what they do best. As our study of American high schools documents, the freer schools are from external control the more likely they are to have effective organizations.

Only at this late stage of the game do we begin to part company with the mainstream. While most observers can agree that the public schools have become too bureaucratic and would benefit from substantial grants of autonomy, it is also the standard view that this transformation can be achieved within the prevailing framework of democratic control. The implicit assumption is that, although political institutions have acted in the past to bureaucratize, they can now be counted upon to reverse course, grant the schools autonomy, and support and nurture this new population of autonomous schools. Such an assumption, however, is not based on a systematic understanding of how these institutions operate and what their consequences are for schools.

POLITICAL INSTITUTIONS

Democratic governance of the schools is built around the imposition of higher-order values through public authority. As long as that authority exists and is available for use, public officials will come under intense pressure from social groups of all political stripes to use it. And when they do use it, they cannot blithely assume that their favored policies will be faithfully implemented by the heterogeneous population of principals and teachers below—whose own values and professional views may be quite different from those being imposed. Public officials have little choice but to rely on formal rules and regulations that tell these people what to do and hold them accountable for doing it.

These pressures for bureaucracy are so substantial in themselves that real school autonomy has little chance to take root throughout the system. But they are not the only pressures for bureaucracy. They are compounded by the political uncertainty inherent in all democratic politics: those who exercise public authority know that other actors with different interests may gain authority in the future and subvert the policies they worked so hard to put in place. This knowledge gives them additional incentive to embed their policies in protective bureaucratic arrangements—arrangements that reduce the discretion of schools and formally insulate them from the dangers of politics.

These pressures, arising from the basic properties of democratic control, are compounded yet again by another special feature of the public sector. Its institutions provide a regulated, politically sensitive setting conducive to the power of unions, and unions protect the interests of their members through formal constraints on the governance and operation of schools—constraints that strike directly at the schools' capacity to build well-functioning teams based on informal cooperation.

The major participants in democratic governance—including the unions—complain that the schools are too bureaucratic. And they mean what they say. But they are the ones who bureaucratized the schools in the past, and they will continue to do so, even as they tout the great advantages of autonomy and professionalism. The incentives to bureaucratize the schools are built into the system.

MARKET INSTITUTIONS

This kind of behavior is not something that Americans simply have to accept, like death and taxes. People who make decisions about education would behave differently if their institutions were different. The most relevant and telling comparison is to markets, since it is through democratic control and markets that American society makes most of its choices on matters of public importance, including education. Public schools are subject to direct control through politics. But not all schools are controlled in this way. Private schools—representing about a fourth of all schools—are subject to indirect control through markets.

What difference does it make? Our analysis suggests that the difference is considerable and that it arises from the most fundamental properties that distinguish the two systems. A market system is not built to enable the imposition of higher-order values on the schools, nor is it driven by a democratic struggle to exercise public authority. Instead, the authority to make educational choices is radically decentralized to those most immediately involved. Schools compete for the support of parents and students, and parents and students are free to choose among schools. The system is built on decentralization, competition, and choice.

Although schools operating under a market system are free to organize any way they want, bureaucratization tends to be an unattractive way to go. Part of the reason is that virtually everything about good education—from the knowledge and talents necessary to produce it, to what it looks like when it is produced— defies formal measurement through the standardized categories of bureaucracy.

The more basic point, however, is that bureaucratic control and its clumsy efforts to measure the unmeasurable are simply *unnecessary* for schools whose primary concern is to please their clients. To do this, they need to perform as effectively as possible, which leads them, given the bottom-heavy technology of education, to favor decentralized forms of organization that take full advantage of strong leadership, teacher professionalism, discretionary judgment, informal cooperation, and teams. They also need to ensure that they provide the kinds of services parents and students want and that they have the capacity to cater and adjust to their clients' specialized needs and interests, which this same syndrome of effective organization allows them to do exceedingly well.

Schools that operate in an environment of competition and choice thus have strong incentives to move toward the kinds of "effective-school" organiza-tions that academics and reformers would like to impose on the public schools. Of course, not all schools in the market will respond equally well to these incentives. But those that falter will find it more difficult to attract support, and they will tend to be weeded out in favor of schools that are better organized. This process of natural selection complements the incentives of the marketplace in propelling and supporting a population of autonomous, effectively organized schools. . . .

EDUCATIONAL CHOICE

It is fashionable these days to say that choice is "not a panacea." Taken literally, that is obviously true. There are no panaceas in social policy. But the message this aphorism really means to get across is that choice is just one of many reforms with something to contribute. School-based management is another. So are teacher empowerment and professionalism, better training programs, stricter accountability, and bigger budgets. These and other types of reforms all bolster school effectiveness in their own distinctive ways—so the reasoning goes—and the best, most aggressive, most comprehensive approach to transforming the public school system is therefore one that wisely combines them into a multi-faceted reformist package.

Without being too literal about it, we think reformers would do well to entertain the notion that choice *is* a panacea. Of all the sundry education reforms that attract attention, only choice has the capacity to address the basic institutional problem plaguing America's schools. The other reforms are all system-preserving. The schools remain subordinates in the structure of public authority—and they remain bureaucratic.

In principle, choice offers a clear, sharp break from the institutional past. In practice, however, it has been forced into the same mold with all the other reforms. It has been embraced half-heartedly and in bits and pieces—for example, through magnet schools and limited open enrollment plans. It has served as a means of granting parents and students a few additional options or of giving schools modest incentives to compete. These are popular moves that can be accomplished without changing the existing system in any fundamental way. But by treating choice like other system-preserving reforms that presumably make democratic control work better, reformers completely miss what choice is all about.

Choice is not like the other reforms and should not be combined with them. Choice is a self-contained reform with its own rationale and justification. It has the capacity *all by itself* to bring about the kind of transformation that reformers have been seeking to engineer for years in myriad other ways. Indeed, if choice is to work to greatest advantage, it must be adopted *without* these other reforms, since they are predicated on democratic control and are implemented by bureaucratic means. The whole point of a thoroughgoing system of choice is to free the schools from these disabling constraints by sweeping away the old institutions and replacing them with new ones. Taken seriously, choice is not a system-preserving reform. It is a revolutionary reform that introduces a new system of public education.

A PROPOSAL FOR REAL REFORM

The following outline describes a choice system that we think is equipped to do the job. Offering our own proposal allows us to illustrate in some detail what a full-blown choice system might look like, as well as to note some of the policy decisions that must be made in building one. More important, it allows us to suggest what our institutional theory of schools actually entails for educational reform.

Our guiding principle in the design of a choice system is this: public authority must be put to use in creating a system that is almost entirely beyond the reach of public authority. Because states have primary responsibility for American public education, we think the best way to achieve significant, enduring reform is for states to take the initiative in withdrawing authority from existing institutions and vesting it directly in the schools, parents, and students. This restructuring cannot be construed as an exercise in delegation. As long as authority remains "available" at higher levels within state government, it will eventually be used to control the schools. As far as possible, all higher-level authority must be eliminated.

What we propose, more specifically, is that state leaders create a new system of public education with the following properties.

The Supply of Schools

The state will be responsible for setting criteria that define what constitutes a "public school" under the new system. These criteria should be minimal, roughly corresponding to the criteria many states now use in accrediting private schools—graduation requirements, health and safety requirements, and teacher certification requirements. Any educational group or organization that applies to the state and meets these minimal criteria must then be chartered as a public school and granted the right to accept students and receive public money.

Existing private schools will be among those eligible to participate. Their participation should be encouraged, because they constitute a supply of already effective schools. Our own preference would be to include religious schools too, as long as their sectarian functions can be kept clearly separate from their educational functions. Private schools that do participate will thereby become public schools, as such schools are defined under the new choice system.

School districts can continue running their present schools, assuming those schools meet state criteria. But districts will have authority over only their own schools and not over any of the others that may be chartered by the state.

Funding

The state will set up a Choice Office in each district, which, among other things, will maintain a record of all school-age children and the level of funding—the "scholarship" amounts—associated with each child. This office will directly compensate schools based on the specific children they enroll. Public money will flow from funding sources (federal, state, and district governments) to the Choice Office and then to schools. At no point will it go to parents or students.

The state must pay to support its own Choice Office in each district. Districts may retain as much of their current governing apparatus as they wish—superintendents, school boards, central offices, and all their staff. But they have to pay for them entirely out of the revenue they derive from the scholarships of those children who voluntarily choose to attend district-run schools. Aside from the governance of these schools, which no

one need attend, districts will be little more than taxing jurisdictions that allow citizens to make a collective determination about how large their children's scholarships will be.

As it does now, the state will have the right to specify how much, or by what formula, each district must contribute for each child. Our preference is for an equalization approach that requires wealthier districts to contribute more per child than poor districts do and that guarantees an adequate financial foundation to students in all districts. The state's contribution can then be calibrated to bring total spending per child up to whatever dollar amount seems desirable; under an equalization scheme, that would mean a larger state contribution in poor districts than in wealthy ones.

While parents and students should be given as much flexibility as possible, we think it is unwise to allow them to supplement their scholarship amounts with personal funds. Such "add-ons" threaten to produce too many disparities and inequalities within the public system, and many citizens would regard them as unfair and burdensome.

Complete equalization, on the other hand, strikes us as too stifling and restrictive. A reasonable trade-off is to allow collective add-ons, much as the current system does. The citizens of each district can be given the freedom to decide whether they want to spend more per child than the state requires them to spend. They can then determine how important education is to them and how much they are willing to tax themselves for it. As a result, children from different districts may have different-sized scholarships.

Scholarships may also vary within any given district, and we strongly think that they should. Some students have very special educational needs—arising from economic deprivation, physical handicaps, language difficulties, emotional problems, and other disadvantages—that can be met effectively only through costly specialized programs. State and federal programs already appropriate public money to address these problems. Our suggestion is that these funds should take the form of add-ons to student scholarships. At-risk students would then be empowered with bigger scholarships than the others, making them attractive clients to all schools—and stimulating the emergence of new specialty schools.

Choice Among Schools

Each student will be free to attend any public school in the state, regardless of district, with the student's scholarship—consisting of federal, state, and local contributions—flowing to the school of choice. In practice most students will probably choose schools in reasonable proximity to their homes. But districts will have no claim on their own residents.

To the extent that tax revenues allow, every effort will be made to provide transportation for students who need it. This provision is important to help open up as many alternatives as possible to all students, especially the poor and those in rural areas.

To assist parents and students in choosing among schools, the state will provide a Parent Information Center within its local Choice Office. This center will collect comprehensive information on each school in the district, and its parent liaisons will meet personally with parents in helping them judge which schools best meet their children's needs. The emphasis here will be on personal contact and involvement. Parents will be re-quired to visit the center at least once, and encouraged to do so often. Meetings will be arranged at all schools so that parents can see firsthand what their choices are.

The Parent Information Center will handle the applications process in a simple fashion. Once parents and students decide which schools they prefer, they will fill out applications to each, with parent liaisons available to give advice and assistance and to fill out the applications themselves (if necessary). All applications will be submitted to the Center, which in turn will send them out to the schools.

Schools will make their own admissions decisions, subject only to non-discrimination requirements. This step is absolutely crucial. Schools must be able to define their own missions and build their own programs in their own ways, and they cannot do that if their student population is thrust on them by outsiders.

Schools must be free to admit as many or as few students as they want, based on whatever criteria they think relevant—intelligence, interest, motivation, special needs—and they must be free to exercise their own, informal judgments about individual applicants. Schools will set their own "tuitions." They may choose to do so explicitly, say, by publicly announcing the minimum scholarship they are willing to accept. They may also do it implicitly by allowing anyone to apply for admission and simply making selections, knowing in advance what each applicant's scholarship amount is. In either case, schools are free to admit students with different-sized scholarships, and they are free to keep the entire scholarship that accompanies each student they have admitted. That gives all schools incentives to attract students with special needs, since these children will have the largest scholarships. It also gives schools incentives to attract students from districts with high base-level scholarships. But no school need restrict itself to students with special needs, nor to students from a single district.

The application process must take place within a framework that guarantees each student a school, as well as a fair shot at getting into the school he or she most wants. That framework, however, should impose only the most minimal restrictions on the schools.

We suggest something like the following. The Parent Information Center will be responsible for seeing that parents and students are informed, that they have visited the schools that interest them, and that all applications are submitted by a given date. Schools will then be required to make their admissions decisions within a set time, and students who are accepted into more than one school will be required to select one as their final choice. Students who are not accepted anywhere, as well as schools that have yet to attract as many students as they want, will participate in a second round of applications, which will work the same way.

After this second round, some students may remain without schools. At this point, parent liaisons will take informal action to try to match up these students with appropriate schools. If any students still remain unassigned, a special safety-net procedure—a lottery, for example—will be invoked to ensure that each is assigned to a specific school.

As long as they are not "arbitrary and capricious," schools must also be free to expel students or deny them readmission when, based on their own experience and standards, they believe the situation warrants it. This authority is essential if schools are to define and control their own organizations, and it gives students a strong incentive to live up to their side of the educational "contract."

Governance and Organization

Each school must be granted sole authority to determine its own governing structure. A school may be run entirely by teachers or even a union. It may vest all power in a principal. It may be built around committees that guarantee representation to the principal, teachers, parents, students, and members of the community. Or it may do something completely different.

The state must refrain from imposing *any* structures or requirements that specify how authority is to be exercised within individual schools. This includes the district-run schools: the state must not impose any governing apparatus on them either. These schools, however, are subordinate units within district government—they are already embedded in a larger organization—and it is the district authorities, not the schools, that have the legal right to determine how they will be governed.

More generally, the state will do nothing to tell the schools how they must be internally organized to do their work. The state will not set requirements for career ladders, advisory committees, textbook selection, in-service training, preparation time, homework, or anything else. Each school will be organized and operated as it sees fit.

Statewide tenure laws will be eliminated, allowing each school to decide for itself whether or not to adopt a tenure policy and what the specifics of that policy will be. This change is essential if schools are to have the flexibility they need to build well-functioning teams. Some schools may not offer tenure at all, relying on pay and working conditions to attract the kinds of teachers they want, while others may offer tenure as a supplementary means of compensating and retaining their best teachers.

Teachers, meantime, may demand tenure in their negotiations (individual or collective) with schools. And, as in private colleges and universities, the best teachers are well positioned to get it, since their services will be valued by any number of other schools. School districts may continue to offer districtwide tenure, along with transfer rights, seniority preference, and whatever other personnel policies they have offered in the past. But these policies apply only to district-run schools and the teachers who work in them.

Teachers will continue to have a right to join unions and engage in collective bargaining, but the legally prescribed bargaining unit will be the individual school or, as in the case of the district government, the larger organization that runs the school. If teachers in a given school want to join a union or, having done so, want to exact financial or structural concessions, that is up to them. But they cannot commit teachers in other schools, unless they are in other district-run schools, to the same things, and they must suffer the consequences if their victories put them at a competitive disadvantage in supplying quality education.

The state will continue to certify teachers, but requirements will be minimal, corresponding to those that many states have historically applied to private schools. In our view, individuals should be certified to teach if they have a bachelor's degree and if their personal history reveals no obvious problems. Whether they are truly good teachers will be determined in practice, as schools decide whom to hire, observe their own teachers in action over an extended period of time, and make decisions regarding merit, promotion, and dismissal.

The schools may, as a matter of strategy, choose to pay attention to certain formal indicators of past or future performance, among them: a master's degree, completion of a voluntary teacher certification program at an education school, or voluntary certification by a national board. Some schools may choose to require one or more of these, or perhaps to reward them in various ways. But that is up to the schools, which will be able to look anywhere for good teachers in a now much larger and more dynamic market.

The state will hold the schools accountable for meeting certain procedural requirements. It will ensure that schools continue to meet the criteria set out in their charters, that they adhere to non-discrimination laws in admissions and other matters, and that they collect and make available to the public, through the Parent Information Center, information on their mission, their staff and course offerings, standardized test scores (which we would make optional), parent and student satisfaction, staff opinions, and anything else that would promote informed choice among parents and students.

The state will not hold the schools accountable for student achievement or other dimensions that call for assessments of the quality of school performance. When it comes to performance, schools will be held accountable from below, by parents and students who directly experience their services and are free to choose. The state will play a crucial supporting role here in monitoring the full and honest disclosure of information by the schools—but it will be only a supporting role.

CHOICE AS A PUBLIC SYSTEM

This proposal calls for fundamental changes in the structure of American public education. Stereotypes aside, however, these changes have nothing to do with "privatizing" the nation's schools. The choice system we outline would be a truly public system—and a democratic one.

We are proposing that the state put its democratic authority to use in creating a new institutional framework. The design and legitimation of this framework would be a democratic act of the most basic sort. It would be a social decision, made through the usual processes of democratic governance, by which the people and their representatives specify the structure of a new system of public education.

This framework, as we set it out, is quite flexible and admits of substantial variation on important issues, all of them matters of public policy to be decided by representative government. Public officials and their constituents would be free to take their own approaches to taxation, equalization, treatment of religious schools, additional funding for disadvantaged students, parent add-ons, and other controversial issues of public concern, thus designing choice systems to reflect the unique conditions, preferences, and political forces of their own states.

Once this structural framework is democratically determined, moreover, governments would continue to play important roles within it. State officials and agencies would remain pivotal to the success of public education and to its ongoing operation. They would provide funding, approve applications for new schools, orchestrate and oversee the choice process, elicit full information about schools, provide transportation to students, monitor schools for adherence to the law, and (if they want) design and administer tests of student performance. School districts, meantime, would continue as local taxing jurisdictions, and they would have the option of continuing to operate their own system of schools.

The crucial difference is that direct democratic control of the schools—the very *capacity* for control, not simply its exercise—would essentially be eliminated. Most of those who previously held authority over the schools would have their authority permanently withdrawn, and that authority would be vested in schools, parents, and students. Schools would be legally autonomous: free to govern themselves as they want, specify their own goals and programs and methods, design their own organizations, select their own student bodies, and make their own personnel decisions. Parents and students would be legally empowered to choose among alternative schools, aided by institutions designed to promote active involvement, well-informed decisions, and fair treatment.

DEMOCRACY AND EDUCATIONAL PROGRESS

We do not expect everyone to accept the argument we have made here. In fact, we expect most of those who speak with authority on educational matters, leaders and academics within the educational community, to reject it. But we will regard our effort as a success if it directs attention to America's institutions of democratic control and provokes serious debate about their consequences for the nation's public schools. Whether or not our own conclusions are right, the fact is that these issues are truly basic to an understanding of schools, and they have so far played no part in the national debate. If educational reform is to have any chance at all of succeeding, that has to change.

In the meantime, we can only believe that the current "revolution" in public education will prove a disappointment. It might have succeeded had it actually been a revolution, but it was not and was never intended to be, despite the lofty rhetoric. Revolutions replace old institutions with new ones. The 1980s reform movement never seriously thought about the old institutions and certainly never considered them part of the problem. They were, as they had always been, part of the solution—and, for that matter, part of the definition of what democracy and public education are all about.

This identification has never been valid. Nothing in the concept of democracy requires that schools be subject to direct control by school boards, superintendents, central offices, departments of education, and other arms of government. Nor does anything in the concept of public education require that schools be governed in this way. There are many paths to democracy and public education. The path America has been trodding for the past half-century is exacting a heavy price—one the nation and its children can ill afford to bear, and need not. It is time, we think, to get to the root of the problem.

NO   Bill Honig

WHY PRIVATIZING PUBLIC EDUCATION
IS A BAD IDEA

One of the loudest salvos in the ongoing battle over "choice" in public schools came this year from theoreticians John E. Chubb and Terry M. Moe in *The Brookings Review* ("America's Public Schools: Choice *Is* a Panacea," summer issue). Chubb and Moe propose to transform our public schools from democratically regulated to market-driven institutions. They argue that the past decade has seen the most ambitious period of school reform in the nation's history, but that gains in test scores or graduation rates are nil. Their explanation: government, with its politics and bureaucracy, so hampers schools' ability to focus on academic achievement that improvement efforts are doomed.

Using data from the early eighties, Chubb and Moe contend that freeing schools from democratic control boosts performance a full grade level. Thus, they would give students scholarships for any public, private, or newly formed school; prohibit states or school districts from establishing organizational or effective curricular standards or assessing school performance; and allow schools to restrict student entry. They assert that parent choice alone will assure quality.

What's wrong with this proposal to combine vouchers with radical deregulation? Everything.

In the first place, Chubb and Moe's basic charge that current reform efforts have not succeeded is dead wrong and, consequently, the need for risky and radical change unjustified. While their data say something useful about the dangers of rigid bureaucracy and the overpoliticization of education, their findings cannot be used to judge the reform effort, since the students in their study were tested before reforms began. Evidence gathered more recently points to substantial gains.

For example, in 1983 California began refocusing on academic excellence, reducing bureaucracy, enhancing professional autonomy, and moving away from a rule-based to a performance-driven system. We raised standards; strengthened curriculum and assessment; invested in teacher and principal training; established accountability, including performance targets and incentives for good results and penalties for bad; provided funds for team building at the school; pushed for better textbooks; and forged alliances with parents, higher education, and the business community.

The result of this comprehensive approach has been real progress. In 1989, in reading and math, California high school seniors scored *one year* ahead of seniors in 1983, the exact improvement that Chubb and Moe say their proposal would achieve and just what they argue could not be accomplished within the existing system.

Since 1986, California eighth grade scores have risen 25 percent, the pool of dropouts has decreased 18 percent, and the number of high school graduates meeting the University of California entrance requirements has risen 20 percent. Since 1983, the number of seniors scoring about 450 in the verbal section of the Scholastic Aptitude Test has grown 19 percent, the number scoring above 500 has increased 28 percent, and the rate of seniors passing Advanced placement tests has jumped 114 percent—to more than 50,000 students a year.

California educators achieved these results even though the number of students in poverty doubled, the number of those who do not speak English doubled to one out of five, and California's student population grew explosively.

Impressive gains were also made nationally during the 1980s. The dropout pool shrunk by a third; the number of graduates attending college grew 18 percent; and on the National Assessment of Educational Progress, the number of 17-year-olds able to solve moderately complex problems increased 22 percent in mathematics, and 18 percent in science.

Reading and writing scores, however, grew less.

Further evidence of improvement in the performance of college-bound American youngsters is that Advanced Placement courses taken have nearly doubled since 1982. The number of students taking the more demanding curriculum, suggested by *A Nation at Risk,* of four years of English; three years of social studies, science, and math; and two years of foreign languages more than doubled between 1982 and 1987, from 13 percent to 29 percent of high school graduates. In science, the number of graduates taking chemistry grew 45 percent to nearly one of every two students, and the number taking physics expanded 44 percent to one of every five students.

Certainly, these gains are not sufficient to prepare American youngsters for the changing job market, to reach their potential, to participate in our democracy, or to keep up with international competition. We still have a long way to go. But that is not the issue. Educators are being challenged on whether we have a strategy that can produce results. We do, and this nation should be discussing how best to build on this record and accelerate the pace of reform—not how to dismantle public education.

IT IS NO EXAGGERATION TO SAY THAT CHUBB and Moe's ideas for change would jeopardize our youngsters and this democracy. Any one of the following objections should be enough to sink their plan.

First, the proposal risks creating elite academies for the few and second-rate schools for the many. It allows schools to exclude students who do not meet their standards—almost guaranteeing exacerbation of existing income and racial stratification. We had such a two-tiered system in the 19th century before mass public education helped make this country prosperous and free. We should not go back 100 years in search of the future.

Second, cult schools will result. Nearly 90 percent of American youngsters attend public schools, which are the major institutions involved in transmitting our democratic values. By prohibiting common standards, Chubb and Moe enshrine the rights of parents over the needs of children and society and encourage tribalism. Is it good public policy to use public funds to support schools that teach astrology or creationism instead of science, inculcate antiminority or antiwhite attitudes, or prevent students from reading *The Diary of Anne Frank* or *The Adventures of Huckleberry Finn*? Absent democratic controls, such schools will multiply.

Third, their plan violates the constitutional prohibition against aiding religious schools.

Fourth, the lack of accountability and the naivete of relying on the market to protect children is alarming. In the 19th century the slogan was "let the buyer beware," and meat packers sold tainted meat to consumers. In the 20th century deregulation produced the savings and loan debacle. Nobody seriously proposes rescinding environmental safeguards—why should our children not be similarly protected? Look at private trade schools. Regulation is weak, and scholarships are available. The results: widespread fraud and misrepresentation. Similar problems occurred when New York decentralized its school system. Corruption and patronage surfaced in its local boards of education. All

across the nation there are calls for *more* accountability from our schools, not less.

Fifth, the plan would be tremendously chaotic. Vast numbers of new schools would have to be created for this plan to succeed; yet most new enterprises fail. Many youngsters will suffer during the transition period, and with no accountability we will not even know if the experiment was successful.

Sixth, taxpayers will have to pay more. Chubb and Moe maintain that competition will produce savings, but they offer no proof. A potent counter-example: colleges compete, yet costs are skyrocketing. Furthermore, if this plan is adopted nationwide, a substantial portion of the cost of private school students—about $17 billion a year—currently paid for by their parents will be picked up by taxpayers (unless public school expenditures are reduced 10 percent, which would make the plan doubly disastrous). In addition, the proposal includes expensive transportation components and the creation of a new level of bureaucracy—Choice Offices. These offices will include Parent Information Centers, where liaisons will meet with parents and students to advise them on what schools to choose. But how many employees will be necessary for this process if parents are to receive the information they need in a timely manner?

IF THIS COUNTRY IS WILLING TO SPEND BIL-lions to improve education, there are much better investments with proven returns than Chubb and Moe's fanciful idea. One is providing funds to bring teachers up to speed in math, science, and history. Investing in team-building efforts, technology, improving assessment, Headstart programs, or prenatal care also offers proven returns for the dollar spent.

Chubb and Moe misread the evidence on choice and claim it is the only answer. We *should* give public school parents more choice, either through magnet schools or through open-enrollment plans. Choice builds commitment of parents and students and keeps the system honest. But limits are necessary to prevent skimming of the academic or athletically talented or furthering racial segregation. More important, where choice has been successful, such as in East Harlem, it has been one component of a broader investment in quality.

This country has an incredible opportunity to build a world-class school system. Public schools have turned the corner, educators have developed an effective game plan for the nineties, and promising ideas to encourage further flexibility within a context of vision and accountability are being implemented. If our leaders support that plan instead of chasing will-o'-the-wisp panaceas, come the year 2000, America's children will enjoy the schools they deserve.

POSTSCRIPT

Is Choice a Panacea for the Ills of Public Education?

Those of us who have attended public schools know firsthand the strengths and weaknesses of that part of the public education system we have experienced. Others of us are the products of private schools and likewise may hold strong beliefs as to the strengths and weaknesses of the system to which we have been exposed. Care must be taken, however, in generalizing from personal experience. One person's school experience may not be reflective of the system at large, and knowledge of the alternative system may not be complete. Good social science demands that we examine the broader experience with public and private schools.

In their examination of the broader experience, Chubb and Moe conclude that bureaucratic control of public schools is the "fundamental [cause] of poor academic performance." They maintain that the monopoly position of these bureaucrats should be challenged and that allocation decisions should be returned to individuals who can make their choices known through the operation of a market mechanism.

Honig thinks this is a bad idea. He believes that Chubb and Moe's proposals would have devastating effects, ranging from the creation of schools for elites to chaos in the remaining portions of the system. What he finds most damaging to Chubb and Moe's argument is that they employed data gathered before the impact of the reforms could possibly be felt. His data suggest that test scores are rising and dropout rates are falling, in spite of the increase in the number of students who live in poverty and in the number of students whose first language is not English.

Thus, we are again confronted with authors who provide conflicting evidence. It is our responsibility to analyze this evidence carefully and to read other studies that discuss this issue. Since privatizing education is an extremely popular proposal among market-oriented policymakers, there is much written about the benefits of "choice" in editorials of business newspapers such as the *Wall Street Journal* and in the publications of conservative-leaning think tanks such as the Cato Institute, the American Enterprise Foundation, or the Hoover Institute. We suggest that you begin, however, by reading the 1983 report, *A Nation at Risk*, by the National Commission on Excellence in Education, which details the failures of the system. You might then turn to a collected set of essays on this topic such as William Lowe Boyd and Herbert Walberg, eds., *Choice in Education: Potential and Problems* (McCutchan, 1990), and end with Deborah W. Meier, "Choice Can Save Public Education," *The Nation* (March 4, 1991).

PART 2

Macroeconomic Issues

Government policy and economics are tightly intertwined. Fiscal policy and monetary policy have dramatic input on the economy as a whole, and the state of the economy can often determine policy actions. Decisions regarding welfare payments or tax rates must be made in the context of broad macroeconomic goals, and the debates on these issues are more than theoretical discussions. Each has a significant impact on our economic lives.

Did Reaganomics Fail?
_____

Do Federal Budget Deficits Matter?
_____

Should the Federal Reserve Target Zero Inflation?
_____

Does the United States Save Enough?
_____

Should the Capital Gains Tax Be Lowered?
_____

Is Workfare a Good Substitute for Welfare?

ISSUE 9

Did Reaganomics Fail?

YES: Samuel Bowles, David M. Gordon, and Thomas E. Weisskopf, from "Right-Wing Economics Backfired," *Challenge* (January/February 1991)

NO: Paul Craig Roberts, from "What Everyone 'Knows' About Reaganomics," *Commentary* (February 1991)

ISSUE SUMMARY

YES: Economists Samuel Bowles, David M. Gordon, and Thomas E. Weisskopf believe that the economic policies of the Reagan administration failed to reverse the long-term deterioration of the U.S. economy due to the inability of Reaganomics to escape the contradictions of right-wing economics. The policies created an economic environment that hindered rather than stimulated investment.

NO: Paul Craig Roberts, an economist and former government policymaker, believes that Reaganomics was a success: It was not the cause of increased government budget deficits; careful analysis of the data suggests that the United States does not save or invest too little; it created an improved investment environment; and some 20 million jobs were created during the Reagan era.

Nineteen-eighty was a year of recession: The output of goods and services fell and the unemployment rate for the year increased to 7.1 percent from 5.8 percent in 1979. The recession impacted the federal government's budget, with the deficit increasing to more than $60 billion from $16 billion in 1979. To make matters worse, inflation remained in the double-digit range: The Consumer Price Index increased by more than 12 percent during 1980.

The economy and economic policy became major issues during the 1980 presidential election campaign. Republican candidate Ronald Reagan promised policies that would restore economic growth and employment, reduce inflation, and bring balance to the federal government budget, and he defeated Democratic incumbent Jimmy Carter. According to the Reagan administration, there were four major components of its economic program, or Reaganomics: a reduction in income tax rates, a reduction in the rate of growth in government spending, a reform of business regulation, and coordination with the Federal Reserve System to achieve noninflationary growth in money. Because certain elements of the program sought to improve work incentives and increase the nation's productive capacity, the program was also referred to as "supply-side economics." In August 1981 President Reagan signed into law the Economic Recovery Tax Act which lowered income tax rates, and the Omnibus Budget Reconciliation Act, which reordered spending priorities. The significance of these two pieces of legislation to the Reagan program was indicated by the fact that Reagan signed both pieces of legislation into law on the same day with much fanfare. Reagan won reelection in 1984, defeating Democratic challenger Walter Mondale. Reagan believed that his reelection represented a vote of support for his macroeconomic policies by the American people. An important piece of legislation passed during Reagan's second term was the Tax Reform Act of 1986, which lowered income tax rates even more. The years from 1981 through 1988 were known as the Reagan era, the era of Reaganomics.

During the Reagan years there were extensive debates regarding the advisability of the various actions that constituted Reaganomics, and there was even more debate on exactly what these actions wrought. Now, some four years after the end of the Reagan era, these debates continue. The actual behavior of the economy during the 1980s is a matter of history. Supporters of Reaganomics focus on the positives of macroeconomic performance—the increase in the number of jobs, a reduction in the rate of inflation, and the longest peacetime business expansion in U.S. economic history. Critics of Reaganomics point to the negatives—federal government budget deficits, the trade deficit and the increased foreign indebtedness of the United States, and an increase in income inequality. Academic economists Samuel Bowles, David M. Gordon, and Thomas E. Weisskopf are radical critics of Reaganomics. They argue that the Reagan policies failed and that the failure can be traced to fundamental contradictions in these right-wing economic policies. Paul Craig Roberts was a part of the Reagan administration, serving as assistant secretary of the Treasury in 1981–83. He argues that Reaganomics was a success and that it did, in fact, improve economic conditions.

YES

Samuel Bowles,
David M. Gordon, and
Thomas E. Weisskopf

RIGHT-WING ECONOMICS BACKFIRED

The right-wing economic program on which Ronald Reagan rode to the presidency ten years ago seemed to many at the time to promise an end to the stagflation of the 1970s and the beginning of a new era of economic prosperity. The Reagan Administration did indeed succeed in reversing many of the economic policies of the 1970s, yet the new policies now appear to have driven the U.S. economy not to new heights of achievement but to an ignominious impasse.

The human costs of the period of "business ascendancy" in the 1980s have been amply documented elsewhere; right-wing economics worked very well for the richest American families, but for a majority of Americans it meant a decline in real well-being. Yet defenders of the right-wing program ask us to focus not on the immediate impact on people's well-being but on the overall macroeconomic record. For all of its short-term human costs, did not the right-wing program succeed in reversing the long-term deterioration in macroeconomic performance of the U.S. economy since the mid 1960s? The evidence suggests that it failed to do so. In spite of winning most of the battles to implement its right-wing program, the Reagan Administration lost the war against economic stagnation.

THE RECORD IN PERSPECTIVE

In order to place the 1980s in historical perspective, it is helpful to compare the recent period of business ascendancy with the three previous periods of the postwar era: the boom, running from 1948 to 1966; the erosion of the social structure of accumulation, from 1966 to 1973; and the political stalemate, from 1973 to 1979. Each period represents one or more completed business cycles ruining from peak to peak; we thus avoid confusing cyclical movements with cross-cycle trends.

Table 1

The Deteriorating Performance of the U.S. Postwar Macroeconomy

	Phase Averages			
	1948–66	1966–73	1973–79	1979–89
[1] Real GNP growth rate (%)	3.8	3.1	2.5	2.6
[2] Rate of capital accumulation (%)	3.6	4.4	3.5	2.6
[3] Real productivity growth rate (%)	2.6	1.8	0.5	1.2
[4] Federal deficit as percent of GNP	−0.2	−0.6	−1.2	−2.5
[5] Trade balance as percent of GNP	0.4	0.1	0.0	−1.8
[6] Net national savings rate (%)[a]	9.6	10.8	8.5	3.2

Growth rates are annual rates, calculated as logarithmic growth rates. Levels are calculated as average annual levels.
[a]Figure is for peak year at end of cycle rather than for cycle average.
Sources: [1] Rate of growth of real gross national product ($ 1982). *Economic Report of the President, 1990 (ERP)*, Table C-2. [2] Rate of growth, net fixed NFCP nonresidential capital stock: Dept. of Commerce, *Fixed Reproducible Tangible Wealth in the United States, 1925–85* (Washington, DC: U.S. Government Printing Office, 1987), A6; *Survey of Current Business*, August 1989, Table 7. [3] Rate of growth of output per hour of all persons, nonfarm business sector (1977 = 100): *ERP* Table C-46; 1989 figure from unpublished update. [4] Federal surplus (+) or deficit (−) as percent of gross national product: *ERP*, Tables C-76, C-1. [5] Trade surplus (+) or deficit (−) on current account, as percent of gross national product: *ERP*, Tables C-102, C-1. [6] Personal, business, and government savings (net of depreciation) as percent of net national product: *ERP*, Tables C-26, C-22.

The measures selected for presentation in Table 1 represent those that economists conventionally emphasize as indicators of macroeconomic performance: the growth of real gross national product; the growth of real capital stock; and the growth of productivity. In addition, we have included three widely discussed measures that we consider to be symptoms of macroeconomic health or illness: the federal budget deficit; the international trade deficit; and the net national saving rate.

Even a cursory glance at Table 1 reveals the main message of the data. The leaders of the right-wing economic program inherited an economy that had been in serious trouble since the mid-1960s; they promised to reverse its decline but they failed to deliver on that promise. It *was* broke, and they did not fix it. If anything, they hastened its deterioration.

CONTOURS OF ECONOMIC FAILURE

Whether in its devastating impact on the lives of the vast majority of people in the United States, its lackluster macroeconomic record, or its buy-now/pay-later character, right-wing economics has failed. Why?

There can be little doubt that the right-wing agenda was implemented to a substantial extent. Indeed, the right won almost all of its significant political battles through much of the previous decade. The monetarists drove up real interest rates. No one in the labor movement could deny the toll that right-wing economics exacted from workers. The free-marketeers trimmed the government's regulatory sails. The supply-siders achieved dramatic reductions in tax rates for the wealthy. And the hawks produced soaring military expenditures.

But if they won all the battles, how could they have lost the war?

There are two ways to answer this question. The superficially most obvious answer is that they may not have been fighting the war they had proclaimed. The right may not have even cared about the long-term health of the U.S. economy or the well-being of the majority of its people. They may have sought, instead, to concentrate power and wealth in the hands of the wealthiest families and the major U.S. corporations—preferring a larger slice of a smaller pie—rather than to take their chances with the kinds of policies that would have been required to revitalize the U.S. economy. If redistribution was their objective, the battles they fought—for higher interest rates, for weaker unions, for less regulation of business, for lower taxes on the affluent, and for larger military expenditures—were not won in vain. This answer has simplicity to recommend it: it assumes that the right-wing forces knew what they were doing, and that they got for their troubles more or less what they set out to get. They won their war.

A quite different answer—and the one toward which we incline—is that they did indeed seek to reverse the economic decline they inherited from the 1960s and 1970s, but that they failed in this objective because the policy package they adopted was ill-suited for the job. Whatever the objectives of the leaders of right-wing economic policy, their dismal macroeconomic record and its buy-now/pay-later character may be attributed to five major shortcomings. These shortcomings suggest that the logic of right-wing economics—its reliance on trickle-down economics, the discipline of the whip, the invisible hand, and the global big stick—was fundamentally flawed.

• First, the idea that savings could be enhanced by redistributing income to the top—a key element in the trickle-down strategy—proved to be wildly off the mark. The policies that distributed income upward also had the effect of reducing net saving (see row 6 in Table 1). This was particularly true of tax cuts for the rich, which exacerbated the government deficit and thus reduced national saving, and the declining real after-tax wage, which compelled families to borrow on a grand scale—running down national saving even further—in order to try to sustain their standards of living.

• Second, the right-wing attachment to the discipline of the whip—the top-down approach to labor relations—is out of date; an outmoded hierarchical and conflictual system of labor relations lies at the root of the continuing inability of the United States to solve the productivity problem. During the 1980s, the United States was consistently outpaced on the productivity front by nations that have adopted more meaningful forms of worker participation in decision making, job security, and collective bargaining. In the United States, the right-wing approach to the problem—relying on the threat of unemployment and intensive workplace supervision to keep workers on their toes—has prevailed. But, as one might have expected, productivity growth barely responded to this heavy dose of the old-time religion; as we have seen in Table 1, it inched back up to less than one-half the rate of the postwar boom.

• Third, the right-wing ideological commitment to the invisible hand is simply out of step with the way the world now works. Even setting aside the economic injustice fostered by the laissez-faire approach, to leave economic decision making entirely to private profit-and-loss calculations is just not a smart way to run an economy. A passive, noninterventionist government simply cannot cope with the unfolding environmental crisis, nor can it provide the needed guidance and support for the basic research and human-resource development essential to future economic well-being.

• Fourth, the military buildup undergirding use of the global big stick, coupled with major tax cuts designed to reduce the size of the government, forced the reductions in public investment. Economists often worry about government expenditures "crowding out" private investment. During the 1980s, however, we saw a new kind of crowding out: military expenditures crowded out *public* investment.

• Finally, the economic environment fostered by the right-wing economic strategy was an obstacle rather than a stimulus to private investment (see row 2 of Table 1). This is perhaps the most surprising failure of the right-wing strategy. One might have thought that lower taxes, weaker unions, and a free hand to pursue profits while ignoring the social or environmental consequences would be just what the doctor ordered to revive ailing private investment. And this was exactly what the right-wing supply-siders promised at the beginning of their reign. Unraveling the puzzle of their unfulfilled promise will take us to the heart of the right-wing failure.

PROFITABILITY AND INVESTMENT

The right-wing economists were not mistaken in their emphasis on the connection between after-tax profitability and private investment. . . .

As the investment boom of the 1960s was a response to a profit surge, so the stagnation of investment in the 1980s is clearly related to the surprisingly lackluster performance of the after-tax profit rate. But the data for 1986 through 1989 suggest that the poor showing of after-tax profits during the 1980s may not be the whole story. Profitability was relatively strong during these years, yet investment continued to falter nonetheless.

We are left with two questions: why did after-tax profits respond so weakly to the political victories scored by the right-wing program? And why did the profit surge after the recession of 1983 not set off a correspondingly resurgent investment boom? Table 2 presents data that will help us answer these two questions. . . .

To work toward an understanding of this sluggish recovery of after-tax profitability, it is helpful to distinguish between the profit *share* of output (or profits divided by total output) and the profit *rate* (profits divided by the capital stock). The profit rate is equal to the profit share times the level of output per unit of capital stock; this relationship is simply an algebraic identity, with the output/capital ratio establishing a bridge between the profit share and the profit rate. The simple answer to our first question, then, is that the profit share of total output increased—reflecting right-wing political victories—but the profit rate failed to rise anywhere near as much because the ratio of output to the capital stock fell. . . .

Taking account of all three determinants of private investment—the after-tax profit rate, the rate of capacity utilization, and the real interest rate—the poor performance of investment in the 1980s is no surprise. As can be seen from Table 2,

Table 2

Tracing the Contours of Macroeconomic Failure

	Phase Averages			
	1948–66	1966–73	1973–79	1979–89
[1] After-tax profit rate (%)	6.9	7.0	5.5	6.0
[2] Percent change, cost of job loss	–0.5	–2.3	–1.4	4.3a
[3] Percent change, relative import price	–1.4	–0.3	5.2	–1.7
[4] Effective rate of profits taxation (ratio)	0.49	0.46	0.49	0.40
[5] After-tax profit share (%)	9.4	9.3	8.6	9.2
[6] Rate of capacity utilization (ratio)	0.98	0.99	0.96	0.94
[7] Real interest rate (%)	–0.3	1.7	0.8	4.8

Levels are calculated as average annual levels.
aFigure is for 1979–1987 (instead of 1979–1989) for reasons of data availability.
Sources: [1] Rate of net after-tax profit, nonfinancial corporate business sector (NFCB), defined as (adjusted profits – profits tax liability + net interest)/(net capital stock + inventories): Numerator from *ERP,* C-12; capital stock same as row [2], Table 10.1; inventories from unpublished tables, Bureau of Economic Analysis. [3] Average annual rate of change of ratio of import price deflator to GNP price deflator: *ERP,* Table C-3. [4] Ratio of profits tax liability to adjusted before-tax profits: *ERP,* C-12. [5] Net after-tax profit share of NFCB domestic output, defined as (adjusted profits – profits tax liability + net interest)/(NFCB gross domestic product): *ERP,* C-12. [6] Ratio of actual output to potential output, private business nonresidential sector: for method and sources, see Samuel Bowles, David M. Gordon, and Thomas E. Weisskopf, "Business Ascendancy and Economic Impasse: A Structural Retrospective on Conservative Economics, 1979–87," *Journal of Economic Perspectives,* Winter 1989, pp. 107–134, Data Appendix. [7] Federal fund rate minus expected rate of inflation: federal funds rate form *ERP,* Table C-71 (with N.Y. Fed discount rate used for 1948–54); expected rate of inflation calculated from three-year distributed lag on past rate of change of GNP price deflator, *ERP,* C-1.

rows 7 and 6, respectively, real interest rates were unprecedentedly high (the consequence of monetarist tight money policies) and, partly as a result, the level of capacity utilization dipped to its lowest average among the four phases of the postwar period. The slightly higher after-tax profit rate during the 1980s simply was not enough of a boost to offset these two negative influences on investment.

Are we to conclude, then, that the failure of the right-wing program to jump-start the stalled accumulation process was simply a mistake, the result of ill-conceived economic policies based on a misunderstanding of what it takes to stimulate private investment? It would be nice if the answer were yes, for a

mistake as simple as this could easily be corrected. But, as we will see, the truth lies elsewhere: the right-wing program failed to stimulate investment because under conditions prevailing in the 1980s (and 1990s) there is no way that all three of the determinants of investment—the after-tax profit rate, the real interest rate, and the rate of capacity utilization—can be made to move in the right direction at the same time. Thus, the failure was not a mistake; it was a result of the bind that eventually straitjacketed the right-wing strategy.

CRITICAL TRADE-OFFS

The contradictions of right-wing economics result from the fact that policies that support a high profit *share* are generally inconsistent with policies that promote high levels of capacity utilization and policies that promote low interest rates. But, as we have already seen, raising the profit share will not secure a high profit rate *unless* it is also accompanied by a high level of capacity utilization. Worse still, it will not generate a high level of investment *unless* it is also accompanied by low interest rates.

There are thus two critical trade-offs that generate contradictions for right-wing economics. The first involves a conflict between (1) the desirability of having a high level of capacity utilization to translate a high profit share into a high profit rate and to stimulate investment, and (2) the desirability of having a low level of capacity utilization to sustain high unemployment as a way of maintaining labor discipline and thereby contributing to a high profit share. The second involves a conflict between (1) the desirability of having a low real interest rate to promote investment, and (2) the desirability of having a high real interest rate to maintain the value of the dollar as a way of lowering the real price of imports and thereby contributing to a high profit share. Let's explore each of these two sources of tension.

CAPACITY UTILIZATION

The threat of unemployment plays a crucial role in keeping wages down, promoting the labor discipline necessary to enforce high levels of work effort, and thus supporting a high profit share. For the threat of unemployment to have teeth, however, the loss of a job must cost the worker a substantial amount in lost income, involving what we have called a high cost of job loss. When jobs

are plentiful, this threat does not have much bite.

But that is just the problem: when capacity utilization is high, jobs are also plentiful and the threat of job dismissal is correspondingly low. The result is a trade-off between the level of capacity utilization and the cost of job loss. Increases in each would raise the profit rate. However, the economy can have high levels of capacity utilization, or it can have a high cost of job loss, but it cannot generally have both at the same time.

. . . Combinations of capacity utilization and cost to job loss that were possible during the 1960s were unattainable during the 1970s.

The shift in the trade-off reflects the erosion of the social structure of accumulation in the late 1960s, and it sharply limited the options open to economic policymakers in the 1970s. The recession of the mid-1970s greatly raised the cost of job loss, but it did so at a cost of even lower levels of capacity utilization. The Cold Bath recession of the early 1980s was no different: the price of a frightened work force was idle factories. For the right-wing economic strategy to escape this bind, their policies would have had to shift the trade-off, . . . allowing more favorable levels of both capacity utilization and the cost of job loss to be attained. And, despite greatly reduced unemployment insurance coverage, they failed to do this: the rules of the economic game defining the options open to policymakers in the 1980s were in this respect no different than in the 1970s.

INTEREST RATES

The second critical tradeoff underlying the contradictions of right-wing economics is similar. High real interest rates in the United States in the 1980s contributed to the worldwide demand for dollars, driving up the price of dollars in terms of other currencies. The higher exchange rates that flowed from this rising dollar value meant that imports into the U.S. economy were cheaper. And cheaper imports—particularly imports of materials and other goods used in production—raised the profit share.

Taken by itself this should have contributed to a higher profit rate and subsequently to a rapid accumulation of capital. But here's the rub: the higher real interest rates also discouraged private investment and depressed consumer borrowing below what they would have been otherwise. The negative effect of high real interest rates on investment lands a one-two punch; not only do high rates directly depress investment, but the lower level of consumer demand reduces capacity utilization, further dampening the incentive to invest.

The economic logic behind these contradictions of right-wing economics is summarized in Figure 1. In that graph, arrows with a plus sign indicate a positive causal relationship; arrows with a negative sign indicate a negative causal relationship. When capacity utilization rises, for example, the profit share falls. The top part of the figure presents the tension flowing from the tradeoff between the rate of capacity utilization and the cost of job loss, while the bottom part illustrates the tension resulting from the trade-off between the real interest rate and the real price of imports.

We can now see why the right-wing attempt to stimulate private investment failed. The high unemployment rates, high real interest rates, and high value of the dollar—all of which were key weapons

Figure 1

The Contradictions of Right-Wing Economics

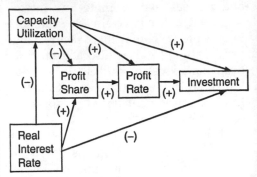

Source: Author's construction.

in the right-wing arsenal—did indeed hit their targets. Wages were kept down, labor discipline was tightened, and U.S. firms were able to buy cheap and sell dear on a global scale; thus, the profit *share* rose. But these weapons also backfired, keeping capacity utilization low, depressing the profit *rate*, and discouraging private investment. The game plan that evolved during the late 1970s, and was masterminded from the White House after Ronald Reagan's inauguration, failed to escape the contradictions of right-wing economics.

In short, the right-wing economic program had indeed gained the upper hand for U.S. business. But it had done so at a price so heavy that the victory was nothing to celebrate, even for the winners.

NO
Paul Craig Roberts

WHAT EVERYONE "KNOWS" ABOUT REAGANOMICS

What everyone "knows" about Reaganomics is that it failed. As the almost universally accepted story goes, the Reagan administration, influenced by supply-side theory, made a "Laffer-curve forecast" that its tax cuts would pay for themselves. Instead they produced surging budget deficits which saddled the U.S. with massive debt, financed by foreigners, to be repaid by future generations. The tax cuts also—so the story continues—fueled a consumption boom at the expense of savings and investment. Overconsumption at home led to an increase in imports, thereby adding a balance-of-trade deficit to the domestic budget deficit. These "twin deficits" were accompanied by a shift of the tax burden from upper- to lower- and middle-income classes, while unleashing a decade of greed on the one hand and, on the other, rising poverty and stagnation in median family income, all leading ultimately to a great crash.

We have all heard this litany of failure countless times from TV pundits and read it countless times in newspaper columns. Moreover, it has come at us not only from the Left but from across the full range of the political and ideological spectrum. Indeed, the most convincing purveyors of the litany have been members of Ronald Reagan's own entourage, such as his first Budget Director, David Stockman, as well as moderate Republicans like Richard Nixon's Secretary of Commerce, Peter G. Peterson, Senate Minority Leader Robert Dole, and House Minority Leader Bob Michel.

Turning to academia, we find that practically every economist anyone has ever heard of has jumped on Reaganomics with both feet. A typical example is Benjamin Friedman of Harvard in his book, *Day of Reckoning: The Consequences of American Economic Policy Under Reagan and After* (1988). Friedman's "most favorable construction" is that Reagan and his administration genuinely believed that "the incentive effects of across-the-board cuts in personal tax rates would so stimulate individuals' work efforts and business initiatives that lower tax rates would deliver higher tax revenues." His "darker assessment" is that the Reagan administration was not that stupid, and that the deficit was deliberately created to "mortgage the nation's future as a means of forcing Americans to give up government activities which they would otherwise have been able to afford."

According to Professor Friedman, then, the only two possibilities are that Reagan was either a fool or a knave:

> We shall probably never know which of these alternative accounts of the origins of the Reagan fiscal policy better describes what really happened. On one construction, it was an intellectual error of the first magnitude. On the other, it was deliberate moral irresponsibility on a truly astonishing scale.

Friedman, a liberal Democrat, was no doubt encouraged in this categorical judgment by the agreement of many Republicans within the profession, again including some who had worked for Reagan. Thus, at the annual meeting of the American Economic Association in 1985, Friedman's Harvard colleague, Martin Feldstein, who had been chairman of Reagan's Council of Economic Advisers, attacked supply-side economists for, among other things, forecasting that the reduction in tax rates would pay for itself in increased revenue. Herbert Stein, who had been a member of Nixon's Council of Economic Advisers, also criticized Reaganomics for this same sin. Even Lawrence B. Lindsey, whose book, *The Growth Experiment* (1989), is a definitive account of the success of Reaganomics, states matter-of-factly that enthusiastic supply-siders claimed the tax cut would pay for itself.

Something is wrong when the American babble of competing voices can produce a uniformly inaccurate picture of the most discussed economic policy of this generation. For all these things that everyone "knows" with such certainty

lack any basis in fact—and I stress that what is at issue here are precisely the basic facts of the case, not debatable interpretations of data. In particular, the Reagan administration did *not* predict that the tax cuts would be self-financing. It predicted the exact opposite—that every dollar of tax cut would lose a dollar of revenue. Moreover, as far as I can ascertain, no supply-side economist inside or outside the Reagan administration ever said that tax cuts would pay for themselves.

PRESIDENT REAGAN'S ECONOMIC PROGRAM was set forth in an inch-thick document, "A Program for Economic Recovery," made available to the public and submitted to Congress on February 18, 1981. Tables in the document make it unmistakably clear that the administration expected the forthcoming tax cut to reduce revenues substantially below the amounts that would be collected in the absence of such a cut. Without the tax cut, revenues were projected as rising from $609 billion in 1981 to $1,159.8 billion in 1986. With the tax cut, they were projected to rise from $600.2 billion in 1981 to $942 billion in 1986. The total six-year revenue cost of the tax cut was thus estimated as $718.2 billion.

As the tax-rate reduction was expected to slow the growth of revenues, receipts as a percentage of GNP were expected to fall from 21.1 percent in 1981 to 19.6 percent in 1986. Accordingly, the document spelled out the necessity of slowing the growth of spending in order to avoid rising deficits. The administration planned to hold the annual growth of spending to 6 percent during 1981–84 and to 9 percent during 1984–86. On this basis, the Reagan budget projected a rise in spending (including the defense build-up) from

$654.7 billion in 1981 to $912.1 billion in 1986.

A summary fact sheet showing the expected revenue losses and planned spending reductions was put out for wire transmission. Months of testimony and debate followed, during the course of which the massive revenue losses were in the forefront. After the Economic Recovery Tax Act of 1981 was passed, the Treasury Department issued to the media a comprehensive report on the legislation, including a three-page table detailing the revenue loss for each of its provisions. (Between introduction and final passage of the bill, the estimated total six-year revenue cost had grown slightly, from $718.2 to $726.6 billion.)

But if Reagan in office never predicted self-financing tax cuts, what about Reagan on the campaign trail? Surely he made that claim?

As a matter of fact, he did not. In *Revolution* (1988), Martin Anderson of the Hoover Institution reproduces the economic plan issued by Reagan and his economic advisers (of whom Anderson himself was one) during the 1980 presidential campaign. That plan estimated that 17 percent of the revenues lost by marginal tax-rate reduction would be recouped by increased economic growth. In other words, far from claiming that tax cuts would pay for themselves, Reagan on the campaign trail predicted that they would forfeit 83 percent of the revenues which would otherwise have accrued.

If, however, Reagan officials and economists never made the infamous claim, surely proponents of the supply-side theory like Jude Wanniski, George Gilder, and Jack Kemp did?

But again, as a matter of fact, they did not. In 1975, in an article in the *Public*

Interest entitled "The Mundell-Laffer Hypothesis," Wanniski claimed only that "sufficient tax revenues will be recovered to pay the interest on the government bonds used to finance the deficit" caused by cutting tax rates. In his book, *An American Renaissance* (1979), Jack Kemp used the Laffer curve only to explain why rising marginal tax rates are a disincentive and to argue against static revenue forecasts that ignore the effects of taxation on incentive. And in a letter to the *Wall Street Journal* in March 1980, Kemp said: "Under some circumstances, cutting tax rates will increase revenue; under others, reduce it."

True, in *Wealth and Poverty* (1981), George Gilder wrote that "lower tax rates can so stimulate business and so shift income from shelters to taxable activity that lower rates bring in higher tax revenue." But this was a nonspecific claim supported by studies of reductions in the top income bracket and in the capital-gains tax rates. Gilder also argued (as did Wanniski in his book *The Way the World Works*) that when the top tax rate is reduced, the earnings of the rich rise, "and they pay more taxes in absolute amounts"—a contention that has since been substantiated by Internal Revenue Service statistics demonstrating unequivocally that during the 1980's, when the top tax rate was cut from 70 to 28 percent, the share of the income-tax revenues collected from the top 1 percent of taxpayers rose by 54 percent.

The kindest way to interpret the allegation that supply-siders predicted that the Reagan tax cut would pay for itself is that critics confused an exposition of the upper portion of the Laffer curve with a prediction of the revenue effects of specific legislation. To do so, however, they had to overlook what the supply-siders themselves were actually saying. In a piece of my own in the *Wall Street Journal* (April 24, 1980), I wrote: "The tax-cut movement in the Congress wasn't based on getting all of the revenues back so the government could keep on spending. Much less were tax cuts advocated as a revenue-raising measure. The issue was whether you got any revenues back as a result of incentive effects operating on the supply side of the economy. And in an earlier *Wall Street Journal* article (August 1, 1978), I argued that the combination of revenue feedbacks and increased saving would not result in inflationary deficits "if government spending in real terms could be held to current levels for about two years."

It is possible that some members of Congress may have avoided the question of whose ox would be gored with lower spending growth by hiding behind the Laffer curve. However, it is shoddy work for academic economists and financial reporters to misrepresent any such political statement as a government forecast. Moreover, none of the supply-side legislative measures ever claimed that tax cuts would pay for themselves. The two most successful such measures, the Holt Amendment (1977–78) in the House and the Nunn Amendment (1978) in the Senate, explicitly linked marginal tax-rate reduction with spending limits. There is thus literally no basis for the caricature of supply-side economics as the belief that tax cuts pay for themselves.

AS FOR THE REAGAN BUDGET DEFICITS, close inspection shows them to be the product of an unsurprising failure and an unexpected success. The failure was on the spending side. During 1981–86 federal spending exceeded not only Rea-

gan's targets but also the current policy projections. Instead of spending cuts from the projected baseline, there were—thanks mainly to Congress—spending add-ons. On the revenue side, conversely, there was a shortfall relative to the budget projections. But this was due not to overestimating the incentive effects of tax reduction, but to overestimating the inflation rate.

The accuracy of revenue forecasts is dependent upon the accuracy of forecasts of nominal GNP, which in turn depend on the forecasts of inflation and real economic growth. In the beginning of 1981 the Reagan administration forecast 11.1 percent inflation for the year, as measured by the consumer price index (CPI), and foresaw inflation falling to 8.3 percent in 1982, 6.2 percent in 1983, 5.5 percent in 1984, 4.7 percent in 1985, and 4.2 percent in 1986. At the time, these forecasts were ridiculed as a "rosy scenario," because they combined falling inflation with sustained real growth—an impossibility according to the "Phillips-curve" relationship which claimed to show that growth in employment and GNP had to be paid for with rising rates of inflation (just as lower inflation had to be paid for by rising rates of unemployment). Since most economists were under the sway of this theory, they refused to believe that the economy could expand for six years without sending inflation substantially higher. Indeed, in their view, to fuel spending through a tax cut when the CPI was already in double digits and when there was an inherited deficit of $70 billion, added up to a prescription for massive inflation.

As it turned out, the administration's inflation forecast was not optimistic but pessimistic. For 1981 the CPI came in at 10.3 percent, almost a point below the forecast. In 1982 inflation measured 6.2 percent, more than 2 points (or 25 percent) below the forecast. In 1983 the inflation rate was 3.2, only half the amount forecast. In 1984 inflation measured 4.3 percent, 1.2 percentage points below forecast. In 1985 the inflation rate fell to 3.6 percent, almost a full point below forecast, and in 1986 it came in at 1.9 percent, less than half the rate forecast.

The cumulative effect of the unanticipated disinflation was a substantial reduction in the levels of nominal GNP, and hence in the tax base. By 1983 and 1984 nominal GNP was running $300 billion below forecast. In 1985 GNP was $500 billion below projections, and it was about $700 billion below in 1986. (In addition to all this, the 1982 recession, brought about by the Federal Reserve Board's fear of inflation, contributed to the loss of revenues by shrinking real output by 2.5 percent in that year.)

In short, intentionally or unintentionally, critics of Reaganomics misinterpreted the revenue shortfalls caused by the unexpected collapse of inflation and attributed them entirely to the tax cuts.

The insistence by Reagan's critics that the essence of supply-side economics consists of the belief that tax cuts pay for themselves is easy to understand. Without this strawman, there is no way to blame Reagan and supply-side economics for the budget deficits and alleged associated ills that have been used to paint a false picture of the 80's as a decade of failure. For if—as is the fact—Reagan predicted that the tax cut would lose revenues, then it was the conventional Phillips-curve economists who produced the revenue shortfall by overpredicting inflation. It was Paul Volcker, then head of the Federal Reserve Board, who drove down revenues by collapsing the real

economy in 1982 in a mistaken attempt to counteract "inflationary tax cuts." It was Congress which inflated the deficit by busting every Reagan budget. And it was Reagan's "pragmatic" advisers, romanticized in the media for refusing to let Reagan be Reagan and veto congressional spending, who allowed the debt to grow out of control.

No matter where one looks, then, the facts contradict what everyone "knows" about the "failure" of Reaganomics.

JUST AS THE CASE AGAINST SUPPLY-SIDE ECONomics collapses once there is no Laffer-curve forecast to blame for the deficits, so the debt-fueled-consumption/foreign-dependence argument unravels under close examination. Indeed, it appears that the same economists and pundits who lack the ability to look up the Reagan forecasts in public documents also lack the ability to read balance-of-payments statistics.

Between 1982 and 1983, when the U.S. became a net importer of capital, distinguished academic economists put out the story of foreign money pouring into America to finance overconsumption caused by the Reagan tax-rate reduction. This story became firmly fixed in the world's consciousness and was seen as further evidence that supplyside economics was just an extreme form of Keynesianism leading to excessive, unhealthy consumption. But this story also lacks any basis in fact.

Between 1982 and 1983 foreign-capital inflow into the U.S. actually *fell* by $9 billion. The change in the capital account of the balance of payments resulted from a $71-billion fall in U.S. capital outflows. During 1982–84 there was no significant change in the inflow of foreign capital into the U.S. However, U.S. capital outflows dropped, from $121 billion to $24 billion—a decline of 80 percent—throwing the U.S. capital account into a $100-billion surplus. It was this collapse in U.S. capital outflow that created the large trade deficit, which by definition is a mirror image of the capital surplus.

Why did American investors suddenly cease exporting their capital and instead retain it at home where it supposedly was subject to reckless policies of inflationary debt accumulation? After all, such a dangerous program as Reagan's was said to be would normally result in capital flight. Why then the sudden preference of American capital for the U.S. as compared, for example, to West Germany, a country with an economic policy that everyone considered sound?

The answer is so obvious that the only mystery is how economists and financial writers could have missed it. The 1981 business-tax cut and the reductions in personal income-tax rates in 1982 and 1983 raised the after-tax earnings on real investment in the U.S. relative to the rest of the world. Instead of exporting capital, the U.S. retained it and financed its own deficit.

As in the case of the tax-revenue shortfall, we are confronted with the spectacle of almost every economist misinterpreting the source of the capital surplus. Economists looked at the net figure, ignored its composition, and, seeing what they wanted to see, erroneously concluded that the net inflow was foreign money financing American overconsumption.

After convincing themselves and many others on the basis of this fundamental error that the U.S. was dangerously dependent on foreign capital, economists began warning of the consequences. The inflow of foreign money to finance our consumption, they declared, was keep-ing the dollar high, thus wrecking the competitiveness of U.S. industry. Furthermore, our addiction to foreign capital meant that the U.S. would have to maintain high interest rates in order to continue to attract the money, thus undermining U.S. investment and de-industrializing America. If U.S. interest rates or the dollar were to fall, foreign capital would flee, depriving us of financing for the "twin deficits."

This doomsday scenario was rapidly picked up by financial journalists and kept international financial markets unnerved. U.S. economic policy came under ever stronger criticism from our allies. America's "twin deficits" became the scapegoat for every country's problems.

Then, in the autumn of 1985, Secretary of the Treasury James A. Baker 3d engineered the political fall of the dollar, which plunged, along with U.S. interest rates, in 1986 and 1987. Remarkably, foreign capital inflows to the U.S. promptly doubled.

THERE ARE OTHER PROMINENT STARS IN THE constellation of misinformation: the U.S. is the world's largest debtor nation; the U.S. has the world's largest budget deficit; and debt-fueled consumption brought on a U.S. savings crisis. Each of these widely believed allegations is a product of the economists' ability to mislead themselves and the public by failing to examine the data.

According to the conventional wisdom, the U.S. became a debtor nation in 1985. By 1988, we were $532 billion in debt to foreigners, as measured by the difference between their investments in the U.S. and our investments abroad. These allegations of massive indebtedness were used to demoralize Americans and to convince them that Reagan produced a temporary prosperity stolen from future living standards, as we would be forced to divert income to the service of foreign debts.

Yet even as economists and financial writers were painting this dismal picture of the U.S. as the world's largest debtor, official statistics showed the U.S. receiving billions of dollars in net creditor income. As it is not possible for a net debtor to have a net creditor's income, something was obviously wrong here. It was this: the data showing us to be a debtor nation were based on historical prices or book values that understated the market value of U.S. foreign investments by hundreds of billions of dollars.

It would have been correct for economists to point out the decline in the net-creditor position of the U.S. as foreigners found America during Reagan's second term a more promising place to invest than their own countries. But this perspective would have pointed to our success rather than to our failure. And in any case, the solution to the problem, if that is what it was, was not for the U.S. to wreck its own investment climate with higher taxes, but for foreigners to cut *their* tax rates so as to make their economies more attractive to their own capital.

During the 1980's economists made the U.S. budget deficit the scapegoat for the failure of European economies to create new jobs. Sucking away their capital to finance our deficit, it was said, saddled Europe with high unemployment rates. After listening to this story, our allies began demanding that the U.S. become a good world citizen and start cutting its budget deficit. Yet while in absolute dollar amounts, the U.S. in the 1980's did have the world's largest budget deficit, when measured as a percentage of GNP, which is the way economists usually measure deficits, the U.S. budget deficit throughout the 1980's was below the Organization for European Cooperation and Development (OECD) average (as the internationally comparable general government budget balances published twice a year by the OECD made perfectly clear).* For example, Canada, Holland, and Spain consistently ran deficits twice as large as others, while Italy's was four times larger. British, French, and German deficits were not significantly lower, and the Japanese deficit had been lower only since 1984.

As a corollary to the budget deficit, there was the accumulated federal debt, which tripled under Reagan and became a "crisis" that would "doom our future." Yet under Reagan the federal debt as a percentage of GNP rose only slightly higher than the percentage which obtained when John F. Kennedy was President, and it was only one-third of the accumulated debt at the end of World War II. As that much higher debt burden did not destroy our economy or prevent the postwar expansion, why should today's much smaller burden do so? One answer, given by the economist Paul Samuelson and others, was that we owed this earlier debt to ourselves, whereas we owed the Reagan debt to foreigners. Yet official statistics reveal that the proportion of U.S. debt held by foreigners peaked in 1979, prior to Reagan.

Nor were these the only numbers ignored by the economists. In the mid-1980's the Bank for International Settlements (BIS) published a table showing federal debt as a share of GNP for the U.S.,

*The hysteria over the U.S. deficit was so pronounced that it eventually spread to the OECD, despite its own published tables.

Canada, Japan, and the European countries. Data were provided for 1973 and 1986 and the percentage increase was calculated. During 1973–86 in the U.S., the ratio of debt to GNP had grown 40.8 percent. However, in Germany and Japan, the supposedly successful countries against which our failure was measured, debt as a share of GNP had increased 121 percent and 194.2 percent respectively.

WHICH BRINGS US TO YET ANOTHER THING everyone "knows": that the Reagan tax cut caused a savings crisis and a drop in investment, with concomitant declines in productivity and median family income accompanied by a rise in poverty. But here yet again the facts tell an entirely different story.

During the 1980's, prices of capital goods in the U.S. rose only about half as fast as the overall U.S. inflation rate. Unless a real or inflation-adjusted measure of investment is used, the decline in the relative price of capital goods can be misinterpreted as a fall in investment's share of GNP. For example, if the economy were adding new factories every year at a 10-percent higher cost, and if other prices were rising by 20 percent, the share of investment as a percentage of GNP would appear to be falling. Economists who have charged that the U.S. is undergoing "disinvestment" have confused themselves and the public by failing to use inflation-adjusted data.

On the surface, measuring investment net of depreciation, or replacement of the capital used in production, seems to be a more appropriate measure than gross investment. However, net investment understates the growth of our productive ability, because it fails to make any adjustment for the shift in the composition of investment from longer-lived as-

sets, such as buildings, to shorter-lived assets, such as equipment, that generate more rapid depreciation. In other words, net investment can appear to be declining when what really is happening is a *shift* in the investment *mix* from plant to equipment. And so it has been in the past twenty-five years, during which equipment's share of investment has increased 25 percent. As a consequence there has been a rise in the depreciation rate. Little wonder that the net measure of investment has been falling as a share of GNP for a quarter-century.

In contrast, gross investment is not affected by a change in its composition. In real terms, gross investment as a share of GNP reached a postwar high in the 1980's. This investment performance greatly contributed to the recovery of U.S. productivity growth from its near standstill in the 1970's. Since 1981 American manufacturing productivity has been especially impressive, growing at almost double the postwar average.

DURING THE PAST YEAR OR SO, A FEW ECONomists have finally begun to challenge the false image of American failures. In a recent issue of the *Quarterly Review* of the Federal Reserve Bank of Minneapolis, Fumio Hayashi of the University of Pennsylvania argues that "the apparent savings-rate gap between Japan and the U.S. is a statistical illusion attributable to differences in the way the two countries compile their national income accounts." Japan values depreciation at historical cost rather than at the higher replacement-cost figure used by the U.S. As a result, Japanese accounting understates the value of assets used in production and makes Japanese investment look higher than it is. The other major source of the savings-gap illusion is the American practice of counting all government expenditures—including roads, bridges, schools, and warships—as consumption, whereas Japan counts such spending as investment. Once the accounting systems are put on an equal footing, Hayashi finds, the notoriously wide difference in the savings rate disappears.

In 1989 two other economists, Robert E. Lipsey of Queens College and Irving B. Kravis of the University of Pennsylvania, who studied savings and investment rates in industrialized countries, reported to the Western Economic Association that the reputation of the U.S. as a nation of spendthrifts depends on careless comparisons and narrow measures of investment. When U.S. savings and investment are broadened to include education, military capital, consumer durables, and research and development, the U.S. rate of capital formation, on a per-capita basis, is seen to be 25 percent higher than the average of industrialized countries. They report that Japan is "at the bottom of the list in the share of investment going into education."

Other economists have exposed as seriously misleading the Census Bureau's statistics trumpeting the growth of poverty. These statistics, it turns out, omit from poor people's income $158 billion of in-kind assistance. As a recent Heritage Foundation report demonstrates, there are many other paradoxical elements in the Census Bureau's definition of poverty as well. For example, according to official government figures, 38 percent of the persons identified as poor by the Census Bureau own their own homes, of which more than 100,000 are valued in excess of $200,000; 62 percent of poor households own a car, with 14 percent owning two or more; nearly half of all poor households have air-condi-

tioning; 31 percent of poor households have microwave ovens; 22,000 poor households have heated swimming pools or hot tubs. In real terms, Heritage calculates, per-capita expenditures of the lowest income fifth of the U.S. population in 1988 exceeded the per-capita income of the median American household in 1955. And international comparisons reveal that poor Americans eat more meat and live in larger houses and apartments than the average West European.

It is thus not unlikely that a significant percentage of the alleged 31.5 million poor Americans are poor only in a relative sense. But whatever their true number, it is certain that the long Reagan economic expansion, which created 20 million jobs without any rise in the rate of inflation, did not increase poverty.

THE MISINTERPRETATION OF REAGANOMICS by American economists and financial journalists is in some ways comparable to the misrepresentation by many intellectuals of Soviet experience, now fully exposed by Gorbachev's glasnost—only it is worse, because the evidence showing the origins of the U.S. budget deficit and capital surplus was readily available. The economists and the journalists simply ignored it and launched a crusade to drive out the devil of Reaganomics, which (among its other sins) had been guilty of doing what they said could never be done—creating 20 million new jobs without causing an increase in inflation.

Thanks to the accumulated economic misinformation and disinformation from the 1980's, the Bush administration—taking a step no administration has taken since the Great Depression—has supported tax increases as the economy was moving into recession. Pressed by conventional economists demanding tighter fiscal policy (that is, smaller budget deficits) and looser monetary policy (more money creation), President Bush agreed to raise taxes in exchange for lower interest rates. The combination of high taxes and easy money is the same policy mix that eventually produced the stagflation of the 1970's, from which Reaganomics extricated us, and it is bound to do us harm again.

Conventional economists, ignoring the lessons of their own textbooks (including even Keynes), have pronounced this disastrous policy mix a great victory for the economy. In the course of 1991 they will forget their role, of course, and blame the recession on Reagan's supply-side tax cut of a decade ago. And everyone will come to buy that story, too.

POSTSCRIPT

Did Reaganomics Fail?

The Reagan program to improve the macroeconomic performance of the U.S. economy represented a significant change in economic policy. These policies began in 1981 and continued through the end of Reagan's second term as president. Bowles, Gordon, and Weisskopf (BGW) compare macroeconomic performance during the Reagan era with macroeconomic performances of earlier periods and conclude that Reaganomics failed to reverse the long-term deterioration of the U.S. economy. Why did these actions—higher interest rates, less regulation for business, weaker unions, increased military expenditures, and lower taxes for the rich—fail to turn the economy around? BGW think the answer to this question lies in the inability of Reaganomics to escape the contradictions of right-wing economics. In particular, actions taken to increase the profit share of output did not increase the after-tax profit rate.

Roberts begins his defense of Reaganomics by examining what he calls the conventional wisdom regarding Reaganomics. He states that this conventional wisdom—particularly the idea that Reaganomics promised that cuts in tax rates would stimulate such a large increase in revenues that budget deficits would fall—is inaccurate. He then examines the problems blamed on Reaganomics: The budget deficits were caused by the Federal Reserve and Congress; the increase in U.S. foreign indebtedness, to the extent that it is accurately reflected by the data, was due to the more attractive investment environment created by Reaganomics; and the assertions that the United States saves and invests too little are based on careless use of data. In addition, Roberts believes that Reaganomics was a success because it created some 20 million jobs.

There is no shortage of readings regarding Reaganomics. In defense of Reaganomics there is no better source than various issues of *The Economic Report of the President* (Government Printing Office) published during the Reagan era. For a series of arguments for and against Reaganomics as they arose during Reagan's first term in office, see T. R. Swartz, F. J. Bonello, and A. F. Kosak, eds., *The Supply Side: Debating Current Economic Policies* (The Dushkin Publishing Group, 1983). More recent assessments include "The New Right and the U.S. Economy in the 1980s: An Assessment of the Economic Record of the Reagan Administration," by Philip Arestis and Mike Marshall, *International Review of Applied Economics* (January 1990); "Ten Years of Kemp-Roth," by Paul Craig Roberts, *The Wall Street Journal* (August 13, 1991); "Reagan's America: A Capital Offense," by Kevin P. Phillips, *The New York Times Magazine* (June 17, 1990); and "Promises the Supply-Siders Made—and Didn't," by Martin Anderson, *The Wall Street Journal* (August 13, 1991).

ISSUE 10

Do Federal Budget Deficits Matter?

YES: Alan Greenspan, from "Deficits Do Matter," *Challenge* (January/February 1989)

NO: Robert Eisner, from "Our Real Deficits," *Journal of the American Planning Association* (Spring 1991)

ISSUE SUMMARY

YES: Federal Reserve chairman Alan Greenspan believes that federal government budget deficits, in the long run, hurt the economy. The deficits crowd out or reduce net private domestic investment, which means a reduction in the rate of growth in the nation's capital stock. This, in turn, means less capital per worker and a reduction in labor productivity, the result of which is that the output of goods and services is smaller and persons are worse off.

NO: Economics professor Robert Eisner believes that if the budget position of the government is measured appropriately, then, in "a fundamental, long-run sense, . . . the total budget is now in balance." The real problems of the U.S. economy are not budget deficits but a lack of expenditures on "human capital and in public investment."

The Full Employment and Balanced Growth Act of 1978 lists a number of economic goals for the federal government. Besides the familiar objectives of full employment, price stability, and increased real income, the act specifically mentions the goal of a balanced federal budget. This means that the government is to collect in taxes an amount equal to its expenditures. Despite this legislative call to action, the federal government has failed to balance its budget, and recent deficits have been of record proportions. For example, between the years 1940 and 1975, there were only two instances when the deficit was in excess of $50 billion. For the years 1980 through 1990 the federal government deficit has averaged about $140 billion; the projected deficit for fiscal year 1992 is almost $400 billion.

When the federal government runs a deficit, it sells securities: treasury bills, notes, and bonds. In this respect, the government is just like a business firm that sells securities to raise funds. The total of outstanding government securities is called the public or national debt. Thus, when the federal government runs a deficit, the public debt increases by the amount of the deficit, and the public debt at any point in time is a summary of all prior deficits (offset by the retirement of securities if the government chooses to repurchase its securities when it has a budget surplus). By September 1991 the gross federal debt was approximately $3.7 trillion. The debt is owned by (has been purchased by) different groups, including individuals, commercial banks, pension funds, life insurance companies, federal government agencies, state and local governments, and corporations. Some securities are also sold to foreign individuals, businesses, and governments.

There are three major questions regarding federal government budget deficits and debt, and they are all discussed in the following selections. The first concerns measurement. For example, to adjust for the impact of the business cycle on the government's budget, economists have developed the concept of the cyclically adjusted budget. But there are other adjustments that economists have suggested are in order to obtain a correct measure of the government's fiscal position. Robert Eisner discusses these and, after making these adjustments, concludes that, in a fundamental sense, the government's budget is in balance. Alan Greenspan accepts one of these adjustments but still believes that there is a deficit.

The second question concerns the causes of the deficit. One possibility is that the government spends more than it collects in revenues because it does not exercise fiscal restraint. That is, it is easy for politicians to spend money but difficult for them to increase taxes to fund the increased spending. Every elected official wants to point to the benefits of increased spending—new roads or increased Social Security payments—and no politician wants to be attacked in a bid for reelection as someone who increased taxes. But the budget position of the government is also influenced by the state of the economy. The deficit is likely to increase if the economy enters a recession. A downturn in economic activity will decrease tax revenues and will increase government spending. Because a deficit can arise for different reasons, it is important to understand exactly what forces create a deficit.

The third major question about deficits concerns the economic consequences of deficits. Some persons perceive the deficits as harmful. With a deficit, the government borrows funds that otherwise would have been available to business firms who would have built new factories and purchased new machinery with the borrowed funds. This is referred to as "crowding out," since government borrowing to finance deficits reduces private investment. The reduction in investment slows the growth of productivity, and this means that the ability of the economy to produce goods and services is also reduced. Greenspan argues in this fashion.

In reading these opposing views, keep these three questions in mind. Greenspan accepts the conventional definition of deficit and Eisner does not. Greenspan believes that deficits must be reduced because they are harming the economy. Eisner believes that there is no real deficit problem and all the talk about deficit reduction is diverting attention away from the true economic problems of too little human and public investment.

YES
Alan Greenspan

DEFICITS DO MATTER

There is a significant view being expressed lately, fortunately to date a minority opinion, that federal government deficits do not matter much. Or in any event, there is no urgency in coming to grips with them. In fact, deficits do matter. Over the long term, they have a corrosive effect on the economy, and it is from this perspective that the case for bringing down the deficit is compelling. More important, the long run is rapidly turning into the short run. If we do not act promptly, the imbalances in the economy are such that the effects of the deficit will be increasingly felt and with some immediacy.

It is beguiling to contemplate the strong economy of recent years in the context of very large deficits and to conclude that the concerns about the adverse effects of the deficit on the economy have been misplaced. But this argument is fanciful. The deficit already had begun to eat away at the foundations of our economic strength. And the need to deal with it is becoming ever more urgent. To the extent that some of the negative effects of deficits have not as yet been felt, they have been merely postponed, not avoided. Moreover, the scope for further such avoidance is shrinking.

To some degree, the effects of the federal budget deficits over the past several years have been muted by two circumstances, both of which are currently changing rapidly. One was the rather large degree of slack in the economy in the early years of the current expansion. This slack meant that the economy could accommodate growing demands from both the private and public sectors. In addition, to the extent that these demands could not be accommodated from U.S. resources, we went abroad and imported them. This can be seen in our large trade and current-account deficits.

By now, however, the slack in the U.S. economy has contracted substantially. And, it has become increasingly clear that reliance on foreign sources of funds is not possible or desirable over extended periods. As these sources are reduced along with our trade deficit, other sources must be found, or demands for saving curtailed. The choices are limited; as will become clear, the best option for the American people is a further reduction in the federal budget deficit, and the need for such reduction is becoming more pressing.

Owing to significant efforts by the administration and the Congress, coupled with strong economic growth, the deficit has shrunk from 5 to 6 percent of gross national product a few years ago to about 3 percent of GNP today. Such a deficit, nevertheless, is still very large by historical standards. Since World War II, the actual budget deficit has exceeded 3 percent of GNP only in the 1975 recession period and in the recent deficit experience beginning in 1982. On a cyclically adjusted or structural basis, the deficit has exceeded 3 percent of potential GNP only in the period since 1983.

THE SAVING FACTOR

Government deficits, however, place pressure on resources and credit markets, only if they are not offset by saving elsewhere in the economy. If the pool of private saving is small, federal deficits and private investment will be in keen competition for funds, and private investment will lose.

The U.S. deficits of recent years are threatening precisely because they have been occurring in the context of private saving that is low by both historical and international standards. Historically, net personal plus business saving in the United States in the 1980s is about 3 percentage points lower relative to GNP than its average in the preceding three decades.

Internationally, government deficits have been quite common among the major industrial countries in the 1980s, but private saving rates in most of these countries have exceeded the deficits by very comfortable margins. In Japan, for example, less than 20 percent of private saving has been absorbed by government deficits, even though the Japanese general government has been borrowing almost 3 percent of its gross domestic product in the 1980s. In contrast, over half of private U.S. saving in the 1980s has been absorbed by the combined deficits of the federal and state and local sectors.

Under these circumstances, such large and persistent deficits are slowly but inexorably damaging the economy. The damage occurs because deficits tend to pull resources away from net private investment. And a reduction in net investment has reduced the rate of growth of the nation's capital stock. This in turn has meant less capital per worker than would otherwise have been the case, and this will surely engender a shortfall in labor productivity growth and, with it, a shortfall in growth of the standard of living.

POWER OF GOVERNMENT

The process by which government deficits divert resources from net private investment is part of the broader process of redirecting the allocation of real resources that inevitably accompanies the activities of the federal government. The federal government can preempt resources from the private sector or direct their usage by a number of different means. The most important are: 1) deficit spending, on- or off-budget; 2) tax-financed spending; 3) regulation mandating private activities such as pollution control or safety equipment installation, which are financed by industry through the issuance of debt instruments; and 4) government guarantees of private borrowing.

What deficit spending and regulatory measures have in common is that the extent to which resources are preempted by government actions, directly or indirectly, is not sensitive to the rate of interest. The federal government, for example, will finance its budget deficit in full, irrespective of the interest rate it must pay to raise the funds. Similarly, a government-mandated private activity will almost always be financed irrespective of the interest rate that exists. Borrowing with government-guaranteed debt may be only partly interest-sensitive, but the guarantees have the effect of preempting resources from those without access to riskless credit. Government spending fully financed by taxation does, of course, preempt real resources from the private sector, but the process works through channels other than real interest rates.

Purely private activities, on the other hand, are, to a greater or lesser extent, responsive to interest rates. The demand for mortgages, for example, falls off dramatically as mortgage interest rates rise. Inventory demand is clearly a function of short-term interest rates, and the level of interest rates, as they are reflected in the cost of capital, is a key element in the decision on whether to expand or modernize productive capacity. Hence, to the extent that there are more resources demanded in an economy than are available to be financed, interest rates will rise until sufficient excess demand is finally crowded out.

The crowded-out demand cannot, of course, be that of the federal government, directly or indirectly, since government demand does not respond to rising interest rates. Rather, real interest rates will rise to the point that private borrowing is reduced sufficiently to allow the entire requirements of the federal on- and off-budget deficit, and all its collateral guarantees and mandated activities, to be met.

A FISCAL FACT

In real terms, there is no alternative to a diversion of real resources from the private to the public sector. In the short run, interest rates can be held down if the Federal Reserve accommodates the excess demand for funds through a more expansionary monetary policy. But this will only engender an acceleration of inflation and, ultimately, will have little if any effect on the allocation of real resources between the private and public sectors.

The Treasury has been a large and growing customer in financial markets in recent years. It has acquired, on average, roughly 25 percent of the total funds borrowed in domestic credit markets over the last four years, up from less than 15 percent in the 1970s. For the Treasury to raise its share of total credit flows in this fashion, it must push other borrowers aside.

The more interest-responsive are the total demands of these other, private borrowers, the less will the equilibrium interest rate be pushed up by the increase in Treasury borrowing. That is, the greater the decline in the quantity of funds demanded, and the associated spending to be financed, for a given rise in interest rates, the lower will be the rate. In contrast, if private borrowing and spending are resistant, interest rates will have to rise more before enough private spending gives way. In either case, private investment is crowded out by higher real interest rates.

Even if private investment were not as interest-elastic as it appears to be, crowding out of private spending by the budget deficit would occur dollar-for-dollar if the total supply of saving were fixed. To the extent that the supply of saving is induced to increase, both the equilibrium rise in interest rates and the amount of crowding out will be less. However, even if more saving can be induced in the short run, it will be permanently lowered in the long run to the extent that real income growth is curtailed by reduced capital formation.

SHORT-TERM MENTALITY

But aggregate investment is only part of the process through which the structure of production is affected by high real interest rates. Higher real interest rates also induce both consumers and business to concentrate their purchases disproportionately on immediately consumable goods and, of course, services. When real interest rates are high, purchasers and producers of long-lived assets, such as real estate and capital equipment, pull back. They cannot afford the debt-carrying costs at high interest rates, or if financed with available cash, the forgone interest income resulting from this expenditure of the cash. Under such conditions, one would expect the GNP to be disproportionately composed of shorter-lived goods, such as food, clothing, services, etc.

Indeed, statistical analysis demonstrates such a relationship—that is, a recent decline in the average service life of all consumption and investment goods and a systematic tendency for this average to move inversely with real rates of interest. In other words, the higher real interest rates, the heavier the concentration on short-lived assets. Parenthetically, the resulting shift toward shorter-lived investment goods means that more *gross* investment is required to provide for replacement of the existing capital stock, as well as for the *net* investment neces-

sary to raise tomorrow's living standards. Thus, the current relatively high ratio of gross investment to GNP in this country is a deceptive indicator of the additions to our capital stock.

Not surprisingly, we have already experienced a disturbing decline in the level of net investment as a share of GNP. Net investment has fallen to 4.7 percent of GNP in the 1980s from an average level of 6.7 percent in the 1970s, and even higher in the 1960s. Moreover, it is low, not only by our own historical standards, but by international standards as well.

International comparisons of net investment should be viewed with some caution because of differences in the measurement of depreciation and in other technical details. Nevertheless, the existing data do indicate that total net private and public investment, as a share of gross domestic product over the period between 1980 and 1986, was lower in the United States than in any of the other major industrial countries except the United Kingdom.

TEMPORARY REPRIEVES

It is important to recognize, as I indicated earlier, that the negative effects of federal deficits on growth in the capital stock may be attenuated for a while by several forces in the private sector. One is a significant period of output growth in excess of potential GNP growth—such as occurred over much of the past six years—which undoubtedly boosts sales and profit expectations and, hence, business investment. Such rates of output growth, of course, cannot persist, making this factor inherently temporary in nature.

Another factor tending to limit the decline in investment spending would be any tendency for saving to respond positively to the higher interest rates that deficits would bring. The supply of domestic private saving has some interest elasticity, as people put off spending when borrowing costs are high and returns from their financial assets are favorable. But most analysts find that this elasticity is not sufficiently large to matter much.

Finally, net inflows of foreign saving can be, as recent years have demonstrated, an important addition to saving. In the 1980s, foreign saving has kept the decline in the gross investment-GNP ratio, on average, to only moderate dimensions (slightly more than one-half percentage point) compared with the 1970s, while the federal deficit rose by about 2 1/2 percentage points relative to GNP. Net inflows of foreign saving have amounted, on average, to almost 2 percent of GNP, an unprecedented level.

Opinions differ about the relative importance of high U.S. interest rates, changes in the after-tax return to investment in the United States, and changes in perception of the relative risks of investment in various countries and currencies in bringing about the foreign capital inflow. Whatever its source, had we not experienced this addition to our saving, our interest rates would have been even higher and domestic investment lower. Indeed, since 1985, when the appetite of private investors for dollar assets seems to have waned, the downtrend in real long-term rates has become erratic, tending to stall with the level still historically high.

Looking ahead, the continuation of foreign saving at current levels is questionable. Evidence for the United States and for most other major industrial nations over the last 100 years indicates that such sizable foreign net capital inflows have not persisted and, hence, may not be a reliable substitute for domestic saving on a long-term basis. In other words, domestic investment tends to be supported by domestic saving alone in the long run.

Clearly, the presumption that the deficit is benign is false. It is partly responsible for the decline in the net investment ratio in the 1980s to a sub-optimal level. Allowing the deficit to persist courts a dangerous corrosion of our economy. Fortunately, we have it in our power to reverse this process, thereby avoiding potentially significant reductions in our standard of living.

NO   Robert Eisner

OUR REAL DEFICITS

Budget deficits of $300 billion! A federal debt over $3 trillion! Repeated trade deficits that have made the United States "The World's Greatest Debtor Nation!" A savings and loan bailout to "cost the taxpayer" $500 billion! What are we to make of these astronomical numbers and apocalyptic proclamations? They are dear to politicians, press, and assorted pundits, but what is their substance? Is the overweening attention they attract obscuring the real issues facing our nation and its economy? And is it preventing vital policy planning and decisions?

This is not going to be an article of gloom and doom. As I write, we have apparently slipped into a recession that costs more than 200,000 jobs in one month, and promises to get worse—no one can honestly say how much worse—before it gets better. Justified concern has been expressed both about where we are now and whether we are providing properly for our future. We also slipped into a brief but fairly expensive war, with initial "off-budget" funding requests running over $60 billion and uncounted billions more anticipated to replenish military stockpiles and compensate for at least some of the war's destruction and political consequences. Paradoxically, war expenditures serve generally to combat recessions, but they also drain resources from investment in the future.

Still the United States remains the globe's greatest economic power. We are the nation with the greatest total wealth and the highest average standard of living—whatever that means—with the exception of any surviving oil sheikdoms and possibly Sweden and Switzerland. We are the envy of much of the world. We are the (probably misunderstood) model for many of our former antagonists in the old communist empire, as their efforts at a transition from Stalinist command socialism to a market (and capitalist?) economy make matters worse before, it is hoped, they get better.

Our economy, though, is far from perfect. There is trouble now, and there is trouble ahead. To find a cure for our troubles we shall have to disabuse ourselves of some very widespread myths and face up to some ignored realities.

From Robert Eisner, "Our Real Deficits," *Journal of the American Planning Association*, vol. 57, no. 2 (Spring 1991). Copyright © 1991 by The American Planning Association. Reprinted by permission.

FAULTY CONCEPTS AND FAULTY MEASURES

It is hard to know where to start on the myths of deficits and debt. Many people talk about them; few know, literally, what they are talking about. First, the numbers and statements in our opening paragraph, however closely they reflect widespread assertions, are false on their face. Even without basic revisions to give them real economic content, the official deficit should be put not at $300 billion but at $162 billion. The relevant measure of the federal debt is not the total gross public debt of $3.2 trillion but the debt held by the public, a more modest $2.5 trillion, from which might well be subtracted some $235 billion of Treasury securities held by the Federal Reserve.

The figures purporting to make the United States the world's greatest debtor nation have little to do with debt. They are calculated as the difference between the value of foreign investments in the United States and investment by Americans in the rest of the world. These values have been so inappropriately and inconsistently calculated that the source of the figures, the Bureau of Economic Analysis of the U.S. Department of Commerce, has ceased publishing their totals pending a review and revision of the underlying methodology. The savings and loan bailout figure of $500 billion is put forth on the basis of double-counting—the original capital amount plus accruing interest. By that measure the federal debt, if it is not paid off, is infinite, because interest payments will keep accumulating forever.

The Deficit and the Real Change in Debt

Many observers, including countless TV newspeople and newspaper headline writers, do not even seem able to distinguish between the federal deficit and the national debt. The deficit, of course, is in principle the change in debt. If an individual starts with a debt of $100,000 and spends $40,000 when his income is $30,000 he must borrow $10,000 to finance the shortfall (or sell off assets) and his (net) debt goes to $110,000.

So it is too, or would be if we measured right, for the federal government. With a current debt held by the public, that is, outside of the government itself, of close to $2,500 billion and a deficit of, say, $200 billion over the year, the debt at the end of fiscal 1991 would go to $2,700 billion. And here we stumble on one of the critical failures of official measures of the deficit; they do not adjust the value of the debt for inflation.

To understand the necessity and nature of the needed inflation correction, we have to recognize first that the central significance of the federal government's net debt is not to the government itself but to the holders of that debt, essentially the American people and their businesses, banks, insurance companies, and pension funds; contrary once more to popular mythology, the proportion of that debt held by foreigners remains little more than 15 percent, less than it was a decade ago. The greater the federal debt, therefore, the wealthier, in holdings of Treasury securities, are the American people.

A federal deficit of $200 billion in effect showers the United States with close to $200 billion in *assets* in the form of Treasury bills, notes, and bonds or, if the securities end up owned by Federal Reserve banks, the money that they back. The effect of this increase in perceived wealth (except for the unlikely incidence of worry that taxes will be higher in the future as a consequence of the increase in debt) is to make us less inclined to save and more inclined to spend. It is in this way that deficits generally prove stimulative to the economy. By giving us greater wealth in the form of Treasury securities they increase our purchases and keep business humming.

Thus, deficits frequently, in fact much more often than not, prove good for us. Properly measured deficits over the past four decades have been positively correlated with subsequent increases in GNP and *decreases* in unemployment.[1] The one way deficits can be bad is if they are *too* large. But for them to be too large they must be bringing about a demand to purchase more than can be produced. The consequence then is rising prices and inflation. Measures to combat the inflation, such as tight money and higher real estate rates, may then "crowd out" desirable investment.

If deficits are to be seen as significant because they increase debt, it must be the real debt that increases, that is, that debt after adjustment for inflation. Clearly the person who had $100,000 at the beginning of the year and $101,000 at the end of the year will not long see herself as richer if she has to reckon that prices have risen 4 percent. In real terms her $100,000 is now worth only about $97,000 compared to a year ago. That person will spend less, not more.

And what is true for the individual will be true for the economy as a whole. A deficit will increase spending to the extent that public holdings of Treasury securities have risen more than inflation. To gauge how much those holdings have gone up in real terms, and hence how large the *real* deficit is, we must adjust for inflation. With inflation running at about 4 percent and the debt held by the

public at about $2,500 billion, this is an adjustment of some $100 billion, more or less than half, depending on how it is measured, of the anticipated deficit over this year.

Peculiar Accounting
There are further corrections to be made to official measures. For one thing, private business and state and local governments keep separate capital budgets. The business income or profit-and-loss statement includes only "current" expenses, not the outlays for new machinery or the building of factories; it counts only the depreciation on those assets as a current cost. If the federal accounts were to be kept in similar fashion and we were to substitute depreciation for current outlays labeled by the Office of Management and Budget as "investment," we would knock another $70 billion or so off our measure of the deficit.

And if we were to note that some $130 billion of federal outlays are grants-in-aid to state and local governments, we might see it as all the more appropriate to balance federal deficits by at least the $40 billion or so of state and local government surpluses. Adding in this correction would finally move our total government budget to surplus.

Another way of looking at this is to note the ratio of debt to income. For individuals, businesses, or government, since debt is increasing (if only because of inflation but also along with general growth), an appropriate question is whether it is increasing faster than income. For the nation, the relevant income is national income, or gross national product. To keep the ratio of debt to GNP constant, debt must grow at the same rate as GNP. For our recent 7-percent growth of GNP, the deficit that, again, is the increase in debt, would come to $175 billion currently, pretty close to the deficit we are actually running and, since the debt-GNP ratio is now three-sevenths, 3 percent of a growing GNP in the future.[2]

There is plenty of room for the debt-income ratio to rise if we see any reason for that. True, it was considerably less—about 25 percent before the large deficits of the 1980s—but it was well over 100 percent at the end of World War II, which ushered in a period of substantial prosperity and growth. In spite of all the hullabaloo to the contrary, the deficit now is not too large. And reducing it now, as the economy plunges into recession, can only further reduce purchases of the nation's output and aggravate that recession.

Phony New Gramm-Rudman Numbers

The pressure to reduce the deficit is fueled in part by other strange games of accounting. Indeed, the new budget deal, the "Budget Enforcement Act of 1990," compounds existing peculiarities so that, in the face of a "unified budget" deficit of $220 billion for fiscal year 1990, it can raise the old Gramm-Rudman 1991 target from $64 billion to $327 billion and claim a $35-billion deficit reduction.

A major reason for the jump in the Gramm-Rudman numbers is the new edict requiring that these numbers not reflect the unified budget total, but rather be measured exclusive of the net inflow of tax revenues into the social security trust funds. The combined trust fund surplus came to $58 billion in 1990 and is projected in the new budget at $60 billion in 1991. Removing these positive components from the total makes the "deficit," restricted arbitrarily to the rest of the budget, that much higher. Political

rhetoric about protecting the sanctity of social security aside, this requirement does not make economic sense, any more than would excluding defense expenditures of $300 billion from a unified budget reportedly in deficit by $220 billion and then asserting that the budget is truly in surplus by $80 billion. The deficit's impact on the economy relates to the difference between total expenditures and total tax revenues, regardless of where the Congress or the administration chose to deposit them. Hence it relates to the increase in the debt held by the public, not to the accounting entries of debt "held" in trust funds.

Another reason for the spurt in the deficit numbers is the improper inclusion of the "costs" of the S&L bailout. Those came to $58 billion in fiscal 1990 and have been projected at $112 billion for 1991. These amounts, however, are merely financial transactions signifying no new government expenditures or commands on the nation's economic resources. They entail putting on different kinds of paper a debt that the government already has to S&L depositors as a consequence of insurance of those deposits. They do not add to the net wealth of the public, although by preventing S&L depositors from losing their money they do preserve that wealth. They are not properly part of the budget deficit and, despite all the contrary rhetoric, they have nothing to do with "the taxpayer." They are no proper excuse for raising taxes or demanding cuts in government expenditures.

Including social security and excluding the S&L bailout, as is recommended by the Congressional Budget Office,[3] puts both the 1990 deficit and the pre-recession-projected 1991 deficit at $162 billion. Under the criterion of preventing an increase in the debt-GNP ratio, these figures are within the bounds. The war against Iraq, of course, brought a significant increase in the deficit but, unless it leads to more subsequent military spending, that impact may be viewed as a temporary aberration. Stability of the debt-GNP ratio is further disturbed by the recession, which has driven the growth of GNP well below its recent 7-percent per year, and has already contributed to the larger, 1991 figure of $207 billion projected by the administration in its 1992 budget document. A severe recession, though, is just the time when we should allow the debt-GNP ratio, along with the deficit, to grow.

In a fundamental, long-run sense, then, the total budget is now in balance; there is no real deficit. Projections for the years ahead, if legislated expenditure ceilings are observed, in fact indicate a real surplus. And that, as we shall explain, is a matter more for concern than for cheers.

REAL DEFICITS

In a still more fundamental sense, our economy—and our society—are not in balance. The real issues are not mismeasured financial magnitudes. They are rather the distribution of income and product and well-being among our current population. They are the composition of our output as between public and private goods and among public goods. They are the decisions that we make now that will affect life well into the next century.

On the level of the budget, the critical problem is not the amount of spending or how it is financed. It is its composition. Some two-thirds of federal expenditures for goods and services go for "national defense." The great bulk of those

expenditures, aside from their function in preserving "the offensive option" for crises in the Persian Gulf or elsewhere, are shown more than ever, with the inability to curtail them sharply with the end of the cold war, to be related at least as much to preserving jobs and profits as national security.

In the past decade, the inequality of distribution of the national income has increased sharply. The rich have gotten richer, the poor poorer, and those in the middle have been squeezed. Tax changes in the first half of the decade, with huge cuts for upper income groups and investment "incentives" that increased capital gains while the rate at which they were taxed was cut aggravated the inequality, as did the lowering of "safety nets" and the starving of uplift programs. The tax reform of 1986 improved horizontal equity, reducing some of the glaring loopholes, but did little if anything on balance to level the playing field as between traditional winners and losers.

The False Issues of National Saving and Investment

The budget deficits of the eighties did actually contribute significantly to bringing the economy out of its deep recession of 1982–83. Unemployment, which had reached a post–World-War-II high of 10.7 percent, was cut in half before beginning to inch up again in 1990. A widespread lament, however, was that these deficits were bringing on a consumption binge and "crowding out" private domestic investment. To the argument that in fact gross private domestic investment as a percent of GNP remained at or close to its previous highs (16 and 17 percent), the retort was that it was being financed by foreigners. Our net foreign investment had turned negative and, further, depreciation or capital consumption had increased so that national saving, the sum of net private domestic investment and net foreign investment, had declined. We were hence not providing enough for future productivity, and a considerable part of the fruits of that productivity would be going to foreign owners of American stocks, bonds, and real assets.

This argument too, though, is out of focus. As long as we maintain a prosperous, growing economy, without restrictive fiscal or monetary policy, private investment in a reasonably free market economy can and should be expected to take care of itself. Business can be expected to invest in what is productive and therefore profitable. And if foreigners choose to invest here they can do so to a greater extent than we invest abroad only so far as we import more than we export. That jointly determined outcome may, unfortunately, stem from restrictive monetary policy that raises real interest rates and hence the value, and cost, of the dollar, thus making U.S. goods unduly expensive to foreigners and foreign goods unduly cheap for Americans. But if that is not the cause, there is nothing to fear here either.

In contradiction to the statements about our "debtor" status, receipts on U.S. assets abroad in the third quarter of 1990 still exceeded payments on foreign assets in the United States, by 8 percent—$33.08 billion to $30.63 billion, or about a $10-billion surplus at annual rates. Even if the current account deficit—negative net foreign investment—continued at its swollen Gulf-crisis rate of $100 billion a year for five years it would bring only a trivial move to net payments of capital income to foreigners. At a 4-percent real rate of return, the cumulated net acquisition of $500 billion of U.S. assets would entail new net payments to foreigners of only $20 billion per year, which would be well under three-tenths of one percent of our GNP. Given the surplus we are still enjoying, we would then have a net deficit on capital income of not much more than one-tenth of 1 percent of GNP, a level that would hardly justify any of the alarm so often expressed. And indeed, with the dollar allowed to fall, our trade balance would improve and the value of our foreign-currency denominated assets as well as the income from them would grow in relevant, dollar terms, so that even this minimal swing to deficit in our capital income accounts might not eventuate—particularly if we could learn to cut our military expenditures abroad.

The Real Issues

Having put in their proper place, cut down to size, or dismissed most of the deficits that receive so much misguided attention, I must point now to the real and important deficits. . . . Private tangible investment in a free market economy, once government has played its part with nonrestrictive and sufficiently stimulative fiscal and monetary policy, can safely and properly be left to find its own level. The real rub is in intangible investment, including investment in human capital, and in public investment—everything that is not automatically pulled along by the actuality or the lure of private profits.

We can begin to see the wastage and failure to develop human capital in the figures for unemployment. In January 1991, it was counted at over 7,715,000, or 6.1 percent of the total labor force. Unemployment was little over 3 percent during the height of the Vietnam War and close to 1 percent during World War II.

We should not require wars to reach minimum unemployment levels.

Yet those contrasting numbers present only a small part of the problem. The widely cited unemployment numbers include only those people not working at all who are either looking for work or not looking because they are awaiting recall by their employers. Workers reduced to part-time employment "for economic reasons," even to an afternoon a week in a car-wash, constitute 5,510,000 more, not included in the total. Also excluded are "discouraged workers," 941,000 of them in the fourth quarter of 1990, who have despaired of finding another job and hence have stopped looking. And most important, uncounted millions in inner cities as well as outlying ghettos remain outside the labor force, outside the mainstream of the economy, poorly educated if at all, a deadweight loss to society as well as to themselves.

Elimination of this human waste requires public policy and public investment. A private firm cannot take into account social costs when it lays off workers. If a tight government budget or tight money deprive a firm's customers of the purchasing power necessary to buy its products, the firm cuts production and employment. Efforts to reduce the budget deficit as an economy slips into recession, whether by cutting government payments or expenditures or by increasing taxes, only aggravate the deficit in purchases, deepen the recession, and add to unemployment.

Further, since we do not have a slave economy, private employers lack adequate incentive to offer basic educational skills to workers. If they do take a chance on an underprivileged youth, and the investment in his employment is successful, they retain only part of the fruits of that investment. Some of it is retained by the worker and much of the rest goes to his next employer.

There is a similar problem with investment in basic research that will over the long run keep us at an advancing, technological frontier. By its nature, and all the more so in a free society, basic research involves the free and open interchange of ideas. Since the people who undertake it are thus unable to keep its benefits to themselves, it is likely to prove inadequate without public support.

In the way of public investment, the needs are more and more evident in our decaying highway system, in crumbling bridges, in skies crowded with planes waiting to land at overcrowded airports, in staggering problems of waste disposal, in the lack of resources devoted to protecting and improving our environment of land, water, and air. One set of estimates suggests the need to double, from $13 billion to $26 billion annually, the expenditures to attain and maintain minimum standards on existing highways. These estimates also suggest $50 billion needed to repair or replace 240,000 bridges, $1 billion a year more just to maintain existing flying conditions, $11 billion to clean up nuclear and non-nuclear military waste, $3 billion for nonmilitary hazardous waste, and $2.4 billion to comply with the Clean Water Act.

And then there are $2 billion in unmet needs for Head Start and early education, $5 billion for education for "at-risk" youth, $7 billion to support long-term health insurance, $4 billion to repair existing public housing. One estimate has set at least $130 billion annually as the shortfall in the nation's investments to tackle some of these most grievous problems.[4]

The United States, the only developed country without a comprehensive system of health insurance, ranks with the worst in infant mortality. In standardized tests in math and science for 13-year-olds, given in a number of advanced countries in Asia, Europe, and North America, United States students came out dead last. Where will that stand us in international economic competition in the twenty-first century? George Bush declared that he intended to be the "education president." But new resources to put into education are declared not available or, in perhaps a convenient rationalization, unnecessary.

Our so painfully arranged and much ballyhooed Budget Enforcement Act of 1990, pretty much a successor to Gramm-Rudman-Hollings, promised to reduce what it denotes as budget deficits by an average of close to $100 billion annually over five years. It would accomplish this very considerably by sharply limiting increases in the aggregate of real "discretionary" domestic expenditures. Any of the hoped-for "peace dividend" that might remain after the Gulf War and its aftermath can be used only to reduce the deficit. The nonmilitary, domestic expenditures would not even grow with the population or total product, let alone meet any of the needs just indicated.[5] One may doubt whether, with a slowing economy, this law will even reduce the "deficits" to which it refers. It can only stand in the way of reduction of the real deficits faced by our nation and its economy.

NOTES

1. See Robert Eisner and Paul J. Pieper, "A New View of the Federal Debt and Budget Deficits," *American Economic Review*, March 1984: 11–29; Robert Eisner, *How Real Is the Federal Deficit?* (New York: The Free Press, 1986); and, for an update, Robert Eisner, "Deficits and Us and Our Grandchildren," in *The Debt and the Twin Deficits Debate*, ed. James Rock (Mountain View, CA: Bristletone Books/Mayfield, 1991).

2. Noting that the deficit, D, equals the change in the debt, ΔB, and that for a constant ratio of debt to GNP the ratio of the change in debt to the change in GNP must equal that debt-GNP ratio, we can write:

$$\Delta B/GNP = (\Delta B/\Delta GNP)^*(\Delta GNP/GNP),$$

whence we have $d = b^*g$,
where $d = D/GNP$, the constant ratio of deficit to GNP, $b = B/GNP$, the constant ratio of debt to GNP, and $g = \Delta GNP/GNP$, the rate of growth of GNP. With $B = {}^3/_7$ and $g = 0.7$, we then have $d = .03$.

3. See the statement of Robert D. Reischauer, director of the Congressional Budget Office, before the Committee on the Budget, U.S. House of Representatives, December 6, 1990, and "CBO Papers—The 1990 Budget Agreement: An Interim Assessment," December 1980, released with the statement.

4. This last figure is from the center for Community Change, as cited in Tom Wicker, "America's Real Deficit," *New York Times*, Op. Ed. page, November 7, 1990, the secondary source for the numbers offered above. The original figures are variously attributed to a number of public and private agencies: the Congressional Budget Office, the General Accounting Office, the Department of Energy, the Environmental Protection Agency, the Department of Housing, the Federal Aviation Administration, the Ford Foundation, and the W. T. Grant Foundation.

5. A quirk in the law, noted only after its passage, apparently putting certain necessarily rising expenditures within the "discretionary" domestic total, may (in order to keep within the legislated aggregate ceiling) actually force vital public investment to decline.

POSTSCRIPT

Do Federal Budget Deficits Matter?

Greenspan begins by examining the argument that recent budget deficits have been associated with a strong economy and, therefore, can be ignored. He terms this argument "fanciful," for the harmful effects of recent deficits have been "muted" by two special circumstances that cannot be expected to continue: economic slack and large trade and current account deficits. The problem with current deficits is that they have not been "offset by saving elsewhere in the economy" and this has led to higher real interest rates. As a consequence, net investment as a percent of gross national product has been falling, which means that workers will have less capital to work with and productivity will grow less rapidly. The long-term implication is that the ability of the economy to produce goods and services will be reduced and the standard of living of Americans will be less than it could have been.

Eisner believes that in order to obtain an economically correct assessment of the fiscal position of the government, it is necessary to make several adjustments to the published data. One adjustment is for inflation, for if deficits are significant it must be because the real value of the government's debt has increased. Another adjustment requires that the accounting procedures used by the federal government be similar to those used by businesses and state and local governments. A third adjustment is to offset the federal government's budget position with the fiscal position of state and local governments. A fourth adjustment involves a comparison of deficits and debt to the size of the economy, to gross national product. If these adjustments are made and "other strange games of accounting" are ignored, then there are no real deficit or debt problems.

There are any number of readings regarding the budget deficit. One might begin with a look at the federal budget as contained in an annual series entitled *The Guide to the Federal Budget,* by Stanley E. Collender (The Urban Institute Press). Other interesting books include *The Deficit Dilemma,* by Gregory B. Mills and John L. Palmer (The Urban Institute, 1983), and *The Debt and the Deficit,* by Robert Heilbroner and Peter Bernstein (W. W. Norton, 1989). For contrasting views on the need for a constitutional amendment to balance the budget, see Milton Friedman's "Less Red Ink,"*The Atlantic* (February 1983) and Gardner Ackley's "You Can't Balance the Budget by Amendment," *Challenge* (November/December 1982). Other interesting articles include Jonathan Rauch, "Is the Deficit Really So Bad?" *Atlantic Monthly* (February 1989); Richard C. Koo, "America's Budget Deficits: They Don't Crowd Out, They Redistribute Income to the Rich," *The International Economy* (May/June 1991); and Daniel Hage, "Budget Ties That Bind," *U.S. News and World Report* (September 9, 1991).

ISSUE 11

Should the Federal Reserve Target Zero Inflation?

YES: W. Lee Hoskins, from "The Case for Price Stability," *Economic Commentary*, Federal Reserve Bank of Cleveland (March 15, 1990)

NO: Michael Meeropol, from "Zero Inflation: Prescription for Recession," *Challenge* (January/February 1990)

ISSUE SUMMARY

YES: Former Cleveland Federal Reserve Bank president W. Lee Hoskins supports House Joint Resolution 409, which calls for the Federal Reserve to pursue policies to eliminate inflation. Hoskins believes zero inflation would "help markets avoid distortions and imbalances, stabilize the business cycle, and promote the highest sustainable growth in our economy."

NO: Economics professor Michael Meeropol opposes House Joint Resolution 409. He believes that a move to zero inflation will not reduce unemployment and reduce the risk of inflation, it will not produce a higher possible rate of saving and investment, and it may increase income inequality by redistributing income to high-income people from low-income people.

In December 1913 the Federal Reserve Act became law. It created the Federal Reserve System (Fed), which began operations early in 1914. The Fed was designed as an institution that would counter the periodic financial panics that had plagued the U.S. economy. Indeed, the financial panic of 1907 led Congress to establish the National Monetary Commission. Following the Commission's studies, several proposals were advanced and, after extensive debate, the Fed was born.

As originally designed, the Fed had three purposes: "to give the country an elastic currency, provide facilities for discounting commercial credits, and improve the supervision of the banking system." Over time there have been many changes in the Fed. For example, the structure of the Board of Governors of the Fed, whose prime function is the formulation of monetary policy, was changed during the 1930s. Perhaps more important than changes in structure have been the changes in its goals. From the original three purposes, the Fed has extended its purview to include "stability and growth of the economy, a high level of employment, stability in the purchasing power of the dollar, and reasonable balance in transactions with foreign countries." In moving from narrow financial goals to broader macro-economic goals, the Fed has responded to legislative demands, primarily the Employment Act of 1946 and the Full Employment and Balanced Growth Act of 1978. While the Fed is usually described as an independent agency of the federal government, its structure, goals, operations, and, indeed, its very existence are determined by Congress and the president.

The conventional interpretation of the Fed is that it uses its tools—open market operations, discount rate changes, and changes in legal reserve requirements—to engage in countercyclical monetary policy. Thus, the Fed will purchase government securities, lower the discount rate, and/or lower legal reserve requirements in an effort to increase the money supply and lower interest rates in order to stimulate an economy operating at less than full employment. But this conventional interpretation has been under attack for some time. Conservatives, led by monetarists such as Milton Friedman and Anna Schwartz, have argued that the Fed has hurt rather than helped the cause of economic stability. The monetarists point to a number of instances in U.S. economic history where the Fed has made things worse and not better. The moral of U.S. economic history, according to the monetarists, is that the economy would be more stable if the Fed did not engage in countercyclical monetary policy.

House Joint Resolution 409 (HJR 409) can be seen as a logical extension of the monetarist position. Instead of a multiplicity of goals, HJR 409 mandates the Fed to pursue the single goal of eliminating inflation. Once inflation has been eliminated, the Fed is to maintain price stability. In the context of a simple monetarist framework, this would mean that the Fed would increase the money supply at approximately the same rate as the increase in the economy's ability to produce goods and services. In this way, the arguments presented in favor of HJR 409 by W. Lee Hoskins can be viewed as the conservative monetarist position regarding the proper role for the Fed, while the position taken by Michael Meeropol can be interpreted as the conventional liberal view for an activist Fed.

YES

W. Lee Hoskins

THE CASE FOR PRICE STABILITY

Mr. Chairman, I am pleased to appear before this Subcommittee to testify on House Joint Resolution 409. I strongly support your resolution directing the Federal Reserve System to make price stability the main goal of monetary policy. Ultimately, the price level is determined by monetary policy. While economic growth and the level of employment depend on our resources and the efficiency with which they are used, the aggregate price level is determined uniquely by the Federal Reserve.

Efficient utilization of our nation's resources requires a sound and predictable monetary policy. H.J. Res. 409 wisely directs the Federal Reserve to place price stability above other economic goals because price stability is the most important contribution the Federal Reserve can make to achieve full employment and maximum sustainable growth.

THE BENEFITS OF PRICE STABILITY

Price Stability Leads to Economic Stability
An important benefit of price stability is that it would stabilize the economy. High and variable inflation has always been one of the prime causes of financial crises and economic recessions. Certainly U.S. experience since World War II reaffirms the notion that inflation is a leading cause of recessions. Every recession in our recent history has been preceded by an outburst of cost and price pressures and the associated imbalances and distortions.

A monetary policy that strives for price stability, or zero inflation, as mandated by H.J. Res. 409 would help markets avoid distortions and imbalances, stabilize the business cycle, and promote the highest sustainable growth in our economy.

Price Stability Maximizes Economic Efficiency and Output
A market economy achieves maximum production and growth by allowing market prices to allocate resources. Money helps make markets work more

From W. Lee Hoskins, "The Case for Price Stability," *Economic Commentary*, Federal Reserve Bank of Cleveland (March 15, 1990). Copyright © 1990 by The Federal Reserve Bank of Cleveland. Reprinted by permission.

efficiently by reducing information and transactions costs, allowing for better decisions and improved productivity in resource use. Stabilizing the price level would make the monetary system operate more efficiently and would result in a higher standard of living for all Americans. Money is a standard of value. Much of our wealth is held either in the form of money or in claims denominated in and payable in money. Money represents a claim on a share of society's output. Stabilizing the price level protects the value of that claim, while inflation reduces it.

When we borrow, we promise to pay back the same amount with interest. When we allow unpredictable inflation, we arbitrarily take from the lender and give to the borrower. When this condition persists, we create an environment in which interest rates rise once to accommodate expected inflation and again to accommodate the increased risk involved in dealing with an uncertain inflation. When inflation rises and becomes uncertain, people are forced to develop elaborate, complicated, and expensive mechanisms to protect their wealth and income, such as new accounting systems, markets for trading financial futures and options, and cash managers who spend all their time trying to keep cash balances at zero. It would be inefficient to allow the length of a yardstick to vary over time, and it is inefficient to allow inflation to change the yardstick for economic value.

While the evidence that price stability maximizes production and employment is not as direct or as extensive as I would like, it is persuasive to me. One source of evidence can be found in the comparison of inflation and real growth across countries. A number of studies find that higher inflation or higher uncertainty about inflation is associated with lower real growth.

Inflation adds risk to decision-making and retards long-term investments. Inflation causes people to invest scarce resources in activities that have the sole purpose of hedging against inflation. Inflation interacts with the tax structure to stifle investment incentives.

More evidence comes from the extreme cases, the cases of hyperinflation. There we see that economic performance clearly deteriorates with high inflation. Both specialization and trade decline as small firms go bankrupt and people return to home production for a larger share of goods and services.

Even a relatively predictable and moderate rate of inflation can be quite harmful. During the seven years of our economic expansion since 1982, inflation has averaged between 3 and 4 percent. While that is low by the standards of the 1970s, the purchasing power of the dollar has been reduced by about 25 percent. Interest rates continue to include a premium for expected inflation and a premium for uncertainty about inflation.

Research at the Federal Reserve Bank of Cleveland indicates that a fully anticipated inflation, with no uncertainty about future inflation, would reduce the capital stock through taxes on capital income. Using 1985 as a benchmark and using conservative assumptions, we have estimated that the interaction of an expected 4 percent inflation rate with the tax on capital income leads to a present value income loss in the American economy of $600 billion or more. This is an amount much greater than the output loss typically associated with recessions. This estimate is from a policy of a perfectly anticipated 4 percent inflation and includes only the welfare loss associated with the failure to fully index taxes on capital income. It ignores the greater damage done to market efficiency by making our monetary yardstick variable.[1]

Even beyond these costs, I believe that inflation diminishes productivity growth. Because the worldwide slowdown in productivity growth occurred simultaneously with the acceleration in inflation and the oil price shocks, the evidence is very difficult to sort out satisfactorily. But if I am correct in believing that inflation inhibits productivity growth, the present value of lost output from even a very small reduction in the trend of productivity growth would far exceed the adjustment costs associated with the transition to price stability.

THE LIMITATIONS OF MONETARY POLICY

A Fallacious Trade-Off: Inflation for Prosperity

Unfortunately, over the years we have come to believe that we can prolong expansion, or avoid recession, with more inflation. A look at recent history reminds us that there is no trade-off between inflation and recession. Although we don't understand recessions completely, we have seen that they can be caused by monetary policy actions as well as by nonmonetary factors.

In the early 1980s we had recessions caused by monetary policy mistakes.

The policy mistake was the excessive monetary growth of the 1970s, which allowed accelerating inflation and rising interest rates and ultimately led to the need for disinflationary monetary policies. The disinflationary policies were necessary to get our economy back to an acceptable level of real activity. Yet even today, we are apt to blame the recessions on policies that reduced inflation instead of blaming the policies that created the inflation to begin with. While recessions will occur even under an ideal monetary policy, they will not be as frequent or as severe. With price stability, we would not have recessions induced by inflation and the subsequent need to eliminate it.

Even if we thought that eliminating the business cycle was a desirable and healthy long-term goal, I believe it is impossible to do so. There are several reasons that prevent us from using monetary policy to offset nonmonetary surprises. First, we cannot predict recessions. Second, monetary policy does not work immediately or predictably; it works with a lag, and the lag is variable and poorly understood.

The Crystal Ball Syndrome

The limitations of economic forecasting are well-known. Analysis of forecast errors has shown that we often don't know that a recession has begun until it is well under way. At any point in time, the range of uncertainty around economic forecasts of business activity for one quarter in the future is wide enough that both expansion and recession are plausible outcomes.

The people who make forecasts and those who use them often get a false sense of confidence because forecast errors are not distributed evenly over the business cycle. When the economy is doing well, forecasts that prosperity will continue are usually correct. And when the economy is performing poorly, forecasts that the slump will continue are also usually correct. The problem lies in predicting the turning points. However, the turning points are the things we must forecast to prevent recessions.

Monetary Policy's Long and Variable Lags

We don't know exactly how a particular policy action will affect the economy. Macroeconomic ideas about monetary policy and its effect on real output have changed profoundly in the last decade as we have recognized that the effect of monetary policy depends importantly on how economic agents form and alter expectations about policy.

Even if we could predict recessions and wanted to vary monetary policy to alleviate them, we still face an almost insurmountable problem—monetary policy operates with a lag. Moreover, the length of the lag varies over time, depending on conditions in the economy and on public perception of the policy process. The effect of today's monetary policy actions will probably not be felt for at least six to nine months, with the main influence perhaps two to three years in the future. The act of trying to prevent a recession may not only fail, but may also create a future recession—via an inflation—where otherwise there would not have been one.

Economic agents, businessmen and consumers alike, do not act in a vacuum. The political forces operating on a central bank make inflation always a possibility. Uncertainty about future inflation adds risk to future investments. Uncertainty about future inflation will raise real interest rates, drive investors away from long-term markets, and delay the very adjustments needed to end the recession. The more certain people are about the stability of future monetary policy, the more easily and quickly inflation can be reduced and the economy can recover.

Lessons We Should Have Learned

If we have learned anything about economic policymaking in the last 20 years, we ought to have learned to think about policy as a dynamic process. To claim that "in order to reduce inflation, we must have a recession," is a wrongheaded notion that completely ignores the ability of humans to adapt their expectations as the environment changes.

People do their best to forecast economic policies when they make decisions. If the central bank has a record of expanding the money supply in attempts to prevent recessions, people will come to anticipate the policy, setting off an acceleration of inflation and misallocation of resources that will lead to a recession.

An economy often goes into recession following an unexpected burst of inflation because people have made decisions that were based on an incorrect view of the future course of asset prices and economic activity. The central bank can help prevent the need for such adjustments by providing a stable price environment. Moreover, price stability will be the optimal setting for adjustments in business inventories and bad debts, should such adjustments be necessary.

THE IMPORTANCE OF ADOPTING HOUSE JOINT RESOLUTION 409

Sound Policies Minimize Uncertainty

Economic policies must have clear objectives, verifiable outcomes, and rules that are consistently adhered to in order to minimize uncertainty. Predictable, verifiable policies ensure that long-term planning and resource allocation decisions will be efficient. Sound policy thus requires a resolute focus on the long term and resistance to policies that, while expedient in the short run, introduce more uncertainty into an already unpredictable world. If enacted, H.J. Res. 409 would make a valuable contribution to this important objective. In the long run, inflation is the one economic variable for which monetary policy is unambiguously responsible. The zero inflation policy called for in H.J. Res. 409 satisfies the key requirements of sound policy: it is clear, it is verifiable, and it has consistent rules. Unlike other rates of inflation, zero inflation is a policy goal that will be understood by everyone.

Responding to Multiple Goals

The Federal Reserve Reform Act of 1977 amended the Federal Reserve Act so that it now requires the Federal Reserve " . . . to promote effectively the goals of maximum employment, stable prices, and moderate long-term interest rates." However, it is the Federal Reserve's responsibility to decide how best to pursue those goals.

Because of the multiplicity of goals established by Congress for the Federal Reserve, the Federal Reserve can choose which goal it emphasizes at any moment. Such discretion increases the likelihood that political and special-interest groups could try to influence the Federal Reserve to pursue the policy that is currently important to that group.

In this respect, the Federal Reserve's situation is different from that of West Germany's central bank, which is also independent. More than one goal is specified by law for that bank, but West German law states that the goal of price stability is to be given highest priority whenever another goal might conflict with maintaining price stability. This is a major reason why West Germany's price level only doubled between 1950 and 1988, while the U.S. price level quadrupled.

Since current law requires the Federal Reserve to promote maximum employment, stable prices, and moderate long-term interest rates, the Federal Reserve must choose a viable strategy to accomplish this mission. Two approaches seem plausible.

One approach would be for the central bank to try to achieve a balance among its three Congressionally mandated objectives. The Federal Reserve could use its own judgment about what balance among the objectives to pursue, and could change that balance from time to time, depending on its view of how the economy works and what course is broadly acceptable to the public. In essence, this is the practice that the Federal Reserve has followed. It has strived to balance desirable economic conditions such as full employment, economic growth, and low long-term interest rates with low rates of inflation. But the major drawback to this approach is its feasibility. To strike a balance among the mandated goals requires that they be reliably linked to one another. Furthermore, monetary policy would need to be capable of influencing simultaneously all these economic dimensions in the desired directions and quantities.

While monetary policy is capable of influencing the economy in the short to intermediate run, over long periods of time monetary policy can only affect the rate of inflation. The rate of inflation, in turn, affects all dimensions of economic performance, including output, employment, and interest rates. Maximum production and employment and low interest rates can be achieved only with price stability.

By its very nature, a balancing act among complex economic goals causes substantial confusion about the Federal Reserve's intentions. Such confusion could be avoided to a large degree if Congress or the Federal Reserve assigned priorities to the goals.

A more promising approach is to select one objective—the only one that the Federal Reserve can influence directly. Under the provisions of H.J. Res. 409, the Federal Reserve would seek to maintain a stable price level over time. Price stability is defined as an inflation rate so small that it does not systematically affect economic decisions. The definition may appear less specific than some would like, but I believe that the decisions of economic agents will be very important in monitoring success in achieving price stability.

In practice, the size of the inflation premium estimated to be found in long-term interest rates, surveys of the public's inflation expectations, and other market-generated measures of inflation expectations can be very useful. If policy is credible, both the inflation component and the inflation uncertainty risk premium would be eliminated from interest rates. Temporary and unforeseen factors will cause the price level to deviate from the desired course. It would be a mistake to try to keep some inflation index on target each and every quarter, or even each and every year.

Price stability can be achieved by holding the money supply (as measured by M2) on or close to a path which is consistent with price stability over long periods. The relationship between money and the price level over long periods of time is stable and strong. However, the link between money and the economy over periods perhaps as short as a year is loose enough to afford the Federal Reserve considerable leeway in responding to problems and crises—as long as economic agents believe that the future value of money will be stable. Clearly, this resolution would not prevent the Federal Reserve from providing liquidity in times of financial crises, such as the stock market crash in 1987.

Announcing a Commitment to Price Stability

Announcement of a commitment to price stability, as embodied in H.J. Res. 409, would enhance the ability of Congress to hold the Federal Reserve accountable for achieving the goal. Central-bank accountability is appropriate in a democracy and, in fact, Congress has the ultimate authority to change the Federal Reserve's goal.

A legislative commitment to price stability would also enhance the Federal Reserve's independence from political pressures as it pursued that goal. A commitment by Congress to price stability would reduce the effectiveness of political pressure to deviate from that goal. Thus, a distinction can be made between a central bank that is accountable for long-run performance and a central bank that can be influenced to pursue short-run goals that might be incompatible with desirable long-term economic performance.

The commitment to price stability supported by a legislative mandate would foster the credibility of the Federal Reserve. Improving the Federal Reserve's credibility would strengthen the expectation that prices will be stable, and would contribute to price and wage decisions that would make price stability easier to achieve and maintain.

ARGUMENTS AGAINST ADOPTING HOUSE JOINT RESOLUTION 409 ARE WEAK

What About the Transition Costs?

A commitment by Congress and the Federal Reserve to achieve price stability would entail adjustment costs. Adjustment costs would arise from two sources: contractual obligations and the credibility problem, or uncertainty about whether price stability would be achieved and maintained. The contractual costs can be alleviated with an appropriate adjustment period. H.J. Res. 409 recognizes that abrupt policy changes can be disruptive and provides a phase-in period to help reduce adjustment costs.

Much of our day-to-day economic activity is conducted under contracts and commitments that extend over longer periods of time and that embody the expectations of a continuing moderate inflation rate. Most of these contracts will expire in the next few years. The disruption to business and the arbitrary wealth redistribution of an abrupt adjustment to price stability would be greatly reduced by an appropriate phase-in period. H.J. Res. 409 gives us five years to get to price stability—a period long enough to reduce substantially the transition costs.

The second set of adjustment costs emanates from the expectations of economic agents. As the Congressional Budget Office points out in its recent *Economic and Budget Outlook*, if everyone believed that inflation would be reduced to zero, and planned accordingly, these costs would be very low. The Federal Reserve has stated that it intends to reduce inflation to zero or to low levels, but it has not committed to a specific timetable for eliminating inflation, or to a plan for doing so. The result is that the public in general and the markets in particular wonder just how serious we are in those intentions, or whether we will switch our priorities to some other goal, as we have in the past.

Large-Scale Econometric Model Estimates of the Transition Cost

Economists have not made much progress in estimating the transition costs of eliminating inflation. Frequently, econometric models that embody a large number of complex relationships and variables are used to estimate the adjustment costs.

For manageability, econometric models are built with many simplifying assumptions, one of which is the presumption that economic agents are backward-looking in the way they form and change expectations. In these models, expectations, which in effect determine adjustment costs, are formed from past experience, and are changed only slowly as the future unfolds.

The presumption that expectations change only slowly inevitably generates estimates of high transition costs. The real question about a change in policy as specified by H.J. Res. 409 is how forward-looking economic agents would behave under a fully credible and fully understood policy change. Backward-looking models are relatively useless in answering this question.

In almost every case, such models are constructed to display the effects that are consistent with the model builder's theories and biases. Almost all of the large models are based on the dual notion that the only way to eliminate inflation is to raise the unemployment rate. Naturally, these models will find that eliminating inflation is very costly. These exercises have been conducted many times in the past, and they have consistently over-estimated the costs of eliminating infla-tion and ignored the benefits of doing so. I might also observe that those who re-ally believe the analytical structures con-tained in these models logically should advocate an acceleration of inflation be-cause the models would predict great benefits from doing so.

One member of the Council of Eco-nomic Advisers, an expert on such mat-ters, has developed large econometric models with sluggish resource adjust-ment induced by labor contracts. Even in these models, there is almost no short-run cost to eliminating inflation with a credible policy change. The reason is simply that, in these models, people are assumed to change their behavior in re-sponse to the policy change.

As the CBO study states, " . . . inflation could be reduced relatively painlessly by lowering inflationary expectations." A commitment by the Congress and the Federal Reserve would enhance cred-ibility and convince economic agents to begin to base decisions on gradual elim-ination of inflation over a five-year pe-riod. The transitional costs presented elsewhere in the CBO study then would be grossly overestimated.

A consistent commitment to a long-run policy goal of price stability is im-portant. One of the worst things we could do is to eliminate inflation for a while and then return to high inflation later. H.J. Res. 409 would contribute to an important change in the policy pro-cess, focusing it toward consistent long-run goals and away from reactions to each new report of economic activity. Each policy action would become part of a policy process that is consistent with long-run price stability.

Fiscal Policy Is No Obstacle to Price Stability

Federal budget deficits should not com-promise either the Federal Reserve's goal of price stability or the adoption of a specific timetable to achieve it. I do not mean to suggest or imply that current fiscal policy is ideal, appropriate, or the result of bad monetary policy. Savings are too low, at least partly because of budget deficits, and measures to address our savings shortfall must include mea-sures to reduce the deficit. However, while we strive for better fiscal policy, we should recognize that monetary pol-icy cannot offset whatever harm may result from fiscal policy; indeed, it can only add to those costs.

We are all familiar with the argument that large federal budget deficits cause high interest rates, forcing the Fed to ease monetary policy in order to keep interest rates at levels consistent with full employment. This argument ignores the fact that both the federal budget deficit and, more important, government spending, at least measured relative to the economy, have been falling for the past several years and should continue to do so.

There is, of course, legitimate concern that the progress in deficit and expen-diture reduction might cease or even be reversed, for any number of reasons. How should such a reversal influence monetary policy? Even if fiscal policy choices were to put upward pressure on interest rates, and there is little con-sensus among economists that this is the case, it is far from clear that the Federal Reserve can do anything to alleviate the economic consequences of that problem. Ultimately, it is real interest rates that affect the consumption and production decisions of individuals and businesses and the allocation of resources over time. Real rates of return are based on the productivity of labor, capital, and other real assets in a society, and have very little, if any, connection with monetary policy.

In an inflationary environment, nominal rates of return include an inflation premium to compensate lenders for being repaid in money of reduced purchasing power. The correlation between monetary policy and nominal interest rates that dominates discussion in the financial press tells us next to nothing about the relationship between monetary policy and the real interest rates that govern the allocation of resources over time. Every movement in the federal funds rate does not produce equivalent changes in real interest rates, in the productivity of our capital stock, or in any of the other important real variables that affect economic activity. The fact that monetary policy exerts relatively direct control over the federal funds rate does not imply that real interest rates can, similarly, be controlled by monetary policy.

It is unnecessary and undesirable for sound monetary policy choices to await sound fiscal policy choices. Sound fiscal policy decisions, like sound private economic decisions, require the stable inflation environment that H.J. Res. 409 would direct the Federal Reserve to provide. The tax-related distortions and economic complexities associated with even stable, positive rates of inflation argue strongly for price stability.

CONCLUSION

If H.J. Res. 409 is enacted and the Federal Reserve commits to an explicit plan for price stability, the transition period will soon be over, and any costs that arise because of this policy change will be outweighed by the benefits. These benefits will be large and permanent, and will far outweigh the costs of getting there.

H.J. Res. 409, if enacted, would be a milestone in economic policy legislation because it would shift the focus of monetary policy away from short-term fine-tuning to the long term, where it belongs. It would enforce accountability for the one vital objective that the Federal Reserve can achieve. It would officially sanction those sometimes unpopular short-run policy actions that most certainly are in our nation's long-term interest. It would make clear that the Federal Reserve cannot achieve maximum output and employment without achieving price stability. I fully support House Joint Resolution 409.

NOTE

1. David Altig and Charles T. Carlstrom. "Expected Inflation and the Welfare Losses from Taxes on Capital Income," manuscript, Federal Reserve Bank of Cleveland, February 1990.

NO

Michael Meeropol

ZERO INFLATION: PRESCRIPTION FOR RECESSION

I recently received a letter that was sent out to many economists (and perhaps other professionals) from Representative Stephen L. Neal (D-NC) asking for our opinions about a proposed congressional resolution (H.J.R. 409) that would order the Federal Reserve System to make zero inflation the "primary and dominant objective of monetary policy." The *Wall Street Journal* also has taken up the call, noting that Fed Chairman Alan Greenspan "testified in support of Mr. Neal's resolution and said its goal—zero inflation within five years—was attainable."

I submit that virtually every one of the several assertions justifying the resolution is based on an erroneous reading of recent history. Most importantly, they fail to demonstrate any understanding of the difference between real and nominal interest rates.

The preamble of the proposed resolution claims that zero inflation will:
• reduce interest rates to—and maintain them at—their lowest possible levels;

• promote the highest possible sustainable level of employment;

• generate the maximum sustainable rate of economic growth;

• encourage the highest possible rate of saving and investment, thereby boosting productivity and enhancing our standard of living; and

• help stabilize the economy, thereby minimizing risk and uncertainty in economic decision-making and abolishing the need to devote resources, time, and energy to predicting and coping with the consequences of inflation.

As for the first point, it is not true that moving to a zero inflation rate will lower interest rates. If the experience of the 1980s is any indication, there will be a period of rising real interest rates followed by a period of higher than usual real rates. A simple comparison of changes in the consumer price

From Michael Meeropol, "Zero Inflation: Prescription for Recession," *Challenge*, vol. 33, no. 1 (January/February 1990). Copyright © 1989 by M. E. Sharpe, Inc., 80 Business Park Drive, Armonk, NY 10504. Reprinted by permission.

Table 1

Nineteen Years of Real Interest Rates

Year	Column 1 Nominal Interest Rate (prime rate)	Column 2 Inflation Rate (CPI)	Column 3 Real Interest Rate (col. 1–col. 2)	Column 4 Unemployment Rate (all workers)
1970	7.91	5.7	2.21	4.8
1971	5.72	4.4	1.32	5.8
1972	5.25	3.2	2.05	5.5
1973	8.03	6.2	1.83	4.8
1974	10.81	11.0	1.81	5.6
1975	7.86	9.1	1.24	8.5
1976	6.84	5.8	1.04	7.7
1977	6.83	6.5	.33	7.1
1978	9.06	7.6	1.46	6.1
1979	12.67	11.3	1.37	5.8
1980	15.27	13.5	1.77	7.1
1981	18.87	10.3	8.57	7.6
1982	14.86	6.2	8.46	9.7
1983	10.79	3.2	7.59	9.6
1984	12.04	4.3	7.74	7.5
1985	9.93	3.6	6.33	7.2
1986	8.33	1.9	6.43	7.0
1987	8.22	3.6	4.62	6.2
1988	9.32	4.0	5.32	5.5

Sources: Column 1, *Economic Report of the President,* 1989, p. 390; Column 2, *Ibid,* p. 378. Column 4, *Ibid,* p. 532. 1988 data from *Survey of Current Business,* Vol. 69, No. 3 (March 1989), col. 1, p. S-10, col. 2, p. S-5, col. 4, p. S-14.

index and the prime lending rate shows us the last nineteen years of real interest rates (see Table 1).

A substantial rise in real interest rates as a result of Fed tightening even more intensely than in the last two years will undoubtedly reinforce the squeeze on heavily indebted small businesses (especially in agriculture) that has been the hallmark of this recovery.

The business failure rate, which usually falls during recoveries, actually rose to unprecedented levels in the 1983–86 period before declining slightly in 1987. We can expect more of the same if a move toward zero inflation raises the real interest rate.

Zero inflation will not reduce unemployment and minimize the risk of recession. Unemployment averaged 6.17 percent in the inflationary 1970s and 7.49 percent in the low inflation 1980s. Even if we omit the years 1980–82, unemployment averages 7.16 percent in 1983–88. This is true despite the fact that there were more quarters of recession in the 1970s than in the 1980s. The only way we have ever been able to lower inflation in this country is by increasing unemployment.

Claiming that zero inflation will create the highest *sustainable* level of employment is a tidy way of avoiding the evidence, because one can always say that previous low levels of unemployment were "not sustainable." It is important to note that I am not asserting a long-run stable trade-off between inflation and unemployment, only that there are successive short-run trade-offs, each within a historical context. I predict that a move by the Fed toward zero inflation will subject the economy to a short-run trade-off similar to that experienced in the period of the post-1979 Volcker anti-inflation strategy.

LOW INFLATION = SLOWER GROWTH

Meantime, the low inflation 1980s has seen only a marginally faster rate of productivity growth than the high inflation 1970s, a slower rate of real GNP growth, and a slower growth in real wages. Real GNP in 1979 was 31.7 percent higher than in 1969. Real GNP in 1988 was 26 percent higher than in 1979. That averaged out to 3.17 percent per year in the '70s and 2.89 percent in the '80s.

Real wages rose an average of only 0.26 percent in the 1970s, but actually fell an average of 0.44 percent in 1980–87. Even if we omit 1980 from the calculation of the 1980s, we observe an average growth rate of 0.07 percent for the years 1981–87. Productivity growth averaged 1.29 percent in the 1970s and 1.38 percent in the period 1980–87.

Some may object to a comparison between the 1980s and the 1970s since inflation remained quite high for the first two years of the '80s, but we must remember that the Fed's anti-inflationary policy had been in place since November 1979. Even though it took two years for the policy to begin to work on the rate of inflation, the rise in unemployment was already apparent in 1980 and the rise in both unemployment and real interest rates was very clear in 1981. It is the *policy* of

attempting to reach zero inflation that I am attacking, and my evidence is based on our experience with a tight anti-inflationary monetary policy that lasted for the entire decade of the 1980s.

It is also a mistake to suggest that zero inflation will encourage the highest possible rate of saving and investment. The 1970s had higher rates of saving and investment than the 1980s. Comparing saving rates is probably unnecessary, given the widespread publicity of the spectacular failure of supply-side economics to raise the personal saving rate, but investment as a percentage of GNP averaged 16.41 percent in the 1970s and 15.8 percent in the 1980s.

Investment decisions depend on expected rates of return that depend in large part on the current and most recent rate of growth of demand. If the effort to achieve zero inflation raises real interest rates dramatically, it will slow down the growth of demand and thus be associated with lower rates of investment.

The argument that a zero rate of inflation will stabilize the economy would only be true *after* real interest rates fall. So far in the 1980s, they have yet to fall to their historical levels. Until they do, the effort to reach zero inflation will be associated with continued instability. We must remember that consistently achieving any *anticipated* rate of inflation will promote stability. Conversely, when the rate of inflation (whatever it is) is unanticipated, that is destabilizing.

Even if it were to become the policy of the Fed to reach zero inflation, that does not mean business can immediately stop devoting resources to predicting inflation. Even after the unlikely event of the Fed achieving zero inflation, each separate business will still have to devote resources to predicting how their *particu-*

lar costs (specific input prices and their labor costs) and their *specific* products' prices *deviate* from the general rate of inflation, whatever that rate might be.

DON'T GET ME WRONG

In making these arguments, I do not wish to be misunderstood. Obviously, volatile swings in the rate of inflation can produce tremendous uncertainties and hurt real economic performance. Also, because of the differing ability of individuals to insulate themselves from the effects of inflation by indexing their incomes, it would probably be a good thing if we could wave a magic wand and get zero inflation with a lock-step drop in nominal interest rates to prevent a rise in real interest rates.

It was one of the predictions of the rational expectations school that a credible anti-inflation policy would produce such an immediate fall in nominal interest rates. As soon as the Fed's anti-inflation policy was deemed "credible" by the financial community, borrowers would refuse to pay inflation premia on their loans, and lenders would cease insisting on them because they would correctly anticipate the success of the Fed's policy.

The fact that this did not happen in the early 1980s and the persistence of high real interest rates to the end of the decade—even after the Fed put the economy through the wringer of 1981–82—is evidence that the rational expectations approach is incorrect. This experience should be a strong warning to those who support H.J. Res. 409 because they expect an immediate response to the Fed's efforts.

It is also important to note that I am not asserting that the rate of inflation is always negatively correlated with the real interest rate. I am merely suggesting that the inflation premia built into any interest rates are more likely correlated with the recent past than with the predictions of "rational economic theory" about the "credibility" of the Fed's declared policy.

Thus, should Congress adopt the resolution, nominal interest rates will not fall as fast as the rate of inflation, if they fall at all. In fact, they will undoubtedly rise in the short-run until the recession becomes apparent. This is particularly true given the continued expansiveness of Federal fiscal policy.

NEAL'S ARGUMENT

Congressman Neal included in his questionnaire a speech he made on the House floor on August 1, 1989. In it, he attempted to anticipate some of the criticisms I have mentioned. He noted that many " . . . fear that the cost in terms of recession and slow growth would be intolerable." He then argued that inflationary surges are followed by big increases in unemployment.

Neal then correctly anticipated the counter that this unemployment is caused by draconian anti-inflationary policies rather than the inflation itself. His only argument to that was "the public in developed economies will sooner or later turn against governments that tolerate rising inflation, and elect leaders willing to rein it in, even at the cost of recession."

But, in the United States, the voters never turned against rising inflation *in support of* what turned out to be the Volcker-Carter-Reagan policy. No one elected Paul Volcker to be head of the Fed and to put the economy through the cold shower anti-inflation treatment of

1979–83. Jimmy Carter was defeated in large part because of his role in permitting the *recession* of 1980, not the inflation of the previous year.

Ronald Reagan was elected on a promise to cut taxes, cut inflation, cut unemployment, restart our productivity engines, stimulate investment, increase saving, and ultimately balance the budget by 1984. He was not elected to preside over the worst recession since the 1930s. The utter failure of Reaganomics on its own terms has been obscured by the length of the recovery from the 1981–82 recession, but even that long recovery has not made the '80s a better decade than the 1970s in terms of economic growth, investment, and unemployment.

Recipients of interest income have benefited most from the reduction in inflation. (Net interest as a percentage of personal income reached a maximum of 10.9 percent in 1979, jumped to 12 percent in 1980, to 13.3 percent in 1981, and peaked at 14.3 percent in 1985 and 1986. In 1988, it was still at 14 percent.) Debtors who contracted their debt during the years of high nominal interest rates (1978 to 1984) have been particularly hard hit by that reduction. Included in this group, of course, has been the biggest debtor in the country, the federal government.

As Robert Eisner showed in *How Real Is the Federal Deficit?* (Free Press, 1986), inflation reduces the real burden of the federal debt on the taxpayers. The reduction of inflation has raised that real burden in the 1980s. A zero inflation rate will end the automatic erosion in the real burden of the debt, increasing again the advantages of interest recipients while raising the interest burden on the average taxpayer.

It is not a very popular point to make, but inflation in the 1970s actually bene-fited the majority of people in the country because the majority of people in the country were (and still are) net debtors. Inflation made property owners with low interest mortgages wealthy by reducing their real interest rates (in some instances to negative values) while the values of their homes rose faster than inflation. It also eased the burden of debt on small businesses, permitting a relatively rapid expansion of activity. This is why investment as a percentage of GNP was actually higher in the inflationary 1970s than in the low inflation 1980s.

Obviously, a stated policy of moderate inflation would not produce this same result once inflation premia had been built into interest rates. Here, however, an easy money policy by the Fed can actually force nominal interest rates down or at least slow their rise, permitting that moderate inflation to once again produce a relatively painless redistribution of income back from the rentiers to the rest of us.

Given a real choice between the slow erosion of the real burden of debt associated with moderate inflation and the unprecedented real interest rates and the accompanying high levels of unemployment we have experienced for the last decade, perhaps American voters might surprise Mr. Neal. However, given what passes for economic discourse by our politicians, it is most unlikely our voters will ever be given such a clear choice.

Finally, it is essential that we recognize that associated with a move toward zero inflation would be an increased redistribution of income away from low income people toward high income people. Low and moderate income people are net debtors. Net creditors are generally high income people and heavily cap-italized financial institutions, like insurance companies. Though the poor are not able to carry much debt because they usually do not qualify, they are harmed by the unemployment associated with the anti-inflationary struggle.

The 1980s has seen a significant drift toward greater inequality in the distribution of income and in the quality of life for our low income citizens. A rising percentage of American children live in poverty. Traditional income redistribution programs for the poor have been cut in real terms, even in the era of lower inflation. The poor kept pace with the rest of society during the inflationary 1970s in terms of health, nutrition, housing, and income support. The percentage of the population living in poverty did not rise dramatically despite the inflation of the 1970s, yet it did rise despite the reduction of inflation in the 1980s.

I hope the majority of my colleagues in the profession will let their member of Congress know that the move to zero inflation would be exactly the wrong kind of medicine for the economy. It appears that the economy will enter a recession some time in 1990 or at least experience very sluggish growth. This is not the time to compound that sluggishness with a big run-up in real interest rates.

We are still waiting for the end of the "short-run" transition from high inflationary expectations in the early '80s to the low inflationary expectations of the late '80s. Meanwhile, real interest rates have remained above their historic averages for the entire decade. Do we have to, indeed, wait for death before the "long-run" and low real interest rates arrive?

POSTSCRIPT

Should the Federal Reserve Target Zero Inflation?

Hoskins begins his statement of support for House Joint Resolution 409 (HJR 409) by asserting that the behavior of the aggregate price level, the rate of inflation, is uniquely determined by the Federal Reserve. He further asserts that "the most important contribution the Federal Reserve can make to achieve full employment and maximum sustainable growth" is to achieve price stability. Price stability or zero inflation promotes these ends by "helping markets avoid distortions and imbalances." Hoskins cites three reasons for adopting HJR 409: It specifies a policy that minimizes uncertainty, eliminates multiple goals and posits instead a single goal that the Federal Reserve can achieve, and enhances Federal Reserve accountability to Congress. Hoskins admits that there may be some transition costs but these are minimized by HJR 409, for it provides for a five-year transition to zero inflation.

Meeropol argues that the claims made on behalf of HJR 409 are not supported by recent economic history. He also argues that low or zero inflation will do little to increase saving and investment and stabilize the economy. These conclusions are both based on a comparison of the high-inflation 1970s and the low-inflation 1980s. Finally, Meeropol argues that inflation tends to benefit debtors at the expense of creditors and, given that low-income persons are net debtors, the elimination of inflation will work to the benefit of high-income creditors. This increase in economic inequality will be made worse if the reduction of inflation generates a recession, for it will be low-income persons who will experience unemployment.

For a complete discussion of the Federal Reserve System, see *The Federal Reserve System: Its Purposes and Functions* (AMS Press, 1984). For a critical evaluation of the Federal Reserve, see *Secrets of the Temple: How the Federal Reserve Runs the Country*, by William Greider (Simon & Schuster, 1987). HJR 409 is reprinted on page 56 of the January/February 1990 issue of *Challenge*. For additional arguments by Hoskins in support of HJR 409 and zero inflation, see "Defending Zero Inflation: All For Naught," *Economic Commentary*, Federal Reserve Bank of Cleveland (April 1, 1991) and "Some Observations on Central Bank Accountability," *Economic Commentary*, Federal Reserve Bank of Cleveland (April 15, 1991). For further arguments against HJR 409 and zero inflation, see S. Roo, "Response to a Defense of Zero Inflation," *Quarterly Review*, Federal Reserve Bank of Minneapolis (Spring 1991).

ISSUE 12

Does the United States Save Enough?

YES: Fred Block, from "Bad Data Drive Out Good: The Decline of Personal Savings Reexamined," *Journal of Post Keynesian Economics* (Fall 1990)

NO: William D. Nordhaus, from "What's Wrong With a Declining National Saving Rate?" *Challenge* (January/February 1990)

ISSUE SUMMARY

YES: Sociology professor Fred Block argues that savings should be calculated using the Federal Reserve's flow of funds data rather than the conventional National Income and Product Accounts data, and that the former data indicate that savings are adequate.
NO: Economics professor William D. Nordhaus believes that increased amounts of saving and investment are necessary if the United States is to avoid a substantial decrease in its standard of living.

When Ben Franklin said "A penny saved is a penny earned," he was extolling the virtues of individual thrift. To spend less than is earned, to save, means that a person can have funds available for future spending. If the savings can be lent to someone else and interest earned on the amount lent, then future consumption could increase by even more than the amount saved. However, to extol the benefits of saving is not to declare how much should be saved.

When the discussion shifts from the individual perspective to the national economy, much the same argument can be made concerning the benefits of saving. In the case of the national economy, savings become investment, and investment means that the nation's capital stock is increasing. This, in turn, means that the nation's ability to produce goods and services increases. Thus, more future production and consumption is possible.

But this analysis suggests that it is always better to save more. There is an opposite side to the saving coin. Because saving is not automatically translated into investment, it is possible that increased saving may decrease total spending in the economy, and the reduction in total spending or aggregate demand may mean a decrease in current production and an increase in unemployment. So it is possible to save too little (impeding investment and future production and consumption) or too much (generating a recession).

Before deciding whether the national saving rate is too high or too low, it must be measured. This is no easy task for several reasons. First, saving is an activity undertaken by various sectors of the economy. For example, a business firm wishing to invest in a new factory can borrow the funds from or use the savings of four different sectors. It can borrow or use the savings of individuals (personal savings), the savings of other business firms (business savings), the savings of the federal, state, and local governments (government savings), or the savings of foreigners (foreign savings). A second complicating factor is that there are different ways of measuring the amount of savings available from the four sectors, particularly personal savings. The conventional approach is to use the National Income and Product Accounts, where personal savings is defined as the difference between personal income and personal outlays. Another, nonconventional, approach relies on the flow of funds data generated by the Federal Reserve. Fred Block uses this alternative approach, which yields a much higher estimate of personal savings, and concludes that the United States is saving enough. William D. Nordhaus relies on the conventional approach to measuring personal savings in his argument that the United States saves too little and that action should be taken to raise the saving rate.

YES

Fred Block

BAD DATA DRIVE OUT GOOD: THE DECLINE OF PERSONAL SAVINGS REEXAMINED

The adequacy of private savings in the United States has become a major topic of debate among economists. The consensus view is that private savings—and especially household savings—declined sharply during the 1980s. This view is given strong support by data in the National Income and Product Accounts (NIPA), which show that personal savings as a percentage of disposable personal income dropped from 7.5 percent in 1981 to a low of 3.2 percent in 1987. However, the consensus view has been challenged by a number of economists who have raised questions about the appropriate way to measure private savings (Eisner, 1989; Lipsey and Kravis, 1987; Blecker, 1990).

This paper also challenges the conventional view by examining several problems with the NIPA and by turning to an alternative data source—the Federal Reserve Board's Flow of Fund data. With some modifications, the Federal Reserve data can be used to generate an Alternative Personal Savings (APS) measure that is conceptually similar to the NIPA measure. Significantly, these two measures are very similar for the period from 1953 to 1974, and then they diverge sharply. By 1987—the low point for the NIPA figure—the alternative measure is three times as great as the NIPA measure.

Since personal savings represent a large share of total private savings, whether personal savings in 1988 were $144.7 billion or $367.3 billion has extremely serious implications for economic analysis and economic policy. The former figure supports a view of money capital in the United States as an extremely scarce resource. The latter figure suggests that money capital in the United States is abundant relative to the opportunities for productive investment. These different interpretations will be addressed in the paper's conclusion.

From Fred Block, "Bad Data Drive Out Good: The Decline of Personal Savings Reexamined," *Journal of Post Keynesian Economics*, vol. 13, no. 1 (Fall 1990). Copyright © 1990 by M. E. Sharpe, Inc., 80 Business Park Drive, Armonk, NY 10504. Reprinted by permission.

PERSONAL SAVINGS IN THE NIPA

Personal savings are calculated by subtracting the total of personal consumption expenditures from disposable personal income. It is well known that such a residual calculated by subtracting one large figure from another large figure is extremely sensitive to small changes in either of the large numbers. For example, if the disposable personal income figure for 1983 were 10 percent higher, the personal savings figure would increase by more than 217 percent. Both disposable personal income and personal consumption expenditures are estimated on the basis of a great deal of direct data, but the government economists make the best approximations they can for a variety of components where direct data are insufficient or inaccurate.

There would be no problem with this procedure if the government economists had a means to cross-check their data against other data sources. As we shall see, when such a comparison is carried out with Federal Reserve Board Flow of Funds' data on financial savings by households, it becomes clear that there is something seriously wrong with the NIPA data.

One problem with the NIPA data centers on the treatment of pension and welfare funds. The architects of the National Income accounts decided to include private employer contributions to pension and social insurance funds, categorized as "other labor income," as a component of personal income, despite the fact that these funds do not go directly into employees' paychecks. At the time that the accounts were constructed, all of these flows were tiny, but with the expansion of pension and health insurance, these items are now enormous.

While the initial decision was logical in terms of the overall system of accounts, it creates a problem for accurately measuring personal savings.

The problem is that the income individuals actually receive—and that can be used for savings—in any given year are the benefits that employees or retirees receive from these funds. These benefit flows are not included in personal income in order to avoid double counting. However, it turns out that employer contributions exceeded benefits for every year until 1984, and since then benefits have risen more rapidly than contributions. By 1988, benefits exceeded contributions by $93.8 billion (*Survey of Current Business*, July 1989). Since the annual growth of private pension fund assets, exclusive of capital gains, has been healthy in this period, it would seem that NIPA procedures understate the total contribution of private pensions to personal savings.[1]

At the same time, the NIPA data neglect employer contributions to those public sector pension funds at the state or local levels that are organized in the same way as private pension funds. In 1985, according to one recent study, including public sector pension funds in the accounts would raise NIPA savings as a percentage of disposable income by almost two full percentage points (Holloway, 1989, p. 60). In 1988, this adjustment would increase NIPA savings rate as a percentage of GNP to 4.4 percent.[2]

Another serious problem with the NIPA data is the classic problem of underreporting of legally earned income. During the Reagan years, IRS funding was cut back severely and the probability of being audited diminished substantially.[3] At the same time, personal enrichment was glorified as the ultimate value. In such a context, it seems likely that tax cheating increased, despite the reduction in marginal rates in 1981. If the chances of being caught diminish substantially, a 0 percent marginal rate will be preferred to a 25 percent marginal rate. However, an increase in the rate of noncompliance with the tax code will mean that NIPA figures understate personal income and personal savings.

The problem of underreporting income is largely concentrated in nonfarm proprietorships, since most wage and salary income is reported directly to the IRS by employers. In its 1985 comprehensive revision of the national accounts, Bureau of Economic Analysis [BEA] economists made substantial upward revisions of nonfarm proprietor income, which had the effect of increasing the personal savings rate above the previously published level by 1 percentage point per year for 1978–80.[4] . . .

A final problem with the NIPA data is its treatment of spending by households on real estate, including the purchase of owner-occupied housing. In theory, the personal savings figure should include both the acquisition of financial and real assets by households, since only consumption expenditures are being subtracted from disposable income. However, the national income accountants treat owner-occupiers as though they rented their homes and an imputed rent figure for owner-occupiers ($339.3 billion in 1988) is added to actual rents of tenants as an important component of personal consumption expenditures. Some fraction of this imputed rent is also credited to owner-occupiers as a component of personal income, but with the inclusion of depreciation, this figure has actually been negative in recent years.[5] It is difficult to sort out how these figures relate to the actual housing expenditures of owner-occupiers, but the BEA figure seems too high. Moreover, the final cost of owner-occupied housing as a percentage of disposable personal income rose from 4.4 percent in 1960 to 5.2 percent in 1988. While the issue of housing does not play a central role in the rest of this paper, it is of critical importance for comparisons of savings rates across countries. Procedures for handling owner-occupied housing and imputing rents vary across countries, and it is entirely possible that these differences in methodology explain a portion of the substantial differences in savings rates across countries.[6]

ALTERNATIVE DATA

There is an alternative data source that can be used to assess these problems with the NIPA data on personal savings. The Federal Reserve Board [FRB] compiles data on the amount of money flowing from households into a variety of financial instruments. These data are also largely indirect; in analyzing data from banks, insurance companies, pension funds, and so forth, the board's economists attribute to households those flows that are not otherwise accounted for.[7] These data are readily available; they are published annually in the *Economic Report to the President* in a table entitled "Savings by Individuals."[8]

In this series, the Federal Reserve economists add the increase in financial assets by households to net investments in housing and consumer durables, and then subtract increases in personal debt, such as home mortgages and consumer credit. Conceptually, this series is comparable to the NIPA series in that both are measures of net savings; an allowance for the depreciation of physical assets is not included.[9] However, the FRB economists differ from the NIPA economists in treating purchases of consumer durables as a form of savings.

However, since the underlying issue in the debate about savings is the ability of households to provide a financial surplus that is available for investment by the business sector, it makes sense to focus only on the net acquisition of financial assets by households. The alternative personal savings figure presented in Table 1 modifies the FRB data by dropping out purchases of consumer durables, spending on owner-occupied housing, and the net increases in mortgage debt.

Mortgage debt is subtracted out for reasons of symmetry. It would be illogical to exclude the accumulation by households of tangible assets—housing —while including the liabilities (the mortgages) incurred in purchasing those assets. In fact, the quantity of the mortgage debt directly reflects not just flows of savings into real estate, but the annual appreciation of real estate values. In order to balance the annual increase in mortgage debt appropriately, one would have to compare it to the annual change in the total value of owner-occupied housing—a figure that rose rapidly in the 1981–88 period.

One can also gain some leverage on this issue by thinking about the comparison between the United States and a country such as Japan, where mortgage financing is scarce. In the absence of readily available mortgages, many housing transactions are financed through loans from other family members (Makin, 1986, p. 103). A buyer might provide 40 percent of the purchase price at the time of sale, and then promise to pay off the

Table 1

NIPA Savings versus APS

Year	APS (billions of $)	NIPA/ GNP	APS/ GNP	Difference as % of NIPA
1947	6.6	2.2%	2.8%	− 26.9%
1948	3.2	4.2%	1.2%	71.2%
1949	3.4	2.8%	1.3%	54.1%
1950	4.6	4.4%	1.6%	63.5%
1951	13.7	5.0%	4.1%	17.5%
1952	20.0	4.9%	5.7%	− 14.9%
1953	18.1	5.0%	4.9%	1.6%
1954	14.5	4.4%	3.9%	11.6%
1955	15.5	3.9%	3.8%	3.1%
1956	23.6	5.0%	5.5%	− 10.8%
1957	23.0	5.0%	5.1%	− 1.3%
1958	25.3	5.3%	5.5%	− 4.1%
1959	20.7	4.4%	4.2%	5.0%
average 1947–59		4.4%	3.8%	13.0%
1960	22.6	4.0%	4.4%	− 8.7%
1961	26.3	4.7%	4.9%	− 5.6%
1962	27.4	4.5%	4.8%	− 5.8%
1963	26.8	4.1%	4.4%	− 8.9%
1964	34.3	4.8%	5.3%	− 8.9%
1965	34.9	4.9%	4.9%	− 1.7%
1966	42.5	4.7%	5.5%	− 18.1%
1967	47.4	5.5%	5.8%	− 5.1%
1968	42.7	4.8%	4.8%	− 0.5%
1969	35.4	4.4%	3.7%	16.1%
average 1960–69		4.6%	4.8%	− 4.7%
1970	55.5	5.7%	5.5%	3.8%
1971	58.2	6.0%	5.3%	12.2%
1972	67.2	5.1%	5.5%	− 9.4%
1973	95.4	6.5%	7.0%	− 7.2%
1974	81.9	6.6%	5.6%	15.3%
1975	134.5	6.5%	8.4%	− 28.6%
1976	137.3	5.4%	7.7%	− 43.4%
1977	152.3	4.6%	7.7%	− 67.9%
1978	152.8	4.9%	6.8%	− 38.7%
1979	168.3	4.7%	6.7%	− 42.5%
average 1970–79		5.6%	6.6%	− 20.6%
1980	208.5	5.0%	7.6%	− 52.3%
1981	206.0	5.2%	6.7%	− 29.2%
1982	247.8	4.9%	7.8%	− 61.0%
1983	316.2	3.8%	9.3%	−142.1%
1984	319.4	4.4%	8.5%	− 94.6%
1985	287.5	3.1%	7.2%	−129.3%
1986	331.6	3.0%	7.8%	−165.5%
1987	316.3	2.3%	7.0%	−210.7%
1988	367.3	3.0%	7.5%	−153.8%
average 1980–88		3.8%	7.7%	−110.6%

Source: All data are from the *Economic Report to the President, 1990.*

other 60 percent over the next twenty years at a particular interest rate. Such private transactions, however, would have no impact at all on the household savings rate, since one household's assets are directly offset by the other's liabilities. In other words, the transfer of existing housing between individuals does not influence the total supply of household savings available for other purposes. The same would appear to be true even when the transactions are mediated through banking institutions.

It is true, however, that tax law changes that reduced the deductibility of consumer debt have led to some substitution of mortgage debt—in the form of second mortgages and home equity loans—for consumer credit. Between 1985 and 1988, annual increases in consumer credit dropped from $82.5 billion to $51.1 billion, while mortgage indebtedness rose relative to personal income. In calculating alternative personal savings, an adjustment for this substitution has been made by assuming that new mortgage debt for 1986 through 1988 was in the same ratio to disposable personal income as in 1985, and increases over that amount were attributed to increases in consumer debt. This adjustment has the effect of lowering alternative personal savings for 1986 through 1988.

In comparing the alternative personal savings figure to the NIPA figure, it is clear that the two series are quite similar in magnitude and direction of change in the period from 1953 until 1974. In the 1960s, for example, the discrepancy between the two series averaged only 4.7 percent of NIPA savings. This similarity provides substantial support for the claim that these two very different series are measuring the same thing. However, starting in the mid 1970s and accelerating in the 1980s, the two series diverge rapidly. Moreover, the alternative figure has clearly risen as a percentage of GNP,

with the levels of the 1980s representing historic highs.

It seems probable that the treatment of pensions, the treatment of owner-occupied housing in the NIPA system, and the underreporting of legally earned income explain much of this discrepancy.[10] It has been argued, however, that the NIPA data are superior to the FRB data, because the latter source has been contaminated by unrecorded inflows of foreign capital (de Leeuw, 1984). The idea is that foreign acquisitions of financial assets in the United States that are not properly reported end up being attributed to U.S. households, thus improperly inflating the estimate of U.S. household savings. While this argument seems plausible, there is one serious problem. The assets accumulated by pension funds and insurance reserves represent a rising share of all of the financial asset acquisitions reported in the Federal Reserve data; they rose from 57 percent of alternative personal savings in 1981 to 61.1 percent in 1988. In short, the component of alternative personal savings that is measured most directly and is most likely to represent holdings of U.S. households has been rising. This makes it implausible that the Federal Reserve figure has been significantly inflated by unrecorded capital inflows.

One final point deserves mention here. The alternative savings series focuses only on financial savings, while the NIPA figure probably does the same by virtue of its treatment of owner-occupied housing. However, one of the most important ways in which individuals save is by raising the quality of their "human capital." A substantial component of what individuals spend for education and for health care can reasonably be seen as this kind of "intangible" savings. One recent study calculated these types of savings to be $348.6 billion in 1981 and found that intangible savings by households have been rising as a percentage of GNP (Eisner, 1985). Other studies that have sought to measure the value of these forms of intangible household savings through calculations of the returns to education over the life course have generated much higher annual estimates that overwhelm the other components of personal savings (Kroch and Sjoblom, 1986; Jorgenson and Pachon, 1983). The neglect of these other forms of household savings in the official data is another reason for extreme caution in drawing policy conclusions from the movements of these series.

SIGNIFICANCE OF THE DATA

In the current debate about the decline of personal savings, the key argument is that the low rate of personal savings in the United States creates difficulties for the financing of productive investment. There are several versions of the argument. In one, the point is that the scarcity of personal savings in the United States makes capital more expensive in the United States relative to countries such as Japan, where the personal savings rate is higher. The higher interest rates discourage certain types of productive investment that would occur at lower interest rates (Hatsopoulos, Krugman, and Summers, 1988). In another, the low savings rate in the United States has forced the United States to borrow capital from abroad to finance new investment—a move that cannot be continued indefinitely (*Economic Report to the President, 1990*, pp. 123–129).

All of these arguments rest on a comparison between trends in personal and private savings and trends in domestic private investment. Such comparisons rarely involve a developed theory about how different kinds of savings flows are used to finance different types of investment. However, when the NIPA data on personal savings are used, the impact of these impressionistic comparisons is powerful; they suggest a significant shortfall of personal savings. Hence, it seems useful to make the same kind of impressionistic comparison of the alternative personal savings figures with private investment trends in the economy. To be sure, domestic investments can be financed by international capital flows, but the international capital markets do not work perfectly. In fact, some of the leading theorists of the savings shortfall in the United States have noted that there remains a strong relationship between domestic savings rates and domestic investment rates, indicating that we are still far from a world of perfect mobility of money capital across international lines (Hatsopoulos, Kragman, and Summers, 1988).

. . . For the years from 1975 to 1988, when APS diverges from NIPA savings, APS grows as a percentage of gross private investment and it rises significantly in relation to net private investment.[11] A number of analysts have recently noted the sharp decline in net investment relative to gross investment in the U.S. economy. This increase in the percentage of investment attributed to depreciation has been explained in terms of the shortening of the service lives of capital goods (Blecker, 1990; Summers, 1983).[12] But whatever the cause, the result is that the use of new investment funds has diminished relatively, so that by the 1980s APS exceeded net private investment in every year. The data suggest an increasing supply of personal savings relative to the amount of net private investment actually taking place. This is a picture that runs directly against the conventional wisdom that household savings are increasingly in short supply. Moreover, when undistributed corporate profits (with inventory valuation adjustment and capital consumption adjustment) are added to APS to create a private savings series, the results are even more dramatic.

To be sure, a complete account of national savings requires including the role of the public sector. However, the proper way to measure public sector savings or dissavings is a controversial issue that is well beyond the scope of this paper (see Eisner, 1986; Heilbroner and Bernstein, 1989). At the very least, available data would have to be adjusted to include government civilian investment as a contribution to national savings.[13] It is relevant, however, to note that for every year of the 1980s, private savings exceeded net private domestic investment by an amount larger than the total government deficit—including off-budget items—reported in the NIPA, and in some years, the surplus exceeded $100 billion.

INTERPRETATION AND CONCLUSION

The obvious objection that will occur to most readers is that, since real interest rates have remained at relatively high levels in the 1980s, it follows that the kind of abundance of savings the data describe could not exist. Yet such an argument represents a partial and misleading application of the law of supply and demand. If private savings are large and expanding relative to real investment, the likely consequence is a rapid bidding up of the prices of assets such as real estate and corporate stocks. As long as the flows of new savings are continuous, this appreciation of asset values will be continuous and highly profitable for investors. The result is a virtually inelastic supply of speculative investment opportunities with a high rate of return. For example, in 1988, the stock market provided a total return (price increases plus reinvested dividends) of 16.5 percent.

Moreover, as long as investors can make 16.5 percent on their capital in the market in a given year, demand for credit will remain strong. People and institutions will cheerfully borrow billions at 10 or 12 percent in order to gain returns of 16.5 percent. This demand for credit will, in turn, slow any significant decline in interest rates. Those selling fixed income securities such as bonds will be forced to pay a higher interest rate to prevent investors from shifting into those speculative assets that offer significantly higher rates of return. To be sure, markets based on this kind of dynamic are likely to be extremely volatile, since prices are based not on expectations about real returns, but on expectations for continuing speculative profits. Yet as we learned from October 1987, even when such a market crashes, the ample supply of savings reasserts itself and drives prices back up.[14]

While this is not the place to elaborate a theory of how an economy with ample supplies of private savings operates, a few final comments are in order. First, the argument being advanced here draws support from an unlikely source—Michael Milken, the now convicted junk bond king. In her book, *The Predators' Ball*, Connie Bruck writes, "The common perception is that capital is scarce, Milken declared in his timeworn message, but in fact capital is abundant; it is vision that is scarce" (p. 272). Milken's genius was to understand the reality of a capital-abundant economy and to devise new financial instruments that took advantage of the abundance of personal savings to create enormous wealth for himself and the corporate takeover artists he financed.

Second, this analysis indicates that the reduction in the capital gains tax being proposed by the Bush administration is doubly wrong. Not only is it unnecessary to create incentives for personal savings that already exist in ample supply, but a cut in the capital gains tax would simply encourage more speculative investments in stocks and real estate that have little to do with the production of real wealth. On the contrary, the fever of speculation and the closely related takeover craze have caused firms to avoid equity financing and shift to debt financing to avoid corporate raiders. Yet whichever way they turn, firms are under mounting pressure to sacrifice long-term considerations for short-term profits (Dertouzos, Lester, and Solow, 1989, chapter 4).

Moreover, the rise of personal savings in the 1980s indicated by the APS data is a direct consequence of the Reagan administration's success in shifting income from the poor to the rich. The share of income earned by the top quintile of families increased from 41.9 percent in 1981 to 43.7 percent in 1986. A reduction in the capital gains tax would further increase this maldistribution of income. The unequal distribution of income makes the economy extremely vulnerable to a shortfall in consumer demand because of the restricted purchasing power of the majority of consumers.

Finally, these findings remind us of Keynes' anticipation of "the euthanasia of the rentier" as capitalist development reduced the scarcity of money capital (Keynes, 1936). The irony is that while the supply of private savings relative to investment has apparently increased, the rentier is more powerful than ever. It would seem that, here again, government action is required to redress the market failures produced by this phase in the development of a market society.[15]

NOTES

1. NIPA does include interest and dividends earned by private pensions as part of personal income. However, an ideal accounting of pension funds would capture both the annual net increase in pension funds assets and the flow of services received as benefits. Data on annual increases in pension fund assets are provided in the Federal Reserve Board, Flow of Funds Section, *Flow of Funds Accounts*.

2. To be sure, changing the accounting of public sector pension funds has the effect of increasing the public sector deficit. The 1988 calculation is based on unpublished data provided by the Bureau of Economic Analysis, U.S. Department of Commerce.

3. The audit rate dropped from 2.12 percent in 1980 to 1.03 percent in 1988 (Kagan, 1989, p. 116; Lasser, 1989, p. 384).

4. The methodology of the revisions is described in Parker (1984). See Holloway (1989, p. 51) for the revision to the savings figures.

5. It seems likely that the BEA's replacement cost adjustment for calculating depreciation exaggerates the growth of depreciation in the entire economy since 1974. This would also contribute to the understating of personal savings in the National Income and Product Accounts.

It should also be noted that another fraction of the imputed rent on owner-occupied housing is attributed to individuals as interest income.

6. There are also significant differences across countries in the relative cost of land. It seems quite likely that a significant portion of the United States–Japan difference in personal savings rates can be traced to the higher price of land in Japan. Goldsmith (1985, p. 122) reports that in 1978 land represented twice as large a percentage of all tangible assets in Japan as in the United States.

7. However, the board also carries out a periodic survey of consumer finance that generates a large amount of data on the actual financial behavior of a sample of households.

8. This series combines savings by households, personal trust funds, nonprofit institutions, farms, and other noncorporate businesses. This makes the series broader than the BEA measure of personal savings, although household savings is by far the dominant component of the FRB series. Nevertheless, this broader coverage seems appropriate in relation to the underlying question of the capacity of the noncorporate part of the economy to contribute resources to finance corporate investment.

9. Both of these series also omit capital gains, although the FRB does provide another series that estimates annual appreciations of asset values. (See Federal Reserve Board, Flow of Funds Section, *Balance Sheets for the U.S. Economy*.)

10. One other possibility is that the divergence has to do with the expansion of the illegal drug trade. NIPA data deliberately exclude income produced in such illegal activities as drug trafficking. However, the FRB data include flows of funds into financial instruments regardless of their legality. Yet this seems unlikely to explain much of the discrepancy, since drug profits that remain in the country enter the legitimate economy and are eventually reflected in the NIPA figures.

11. The strength of APS relative to gross private domestic investment is significant in light of the Council of Economic Advisors' conclusion that: "During the long expansion since 1982, however, U.S. real gross investment performance has been quite strong" (*Economic Report to the President, 1990*, p. 119).

12. Another possibility is that the decline of net investment can be traced to some combination of changes in the tax laws and weaknesses in the NIPA adjustments for the replacement costs of capital goods. On the latter point, see Eisner (1983).

13. Published data would also have to be adjusted to compensate for the fact that the FRB series does include public employer contributions to pension fund reserves. This requires a compensating adjustment to governmental budget figures.

14. These speculative markets have also attracted inflows of savings from abroad. This helps explain how the United States can be a net importer of capital at the same time that private domestic savings exceed net investment.

15. Reorientations of policy in response to changes in the organization of the economy are developed further in Block (1990).

REFERENCES

Blecker, Robert A. *Are Americans on a Consumption Binge? The Evidence Reconsidered*. Washington: Economic Policy Institute, 1990.

Block, Fred. *Postindustrial Possibilities: A Critique of Economic Discourse*. Berkeley: University of California Press, 1990.

Bruck, Connie. *The Predators' Ball: The Junk Bond Raiders and the Man who Staked Them*. New York: Simon and Schuster, 1988.

de Leeuw, Frank. "Conflicting Measures of Private Saving." *Survey of Current Business*, November 1984.

Dertouzos, Michael L.; Lester, Richard K.; and Solow, Robert M. *Made in America: Regaining the Productive Edge*. Cambridge, MA: MIT Press, 1989.

Eisner, Robert. "Discussion." In Federal Reserve Bank of Boston, *Saving and Government Policy*. Boston: Federal Reserve, 1983, 104–109.

___. "The Total Incomes System of Accounts." *Survey of Current Business*. January 1985, 24–48.

___. *How Real is the Federal Deficit?* New York: Free Press, 1986.

___. "The Real Rate of National Saving." Paper presented at the American Economic Association, December 1989.

Goldsmith, Raymond W. *Comparative National Balance Sheets: A Study of Twenty Countries, 1688–1978*. Chicago: University of Chicago Press, 1985.

Hatsopoulos, George N.; Krugman, Paul; and Summers, Lawrence H. "U.S. Competitiveness: Beyond the Trade Deficit." *Science*, July 1988, 241, 299–307.

Heilbroner, Robert, and Bernstein, Peter. *The Debt and the Deficit: False Alarms/Real Possibilities*. New York: W. W. Norton, 1989.

Holloway, Thomas M. "Present NIPA Saving Measures: Their Characteristics and Limitations." In *The Measurement of Saving, Investment, and Wealth*, Robert E. Lipsey and Helen Stone Tice, eds. Chicago: Univ. of Chicago Press, 1989, 21–100.

Jorgenson, D., and Pachon, A. "The Accumulation of Human and Non-Human Capital." In *The Determinants of National Savings and Wealth*, Franco Modigliani and Richard Hemming, eds. New York: St. Martin's Press, 1983, 302–350.

Kagan, Robert A., "On the Visibility of Tax Law Violations." In *Taxpayer Compliance Volume 2: Social Science Perspectives*, Jeffrey A. Roth and John T. Scholz, eds. Philadelphia: University of Pennsylvania Press, 1989, 76–125.

Keynes, John Maynard, *The General Theory of Employment, Interest, and Money*. New York: Harcourt, Brace & World, 1964 [1936].

Kroch, Eugene, and Sjoblom, Kriss. "Education and the National Wealth of the United States." *Review of Income and Wealth*, March 1986, 32 (1), 87–106.

Lasser, J. K. *Your Income Tax*. New York: Simon and Schuster, 1989.

Lipsey, Robert, and Kravis, Irving. *Saving and Economic Growth: Is the United States Really Falling*

Behind? American Council of Life Insurance and The Conference Board, 1987.

Makin, John H. "Savings Rates in Japan and the United States: The Role of Tax Policy and Other Factors." In *Savings and Capital Formation: The Policy Options*, F. Gerard Adams and Susan M. Wachter, eds. Lexington, MA: D. C. Heath, 1986, 91–126.

Parker, Robert P. "Improved Adjustments for Misreporting of Tax Return Information Used to Estimate the National Income and Product Accounts, 1977." *Survey of Current Business*, June 1984, 17–25.

Roth, Jeffrey A.; Scholz, John T.; and Witte, Ann Dryden, eds. *Taxplayer Compliance Volume 1: An Agenda for Research*. Philadelphia: University of Pennsylvania Press, 1989.

Summers, Lawrence H. "Issues in National Savings Policy." In Federal Reserve Bank of Boston, *Saving and Government Policy*, Boston: Federal Reserve, 1983, 65–88.

NO

William D. Nordhaus

WHAT'S WRONG WITH A DECLINING NATIONAL SAVING RATE?

The 1980s was the "Cheerful Decade," a period of restored faith in America, of rapid economic growth, of robust consumption. During the euphoric Reagan expansion of 1982–1988, unemployment fell by half, and real per capita personal consumption expenditures grew 3 percent annually. America was enjoying a perpetual Christmas, and believing, as President Reagan stated in his valedictory *Economic Report*, that "America is brimming with self-confidence and a model for other countries to emulate."

Amid this bonhomie, however, the world's economists and central bankers, like a chorus of nagging Scrooges, kept repeating that "we are living on borrowed time and borrowed money." The United States has been saving less and less for the future, and the bill for our Cheerful Decade eventually will be rendered in the form of reduced growth, even a decline in living standards for the future.

TRENDS IN U.S. SAVING

. . . The recent history of the saving rate (see Table 1) reveals the extent of the problem. Net private national saving and investment as a percent of net national product [NNP] ("the net national saving rate") averaged around 8 percent for three decades after 1950. Then, in the early 1980s, the net national saving rate began to fall, reaching a postwar low of 2.4 percent in the past two years.

Three components of decline in national saving stand out, including a decline in government saving, a decline in the personal saving rate, and a decline in business saving. The decline in government saving constitutes the sharpest change during the 1980s. The net saving position of all levels of government was roughly zero over most of the period from 1950 to 1980. Since that time, however, the federal budget swung sharply toward deficit, while the surpluses of state and local governments changed but little. Although economists continue to dispute the source of the rising federal

From William D. Nordhaus, "What's Wrong With a Declining National Saving Rate?" *Challenge*, vol. 33, no. 1 (January/February 1990). Copyright © 1990 by M. E. Sharpe, Inc., 80 Business Park Drive, Armonk, NY 10504. Reprinted by permission.

Table 1

The Net Savings Rate, 1950–88

Period	Net national savings rate (national saving as percent of NNP)
1950–59	8.4 percent
1960–69	8.4
1970–79	7.8
1980–86	3.8
1987–88	2.4

Source: National saving equals net private domestic investment plus net foreign investment. Data from Department of Commerce, National Income and Product Accounts.

deficit, it seems clear that Lafferism and unrealistic hopes for expenditure cuts helped launch the deficit-bound fiscal experiment of the 1980s.

Although the decline in the personal saving rate is well known, causes are elusive. After averaging around 7 percent of personal disposable income for the period 1950–1980, the personal saving rate headed downhill, troughing at 3.2 percent in 1987. Barry P. Bosworth suggests that part of the decline in personal saving is due to the inclusion of corporate pension contributions in household saving, while consumer spending may have been buoyed by the phenomenal rise in the stock market after 1982. But even after allowing for these influences, personal saving declined more than expected over the last decade.

A little-remarked component of our sinking saving is the fall in business saving. Business saving is conventionally measured in the national accounts by retained earnings of corporations. As a percent of GNP, this fell from around 4.5 percent in the mid-1960s to 2.75 percent in the late 1970s, and to 1 percent of GNP in the last two years. An alternative measure of corporate saving constructed by the Federal Reserve (which includes

stock dividends and nondividend cash payments) indicates that corporate saving actually turned *negative* in the last two years with the rash of LBOs and stock repurchases.

What was the impact of these changes on saving and investment patterns? In the past decade, the gross national saving rate declined by 5.2 percent of GNP. By elementary accounting, this must correspond to an equal decline in gross investment. As it turned out, more than half of the decline in investment surfaced as a drop in net foreign investment. Another large decline occurred in business investment, while a small decline occurred in the share of residential housing.

WHAT IS AT STAKE?

To understand the dilemmas posed by lower saving, we need to understand the stakes. Lower saving lowers future living standards in two steps. First, declining national saving reduces our investment for the future. Second, lower investment reduces the growth of output, wages, and living standards. Present pleasures are, in essence, at the expense of future consumption.

Investment in durable productive goods is in the long run determined by the nation's willingness to save. Both investment and saving should be broadly interpreted to include all channels of saving (personal, government, and corporate) and all forms of investment (plant, equipment, R & D, education, and the environment, in the public as well as the private sector). As the nation effectively increases its saving rate, investment in different areas will rise and the stock of tangible, human, and informational capital will increase.

At the same time, we must recognize a loose coupling between attempts to save and higher investment. Keynes argued, in his famous paradox of thrift, that increased saving would reduce aggregate demand, depress the economy, and increase unemployment rather than investment. Keynes's concern may be justified in the short run or in particular historical circumstances. But today, with the Federal Reserve in essence targeting output and inflation, a potentially contractionary higher saving rate will quickly be offset by the Federal Reserve actions so that interest-sensitive components of aggregate demand will rise to take up the slack left by lower consumption.

An additional concern arises, however, because the higher saving will not necessarily be channeled to the most desirable form of investment. Table 2 presents estimates of the impact of a policy shift that reduces the federal deficit while monetary policy maintains the same level of real GNP and unemployment. This result indicates that every dollar of deficit reduction will produce about 90 cents of higher national saving. Most of the higher saving comes in a reduced trade deficit, with but a modest increase in business investment.

These results should give us pause because, while many people emphasize the importance of increasing business investment, Table 2 shows that higher saving is likely to flow primarily into housing and foreign investment. This observation emphasizes the need to buttress saving policies with investment policies, so that the increased saving is channeled into the most productive sectors.

The second link from saving to economic growth is the impact of higher

Table 2

Impact of Changing Fiscal-Monetary Policies on National Savings and Consumption

Sector		Change in output (billions of dollars) (1989 prices)
Investment sectors		$45
Gross private domestic investment	$20	
Housing	10	
Business fixed investment	7	
Net exports	25	
Consumption sectors		−45
Government purchases of goods and services	−19	
Personal consumption expenditures	−26	
Memorandum:		
Change in real GNP	0	
Change in federal deficit	−50	

Source: Simulation of the DRI model in which federal deficit is cut by $50 billion through higher personal taxes and lower federal nondefense expenditures; monetary policy loosened to keep real GNP at the same level. Simulation examines second and third years of the experiment.

investment on productivity growth. As capital is accumulated, the nation will enjoy rising output, real wages, and living standards. How large is this impact?

The impact of higher investment on living standards is difficult to measure exactly, but the "growth-accounting" technique of Solow and Denison gives an approximate quantitative answer. Assume that during the 1980s, the national saving rate (defined as net national saving divided by NNP) had been 7.5 percent instead of 3.5 percent of NNP. Under conventional assumptions, GNP at decade's end would be 3 percent higher, this amounting to around $150 billion in today's prices. . . .

HOW TO INCREASE
NATIONAL SAVING

How should the nation increase its saving rate? How should the increased saving be channeled into the most productive purposes?

First, the nation must take steps to reduce the level of full-employment consumption. Second, we should ensure that the increased potential flow of saving is channeled into high-priority investments. Third, we should balance the needs for intangible and public investment with the value of tangible capital.

There is little dissent today about the need to increase national saving. There are two general sets of policies to promote saving: "income-affecting" policies and "price-affecting" policies. The former include increases in taxation or decreases in government transfers and consumption spending. The latter comprise policies that leave incomes untouched but change relative input or product prices.

Conventional wisdom before the 1980s held that saving is insensitive to the return on saving. The 1980s constituted a grand experiment in the use of "price-affecting" policies to bolster saving. These included higher real interest rates, lower tax rates on income, and special incentives for saving. One measure of the impact of these policies was that the real post-tax return (measured by the real return on tax-free bonds) rose from *minus* 2.5 percent in 1979 to *plus* 3 percent in 1988. Yet personal saving declined. This experiment, along with the volumes of corroborating sophisticated econometric work, should give pause to those who desire to use price-affecting policies to raise our saving rate.

By contrast, conventional wisdom a decade ago held that "income-affecting" measures are an effective tool in changing saving. Such measures would include either direct taxation (e.g., increases in personal taxation) or indirect taxation (e.g., tax increases on consumption). Notwithstanding elegant contrary theoretical arguments, the conventional wisdom has been largely confirmed by the fiscal experiments of the 1980s. It is difficult to find a $2.4 trillion nest egg that individuals have set aside to pay back their share of the federal debt accumulated since 1980.

What "income-affecting" measures would be most effective and efficient in increasing national saving? While some expenditure increases may be possible, the swiftest, simplest, and fairest route to reducing consumption is through higher taxes, particularly taxes on personal income or consumption. I would particularly endorse a stiff tax on gasoline and other forms of energy use, excises on alcohol and tobacco, environmental taxes, and, for fairness, increases in the top rate on individuals and increases in inheritance taxes.

"READ MY LIPS"

To a first approximation, a penny taxed is a penny saved. So what President Bush's lips really are saying is, "No new saving."

But a policy to increase national saving is not enough. We must consider where that saving should go. By coordinating our monetary and fiscal policies we can channel saving into the most productive investments.

I would submit that the priorities for conventional investment should be in two areas: increasing investment in the corporate sector, and reducing our foreign disinvestment. The priority on corporate investment arises from the high private rate of return on those investments, the importance of the corporate sector to international trade, and the potential for social returns that exceed private returns. The priority of the second area is based on the fundamental immorality of the world's richest country draining the world's saving pool, along with the practical proposition that we cannot forever continue to borrow at current levels.

With respect to corporate investment, it is ironic that the Tax Reform Act of 1986, which was designed to level the economic playing field, instead *aggravated* the tax burden on corporate investments. Because of repeal of the Investment Tax Credit and tightening depreciation allowances, the tax rate on corporate investments now approaches historical highs.

I believe that the basic approach to business taxation followed in 1986 was a mistake. In order to channel investment into the corporate sector, we should go back to the drawing boards and redesign an investment tax credit. The new credit should be refundable (to promote startups and unprofitable industries), should apply to net investment only, and should include all capital, not just equipment. Such an expanded investment tax credit would ensure that our increased national saving is channeled into high-return investments.

Popular discussion today concentrates on changes in private investment in plant, equipment, and housing. But the economic welfare of a nation depends equally upon the public capital stock, intangible investments in R & D and education, and environmental investments.

This area deserves greater study, but I will mention only two areas of concern: public capital and R & D. During the Reagan years, real gross federal physical investment was near constant; within this total, military spending rose while civilian investment fell. Curbing productive public investments at a time when the nation is concerned about its declining savings rate represents an accounting fallacy that only measured investment contributes to economic growth. To let roads, bridges, dams, nuclear facilities, and the environment deteriorate in order to cut the deficit, with some fraction of the lower deficit flowing to private investment, is misguided economic management. Moreover, unlike most other forms of investment, public investment is under the direct control of economic policy. There is no slip 'twixt the cup and the lip when expenditures are devoted to public investments.

The most critical investment program for economic growth lies in the area of research and development. Total federal R & D rose from $37.4 billion to $45.8 billion from 1980 to 1986 (all figures here are in constant 1982 prices). Within this, however, military R & D rose from 49.1 percent to 67.8 percent. Civilian federal research fell 23 percent. The largest decreases were in energy, space, and environmental R & D.

The increasing militarization of the federal R & D effort is one of the most pernicious sides of the Reagan military buildup. Half of our national R & D effort is now devoted to military and space. While some claim that military R & D will have beneficial spillovers to the civilian sector, it is challenging to imagine the civilian benefits from projects like enhanced radiation nuclear weapons, space surveillance and target acquisition, and Trident II enhancements. Perhaps a Soviet delegation could tutor us on the desirability of a "dual economy" in which the premier scientific talent is siphoned off into increasingly esoteric projects for enhanced destruction.

Who, then, will pay the bills for the Cheerful Decade? In the end, American consumers will. But the choice to be faced is: Should the payment be made in slow consumption growth over the long run, with mounting foreign debt, stagnant technology, and a crumbling capital stock? Or should the nation take bold steps to curb its consumption now and devote the higher saving to cutting foreign indebtedness, bolstering informational and business capital, and setting in motion renewed long-term growth? The latter path will require the leadership to take painful steps and the judgment to choose wise policies, but it is the only course that will provide a sound economic foundation for America's next century.

POSTSCRIPT

Does the United States Save Enough?

Block argues that there are two ways of measuring personal savings. One method, the conventional method, uses the National Income and Product Accounts (NIPA); personal savings is the difference between personal income and personal outlays. The second method, based on the Federal Reserve's flow of funds, is Alternative Personal Savings (APS); personal savings should represent the "financial surplus available for investment by the business sector" and is measured as "the net acquisition of financial assets by households." Up until 1974 the two measures yielded comparable values for personal savings, but since then the measures have differed sharply. In 1988 the NIPA method yielded a personal savings figure of $144.7 billion while the APS estimate was $367.3 billion. Block believes that the APS method is more appropriate. He indicates several problems with the NIPA method, including the treatment of pension and welfare funds as well as spending by households on real estate and the underreporting of legally earned income. When the APS figure is combined with business savings, Block finds "that for every year of the 1980s private savings exceed net private domestic investment by an amount larger than the total government deficit." Block supports this conclusion by arguing that the abundance of savings is evidenced by the "rapid bidding up of the prices of assets such as real estate and corporate stocks" that took place during the 1980s.

Nordhaus begins by examining the national savings rate (national saving as a percentage of net national product using the National Income and Product Accounts) for various time periods since 1950. It has fallen from 8.4 percent during the 1950–59 period to 3.8 percent during the 1980–86 period, and to 2.4 percent during the 1987–88 period. The decline in the saving rate means a decrease in future living standards and involves a two-step process: (1) falling saving reduces investment for the future and (2) lower investment decreases the growth of output, wages, and living standards. To prevent this, actions must be taken to increase the national saving rate and to ensure that the additional saving is "channeled into the most productive purpose." To increase the saving rate, Nordhaus argues for an increase in taxes: "I would particularly endorse a stiff tax on gasoline and other forms of energy use, excises on alcohol and tobacco, environmental taxes, and, for fairness, increases in the top rate on individuals and increases in inheritance taxes." To get the increased funds to the right sources, Nordhaus wants to target the investment tax credit, increase research and development expenditures, and increase public investment in roads and bridges. Although this means less consumption today, "it is the only course that will provide a sound economic foundation for America's next century."

For readings supporting the view that the United States saves too little, see "The Saving Shortfall," by Lou Ferleger and Jay R. Mandle, *Challenge* (March/April 1989), and "U.S. Net Foreign Saving Has Also Plunged," by Peter Hooper, *Challenge* (July/August 1989). For an analysis that supports Block, see "Explaining the Postwar Pattern of Personal Saving," by Richard W. Kopcke, Alicia H. Munnell, and Leah M. Cook, *New England Economic Review*, Federal Reserve Bank of Boston (November/December 1991). For an altogether different perspective on this issue, see "What Is the 'Right' Amount of Saving?" by Milton Friedman, *National Review* (June 16, 1989). The same issue of the *National Review* contains a number of conservative and liberal responses to Friedman's argument.

ISSUE 13

Should the Capital Gains Tax Be Lowered?

YES: Robert W. Kasten, Jr., from "Lower Capital Gains Rate Will Gain Revenue," *Congressional Record* (February 7, 1989)

NO: John Miller, from "Helping the Rich Help Themselves," *Dollars and Sense* (June 1989)

ISSUE SUMMARY

YES: Senator Robert W. Kasten, Jr. (R-Wisconsin) wants to reduce the tax rate on capital gains because such a reduction will increase government revenues, stimulate the economy and the job market, and bring the U.S. economy more in line with "European and Asian competitors."

NO: Professor of economics John Miller is against a cut in the tax rate on capital gains because he believes that the benefits will primarily go to the rich and that it will not stimulate investment. Instead, he proposes an increase in the tax rate on short-term capital gains.

In his January 28, 1992, State of the Union address President George Bush proposed a number of new initiatives. But one proposal was not new; once again he called for a reduction in the capital gains tax. Speaking with a sense of urgency, he declared, "This time, at this hour, I cannot take 'No' for an answer. You must cut the capital gains tax of the people of our country." President Bush was unsuccessful in accomplishing this particular goal of his 1992 economic agenda.

To understand the current controversy on the capital gains tax, some background on taxation in general and two major pieces of tax legislation passed during the 1980s is useful.

To finance its activities, the federal government has to raise revenue, and the primary vehicle for raising revenue is taxation. But the controversy over taxes is ceaseless for a variety of reasons. There are disagreements over the reasons why government needs revenue and disagreements over the types of taxes that are used to raise revenue. And there are disagreements over the effects of taxes on the allocation of resources and the distribution of income and what constitutes a "good" tax as opposed to a "bad" tax. What one perceives as a good tax, another may view as confiscation. So every year it seems that some part of the tax code is the target of reformers who argue that change is necessary in order to make taxes fairer, to make taxes simpler, to raise more revenue, to stimulate investment, to stimulate savings, or to make the economy more competitive internationally.

In 1981 Congress passed and President Reagan signed into law the Economy Recovery Tax Act. This was a major revision to the federal tax code, which substantially reduced personal tax rates. Every year after this legislation was passed, there were additional changes, and 1986 saw a major overhaul in the federal tax code with the passage and signing of the Tax Reform Act of 1986. Designed to make the tax system fairer and simpler, this legislation brought about another substantial reduction in tax rates. One additional feature of the 1986 Tax Reform Act was that it treated capital gains, long-term as well as short-term, as ordinary income. Given the history of tax controversy, it should not be surprising that various interest groups began seeking modification of the 1986 tax law almost immediately.

To understand capital gains taxation it is necessary to understand capital gains. Capital gains can be simply defined as the profit earned when a person sells an asset at a price higher than that at which it was purchased. Until 1986, tax laws usually distinguished between long-term and short-term capital gains. Short-term capital gains were profits realized within one year; that is, less than one year had elapsed between the purchase of an asset and its sale. Long-term capital gains were profits realized over a year or more. Short-term capital gains were taxed as ordinary income while long-term capital gains were taxed at a lower rate. Why this differential treatment in capital gains tax rates? The logic was that short-term capital gains were the result of speculative activity while long-term capital gains were good for the economy—something to be encouraged by preferential tax treatment.

This distinction ended with the Tax Reform Act of 1986. Almost immediately arguments were raised to reinstitute the preferential treatment of long-term capital gains. During 1989 several different proposals for lowering the tax rate on long-term capital gains were introduced in Congress. President Bush offered his own proposal for a capital gains tax cut. This proposal was almost identical to the one proposed in his 1992 State of the Union address.

Should the tax rate on capital gains be reduced? Although the following readings are based on legislation proposed in 1989, they represent the same arguments that erupted with every call for tax relief on capital gains. Senator Robert W. Kasten, Jr., believes a reduction in capital gains taxation would stimulate the economy, while John Miller believes that such an action would only benefit the rich.

YES

Robert W. Kasten, Jr.

LOWER CAPITAL GAINS
RATE WILL GAIN
REVENUE

President Bush's proposal to reduce the capital gains tax will—once again—spark the debate over capital gains and tax revenues. This debate is becoming as predictable as the annual return of the seasons. We have been through the same debate year in, year out—and some people continue to refuse to learn from American economic history. One year ago, 2 years ago, and even as far back as 1978, we have heard the very same argument against reducing the capital gains tax: That it would somehow lose precious tax revenues for the Federal Government.

Skeptics said about the 1978 capital gains tax cut that it would do little for investment and do much to erode tax revenues. I remember then-Treasury Secretary Michael Blumenthal asserting that the proposed capital gains rate reduction from 50 to 28 percent would cost the Treasury over $2 billion in revenue. He said, "The measure would do little for capital formation and would waste revenues."

Secretary Blumenthal objected. But in Congress, cooler economic heads prevailed—and the House and Senate agreed with my distinguished Wisconsin colleague, the late Congressman Bill Steiger, that it was time to cut the capital gains tax.

That was a cut in the tax on capital gains. Well, what happened? Did revenues go down? We've been through this time, and time, and time again—and you can go through the facts on this until everyone is blue in the face, but people just don't listen.

The fact is, taxes paid on capital gains increased from $9.1 billion in 1978 to $11.7 billion in 1979, and to $12.5 billion in 1980. In 1981, we cut the top rate on

From Robert W. Kasten, Jr., "Lower Capital Gains Rate Will Gain Revenue," *Congressional Record*, vol. 135, no. 12 (February 1989).

capital gains even further to 20 percent, and capital gains tax revenues rose to $12.7 billion in 1981, $12.9 billion in 1982, $18.5 billion in 1983, $21.5 billion in 1984 and $24.5 billion in 1985. Tax revenues to the Treasury were 184 percent higher in 1985 than in 1978.

These are all IRS figures. Nobody denies them. But a lot of people insist on ignoring them—and persist in making statements about revenues that are contrary to facts.

[A]llow me to quote from last week's Washington Post editorial on capital gains: " . . . revenues would certainly drop. Taken all together, over a period of several years, the effect on revenues would be zero at best and possibly a substantial loss." Does this sound familiar? It should—it's the same old discredited nonsense we've been hearing year in, year out since 1978.

[T]his blithe disregard for the facts—a disregard which is no doubt ideologically motivated—does nothing to expand public understanding of this issue. I would like to take this opportunity to explain to my colleagues once again why lower capital gains rates lead to higher tax revenues.

I

This revenue windfall will come from three sources. First, because the tax cost of selling equities will be cut in half, lower capital gains rates will lead to greater realizations by stockholders. These greater realizations will lead to permanently higher receipts from the capital gains tax.

As the historical record shows, capital gains taxes paid continued to climb several years after the tax rate cuts of 1978 and 1981. Many econometric studies of capital gains rates and revenues have quantified this potential realization effect. Harvard Prof. Lawrence Lindsey estimates that a flat 15-percent capital gains rate would increase capital gains taxes paid by $31 billion over 3 years.

II

Second, a lower capital gains tax rate increases the value of stocks. Taxing capital gains at a high rate reduces the potential return on investment—and this future return translates into a lower price for the stock today. Conversely, a lower capital gains rate will increase stock prices, giving the Government more gains to tax.

III

Third, and most important, a lower capital gains rate will raise GNP. Even the Congressional Budget Office admits that "lower rates on gains could increase savings and capital formation and channel more resources into venture capital." What CBO failed to recognize, however, is that this increased capital formations means that the entire tax base will grow even faster—resulting in an even greater increase in overall revenues to the Federal Government.

Most studies and available statistics on the revenue impact of the 1978 and 1981 tax cuts have focused solely on the realization effect and the subsequent increase in capital gains taxes paid. In doing so, they have neglected other important sources of revenue growth—and have, therefore, underestimated the potential revenue gains.

This week, President Bush will propose a cut in the capital gains tax as part of this fiscal 1990 budget plan. The administration will estimate that this proposal will have no revenue effect, or would raise revenue. The opponents of the proposal will once again charge that the tax rate cut will lose billions in tax revenue over the long run.

I am today calling upon the administration to clear the air—to tell the truth, the whole truth on this issue. The President's budget message must make it clear that revenues will rise as a result of this proposal. These revenues will result from increased realizations, and also from the increase in the value of current assets, and the increase in the rate of GNP growth. If Treasury cannot provide a complete, dynamic estimate now, they should promise that one will be furnished in the near future. More than anything else, the resolution of the revenue question will provide a major spark to the capital gains reform movement.

I believe that we can achieve a bipartisan consensus on capital gains this year—just as we did in 1978 and in 1981. Last week, I introduced a capital gains reform bill, S. 171, which would provide a capital gains tax cut for the sale of corporate stock. My bill would also partially index all capital assets for inflation.

In my discussions with administration officials, I have found all concerned to be receptive to my new approach on capital gains. In the 7th year of our recovery, when the odds of continued growth appear to be against us, it is more essential than ever that we do what we can to promote continued economic expansion.

That means we have to come up with a bipartisan, progrowth, projobs, capital gains reform bill. My bill is an olive branch to all sides of this debate—and a call to unity on the goals of American jobs, competitiveness and productivity.

[N]ow more than ever, we must focus on these economic goals. Because of the high capital gains rate, individuals have no incentive to assume the extra risk associated with investment in growth stocks.

As a result, entrepreneurs are finding it more difficult to secure investment funds from private sources. This shortage of startup capital today threatens to rob our economy of innovations, productivity gains, and job opportunities in the future.

Without start-up capital, many of today's dynamic, young companies—such as Apple Computers, Federal Express, and Cray Research, which is an important employer in my State of Wisconsin—never would have made it from the blackboard to the marketplace.

Other countries recognize the benefits of encouraging long-term investment—in fact, many do not tax capital gains at all. Their commitment to long-term investment has created new technologies and new innovations—and better products. We buy their products. They take our money. And U.S. jobs move overseas.

I ask unanimous consent that a table comparing the taxation of capital gains in the United States with our European and Asian competitors be printed in the RECORD.

There being no objection, the material was ordered to be printed in the RECORD, as follows: *(Please turn to tables on next page)*

Table 1

Capital Gains Rates and The Associated Revenue
(In billions of dollars)

Year	Revenue	Tax rate (percent)
1968	$ 5.9	26.9
1969	5.3	27.5
1970	3.2	32.2
1971	4.4	34.4
1972	5.7	45.5
1973	5.4	45.5
1974	4.3	45.5
1975	4.5	45.5
1976	6.6	49.125
1977	8.1	49.125
1978	9.1	49.125
1979	11.7	28
1980	12.5	28
1981	12.7	28
1982	12.9	20
1983	18.5	20
1984	21.5	20
1985	24.5	20
1986	46.4	20

Source: Research Paper No. 8801, U.S. Treasury Department.

Table 2

Comparison of U.S. Taxation of Capital Gains with Some of Our European and Asian Competitors

Country	Percent[2]
United Kingdom	40
United States	33
Sweden	18
Canada	17.51
France	16
West Germany	0
Belgium	0
Italy	0
Netherlands	0
Hong Kong	0
Singapore	0
South Korea	0
Taiwan	0
Malaysia	0
Japan	([1])

[1]No capital gains tax until Mar. 3, 1989 (except for substantial trading or substantial shareholders). After Mar. 3, 1989 shareholder has a choice of a 20 percent national and a 6 percent local tax on net gain at the time of filing, or 1 percent of sales proceeds withheld at source (this option is available only on shares listed for at least 1 year).

[2]Maximum long-term capital gains tax rates.

Source: Arthur Anderson and Co., April 1987.

NO
John Miller

HELPING THE RICH HELP THEMSELVES

Only in a supply-side world would a President propose a tax cut in order to increase government revenues. And only in trickle-down America would this President herald the cut as "tax reform" when 64% of the benefits are targeted to the richest 0.7% of taxpayers, while the bottom 60% of taxpayers would receive less than 3% of the largess. Yet this is precisely what George Bush is proposing with his capital-gains tax cut plan.

A capital gain is income from the sale of a personally owned asset—be it stocks, bonds, real estate, gold, or old paintings—that has gone up in value. Under current laws, effective since the Tax Reform Act of 1986, capital gains are taxed at the same rate as other income. But the Bush administration wants to exempt almost half of some categories of capital gains from taxation, claiming this will spur trading in financial assets, which in turn will lead to growth in tax revenues. Not only that, the Bush team argues that the tax break will trigger more long-term investment, helping to revitalize the economy.

There are a few things wrong here. Most evidence indicates that reducing taxes on capital gains will decrease tax receipts, not boost them. In addition, the tax cut is unlikely to have much effect on long-term investment—and particularly on the productive investments needed to rebuild the U.S. economy. That leaves one reason for the tax cut: to give the rich a bonus. A capital-gains tax break would so overwhelmingly benefit the wealthy that it would make the Reagan tax cuts of the early 1980s seem progressive by comparison.

The Bush administration is right that the capital-gains tax needs reform. But true reform would go in the opposite direction—closing old loopholes, not opening new ones.

THE UNKINDEST CUT OF ALL

Here's how the Bush proposal works. The proposal effectively cuts the capital-gains tax rate from 28% to 15%. Forty-five percent of profits from the sale of most assets held for three years or longer would be excluded from

From John Miller, "Helping the Rich Help Themselves," *Dollars and Sense* (June 1989). Copyright © 1989 by *Dollars & Sense*, 1 Summer Street, Somerville, MA 02143. Reprinted by permission.

taxation. This means that a wealthy tax-payer with capital gains would pay a 28% tax on only the remaining 55% of the income from their long-term capital gains, or the equivalent of a 15.4% tax rate. Actually, the rate would be "capped" at 15%—the same rate currently charged on the taxable income of the poorest families. In a feeble gesture toward curbing speculation, the tax break would not exempt capital gains on real estate and art objects, nor gains on assets held for less than three years.

Setting a lower effective tax rate for capital gains than for other income is not a new idea: capital gains were taxed at bargain rates continuously from 1921 to 1986. But the 1986 Tax Reform Act marked a significant departure. In return for dramatically lower personal income tax rates, the Reagan administration agreed to tax capital gains as ordinary income. As Vice President, Bush promised Congress that broadening the tax base to include all capital-gains income would provide the necessary revenues to offset the revenues lost from lowering tax rates on the wealthy.

Now, as President, Bush wants to keep the new lower personal income taxes for the rich and to reinstitute the preferential treatment of capital gains. The combination of the two would leave the tax on capital gains at its lowest level since 1942. At the same time, Bush asks us to believe that he can now increase revenues by reversing the very measures he argued earlier were necessary to maintain tax revenues.

SUPPLY-SIDE MAGIC

The supply-side rationale behind Bush's revenue claim is simple, if fanciful. The supply-siders claim that if capital-gains taxes are cut, property-owners will suddenly begin to sell previously hoarded assets. They point out that, currently, there is only one way to beat the capital-gains tax: hold onto your assets until you die. When inheritors sell the property, they only pay taxes on capital gains that accrue after the date of inheritance. So, the argument goes, with gains taxes so high, substantial numbers of wealthy individuals have decided to hold onto their property for life—or at least until the tax rate drops. If the capital-gains tax was lowered, many of them would sell the property to realize the capital gains.

In theory, property owners' increased willingness to cash in on capital gains could boost the total amount of taxable capital gains enough to offset the decreased tax rate. Bush administration projections hold that Treasury revenues would rise by nearly $5 billion in the next year (as capital gains increase 120%) and continue to grow for the following two fiscal years.

But in 1980, when presidential candidate Ronald Reagan made similar claims about the effects of cutting income taxes, George Bush denounced them as "voodoo economics." And today, almost no one outside the Oval Office agrees with the Bush administration's projections. If asset owners don't sell more, the annual loss to the Treasury from the tax cut would be $17 billion—increasing the projected deficit by almost one-fifth—and few tax experts believe that they'll sell enough to wipe out this loss.

For instance, two major non-partisan institutions of Congress examined the effects of the proposed changes in the capital-gains tax. The Congressional Budget Office estimated that the Bush scheme could lose from $4 billion to $8 billion a year. The Joint Congressional

Committee on Taxation projected that while the proposal would raise revenues the first year, it would lose $13.3 billion over the next five years.

The history of capital-gains taxation offers confirmation that asset-owners' responsiveness to tax changes is not strong enough to justify Bush's optimistic revenue claims. After Jimmy Carter and a Democratic Congress lowered capital-gains taxes in 1978, stock sales rose in 1979, only to decline in 1980. And since 1986, when capital-gains taxes rose from 20% to 28%, capital gains have not decreased, but rather increased by more than 15% in nominal terms.

REVIVING INVESTMENT?

The Bush administration asserts that in addition to enhancing government revenues, a tax break on capital gains would revive long-term investment in the 1990s—this time by affecting how the wealthy act as buyers. Lower taxes on capital gains would increase investors' rate of return, encouraging more investment and contributing to higher growth rates in the decade ahead. Because the tax cut applies only to gains on property held for three years or more, it allegedly would lengthen the planning horizon of investors. And with lower capital-gains taxes, owners of stocks supposedly would become more active traders, supplying capital to new, more productive uses.

But many in the business world find these arguments almost as far-fetched as the supply-side revenue claim—and progressives have even less reason to accept them. *Business Week* editorialized, "The issue is how to guide [the money of large institutional investors] into long-term investment. . . . It won't be easy,

but tinkering with the capital-gains rate is like pouring buckets of water on a burning house." Other business interests have expressed alarm that cutting the capital-gains tax rate would lead to investment guided by tax avoidance, rather than by market conditions.

Instead of taxing capital gains at a lower rate than ordinary income, *Business Week*, the *Los Angeles Times*, and others have argued that investment can better be stimulated by adjusting capital gains for inflation before taxing them. They contend that inflation has discouraged long-term investment by forcing investors to pay taxes not only on profits but also on capital gains generated by inflation. With inflation indexing, investors could pay taxes only on their "real" capital gains, not on inflation.

From a progressive viewpoint, both the Bush plan and the inflation-indexing alternative fall short as ways of encouraging productive investment. For one thing, both proposals overstate the influence of capital-gains taxation on new investment. These tax-cutting proposals seek to spark new investment by making new stock issues more attractive to investors. But the vast majority of stock sales affected by capital-gains taxes are not new issues but resales of existing stock, which generate no new investment. Furthermore, stock issues finance only a small fraction of new investment. In the 1970s and 1980s less than 10% of the money corporations raised from outside sources has come from selling stock (see "Beyond the Boom," *D&S*, June 1986). Even *Business Week* concludes that "the real problem in venture capital" is not that potential investors are deterred by the high tax rate on gains, but rather that there is "too much money chasing too few opportunities."

Since tax changes have limited effects on the volume of investment, the important question is whether they help to redirect the investment. Cutting capital-gains taxes across the board does nothing to direct capital to productive uses—such as plant, equipment, infrastructure, or education. But cutting capital-gains taxes selectively could affect the character of investment. By denying the capital-gains exemption to income from the sale of non-productive property, the capital-gains tax could discourage financial speculation and direct investment toward more productive uses.

BONANZA FOR THE WEALTHY

While cutting capital-gains taxes is unlikely to increase government revenues or do much for investment, it will certainly succeed in redistributing income—to the rich. Capital gains go almost entirely to the wealthy. The wealthiest 5% of all taxpayers receive 85% of capital gains; the richest .7% of taxpayers receive 70% of capital gains. Five of every six taxpayers with incomes of more than $1 million a year have capital-gains income, but fewer than one in every 20 taxpayers earning $10,000 or less have it.

Thus, cutting capital gain taxes amounts to what Robert McIntyre, Director of Citizens for Tax Justice (CTJ), calls a "bonanza for the wealthy." CTJ estimates that about two-thirds of the benefits of the Bush cut would go to the richest 685,000 people in the nation, or less than 1% of taxpayers. These taxpayers, all with incomes over $200,000, would receive an average tax cut of about $25,000. For the 80% of families earning less than $60,000 a year the average tax savings from the Bush plan would be only $20.

The one-sided distributional effect of cutting capital-gains tax is reinforced in the Bush proposal by the fact it does not apply to the sale of homes, which qualified for the capital-gains exemption prior to 1986. As a sop for the less fortunate, the Bush proposal would allow families with taxable income of less than $20,000 to sell their homes tax free.

FAIR TAXES INSTEAD

A more progressive tax policy would stiffen taxes on capital gains, not cut them. On the national level, Jesse Jackson's "Budget Plan for Jobs, Peace, and Justice" included measures along these lines. Besides proposing to restore personal income taxes on the wealthy to their pre-1986 levels, the Jackson budget favored closing the loophole that allows the rich to avoid capital-gains taxation at death. This makes a lot more sense—and is far more likely to raise revenue—than countering the loophole by lowering gains taxes on the rich as Bush proposes. The Jackson plan also would have imposed a "securities-transfer excise tax" of 0.5% on the sale of certain kinds of financial assets, a tax that would reduce short-term speculative merger and acquisition activity.

Even some investors and economic theorists support such policies. Fifty years ago, John Maynard Keynes, the economist whose theories underpin much of modern economic policy, favored "a substantial securities transfer tax" to mitigate "the predominance of speculation over enterprise in the United States." On Wall Street today, Warren Buffet, the head of Berkshire Hathaway and arguably the most successful securities investor in America, favors "a confiscatory 100% tax on short-term capital gains"—taxing away all short-term gains to remove the incentive for speculation.

Increasing short-term capital-gains taxes has also found support in state and local governments. Since 1973, Vermont has imposed a short-term capital-gains tax on land sales in an attempt to slow the pace of development. Rhode Island also recently considered taxing short-term capital gains on real estate in order to curb housing speculation.

Both the Rhode Island bill, defeated by fierce opposition from the real-estate lobby, and the Vermont law contain several features that could be adopted in a progressive national capital-gains tax:

• To favor long-term investment, impose higher taxes on short-term capital gains, not lower taxes on long-term gains as Bush proposes.

• Define the short term in several different gradations subject to different tax rates, including near-confiscatory rates for the shortest term and most likely speculative investment. The Rhode Island tax proposal defined the short term to be 5 years and imposed tax rates ranging from 80% for six-month investments to 15% for investments held the full five years. The Vermont law has a similar feature and also mandates a tax rate that increases with the amount of profit, similar to the income tax.

• Specify the type of investment subject to the short-term capital-gains tax, directing the flow of investment away from speculative activity. The Rhode Island bill applied only to non-owner-occupied housing, exempting owner-occupied residences from the short-term gains tax.

• Use the revenues from the short-term capital-gains tax to fund domestic spending or non-speculative public investment. In the Rhode Island bill, tax revenues were to go to a neighborhood preservation fund.

Unlike the Bush proposal, these progressive alternatives would promote equality, raise revenues, and strengthen the economy. The burden of a beefed-up capital-gains tax would fall chiefly on those with incomes above $200,000, the same people who benefited most from the Reagan tax cuts. Furthermore, such a tax could be the first step toward a more explicit and progressive industrial policy, cooling speculation and directing investment into needed areas. Selective tax rates could guide resources into more socially worthwhile investments, such as education. Finally, the revenues raised from the capital-gains tax would provide funds to restore the cuts in domestic spending, or to reduce the budget deficit, or even to fund investment in publicly-owned industry. Instead of Bush's thinly disguised giveaway to the wealthy, we could have a capital-gains tax policy that would actually do us all some good.

NOTES

SOURCES: Robert McIntyre, "Tax Americana," *The New Republic*, March 27, 1989; Congressional Budget Office, "How Capital Gains Tax Rates Affect Revenues," 1989; Jesse Jackson, "Paying for Our Dreams: A Budget Plan for Jobs, Peace, and Justice," 1988; and various materials from Citizens for Tax Justice, 1311 L St. NW, Washington, DC 20005.

POSTSCRIPT

Should the Capital Gains Tax Be Lowered?

Kasten begins his case for a reduction in the tax rate on capital gains by arguing that a rate reduction will not reduce the tax revenues of the federal government. To support his argument, he reviews what happened when the capital gains tax rate was cut in 1978 and in 1981: In spite of these cuts, "tax revenues to the Treasury were 184 percent higher in 1985 than in 1978." He offers three reasons why a cut in the tax rate can be expected to increase governmental revenues: (1) a lower rate will stimulate the sale of assets whose price has increased; (2) a lower rate will increase the value or price at which stocks can be sold; and (3) a lower rate will stimulate the economy and thus increase revenues from other tax sources. Kasten also supports a reduction in the tax rate on capital gains because it is "pro-growth and pro-jobs." The final reason why Kasten supports a reduction in the capital gains tax rate involves international considerations. He compares the rate of capital gains taxation in the United States with those imposed by European and Asian competitors. In this comparison only one country, the United Kingdom, has a higher rate, and many countries do not tax capital gains at all. The implication is that if the United States is to remain competitive internationally it must reduce the tax rate on capital gains.

Miller believes that the tax rate on long-term capital gains should not be reduced. Such a reduction, at least in the form proposed by President Bush in 1989, would benefit mainly the rich: "65% of the benefits are targeted to the richest 0.7% of taxpayers." In addition, Miller believes that a cut in the capital gains tax rate will reduce governmental revenues. Here he uses estimates provided by the Congressional Budget Office and the Joint Congressional Committee on Taxation, as well as what happened after 1986 when the tax was lowered. Miller also denies that the tax cut would stimulate productive investment. Here he asserts that capital gains taxation has little effect on productive investment.

Kasten has written several articles that further develop his views, including "Capital Gains: The Right Cuts," *The Washington Post* (February 7, 1989) and "The Kindest Cut of All—Reducing Capital Gains Tax," *Chicago Tribune* (February 22, 1989). For a more balanced perspective, see "Tax Options for 1989: Revising Capital Gains Rates," by Elizabeth Wehr, *Congressional Quarterly* (December 10, 1989). For arguments against a reduction in the capital gains tax, see "Capital Pains," by Laura Sanders, *Forbes* (July 19, 1989), and "Tax Deform," by Robert S. McIntyre, *The New Republic* (August 21, 1989). Also see President Bush's State of the Union address and the Democratic response by House Speaker Thomas Foley in the January 29, 1992, issue of the *New York Times*.

ISSUE 14

Is Workfare a Good Substitute for Welfare?

YES: Lawrence M. Mead, from Statement Before the Subcommittee on Trade, Productivity, and Economic Growth, Joint Economic Committee, U.S. Congress (April 23, 1986)

NO: Morton H. Sklar, from Statement Before the Subcommittee on Trade, Productivity, and Economic Growth, Joint Economic Committee, U.S. Congress (April 23, 1986)

ISSUE SUMMARY

YES: Associate professor of politics Lawrence M. Mead, an advocate of the work ethic, urges Congress to make work a fundamental condition of receiving welfare assistance.
NO: Attorney Morton H. Sklar rejects Mead's contention that work must be a key ingredient in any welfare system. His experience suggests that a work requirement is inappropriate for many welfare recipients and not cost-effective for those who would be asked to work.

Given American society's traditional commitment to a market system and its fundamental belief in self-determination, Americans are not much at ease in enacting social welfare legislation that appears to give someone "something for nothing," even if that individual is clearly in need. Thus, when we trace the roots of the existing U.S. social welfare system back to its origins in the New Deal legislation of President Franklin Roosevelt, created during the Great Depression of the 1930s, we see that many of the earliest programs linked jobs to public assistance. One exception to these early programs was Aid to Families with Dependent Children (AFDC), which is one of the oldest public assistance programs and was established as part of the 1935 Social Security Act. This program provides money to families in which there are children but no breadwinner. In 1935, and for many years thereafter, this program was not particularly controversial because the number of beneficiaries was relatively small and the popular image of an AFDC family was that of a white woman with several young children who had lost her husband as a result of a mining accident, an industrial mishap, or perhaps World War I.

In the early 1960s, as the U.S. economy prospered, poverty and what to do about it captured the attention of the nation. The Kennedy and Johnson administrations focused their social welfare programs on poor individuals— a minority of the population, especially, but not exclusively, a black minority, left behind as the general economy grew and set new record highs. Their policies were designed to address the needs of those who were trapped in "pockets of poverty," a description popularized in the early 1960s in the writings of Michael Harrington (1929–1989), a political theorist and prominent socialist. Between 1964 and 1969 the number of AFDC recipients increased by more than 60 percent, and the costs of the program more than doubled. The number of AFDC families continued to grow throughout the 1970s, and the program became increasingly controversial.

In part, the controversy grew because of the increase in recipients and the increase in costs and in part because the program became increasingly identified in the public mind as a black or ethnic minority program. A welfare mother was now perceived as a woman in a big-city public housing project whose children have been deserted by their father. This change in perceptions, which corresponded only partially with changes in reality, made welfare a controversial issue. It has now become, perhaps, the most controversial of all the many government programs that provide public assistance.

In the 1980s, direct attacks began to be made on AFDC by social critics such as Charles Murray. Murray charged AFDC with encouraging welfare dependency, teenage pregnancies, the dissolution of the traditional family, and, of course, an erosion of the basic American work ethic. These criticisms set the stage for the first major reforms in AFDC in 25 years. In 1988 the Family Support Act was passed. This legislation requires the states to run programs that will help, or so it is thought, persons receiving welfare assistance to break their dependency on welfare assistance. The programs involve work (workfare), education (learnfare), or training. This legislation was and is controversial. The following readings, although written before the Family Support Act was passed, are representative of the continuing controversy. Lawrence M. Mead argues in favor of programs that require people to work for welfare assistance, while Morton H. Sklar holds that workfare is inappropriate for many welfare recipients. What conditions should be imposed upon those who receive welfare checks? Should recipients be asked to work? Is this the most cost-effective means of eliminating poverty? These and other questions are addressed in the readings that follow.

YES

PREPARED STATEMENT OF
LAWRENCE M. MEAD

My name is Lawrence M. Mead. I am an Associate Professor of Politics at New York University. I have been researching federal welfare and employment programs for about ten years. Much of what I will say is drawn from my recent book, *Beyond Entitlement*.[1]

I. THE WORK PROBLEM

While most people who rely on Aid to Families with Dependent Children (AFDC) leave the rolls in under two years, 38% remain on for five years or more.[2] Nonwork is a serious problem on AFDC. Only 15% of welfare mothers work at a given time, according to government surveys, and the rate is still lower among the long-term cases.[3] Nonwork is one of the keys to solving poverty and dependency in the United States. If more of the poor worked, many fewer would need support. There would be more political support for a generous antipoverty policy. Most important, chances for integration would improve.

The traditional explanations for nonwork are no longer persuasive. Most of the long-term poor and dependent are nonwhite,[4] and it could be claimed until recently that they were simply kept out of the job market by discrimination. But in recent decades, a black middle class has appeared, and a number of nonwhite groups—West Indians, Asians—have done conspicuously well economically. Nor can the dysfunctions of today's underclass—crime and illegitimacy as well as nonwork—be seen as "rational" responses to discrimination, since the poor themselves are the main victims.

Some cite other social barriers. Allegedly, the economy does not provide enough employment for the poor. Particularly, the decline of manufacturing has reduced the number of jobs available to the uneducated. Or the poor are kept from working by child care responsibilities or lack of skills. Thus, to raise welfare work levels would take massive new government programs to provide jobs, child care, and training.[5]

From U.S. Congress. Joint Economic Committee. Subcommittee on Trade, Productivity, and Economic Growth. *Workfare Versus Welfare*. Hearing, April 23, 1986. Washington DC: Government Printing Office, 1986.

However, job creation in the service sector has been prodigious in recent decades. The "high tech" economy seems to create nearly as many low- as high-skilled jobs. Many of these positions require little more initially than an ability to read, get to work on time, and take orders. The presence of 5 to 10 million illegal aliens in the country certifies that at least low-skilled work is widely available. There is little evidence that relatively low-placed groups such as blacks, teenagers, and women are confined in unattractive jobs for reasons beyond low skills. Most of their unemployment is due to turnover in jobs rather than lack of jobs. The main reason the long-term poor do not work steadily today is problems of work discipline peculiar to them, not the limitations of the labor market.[6]

Government services are much less critical to work than is often claimed. Training programs have little impact on skills, but in any event mothers with low skills seem to escape welfare through work as often as the better-prepared. And while many working mothers could use child care programs, most arrange, and prefer, informal care through friends and relatives. Mothers with children under 6 are just as likely to work their way off welfare as those with children in school.[7]

Another approach says that nonwork results from the disincentives in welfare. Allegedly, AFDC breaks up families because eligibility is usually limited to single parents with children, and it discourages work because most of what recipients earn is deducted from their welfare grants. Using this reasoning, conservatives demand cuts in welfare for the employable while liberals recommend stronger work incentives—i.e., allowing recipients to keep more of their wages as an inducement to work. More broadly, conservatives blame the generous social programming of the 1960s and 1970s for the increasing behavioral problems among the underclass.[8]

Experience has shown that these proposals are impolitic. The Reagan Administration has achieved only marginal cuts in welfare benefits, while proposals by Presidents Nixon and Carter to reform welfare on work incentive lines were rejected by Congress. More significant, research and experience have not shown that welfare incentives have much effect on work effort either way. Stronger work incentives were added to AFDC in 1967, then largely withdrawn in 1981, without affecting work levels palpably. And if dysfunction among the poor rose when social spending boomed, it has not yet declined even though welfare benefits have fallen by a third, allowing for inflation, in the last 15 years.[9]

A better explanation for nonwork is simply that the dependent poor have seldom been expected to work. Welfare and the other programs that give them income and services have been permissive. They have seldom required their clients to work or otherwise function *in return* for support. This reflects the liberal social analysis of the Great Society period, which attributed all problems of the poor to social forces and refused to hold them accountable even for personal conduct. The onus lay entirely on government to make work happen by providing new benefits to the poor, including cash, education, training, and child support.

Unfortunately, the poor are irresolute about achieving work, and a permissive policy cannot change this. Studies show that they accept mainstream values such as employment, contribution to families, and obedience to the law, but that they less often observe them than the better-off. They feel that difficult circumstances prevent them living by norms that, in principle, they accept. Without setting standards, federal programs could not close this gap between intention and behavior. Instead, they strengthened the "welfare mentality" of the poor—their tendency to see all solutions, like all problems, coming from outside themselves.[10]

II. THE NEED FOR OBLIGATION

The evidence is that work requirements might raise work levels on welfare significantly, though they have not done so yet. The work tests first added to AFDC in 1967 were ineffective mainly because they lacked sufficient authority. In practice, too few of the employable recipients were subject to the Work Incentive (WIN) program, the first work program in AFDC. In 1971, Congress mandated that all employable recipients to WIN, and job entries jumped sharply.[11]

But WIN required at most that employable recipients look for work, on pain of reductions in their welfare grants. In 1981, Congress allowed states to toughen the requirements further. They might now for the first time institute workfare, that is require clients actually to work in return for benefits. About half the states have since instituted more demanding AFDC work programs of some kind. Typically, they mandate that employable recipients, or at least new applicants for AFDC, participate in varying combinations of job search, training, and work in government agencies. According to studies by the Manpower Demonstration Research Corporation (MDRC), programs in San Diego and West Virginia have raised the share of the employable engaged in these activities to over 60%.[12]

According to my own studies of WIN, the participation rate is the key to welfare work, and participation hinges on obligation. To raise participation, an office must provide clients with necessary services (especially child care) and then require them to join in job search or some kind of training or subsidized job program. The higher the proportion of clients so obligated, the higher the proportion that goes to work. Economic factors—the availability of jobs, the employability of clients, the number of staff available to serve them—matter too, but less so than the degree of work obligation. Apparently, nothing improves clients' employment fortunes so much as simply expecting them to work.

Most WIN staff interviewed for these studies had come to similar conclusions. Few believed that the barriers often cited to welfare work were decisive. Few said that jobs were literally unavailable—even in depressed areas of New York City. "Good" jobs were scarce, but low-paid jobs were commonplace. While most supported training for those who could get "better" jobs, many said that WIN had sometimes used training as a substitute for work. Few believed that government child care was essential for mothers to work. Typically, mothers who demanded care from the program were seeking to avoid participation; those who wanted to work arranged care themselves. Staff complained most bitterly, not about the job market or their own resources, but about their limited *legal* ability to penalize, through welfare reductions, the few clients who resisted work.[13]

III. AN ASSESSMENT OF WORKFARE

The MDRC studies permit a preliminary assessment of these new requirements, though experience is still limited. I will use "workfare" here broadly to include any definite requirement to participate in job search, training, or public sector employment in return for welfare benefits.

The traditional question asked by liberals about welfare work is whether the recipients benefit, by conservatives whether the welfare rolls and costs to government are reduced. In these terms, the new programs appear to yield definite but limited gains. Compared to recipients not subject to the new requirements, clients who have been in workfare more often work and earn somewhat more. Lower proportions remain on welfare, and their welfare grants are smaller. Notably, the employment and earnings gains were highest in programs involving required work, not just job search.

Budgetary savings are less clear. Workfare costs more at the outset than plain income maintenance because of the required child care, training, and government jobs. These costs are recouped later in reduced welfare costs as more recipients go to work, either reducing their grants or lifting them off welfare entirely. Of the three programs for which MDRC has complete data, two saved money. All three were worthwhile if other benefits, to society and the recipients, are included.[14] No doubt, testimony from MDRC will explicate these findings.

However, these economic questions are not the most important ones to ask about workfare. They reflect the traditional, "New Deal" preoccupation of American politics with the scale of government. Liberals want larger government to serve the individual, while conservatives want to reduce public burdens on the private sector. Implicitly, both assume that social programs must be benefit-oriented. Liberals tend to regard work or training as another benefit for the recipients alongside case assistance. Conservatives realize this approach is permissive, but their usual response is simply to cut back such programs and let the marketplace impose work discipline.

Neither stance easily appreciates the real point of workfare—to change the *character* of government rather than its scale. Properly understood, work is not another benefit for the recipient but an *obligation* balancing the benefits they are already receiving from society. Neither is it a way to cut back welfare, at least at the outset. The point, rather, is to avoid exempting recipients from normal social obligations, to require that they function *even if* they are dependent.

Viewed politically, the potential of workfare to raise participation levels outweighs all the economic results. Unlike politicians, the public is much more concerned with the character than the extent of welfare. Polls reveal little sentiment either to expand or contract welfare, but intense disquiet at the "abuses" associated with welfare—fraud and abuse, nonpayment of child support by absent fathers, and above all nonwork. The public is humanitarian but *not* permissive. It wants welfare to help the needy but also to uphold social standards. The traditional liberal and conservative positions on welfare violate one side or the other of this public mind. Potentially, workfare could satisfy both. It helps the needy, but in a *demanding* way.

To the public, the moral issues in welfare dwarf the economic ones. The social dysfunction linked to dependency is much more distressing than the cost of welfare. Americans wish they could view AFDC recipients as "deserving" in the same manner as beneficiaries of Social Security and other social insurance programs. More than anything else, higher work levels would make welfare more "respectable." Polls indicate that if assistance could be given by way of work, voters would want to spend *more* on the poor rather than less. Thus, workfare deserves the support of those who seek a generous social policy.[15]

The other critical political fact about workfare is that the recipients themselves accept it. Compared to plain welfare, workfare may not make the recipients much better off economically, but it responds directly to the difficulty they have in living up to the norms they profess. Conservatives tend to say that recipients who fail to work are ripping off the public, while liberals say they have made a "rational" decision not to work in view of the constraints. But these characterizations project on the dependent the self-reliant psychology of the better-off. In fact, the dependent are usually depressed, not cynical, about nonwork. They fail to work, not out of calculation, but because they feel overwhelmed by the logistics of work, as well as by ordinary domestic crises.

By mandating work, workfare helps change employment from an aspiration into a reality. It provides necessary support services, but it also requires that mothers get out of the house in the morning, a spur they need. In my studies, WIN staff said that recipients very seldom contested the work obligation in principle. Nearly always, they accepted it, and they saw participation in WIN as positive. In the MDRC studies, the great majority of workfare clients viewed the participation requirement as fair. They also felt their jobs were meaningful, not "makework." At most, many of those in public positions where they "worked off" their grants would have preferred regular, paid employment.[16]

How do we reconcile these findings with the common view that workfare is "punitive"? One explanation is that critics often see work requirements as invidious in the same way as the restraints on sexual activity that welfare agencies have sometimes tried to impose on recipients. Allegedly, to require work is demeaning in the same manner as raiding a welfare family in the middle of the night to see if there is a man in the house. But the evidence is that recipients view work demands quite differently from intrusions into their personal lives. The latter are private, but work is a public matter about which the agency may inquire, since it affects the size of the welfare grant and the cost to society.[17]

Also, workfare was first used in local general assistance programs intended for groups not eligible for federal welfare, usually two-parent families and single men. In these programs, many more of the employable recipients were men, and many more of them resisted work, than in AFDC. Inevitably, efforts to make them work took on a harsh tone. And when workfare appeared in AFDC, in experimental programs before 1981, the impetus usually came from conservative state officials interested in "program integrity." They saw workfare mainly as a way to deter the employable poor from seeking welfare or to drive them off the rolls, thus limiting assistance to the unemployable or "truly needy."[18] In contrast, the recent AFDC work programs have not been punitive.[19] Their purpose is much more to raise work levels *on* welfare than to limit assistance.

A final explanation is that those who say workfare is punitive are usually quite different from the recipients. That sentiment comes from the leaders of welfare advocacy groups, but typically they are working, not on welfare. Maybe they once were on welfare, but they are now upwardly mobile. Like other self-reliant Americans, they are able to live out the work ethic without either assistance or obligation from government. They would resent being told to work, and so they should. But they err in generalizing from their own experience to that of recipients generally. Most welfare recipients do not resent work demands. Many know they need the structure of workfare programs, with their combination of supports and requirements, actually to achieve work.

The main shortcoming of workfare may be that initially it reaches mainly welfare mothers, not the men who father their children and should normally be supporting them. For constitutional reasons, government cannot force people to work except as a condition attached to benefits it gives them. Since it is usually mothers who receive AFDC, they are the easiest to obligate. There is no comparable benefit for men. While they receive some welfare and training services, they seldom rely on it to live as the women do. Most of their income comes from a combination of erratic work, informal subsidy from the mothers, and "hustling" in the underground economy.

A work policy for men would have to orchestrate a number of lesser obligations, not all of them federal. Some men are on AFDC (either teenagers not in school or unemployed fathers, in states covering them); they can be, and are, required to work in the same way as mothers. Child support enforcement can be strengthened. Work in available jobs can be made an eligibility requirement for federal training programs. Standards in the schools can be raised, to ensure that youths leaving school can read. Perhaps most important, police measures are needed to constrict the underground economy. These steps together might gradually do for men what workfare does for women—cause them to accept available jobs in the legal labor market.

On balance, workfare is certainly worthwhile. The long-term poor are notably unresponsive to the opportunities around them. They have not taken advantage of existing employment, as recent immigrant groups have, nor have benefit-oriented social programs done much to help them. Workfare has drawn a stronger response from this group than anything yet tried. That alone makes it the most promising development in social policy since the Great Society.

IV. IMPLEMENTATION

However, workfare raises substantial implementation questions. The most fundamental of these are political. As mentioned above, federal politicians prefer benefit-oriented programs, or reductions in such programs, to the combination of benefits and requirements represented by workfare. Congress has allowed workfare in AFDC, but it has not yet mandated it, as the Reagan Administration wants. Proposals to do so will arouse continuing resistance, not withstanding the strong evidence for them. Liberals will say they are punitive, and conservatives will say they perpetuate big government.

A lesser, but substantial issue is cost. As mentioned, for a given caseload, workfare usually costs more than plain welfare, at least at the outset. The states that currently impose workfare have financed it fairly easily with a combination of welfare, WIN, and other training monies. But most of these programs cover only the employable among new applicants for AFDC and usually not all of them. The added cost would be greater if all employable applicants and recipients were covered. How much greater is difficult to say, since it is uncertain how recipients would react. If they all waited to be obligated, did nothing for themselves, and were placed in government jobs, a vast public employment structure would be needed. If they all took private sector jobs, costs might even be lower than now, because of welfare savings from earnings. An outcome in the middle is likely. One plausible estimate, by the Ways and Means Committee, is that a serious work program covering the whole caseload would cost $2 billion.[20]

While that is much less than CETA, the major public employment program of the 1970s, it clearly raises an issue in the current fiscal climate. There is danger that even existing training funds, on which workfare has relied, will be eliminated due to budget balancing under Gramm-Rudman-Hollings.

Another major challenge is administrative.[21] To implement serious work requirements would be a strenuous test for existing work and welfare programs at the local level. Handling the increased caseload is only one aspect. Such a policy would have to overcome the considerable resistance, both political and bureaucratic, that these agencies have shown to past work requirements, helping to explain their poor record. While the political climate in welfare is more conservative than a decade or so ago, the priority in welfare administration is still to avoid errors in grants payment rather than to use work to divert people from welfare. Employment programs have not generally given a high priority to mandatory welfare clients, preferring to serve jobseekers who come to them voluntarily. To overcome these impediments from the federal level is difficult, given the frictions inherent in the intergovernmental system.

To overcome the inertia will require a sustained effort at administrative development, not something American government is good at. Washington has to make clear a will to enforce work, and local officials must be made to carry it out. One mechanism here must be stronger fiscal sanctions to force local programs to work actively with more of their caseloads; under WIN, they have to serve no more than 15% of the employable clients. Another need is a number of legal changes to make it easier to obligate the recipients to participate.[22]

The key to successful implementation is voluntary compliance. Once the work mandate is clear to staff and clients alike, they are more likely to conform without pressure, cutting both costs and administrative problems. Voluntary compliance is what makes the income tax system so much more efficient than welfare work. Many of the same poor people who fail to work regularly and face no pressure to do so pay their taxes honestly without prompting, because the obligation is accepted and enforced. While the IRS faces rising tax evasion, it still has to monitor many fewer cases to achieve compliance than work programs would at the outset.

Achieving voluntary compliance is a complex process requiring both political leadership from the top and strong administrative sanctions over a considerable time. It is no accident that the new work programs that have achieved the highest participation are in localities—San Diego and West Virginia—with a long commitment to welfare employment. Work by the dependent will become usual only when it is seen as an inviolable adjunct of welfare—as inevitable as "death and taxes."

In view of the challenges, a political commitment to workfare should be combined with administrative caution. The AFDC law should be changed to mandate active participation in work or training for all employable recipients, but the implementation should be phased in. Raise the share of the employable that work programs must obligate to participate from 15% to perhaps 30%, with gradual increases after that to 50% or more, alongside appropriate funding increases. To obligate half the employable to work or train is probably feasible, and it would establish work rather than nonwork as the norm on welfare, the threshold needed to promote voluntary compliance over the longer term.

In contrast, the Administration has proposed to cut funding for WIN, yet to raise the participation rate required of states to 75%. In the short term at least, it is contradictory to seek more welfare work and expect funding to fall, and 75% participation is impracticable.

To mandate work is a new venture in American social policy. Many politicians and administrators find it distinctly uncongenial. It violates our traditional conception of government as the servant and not the master of the individual. But for the long-term poor, such requirements seem essential to functioning and, thus, to social integration. Welfare work will be enforced when our leaders accept, as the public already seems to, that it is essential to greater equality in American life.

NOTES

1. Lawrence M. Mead, *Beyond Entitlement: The Social Obligations of Citizenship* (New York: Free Press, 1986).
2. Mary Jo Bane and David T. Ellwood, "The Dynamics of Dependence, The Routes to Self-Sufficiency," study prepared for the Department of Health and Human Services (Cambridge, Mass: Urban Systems Research and Engineering, June 1983), ch. 2.
3. *Beyond Entitlement*, pp. 74–5. The proportion of welfare mothers working anytime in the year is higher, perhaps a third or more. And many welfare women work without reporting the income to welfare. These facts indicate a capacity to work, but they do not solve the welfare work problem, since the effort is seldom sustained and working "off-the-books" involves cheating on welfare. See Mildred Rein, *Dilemmas of Welfare Policy: Why Work Strategies Haven't Worked* (New York: Praeger, 1982), chs. 5–6.
4. Greg J. Duncan et al., *Years of Poverty, Years of Plenty, The Changing Economic Fortunes of American Workers and Families* (Ann Arbor: Institute for Social Research, University of Michigan, 1984), tables 2.2, 3.2.
5. William Julius Wilson, *The Declining Significance of Race: Blacks and Changing American Institutions*, 2nd Ed. (Chicago: University of Chicago Press, 1980); Leonard Goodwin, *Causes and Cures of Welfare: New Evidence on the Social Psychology of the Poor* (Lexington, Mass.: D. C. Heath, 1983), ch. 7.
6. *Beyond Entitlement*, chs. 2, 4.
7. Bane and Ellwood, "Dynamics of Dependence," ch. 3; Suzanne H. Woolsey, "Pied-Piper Politics and the Child-Care Debate," *Daedalus*, vol. 106, no. 2 (Spring 1977), pp. 127–45.
8. For the conservative view, see Charles Murray, *Losing Ground: American Social Policy, 1950–1980* (New York: Basic Books, 1984). For the liberal view, see Henry J. Aaron, *Why Is Welfare So Hard to Reform?* (Washington, D.C.: Brookings, 1973).
9. *Beyond Entitlement*, ch. 4.
10. *Beyond Entitlement*, ch. 3; Ken Auletta, *The Underclass* (New York: Random House, 1982), chs. 3–15.
11. *Beyond Entitlement*, pp. 121–4.
12. Judith M. Gueron, *Work Initiatives for Welfare Recipients: Lessons from a Multi-State Experiment* (New York: Manpower Demonstration Research Corporation, March 1986), pp. 10–11.
13. Lawrence M. Mead, "Expectations and Welfare Work: WIN in New York City," *Policy Studies Review;* vol. 2, no. 4 (May 1983), pp. 648–62, and

"Expectations and Welfare Work: WIN in New York State," *Polity*, vol. 18, no. 2 (Winter 1985), pp. 224–52. The latter study is summarized in *Beyond Entitlement*, ch. 7. Preliminary results from a study now underway show similar results for WIN nationwide.

14. Gueron, *Work Initiatives for Welfare Recipients*, pp. 14–19.

15. *Beyond Entitlement*, chs. 9–10.

16. Gueron, *Work Initiatives for Welfare Recipients*, pp. 13–14.

17. Joel Handler and Ellen Jane Hollingsworth, *The "Deserving Poor": A Study of Welfare Administration* (New York: Academic Press, 1973), p. 84.

18. Judith M. Gueron and Barbara Goldman, "The U.S. Experience in Work Relief," (New York: Manpower Demonstration Research Corporation, March 1983), pp. 1–33. For a sophisticated statement of the "program integrity" approach, see Blanche Bernstein, *The Politics of Welfare: The New York City Experience* (Cambridge, Mass.: Abt Books, 1982).

19. Gueron, *Work Initiatives for Welfare Recipients*, p. 13.

20. Rein, *Dilemmas of Welfare Policy*, p. 81.

21. The following discussion summarizes *Beyond Entitlement*, pp. 135–47, 182–6.

22. For details, see *Beyond Entitlement*, pp. 144–6.

NO

Morton H. Sklar

PREPARED STATEMENT OF
MORTON H. SKLAR

Members of the Committee:

My name is Morton Sklar. Since 1978 I have served as Legal Counsel, and Director, of Jobs Watch, a public interest project providing information, clearinghouse, and support services on a variety of issues related to unemployment, with a special emphasis on job training and welfare to work activities. While at Jobs Watch I prepared and published in 1983 the first national survey examining how extensively and in what form the states and localities were attaching workfare requirements to the receipt of welfare benefits. I served as legal counsel on two major lawsuits involving workfare, one of which, the *Milwaukee County* case, produced a finding by the U.S. Seventh Circuit of Appeals that a workfare program had unlawfully displaced regular civil service workers, and had failed to provide workfare participants with a fair and reasonable wage for the work they were required to perform.

Since Jobs Watch lost its funding in August of 1985, I have been continuing to work, on an independent basis, directly with a number of communities involved with the adoption and/or implementation of workfare programs, including California, where the statewide Greater Avenues for Independence (GAIN) program was recently adopted, and New York, where a statewide workfare requirement has been proposed and is now before the legislature. I also have been conducting a statewide evaluation of job training programs generally in the state of Virginia, with the final report due out in June.

Because of the recommendations that I am about to make in this testimony, it is important to stress that the analytical and on-site field work that forms the basis for my assessment is not restricted to workfare. It has covered a broad variety of program policies and initiatives designed to assist welfare recipients and others dealing with longer-term joblessness become gainfully employed.

With this broader perspective in mind, one of the most important suggestions that I can make, and the one overriding thought that I would hope this

From U.S. Congress. Joint Economic Committee. Subcommittee on Trade, Productivity, and Economic Growth. *Workfare Versus Welfare*. Hearing, April 23, 1986. Washington DC: Government Printing Office, 1986.

testimony leaves you with, is that *the debate over federal welfare-to-work policy should not be put in terms of "Workfare Versus Welfare,"* as these hearings have (inappropriately, I think) been titled. I would hope, when the Congress completes its examination of recent experiences with workfare, and has had a chance to review several other welfare to work policy options that have proven far more effective, that they will see that the choice does not boil down to workfare on one hand, or welfare dependency on the other. There are several viable policy and program alternatives that are far more effectively geared to improving the job holding potential of welfare recipients than workfare.

It would be self-defeating, unduly expensive and contradictory to the lessons we have learned about job training in the past few years for Congress to in any way encourage or facilitate the adoption of workfare by states and localities. The goal of Congressional policy and action on the welfare to work issue would be more profitably directed towards encouraging job training approaches that experience has shown to be more effectively directed towards reducing welfare dependency and improving the job holding ability of recipients.

1. What Workfare Is and Isn't

To understand why my principal recommendation is to support policy options other than workfare it is important to see what workfare is (and seeks to do), and what its virtues and deficiencies are in comparison with alternative approaches.

In essence, workfare is similar to the public service jobs type of approach that Congress became disenchanted with in the old Comprehensive Employment and Training Act (CETA) program, and de-

leted under the current Job Training Partnership Act (JTPA) system. But workfare is far less than CETA's public service employment (PSE) effort, since PSE represented paid, full-time (though temporary) jobs with all of the status and benefits of regular civil service employment. Workfare assignments tend to be in lesser skilled positions, and more sporadic in nature than PSE, since the tasks and hours assigned vary for each participant. How can it be that the more legitimate type of work and on-the-job training experiences of PSE are seen as totally discredited by Congress on the one hand, while the much less substantial public service assignments of workfare are now being considered a viable training approach for welfare recipients?

The other aspect of what workfare is and is not that must be borne in mind is that it is not a training program. With an expenditure of less than $600 on average per participant, it is not really intended to deal, nor can it deal, with any of the job skill or academic deficiencies that force people to be on welfare instead of in the labor market. To that extent, workfare seems primarily designed to serve as a penalty or discouragement to the receipt of assistance benefits rather than a way to promote eligibility.

Much has been made of the fact that a goodly proportion of workfare participants report (in the recent Manpower Demonstration Research Corp. survey and elsewhere) a generally positive feeling about their experience. This has more to do with the strong motivation for, and interest in work that the vast majority of welfare recipients already have, than the ability of workfare to stimulate a work ethic.

The assumption that the only thing that keeps welfare recipients on the rolls is a lack of motivation to work is a gross misconception. Half of recipients (and an even higher proportion of the employable recipients that workfare would apply to) find jobs and leave welfare in their own right after a relatively brief stay in the program. The remainder of employable recipients, who make up only approximately 7% of all those receiving welfare, remain in the program for longer than two year stints. But this is the group that is least likely to benefit from workfare, or be motivated by experience, since they face the types of more serious academic and skill deficiencies that are not affected or improved by short-term work assignments.

2. Workfare Does Not Save Money
Another misconception about what workfare is and is not that needs to be addressed is the widespread assumption that the program saves money. Recent experiences with workfare in state after state prove the contrary—that in fact the program costs substantially more than it saves through reduced welfare payments.

State agency audits found:

• in Georgia, that "savings from non-participation and employment" were exceeded by nearly 5 to 1.

• in Florida, that "from the government/taxpayer's perspective, for every dollar spent, only 16 cents was returned, a net loss of 84 cents."

• in Connecticut, that "the program produced direct costs to the state of $6,884,625 . . . and a savings of $1,871,216" for a greater than 3 to 1 cost over savings ratio.

These findings are typical of the independent and government sponsored evaluations of workfare. The promise that proponents of workfare hold out for easy savings through reduced welfare

rolls does not generally pan out in practice. This is partly because of the relatively high costs of administering the program, and in part because workfare does not result in long-lasting job placements—only temporary benefit terminations, or the revolving door of welfare to dead-end job and back to welfare again.

The one study that seems to hold more of a promise for some beneficial effects from workfare is the evaluation conducted by the Manpower Demonstration Research Corporation (MDRC), some of whose initial results were recently summarized in a report written by MDRC's vice-president Judith Gueron. MDRC took an in-depth look at demonstration welfare to work programs in several states, including Arkansas, California, Maryland, Virginia, and West Virginia.

MDRC reported employment gains among participants in two of the more effective programs (San Diego and Baltimore) of from 3 to 8 percentage points relative to other welfare recipients, and a favorable benefits over costs result of from $100 to $2,000 per participant over a five year period. These results seem at variance with my earlier conclusion of workfare being a costly and ineffective program. But MDRC pointed to some important provisos in making their findings. One was that the Baltimore and San Diego programs in particular were not straight workfare. In Baltimore's program, especially, a wide mix of remediation and training activities was added to the workfare component. So it would not be fair to characterize MDRC's favorable findings as applying to workfare in general.

Along the same lines, the MDRC demonstrations were of limited scope in terms of the number of participants. They cautioned readers that it would be unfair and inaccurate to assume that every jurisdiction that attempted a workfare program for larger segments of the welfare population would obtain similar results. MDRC warned that their findings "should not be used to draw conclusions about the quality of programs—or the reactions of welfare recipients—if workfare-type requirements are implemented on a larger scale, are differently designed, or are of longer duration."

Further evidence of the desirability of treating MDRC's findings with caution is the fact that in the program that MDRC viewed as producing the most effective results—San Diego's—earlier findings suggested that cost benefits and employment gains were attributable mostly to other aspects of the San Diego program than workfare.

In sum, it is unlikely that the positive gains that MDRC identified in its best demonstration programs can be duplicated on much larger scale operations, especially when implemented by jurisdictions that do not offer the additional funding and program support elements that were featured in its model experiments. More telling in the debate over the value of straight workfare programs are the preponderantly negative results achieved by every other state where the approach was attempted and evaluated.

3. Workfare Threatens Existing Civil Service Jobs

One of the aspects of the workfare debate that has always irritated, and amused me at the same time, is the claim of supporters of the program that it does not feature make-work assignments, but rather provides valuable work experiences that benefit participant and society alike. What is troubling about this claim is that if it is true then almost by defini-tion we are talking about workfare recipients performing—for the equivalent of the minimum wage—the very same tasks that would otherwise be performed by civil service employees at higher wage rates. What this means is that we would be replacing salaried workers with unsalaried workfare recipients.

This perhaps would produce some savings to the government, but it would strike at the heart of the notion that workfare is designed to promote employment and the work ethic. Instead, to the extent that this type of worker displacement occurs, workfare would cause or promote continued unemployment, and undercut the principle of pay being commensurate with the work performed and prevailing wage rates.

And in fact, we have very concrete evidence that this is exactly what is occurring under workfare. Last August, the U.S. Seventh Circuit Court of Appeals, in the Milwaukee County case, issued the nation's first court finding that a workfare program was illegally displacing civil service personnel, and had failed to pay workfare participants the full and fair value of their work by not meeting prevailing wage requirements. In Lackawana, New York, a similar case has been filed because several city sanitation workers were laid off, and then found themselves assigned to do the very same work as workfare participants, at a lower rate of pay.

Proponents of workfare are fond of claiming that the displacement of workers really is not a problem because there is language in most workfare program statutes prohibiting this result. But the existence of statutory standards does not mean that the prohibited conduct is not taking place, especially when the burden of monitoring the problem and bringing the complicated litigation falls to welfare recipients, and when the temptation for governments to cut corners and costs by using a cheaper workforce is so great. As the attorney who handled the successful *Milwaukee County* case, I can tell you first-hand that even when there is an obvious situation of illegal displacement taking place, it is a difficult matter to prove because the government will always claim that budgetary limits rather than the easy availability of workfare labor was the reason for layoffs in civil service personnel.

The statutory prohibition against displacement, however well drafted, is a difficult tool to use. The only real protection against the practice is to deny the use of, or strictly limit the amount of workfare, because displacement, or the refusal to rehire previously laid off personnel, is almost an inevitable consequence of making a low paid alternative workforce available to government agencies.

If you take a look at a recent report issued by the American Federation of State, County and Municipal Employees Union in New York State (attached), you will see why displacement is almost an inevitable companion of workfare. Their survey of workfare assignments in the state found participants performing virtually the same tasks as regular employees, with exactly the same job titles, except that the word "assistant" was added. The *Milwaukee County* and *Lackawana* cases are not aberrations.

4. Recent Lessons From Experience

It is because of the problems and limits of workfare that states and local jurisdictions have begun to move away from the straight workfare model, and to favor a wider and more effective mix of program approaches. California, Massachusetts and New York are probably the best cases in point. This summer the California legislature rejected their governor's proposed workfare package, substituting what they call GAIN, the Greater Avenues for Independence program. GAIN includes workfare assignments (called pre-employment preparation) as part of a much broader system of more legitimate training activities, but the California Department of Social Services estimated in their legislative material that no more than 15% of participants in GAIN would be assigned to workfare. Instead, recognizing that the underlying problem relates to academic and job skill deficiencies, they *guaranteed* academic remediation as the very first activity for *every participant* that has literacy deficiencies (estimated at 50% of recipients), allowed recipients to enter and complete education and training programs, and made available more effective training components, such as supported work.

The Massachusetts CHOICES program follows the same pattern. An early effort to adopt a statewide workfare program was rejected and replaced with a comprehensive system of training and supportive services. Participants play a major role in determining the most suitable component to fit their needs in order to foster their own commitment to make the program work effectively.

Just this past month, the New York State legislature also rejected Governor Cuomo's proposal to make a straight workfare program a part of the fiscal 1987 budget package, and are likely to adopt a more comprehensive training system along the lines of GAIN later this spring.

The two critical common elements in these experiences is that in all three states:

• a straight workfare proposal was rejected, and

• each state made a commitment to a more effective investment in the employment potential of welfare recipients by stressing more legitimate remediation and training efforts, and by backing up this choice with *additional state funding* to make the remediation activities and necessary supportive services more meaningful.

Let us hope that their message reaches Congress and federal level decision-makers. To phrase the policy debate as a choice between welfare and workfare is to ignore the benefits of what we have learned about the deficiencies of workfare, and to fly in the face of the clear direction that states are moving towards by their own choice.

5. What Are the Alternatives—What Can Congress and the Federal Government Do?

Given the strong popular sentiment against welfare costs, and the strict budgetary constraints we are facing, it is not enough for a federal welfare to work policy to be based on a rejection of the workfare approach. What direction should be taken?

The two models that have shown themselves to be most effective are the supported work program, and the comprehensive training and services approach of the type embodied in the California GAIN and Massachusetts CHOICES programs.

The Supported Work approach was applied on a demonstration basis by MDRC in 1975–1978 in 15 sites. The program was found to be "most effective in preparing for employment a substantial number of women who have been on welfare (AFDC) for many years." Recipients had to have been on welfare for at least 30 of the previous 36 months in order to participate. Their average stay on welfare was 8.5 years. This was clearly the most difficult category of recipients to assist.

After an average of 9.5 months of comprehensive remediation and training assistance, costing approximately $7,000 per participant, the program produced substantial employment and income gains for these long-term welfare mothers. Most important, these results produced long-term net savings to the government of between $3 and $10 thousand per participant.

In other words, if one of the principal purposes of welfare reform is to cut welfare costs, the best way to do it, and the most lasting, is to make a more substantial investment in terms of both time and money. These investments will far more than pay for themselves.

In essence, that is also the principle underlying the GAIN and CHOICE programs. California added $137 million to provide for effective child care services for participants. Massachusetts added $5.8 million earmarked for supported work program assignments, and $18 million more for other training options. California mandated remedial education for every participant needing it, and Massachusetts allocated $2.7 million for a similar purpose.

All these are evidence of the growing recognition that an investment in time and funding is the proper and more effective approach to the employment promotion aspects of welfare reform.

It would be a great shame to see a federal policy that discourages this approach and looks instead to shortcut methods for cutting the welfare rolls, such as workfare. What federal policy should do is to:

1. encourage the type of state discretion that produced the GAIN and CHOICES programs, without imposing mandatory workfare requirements;

2. provide financial support and incentives for states that can show above average employment gains for welfare recipients (and especially for long-term recipients); and

3. encourage the use of the most effective program approaches such as supported work and remedial education.

Of course, the most appropriate question, and one that is close to the top of Congress' concerns, is where the funding for this policy of encouraging longer-term remediation is going to come from. I would suggest two sources.

One, which will probably be viewed as somewhat surprising is the Job Partnership Training Act. What we are learning about JTPA from independent assessments such as the Grinker-Walker study is that, contrary to Reagan Administration claims, the program is not working effectively. At current funding levels, only 3% of eligible unemployed people can participate in JTPA. That fact, plus the strong pressures of the program to produce fast placements at very low cost and in very brief periods of time, have led to creaming—the provision of assistance to those who need service least, and who are already in the best position to find work. This result is a direct contradiction of the stated goal of the program to serve those most in need of employment assistance.

Contractor after contractor, service delivery area official after service delivery area official, private industry council member after private industry council member in Virginia (where I have been working most closely) and elsewhere, all convey the same message—the makeup of the current JTPA program discourages service to the more long-term unemployed, and forces us to concentrate relatively short-term and low-cost efforts on those who are largely job-ready in their own right.

It's true that JTPA produces good participation statistics and good placement rates. But these figures belie the true contribution (or lack of contribution) of the program. Its fast-in and fast-out high volume approach cannot hope to deal with job training needs in a realistic and meaningful way.

I would suggest taking JTPA's funding and remodeling the program to target exclusively on the harder to employ, such as long-term welfare recipients. This would mean reversing JTPA's present orientation by keying the indicators of the program's performance to successful placements of those needing more substantial forms of assistance, rather than those needing only fast-in and fast-out service.

A second funding source that deserves exploration is a revised version of the Unemployment Insurance (UI) program. Roger Vaughn, former assistant director of New York State's employment and training office, was one of the first to suggest using UI as a basis for self-supported, guaranteed training (or retraining) for dislocated workers and others needing this assistance. The virtue of this approach is that it would make training part of a self-insurance system financed primarily by employers and employees themselves, rather than a governmental benefit program that might attach the stigma of a grant-in-aid to the receipt of benefits. There is a great deal of logic in linking training to a system designed to provide for the temporary needs of the unemployed.

What makes Vaughn's proposal different from similar ones that would add training insurance to UI is his suggestion that long-term, unemployed people such as welfare recipients, including those that have been unable to contribute to the training fund because they have been jobless, would also be able to draw on these resources for training purposes. This makes sense because once employed, these recipients would then become paying participants in the UI training fund.

There is one other funding source that also should be mentioned. Employed welfare recipients become taxpayers instead of tax users. Our initial investment in improving their employment potential will be returned several fold through tax payments they will make.

Summary

Summarizing my recommendations to you:

1. The debate over federal welfare-to-work policy should not be put in terms of "Workfare Versus Welfare." Congress should be supporting and seeking to encourage the adoption of policies and programs that are far more effective than workfare in helping welfare recipients become employed on a long-term basis. Workfare is the least effective and probably the most costly (measured in terms of long-term effects) approach.

2. There is not one program or policy approach that is best suited to assist every welfare recipient find work. The fifty percent of welfare recipients who currently find work and leave the program in a short time need little more than job search and referral assistance. Recipients who are long-term unemployed need the type of academic and skill training designed to deal with the barriers that keep them from being considered employable. Few in either category receive any benefits from the type of unpaid public service work experience that workfare represents.

3. What you put in, you get out. You can't expect to produce positive change in the hard-core unemployed with quick, low-investment approaches such as workfare. A person with literacy problems can't be made employable with a 6 to 8 week stint in workfare, or in a low-cost job training program costing $600 per participant. The long-term cost of doing little or nothing to change recipients' basic employability profiles is far greater than making an initial investment in human capital that is designed to improve employability on a more lasting basis. Proven programs such as Supported Work and others that deal with the core issues of academic and job skill deficiencies that keep welfare recipients from becoming employed deserve to be the focus of national welfare-to-work policies.

4. Among the sources of funding that should be considered to support a more effective federal training effort for welfare recipients are:

• a revamped Job Training Partnership Act program that focuses assistance more carefully on the hardest to employ, and encourages (rather than discourages as is presently the case) the type of longer-term remediation that makes the most effective difference in the employability of welfare recipients; and

• an expanded Unemployment Insurance (UI) program that adds a training support component, and makes it available (through UI's joint employer/employee contribution system) to all long-term unemployed or dislocated workers.

I appreciate being given this opportunity to participate in Congress' consideration of welfare reform policy needs, and would be pleased to continue to work with you in any way that you would find useful.

POSTSCRIPT

Is Workfare a Good Substitute for Welfare?

Mead argues that the fundamental problem with AFDC is that welfare mothers are not obligated to work. Since few of these recipients of welfare aid have experienced the discipline of the workplace, they become disinterested and discouraged with all that happens around them. They give up the right of self-determination. They slip out of the American mainstream and get caught in the backwater eddies of "welfare dependency."

Sklar does not reject the importance that Mead attaches to work experience. Rather, he argues that blaming all the problems of welfare on a lack of a work obligation is a "gross misconception." He finds that the problems of those who are welfare dependent are far more complex. Those who seem trapped are those who are least able to compete in the marketplace. They are poorly educated. They have low skill levels. In short, they are the least likely to benefit in a fundamental sense from short-term work experience.

What we find in this discussion are two views of the poor. In a fundamental sense, Mead argues that the poor are poor because they are lazy. If they would just go out and get work, they would no longer need assistance. Sklar attributes idleness to a lack of job skills, not laziness. For him, it is a matter of eliminating the barriers to employment, which, he claims, is not an inexpensive project.

Addressing the problems of those in need is well documented in the literature. Certainly one place to begin is to read the testimony of the other expert witnesses who appeared before the Subcommittee on Trade, Productivity, and Economic Growth in April 1986. Then turn to those who contributed to two turning points in welfare policy—one to the left and one to the right: Michael Harrington, *The Other American* (Macmillan, 1962), and Charles Murray, *Losing Ground: American Social Policy 1950–1980* (Basic Books, 1984). Next, look at the changes in the law concerning work requirements for welfare recipients. For example, in the Omnibus Budget Reconciliation Act of 1981, states were allowed to establish mandatory Community Work Experience Programs (CWEP), where adults could be mandated to participate in CWEP training or jobs as a condition of receiving public assistance. These legislative changes and others are summarized in Statements before the Committee on Ways and Means, *Background Material and Data on Ways and Means*, U.S. House (Washington, DC: U.S. Government Printing Office, 1987). Finally, look at Mead's detailed arguments in his book *The New Politics of Poverty: The Nonworking Poor in America* (Basic Books, 1992). For a review of some preliminary results of the Family Support Act, see Jason De Porle, "Welfare Plan Linked to Jobs is Paying Off, A Study Shows," *The New York Times* (April 23, 1992).

PART 3

International Issues

For many years America held a position of dominance in international trade. That position has been changed by time, events, and the emergence of other economic powers in the world. Decisions that are made in the international arena will, with increasing frequency, influence our lives. Protectionist measures are being discussed in Congress, and the jobs of many Americans may depend on the outcome of those discussions. Relations between the United States and Japan seem to make media headlines every week. Other concerns that currently have the attention of economists and other analysts are the environment and industrial activity.

Should the United States Protect Domestic Industries from Foreign Competition?

Is Japan a Threat to America's Economic and National Security?

Does Global Warming Require Immediate Government Action?

Should a New Military-Industrial Complex Be Developed?

ISSUE 15

Should the United States Protect Domestic Industries from Foreign Competition?

YES: Robert Kuttner, from "The Free Trade Fallacy," *The New Republic* (March 28, 1983)

NO: Michael Kinsley, from "Keep Free Trade Free," *The New Republic* (April 11, 1983)

ISSUE SUMMARY

YES: Columnist Robert Kuttner alleges that David Ricardo's eighteenth-century view of the world does not "describe the global economy as it actually works" in the twentieth century. He says that, today, "comparative advantage" is determined by exploitative wage rates and government action; it is not determined by free markets.

NO: Social critic Michael Kinsley replies that we do not decrease American living standards when we import the products made by cheap foreign labor. He claims protectionism today, just as it did in the eighteenth century, weakens our economy and only "helps to put off the day of reckoning."

The basic logic of international trade has not changed over time. The villains change, the winners and losers change, but the theory remains the same. Thus, do not be alarmed that the readings that follow refer to 10-year-old editorials that appeared in the *Wall Street Journal*, the *New York Times*, or the *Village Voice*. The pleadings made in these articles are almost identical to those that are now being made in the newspapers of the 1990s. As the saying goes, "The more things change, the more they stay the same." It is because of the timelessness of the free trade versus protectionism debate that we have included the Kuttner/Kinsley selections, even though these essays first appeared in print a decade ago. Not only does the basic logic of international trade not change over time, it is indistinguishable from domestic trade: Both domestic and international trade must answer the fundamental economic questions: *"What* to produce?" *"How* to produce it?" and *"For whom* to produce?" The distinction is that the international trade questions are posed in an international arena. This is an arena filled with producers and consumers who speak different languages, use different currencies, and are often suspicious of the actions and reactions of foreigners.

If markets work the way they are expected to work, free trade simply increases the extent of a purely domestic market and, therefore, increases the advantages of specialization. Market participants should be able to buy and consume a greater variety of inexpensive goods and services after the establishment of free trade than they could before free trade. You might ask, Then why do some wish to close the borders and deny Americans the benefits of free trade? The answer to this question is straightforward. These benefits do not come without a cost.

There are two sets of winners and two sets of losers in this game of free trade. The most obvious winners are the consumers of the less expensive imported goods. These consumers are able to buy the low-priced color television sets, automobiles, or steel that is made abroad. Another set of winners are the producers of the exported goods. All the factors in the export industry, as well as those in industries that supply to the export industry, experience an increase in their market demand. Therefore, their income increases. In the United States, agriculture is one such export industry. As new foreign markets are opened, farmers' incomes increase, as do the incomes of those who supply the farmers with fertilizer, farm equipment, gasoline, and other basic inputs.

On the other side of this coin are the losers. The obvious losers are those who own the factors of production that are employed in the import-competing industries. These factors include the land, labor, and capital that are devoted to the production of such items as U.S.–made color television sets, U.S.–made automobiles, and U.S.–made steel. The less expensive foreign imports displace the demand for these products. The consumers of exported goods are also losers. For example, as U.S. farmers sell more of their products abroad, less of this output is available domestically. As a result, the domestic prices of these farm products and other export goods and services rise.

The bottom line is that there is nothing "free" in a market system. Competition—whether it is domestic or foreign—creates winners and losers. Historically, we have sympathized with the losers when they suffer at the hands of foreign competitors. However, we have not let our sympathies seriously curtail free trade. Robert Kuttner argues that we can no longer afford this policy. He maintains that U.S. workers face "unfair foreign competition" and that the international rules of the game have changed. Michael Kinsley replies that this is pure, unadorned protectionism. He concludes that "each job 'saved' will cost other American workers far more than it will bring the lucky beneficiary."

YES
Robert Kuttner

THE FREE TRADE FALLACY

In the firmament of American ideological convictions, no star burns brighter than the bipartisan devotion to free trade. The President's 1983 Economic Report, to no one's surprise, sternly admonished would-be protectionists. An editorial in *The New York Times*, midway through an otherwise sensibly Keynesian argument, paused to add ritually, "Protectionism might mean a few jobs for American auto workers, but it would depress the living standards of hundreds of millions of consumers and workers, here and abroad."

The Rising Tide of Protectionism has become an irresistible topic for a light news day. Before me is a thick sheaf of nearly interchangeable clips warning of impending trade war. With rare unanimity, the press has excoriated the United Auto Workers for its local content legislation. *The Wall Street Journal's* editorial ("Loco Content") and the *Times's* ("The Made-in-America Trap") were, if anything, a shade more charitable than Cockburn and Ridgeway in *The Village Voice* ("Jobs and Racism"). And when former Vice President Mondale began telling labor audiences that America should hold Japan to a single standard in trade, it signaled a chorus of shame-on-Fritz stories.

The standard trade war story goes like this: recession has prompted a spate of jingoistic and self-defeating demands to fence out superior foreign goods. These demands typically emanate from overpaid workers, loser industries, and their political toadies. Protectionism will breed stagnation, retaliation, and worldwide depression. Remember Smoot-Hawley!

Perhaps it is just the unnerving experience of seeing *The Wall Street Journal* and *The Village Voice* on the same side, but one is moved to further inquiry. Recall for a moment the classic theory of comparative advantage. As the English economist David Ricardo explained it in 1817, if you are more efficient at making wine and I am better at weaving cloth, then it would be silly for each of us to produce both goods. Far better to do what each does best, and to trade the excess. Obviously then, barriers to trade defeat potential efficiency gains. Add some algebra, and that is how trade theory continues to be taught today.

To bring Ricardo's homely illustration up to date, the economically sound way to deal with the Japanese menace is simply to buy their entire

From Robert Kuttner, "The Free Trade Fallacy," *The New Republic*, vol. 188, no. 12 (March 28, 1983). Copyright © 1983 by The New Republic, Inc. Reprinted by permission of *The New Republic*.

cornucopia—the cheaper the better. If they are superior at making autos, TVs, tape recorders, cameras, steel, machine tools, baseballs, semiconductors, computers, and other peculiarly Oriental products, it is irrational to shelter our own benighted industries. Far more sensible to buy their goods, let the bracing tonic of competition shake America from its torpor, and wait for the market to reveal our niche in the international division of labor.

But this formulation fails to describe the global economy as it actually works. The classical theory of free trade was based on what economists call "factor endowments"—a nation's natural advantages in climate, minerals, arable land, or plentiful labor. The theory doesn't fit a world of learning curves, economies of scale, and floating exchange rates. And it certainly doesn't deal with the fact that much "comparative advantage" today is created not by markets but by government action. If Boeing got a head start on the 707 from multibillion-dollar military contracts, is that a sin against free trade? Well, sort of. If the European Airbus responds with subsidized loans, is that worse? If only Western Electric (a U.S. supplier) can produce for Bell, is that protection? If Japan uses public capital, research subsidies, and market-sharing cartels to launch a highly competitive semiconductor industry, is *that* protection? Maybe so, maybe not.

Just fifty years ago, Keynes, having dissented from the nineteenth-century theory of free markets, began wondering about free trade as well. In a 1933 essay in the *Yale Review* called "National Self-Sufficiency," he noted that "most modern processes of mass production can be performed in most countries and climates with almost equal efficiency." He wondered whether the putative efficiencies

of trade ne[...] national au[...] world trad[...] of multinat[...] predicted, [...] steel, plas[...] and mach[...] almost anywhere, but by labor[...] with vastly differing prevailing wages.

With dozens of countries trying to emulate Japan, the trend is toward worldwide excess capacity, shortened useful life of capital equipment, and downward pressure on wages. For in a world where technology is highly mobile and interchangeable, there is a real risk that comparative advantage comes to be defined as whose work force will work for the lowest wage.

In such a world, it is possible for industries to grow nominally more productive while the national economy grows poorer. How can that be? The factor left out of the simple Ricardo equation is idle capacity. If America's autos (or steel tubes, or machine tools) are manufactured more productively than a decade ago but less productively than in Japan (or Korea, or Brazil), and if we practice what we preach about open trade, then an immense share of U.S. purchasing power will go to provide jobs overseas. A growing segment of our productive resources will lie idle. American manufacturers, detecting soft markets and falling profits, will decline to invest. Steelmakers will buy oil companies. Consumer access to superior foreign products will not necessarily compensate for the decline in real income and the idle resources. Nor is there any guarantee that the new industrial countries will use their burgeoning income from American sales to buy American capital equipment (or computers, or even coal), all striving to develop their anced, diversified economies. ist this background of tidal change e global economy, the conventional erence for "free trade" is just not helpful. As an economic paradigm, it denies us a realistic appraisal of second bests. As a political principle, it leads liberals into a disastrous logic in which the main obstacle to a strong American economy is decent living standards for the American work force. Worst of all, a simple-minded devotion to textbook free trade in a world of mercantilism assures that the form of protection we inevitably get will be purely defensive, and will not lead to constructive change in the protected industry.

The seductive fallacy that pervades the hand-wringing about protectionism is the premise that free trade is the norm and that successful foreign exporters must be playing by the rules. Even so canny a critic of political economy as Michael Kinsley wrote in these pages that "Very few American workers have lost their jobs because of unfair foreign trade practices, and it is demagogic for Mondale and company to suggest otherwise." But what is an unfair trade practice? The Common Market just filed a complaint alleging that the entire Japanese industrial system is one great unfair trade practice!

To the extent that the rules of liberal trade are codified, they repose in the General Agreement on Tariffs and Trade (stay awake, this will be brief). The GATT is one of those multilateral institutions created in the American image just after World War II, a splendid historical moment when we could commend free trade to our allies the way the biggest kid on the block calls for a fair fight.

The basic GATT treaty, ratified in 1947, requires that all member nations get the same tariff treatment (the "most favored nation" doctrine), and that tariffs, in theory at least, are the only permissible form of barrier. Governments are supposed to treat foreign goods exactly the same as domestic ones: no subsidies, tax preferences, cheap loans to home industries, no quotas, preferential procurement, or inspection gimmicks to exclude foreign ones. Nor can producers sell below cost (dumping) in foreign markets. . . .

In classical free trade theory, the only permissible candidate for temporary protection is the "infant industry." But Japan and its imitators, not unreasonably, treat every emerging technology as an infant industry. Japan uses a highly sheltered domestic market as a laboratory, and as a shield behind which to launch one export winner after another. Seemingly, Japan should be paying a heavy price for its protectionism as its industry stagnates. Poor Japan! This is not the place for a detailed recapitulation of Japan, Inc., but keep in mind some essentials.

The Japanese government, in close collaboration with industry, targets sectors for development. It doesn't try to pick winners blindfolded; it creates them. It offers special equity loans, which need be repaid only if the venture turns a profit. It lends public capital through the Japan Development Bank, which signals private bankers to let funds flow. Where our government offers tax deductions to all businesses as an entitlement, Japan taxes ordinary business profits at stiff rates and saves its tax subsidies for targeted ventures. The government sometimes buys back outdated capital equipment to create markets for newer capital.

The famed Ministry of International Trade and Industry has pursued this essential strategy for better than twenty years, keeping foreign borrowers out of cheap Japanese capital markets, letting in foreign investors only on very restricted terms, moving Japan up the product ladder from cheap labor intensive goods in the 1950s to autos and steel in the 1960s, consumer electronics in the early 1970s, and computers, semiconductors, optical fibers, and just about everything else by 1980. The Japanese government also waives antimonopoly laws for development cartels, and organizes recession cartels when overcapacity is a problem. And far from defying the discipline of the market, MITI encourages fierce domestic competition before winnowing the field down to a few export champions. . . .

The Japanese not only sin against the rules of market economics. They convert sin into productive virtue. By our own highest standards, they must be doing something right. The evident success of the Japanese model and the worldwide rush to emulate it create both a diplomatic crisis for American trade negotiators and a deeper ideological crisis for the free trade regime. As Berkeley professors John Zysman and Steven Cohen observed in a careful study for the Congressional Joint Economic Committee last December, America, as the main defender of the GATT philosophy, now faces an acute policy dilemma: "how to sustain the open trade system and promote the competitive position of American industry" at the same time.

Unfortunately, the dilemma is compounded by our ideological blinders. Americans believe so fervently in free markets, especially in trade, that we shun interventionist measures until an industry is in deep trouble. Then we build it half a bridge.

There is no better example of the lethal combination of protectionism plus market-capitalism-as-usual than the steel industry. Steel has enjoyed some import limitation since the late 1950s, initially through informal quotas. The industry is oligopolistic; it was very slow to modernize. By the mid-1970s, world demand for steel was leveling off just as aggressive new producers such as Japan, Korea, and Brazil were flooding world markets with cheap, state-of-the-art steel.

As the Carter Administration took office, the American steel industry was pursuing antidumping suits against foreign producers—an avenue that creates problems for American diplomacy. The new Administration had a better idea, more consistent with open markets and neighborly economic relations. It devised a "trigger price mechanism," a kind of floor price for foreign steel entering American markets. This was supposed to limit import penetration. The steelmakers withdrew their suits. Imports continued to increase.

So the Carter Administration moved with characteristic caution toward a minimalist industrial policy. Officials invented a kind of near-beer called the Steel Tripartite. Together, industry, labor, and government would devise a strategy for a competitive American steel industry. The eventual steel policy accepted the industry's own agenda: more protection, a softening of pollution control requirements, wage restraint, new tax incentives, and a gentlemen's agreement to phase out excess capacity. What the policy did not include was either an enforceable commitment or adequate capital to modernize the industry. By market standards, massive retooling was not a rational course, because the return on steel investment was well below prevailing yields on other investments. Moreover, government officials had neither the ideological mandate nor adequate information to tell the steel industry how to invest. "We would sit around and talk about rods versus plate versus specialty steel, and none of us in government had any knowledge of how the steel industry actually operates," confesses C. Fred Bergsten, who served as Treasury's top trade official under Carter. "There has never been a government study of what size and shape steel industry the country needs. If we're going to go down this road, we should do it right, rather than simply preserving the status quo." . . .

The argument that we should let "the market" ease us out of old-fashioned heavy industry in which newly industrialized countries have a comparative advantage quickly melts away once you realize that precisely the same nonmarket pressures are squeezing us out of the highest-tech industries as well. And the argument that blames the problem on overpaid American labor collapses when one understands that semiskilled labor overseas in several Asian nations is producing advanced products for the U.S. market at less than a dollar an hour. Who really thinks that we should lower American wages to that level in order to compete?

In theory, other nations' willingness to exploit their work forces in order to provide Americans with good, cheap products offers a deal we shouldn't refuse. But the fallacy in that logic is to measure the costs and benefits of a trade transaction only in terms of that transaction itself. Classical free-trade theory assumes full employment. When foreign, state-led competition drives us out of industry after industry, the costs to the economy as a whole can easily outweigh the benefits. As Wolfgang Hager, a consultant to the Common Market, has written, "The cheap [imported] shirt is paid for several times: once at the counter, then again in unemployment benefits. Secondary losses involve input industries . . . machinery, fibers, chemicals for dyeing and finishing products."

As it happens, Hager's metaphor, the textile industry, is a fairly successful example of managed trade, which combines a dose of protection with a dose of modernization. Essentially, textiles have been removed from the free-trade regime by an international market-sharing agreement. In the late 1950s, the American textile industry began suffering insurmountable competition from cheap imports. The United States first imposed quotas on imports of cotton fibers, then on synthetics, and eventually on most textiles and apparel as well. A so-called Multi-Fiber Arrangement eventually was negotiated with other nations, which shelters the textile industries of Europe and the United States from wholesale import penetration. Under M.F.A., import growth in textiles was limited to an average of 6 percent per year.

The consequences of this, in theory, should have been stagnation. But the result has been exactly the opposite. The degree of protection, and a climate of cooperation with the two major labor unions, encouraged the American textile industry to invest heavily in modernization. During the 1960s and 1970s, the average annual productivity growth in textiles has been about twice the U.S. industrial average, second only to electronics. According to a study done for the Common Market, productivity in the most efficient American weaving operations is 130,000 stitches per worker per hour—twice as high as France and three times as high as Britain. Textiles, surprisingly enough, have remained an export winner for the United States, with net exports regularly exceeding imports. (In 1982, a depressed year that saw renewed competition from China, Hong Kong, Korea, and Taiwan, exports just about equaled imports.)

But surely the American consumer pays the bill when the domestic market is sheltered from open foreign competition. Wrong again. Textile prices have risen at only about half the average rate of the producer price index, both before and after the introduction of the Multi-Fiber Arrangement.

Now, it is possible to perform some algebraic manipulations and show how much lower textile prices would have been without any protection. One such computation places the cost of each protected textile job at several hundred thousand dollars. But these static calculations are essentially useless as practical policy guides, for they leave out the value over time of maintaining a textile industry in the United States. The benefits include not only jobs, but contributions to G.N.P., to the balance of payments, and the fact that investing in this generation's technology is the ticket of admission to the next.

Why didn't the textile industry stagnate? Why didn't protectionism lead to higher prices? Largely because the textile industry is quite competitive domestically. The top five manufacturers have less than 20 percent of the market. The industry still operates under a 1968 Federal Trade Commission consent order prohibiting any company with sales of more than $100 million from acquiring one with sales exceeding $10 million. If an industry competes vigorously domestically, it can innovate and keep prices low, despite being sheltered from ultra-low-wage foreign competition—or rather,

thanks to the shelter. In fact, students of the nature of modern managed capitalism should hardly be surprised that market stability and new investment go hand in hand.

The textile case also suggests that the sunrise industry/sunset industry distinction is so much nonsense. Most of America's major industries can be winners or losers, depending on whether they get sufficient capital investment. And it turns out that many U.S. industries such as textiles and shoes, which conventionally seem destined for lower-wage countries, can survive and modernize given a reasonable degree of, well, protection.

What, then, is to be done? First, we should acknowledge the realities of international trade. Our competitors, increasingly, are not free marketeers in our own mold. It is absurd to let foreign mercantilist enterprise overrun U.S. industry in the name of free trade. The alternative is not jingoist protectionism. It is managed trade, on the model of the Multi-Fiber Arrangement. If domestic industries are assured some limits to import growth, then it becomes rational for them to keep retooling and modernizing.

It is not necessary to protect every industry, nor do we want an American MITI. But surely it is reasonable to fashion plans for particular key sectors like steel, autos, machine tools, and semiconductors. The idea is not to close U.S. markets, but to limit the rate of import growth in key industries. In exchange, the domestic industry must invest heavily in modernization. And as part of the bargain, workers deserve a degree of job security and job retraining opportunities.

Far from being just another euphemism for beggar-thy-neighbor, a more stable trade system generally can be in the interest of producing countries. Universal excess capacity does no country much of a favor. When rapid penetration of the U.S. color TV market by Korean suppliers became intolerable, we slammed shut an open door. Overnight, Korean color TV production shrank to 20 percent of capacity. Predictable, if more gradual, growth in sales would have been preferable for us and for the Koreans.

Second, we should understand the interrelationship of managed trade, industrial policies, and economic recovery. Without a degree of industrial planning, limiting imports leads indeed to stagnation. Without restored world economic growth, managed trade becomes a nasty battle over shares of a shrinking pie, instead of allocation of a growing one. And without some limitation on imports, the Keynesian pump leaks. One reason big deficits fail to ignite recoveries is that so much of the growth in demand goes to purchase imported goods.

Third, we should train more economists to study industries in the particular. Most economists dwell in the best of all possible worlds, where markets equilibrate, firms optimize, the idle resources re-employ themselves. "Microeconomics" is seldom the study of actual industries; it is most often a branch of arcane mathematics. The issue of *whether* governments can sometimes improve on markets is not a fit subject for empirical inquiry, for the paradigm begins with the assumption that they cannot. The highly practical question of *when* a little protection is justified is ruled out *ex ante*, since neoclassical economics assumes that less protection is always better than more.

Because applied industrial economics is not a mainstream concern of the economics profession, the people who study it tend to come from the fields of management, industrial and labor relations, planning, and law. They are not invited to professional gatherings of economists, who thus continue to avoid the most pressing practical questions. One economist whom I otherwise admire told me he found it "seedy" that high-wage autoworkers would ask consumers to subsidize their pay. Surely it is seedier for an $800-a-week tenured economist to lecture a $400-a-week autoworker on job security; if the Japanese have a genuine comparative advantage in anything, it is in applied economics.

Fourth, we should stop viewing high wages as a liability. After World War II, Western Europe and North America evolved a social contract unique in the history of industrial capitalism. Unionism was encouraged, workers got a fair share in the fruits of production, and a measure of job security. The transformation of a crude industrial production machine into something approximating social citizenship is an immense achievement, not to be sacrificed lightly on the altar of "free trade." It took one depression to show that wage cuts are no route to recovery. Will it take another to show they are a poor formula for competitiveness? Well-paid workers, after all, are consumers.

NO

Michael Kinsley

KEEP FREE TRADE FREE

Free trade is not a religion—it has no spiritual value—and Bob Kuttner is right to insist, as he did in TNR two weeks ago, that if it is no longer good for America in practical terms, it is not a sensible policy for liberals anymore. He and I would also agree that a liberal trade policy ought to be good for working people in particular (including people who would like to be working but aren't). The question is whether free trade is just a relic from two happier eras—the period of liberal clarity two centuries ago when Adam Smith and David Ricardo devised the theories of free enterprise and free trade, and the period of American hegemony after World War II when we could dominate world markets—or whether it is still a key to prosperity.

Kuttner argues that Ricardo's theory of "comparative advantage"—that all nations are better off if each produces and exports what it can make most efficiently—no longer applies. Local factors such as climate and natural resources don't matter much anymore. As a result, "most basic products . . . can be manufactured almost anywhere" with equal efficiency. This means, Kuttner says, that the only ways one nation (e.g., Japan) gains comparative advantage over another (e.g., us) these days are through low wages or "government action." Either of these, he says, makes nonsense of Ricardo's theory. In addition, Kuttner says, Ricardo didn't account for the problem of "idle capacity"—expensive factories sitting unused.

"Idle capacity" is an argument against any competition at all, not just from abroad, and has a long history of being carted out whenever established companies (the airlines, for example) want the government to prevent newcomers from horning in on their turf. If you believe in capitalism at all, you have to believe that the temporary waste of capital that can result from the turmoil of competition is more than outweighed by the efficiency of competition in keeping all the competitors on their toes. A capitalist who builds a plant knowing (or even not knowing) that it is less efficient than a rival abroad deserves whatever he gets. As for older plants that are already built—that capital is sunk. If the cost of running those plants is higher than the cost of buying the same output from abroad, keeping them running is more wasteful than letting them sit idle.

This brings us to the real problem; not sunk capital but sunk lives. The middle-class living standard achieved by much of the United States working class is one of the glories of American civilization. Yet Kuttner says, "semi-skilled labor overseas is producing advanced products for the U.S. market at less than a dollar an hour. Who really thinks that we should lower American wages to that level in order to compete?"

We shouldn't, of course. But importing the products of cheap foreign labor cannot lower American living standards as a whole, and trade barriers cannot raise living standards. This is not a matter of morality: it is a matter of mathematics. If widgets can be imported from Asia for a price reflecting labor costs of $1 an hour, then an hour spent making widgets adds a dollar of value to the economy. This is true no matter what American widget makers are being paid. If foreign widgets are excluded in order to protect the jobs of American widget makers getting $10 an hour, $1 of that $10 reflects their contribution to the economy and $9 is coming out of the pockets of other workers who have to pay more for widgets. Nice for widget makers, but perfectly futile from the perspective of net social welfare.

After all, if this economic alchemy really worked, we could shut our borders to all imports, pay one another $1,000 an hour, and we'd all be rich. It doesn't work that way. In fact, as a society, we're clearly better off taking advantage of the $1 widgets. The "comparative advantage" of cheap Asian labor is an advantage to us too. That's why trade is good.

But what about the poor widget makers? And what about the social cost of unemployment? If former widget makers aren't working at all, they aren't even adding a dollar's worth to the economy.

Protectionism is, in effect, a "make work" jobs program—but a ridiculously expensive one, both directly and indirectly. The direct cost, in this example, is $9 an hour. The indirect cost is in reducing the efficiency of the economy by preventing international specialization.

If the disparity between American and foreign wages is really that great, Americans just shouldn't be making widgets. We could pay widget workers at $8 an hour to do nothing, and still be better off. We could put them to work at their current wage doing anything worth more than a dollar an hour. We could spend the equivalent of $9 an hour on retraining. And we owe it to widget workers to try all these things if necessary, because they are the victims of a change that has benefited all the rest of us by bringing us cheaper widgets (and because, as Lester Thurow points out, doing these things will discourage them from blocking the needed change). To protect them while they keep on making widgets, though, is insane.

These suggestions are, of course, overt tax-and-spend government programs, compared to the covert tax-and-spend program of protectionism. In a period of political reaction, the covert approach is tempting. But hypocrisy is not a sensible long-term strategy for liberals, nor is willfully ignoring the importance of economic productivity.

In many basic industries, American wages are not all that far out of line, as Bob Kuttner seems to acknowledge in the case of autos. Modest wage adjustments can save these jobs and these industries for America. It is uncomfortable for a well-paid journalist to be urging pay cuts for blue-collar workers. On the other hand, steelworkers (when they are working) make more than the median American income. Protectionism to preserve wage levels is just a redistribution of national wealth; it creates no new wealth. Nothing is wrong with redistribution, but in any radical socialist redistribution of wealth, the pay of steelworkers would go down, not up. So it's hard to see why the government should intervene to protect steelworkers' wages at the expense of general national prosperity. This is especially true when millions are unemployed who would happily work for much less, and there is no jobs program for them.

But Bob Kuttner believes that protection can be good for general national prosperity even apart from the wage question, in an age when other nations' "comparative advantage" comes from government policies that include protectionism. It is important to separate different strands in the common protectionist argument that we have to do it because Japan does it. Many politicians of various stripes, and William Safire in a recent column, argue (on an implicit analogy between trade war and real war) that only by threatening or building trade barriers of our own can we persuade the Japanese to dismantle theirs and restore free trade. Kuttner, by contrast, thinks that the idea of free trade is outmoded; that the Japanese are *smart* to restrict imports and we would be smart to do the same as part of an "industrial policy."

Both Safire and Kuttner assume incorrectly that free trade needs to be mutual. In fact, the theory of free trade is that nations benefit from their own open borders as well as the other guy's. This may be right or wrong, but the mere fact that Japan is protectionist does not settle the question of what our policy should be.

Certainly, it's worth looking at Japan for clues about how to succeed in the world economy, and certainly one key to Japan's success seems to be a government-coordinated industrial policy. (The current vogue for "industrial policy" is assessed by my colleague Robert Kaus in the February *Harper's*—forgive the plug.) But why must such a policy include trade barriers? One reason Japan thwarts imports is a conscious decision to reduce workers' living standards in order to concentrate national resources on industrial investment. I presume this isn't what Kuttner and other liberal trade revisionists have in mind. Kuttner and others include protectionism in their "industrial policy" for two other reasons. First, as a sort of bribe to get unions to go along with sterner measures—possibly necessary, but not a case for protection on its own merits. Second, to give promising industries a captive market in which to incubate and gather strength before taking on the world.

The trouble with this "nurture" argument is that there's no end to it. Kuttner himself says that it's "not unreasonable" to "treat every emerging technology" this way, and also says that "most of America's major industries can be winners" with the right treatment. After you add the few hopeless loser industries where we must allegedly create barriers to save American wages, you've got the whole economy locked up, and whether this will actually encourage efficiency or the opposite is, at the very least, an open question. And if every major country protects every major industry, there will be no world market for any of them to conquer.

Kuttner's model for "managed trade" is the Multi-Fiber Arrangement, an international agreement that restricts imports of textiles. This, according to Kuttner, permitted the American textile industry to modernize and become productive, to the point where exports exceeded imports—a less impressive accomplishment if you recall that the M.F.A. *restricts* imports.

Kuttner concedes that, despite the productivity gains, textile prices are higher than they would be without protection from cheap foreign labor. (Indeed, the current situation in the textile industry, as Bob Kuttner describes it, seems to vindicate Luddites, who got their start in textiles; human beings could do the work more efficiently, but machines are doing it anyway.) So what's the point? According to Kuttner, "The benefits include not only jobs, but contributions to G.N.P., to the balance of payments, and the fact that investing in this generation's technology is the ticket of admission to the next." Yet Kuttner does not challenge the "algebraic manipulations" he cites that show how each job saved costs the nation "several hundred thousand dollars" in higher textile prices. The only "contribution to G.N.P." from willful inefficiency like this can be the false contribution of inflation. The balance of payments is a measure of economic health, not a cause of it; restricting imports to reduce that deficit is like sticking the thermometer in ice water to bring down a feverish temperature. As for the suggestion that the *next* generation of technology will bring the *real* payoff—well, they were probably promising the same thing two decades ago when the Multi-Fiber Arrangement began.

Kuttner also worries that "without some limitation on imports," Keynesian fiscal policies don't work. This is like the monetarists who worry that financial advances such as money market funds will weaken the connection between inflation and the money supply. Unable to make their theory accord with life, they want the government to make life accord with their theory. There *is* a world economy—which Bob Kuttner seems to recognize as a good thing—and this means Keynesian techniques will increasingly have to be applied internationally. . . .

There can be no pretense that domestic content legislation has anything to do with "industrial policy"—improving the competitive ability of American industry. It is protectionism, pure and unadorned, and each job "saved" will cost other American workers far more than it will bring the lucky beneficiary. Like most protectionist measures, far from aiding America's adjustment to world competition, it just helps put off the day of reckoning.

POSTSCRIPT

Should the United States Protect Domestic Industries from Foreign Competition?

The desirability of free trade is one of few issues on which a large majority of professional economists agree. Survey after survey confirms this: Economists are ardent supporters of free trade. In spite of this general consensus, protectionism is hotly debated. This certainly is the case in these essays that appeared in *The New Republic*.

Kuttner argues two basic points in his essay. First, he contends that the world that English economist David Ricardo modeled in 1817 is starkly different than the world we know today. He describes our world as "a world of learning curves, economies of scale, and floating exchange rates." It is a world where comparative advantage "is created not by markets but by government action." Second, he maintains that although free markets will lead to factor price equalization—that is, wage rates in developing countries will rise and U.S. wage rates will fall as long as there is a differential—we should not, and cannot, allow this to happen. He asks: Do we want wage levels in the United States to fall to a dollar an hour?

Kinsley does not believe that free trade is a relic from the past. He maintains that Kuttner has just forgotten the lessons from his introductory economics course. After looking at the simple mathematics of Kuttner's proposal, Kinsley contends: "Protectionism is, in effect, a 'make work' jobs program—but a ridiculously expensive one, both directly and indirectly." He believes we can achieve the same end without sacrificing the benefits of "international specialization." Kinsley goes on to argue that when "every major country protects every major industry"—the natural consequence of Kuttner's national industrial policy—"there will be no world market for any of them to conquer." He contends that we will return to the isolationists' world, a world that is poorer than it need be.

Since the majority of economists support the notion of free trade, readings supporting this position are very easy to identify. However, if you would like to read an extreme position paper, you might try Paula Stern's "Ronald Reagan: The International Bad Boy on Trade," *The International Economy* (July/August 1991). In this essay she argues that "the essence of Reagan's trade policy became clear: Espouse free trade, but find an excuse on every occasion to embrace the opposite." For a more scholarly discourse, you might read Douglas Irwin's "Retrospectives: Challenges to Free Trade," *Journal of Economic Perspectives* (Spring 1991). Irwin concludes that when all is said and done, the charges leveled at free trade "will not fundamentally challenge the belief of economists in free trade."

ISSUE 16

Is Japan a Threat to America's Economic and National Security?

YES: Stephen D. Cohen, from "United States–Japanese Trade Relations," *Proceedings of the Academy of Political Science* (1990)

NO: Philip H. Trezise, from "Japan, the Enemy?" *The Brookings Review* (Winter 1989–1990)

ISSUE SUMMARY

YES: Professor of international economic relations Stephen D. Cohen concludes that a continuation of our "inferior industrial performance relative to Japan" is a threat to both the "economic [and] national security interests of the United States."

NO: Philip H. Trezise, a senior fellow of the Brookings Institution, replies that "on any rational calculation, economic competition from Japan does not threaten America's national security" or its long-run economic vitality.

In the post–World War II period, Japan flooded the free world market with cheap imitations of American-made goods. There were toy cars and airplanes made out of tin, flimsy dolls dressed in gaudy, rough cotton, watches and clocks that rarely lasted through a year of service, and many, many other consumer items all boldly stamped "made in Japan." In the eyes of most consumers, "made in Japan" was synonymous with "second rate." This was poor-quality merchandise that rarely, if ever, commanded respect.

Gradually, however, this reputation faded. The Japanese genius for copying, modifying, and producing at low cost simple consumer goods was directed toward more sophisticated items. No longer were Japanese industrialists content with competing for the "low end" of the consumer market; they set their sights on the "high end." The transistor, which was first developed in the United States in the early 1960s and licensed to Japanese firms, became the vehicle. This technology was first applied to the radio. Portable radios that were once the size of large suitcases suddenly were squeezed into remarkably small boxes that became extremely popular among beach-goers. The rest of the electronic industry was soon to follow. Relatively inexpensive state-of-the-art television sets, cameras, tape recorders, and calculators produced in Japan literally drove their American counterparts out of the market. For all practical purposes, by the mid-1970s, the U.S. electronics industry was dead.

Other Japanese industrialists turned their attention to the automobile market—an industry dominated by the Big Three American auto makers (General Motors, Ford, and Chrysler). The energy crisis that was initiated by the Organization of Petroleum Exporting Countries (OPEC) in 1973 and 1979 opened the trade door for Japan. From a negligible market share, Japanese exports to the United States rose to 1.2 million cars in 1973, as consumers turned their backs on the American-built gas-guzzlers. By the time the second wave of the energy crisis hit the American coastline, Japanese sales in the United States had risen to 1.7 million cars. This market penetration whetted the American appetite for the fuel-efficient, low-maintenance, inexpensive alternative to the automobiles produced by the Big Three. By 1986, Japanese auto sales rose to a remarkable 3.6 million cars, signaling to all that the U.S. automobile industry was under a direct attack.

Japanese success in the world marketplace is reflected in its trade balances. In 1963, the value of Japanese merchandise exports to North America was essentially equal to the value of Japan's imports from North America. By 1973 this ratio rose to 1.1, or slightly more exports to North America than imports to Japan. Over the next 13 years this ratio grew markedly, so that by 1986 Japan was exporting to North America 3.3 times more than it was importing. This imbalance excited much concern over "American competitiveness" and "Japanese unfair trade practices."

These concerns eventually led to a series of trade concessions on the part of Japan. Most importantly, they agreed to voluntary export quotas on certain commodities, such as automobiles, and explicit policies to open their domestic markets to American firms. Gradually the ratio of Japanese merchandise exports to imports began to fall. By 1989 it was back down to 1.9; but this still represented nearly twice the value of exports to North America compared to the value of her imports from North America.

In the selections that follow, the wisdom of seeking trade concessions is debated. Stephen D. Cohen argues that the presence of Japan's trade surplus is a threat to America's international strength—both military and economic strength. Philip H. Trezise, on the other side, maintains that Japanese success in the world marketplace is beneficial not only to the Japanese but also to Americans.

YES

Stephen D. Cohen

UNITED STATES–JAPANESE TRADE RELATIONS

With the waning of the cold war and the reduced threat of confrontation between the global military superpowers, the United States and Japan arguably constitute the world's most important bilateral relationship. This relationship now consists of a struggle—peaceful to be sure, but for enormous stakes—between economic superpowers. Relations between the United States and Japan feature a close political and military friendship that is being strained by a long-running series of economic frictions. To the dismay of political scientists, most American businesspeople and many American economists are urging their government to take an increasingly harder line with Japan in an effort to receive equitable treatment in what has long been viewed as an unbalanced, inequitable trading relationship.

The economic arguments between the United States and Japan have extraordinary significance. These two countries formed the world's newest and most important bilateral relationship not because of political or military considerations but because global power and influence among nations in the twenty-first century will be determined more by economic and technological strength than by the size and sophistication of weapons stockpiles. Japan and the United States, as the world's largest and strongest economies, will inevitably be the two forces to be most reckoned with in what may be the continuing evolution into a postmilitary international system. This is why the majority of respondents in some recent United States public opinion polls indicated that Japan, not the Soviet Union, represents the greatest long-term threat to American national security. There is an intuitive recognition (not yet fully shared by the United States government) that national security must be defined broadly to include industrial and financial strength.

Japan is the most significant foreign competitor of the United States and vice versa. No other country has mounted such a comprehensive and successful assault on the competitiveness of American industry, once the undisputed colossus of the world. No other country has in so many instances caught up to and surpassed the once unassailable American

From Stephen D. Cohen, "United States–Japanese Trade Relations," *Proceedings of the Academy of Political Science*, vol. 37, no. 4 (1990). Copyright © 1990 by The Academy of Political Science. Reprinted by permission.

leading-edge superiority in the high-tech sector. No other country comes close to Japan in representing a future challenge to United States competitiveness in the critically important new technologies: supercomputers, semiconductors, superconductivity, composite materials, telecommunications equipment and so on.

For most Japanese, friendship with the United States represents political security to a country with a still undefined sense of international mission or function. The United States is also Japan's most important foreign market and a key determinant of its continued prosperity. At the same time, American industry has been a symbolic target for a country that wished to bypass it on the way to becoming an internationally dominant industrial power.

The importance and mutual rewards of the world's largest bilateral trade relationship are not in question. What is in question is whether the likely further escalation of bilateral trade conflict will erupt into damaging unilateral economic actions that in turn will lead to political estrangement. There can be no assurance that the previously successful record of trade-conflict management can continue indefinitely, especially in view of a possible expansion of Japan's industrial superiority in the future. Also not in question is whether, by conventional measurements, the Japanese trade performance has been superior to that of the United States.

What is in question is how the two countries should best respond to a state of affairs that tries everyone's patience. Japan's trade policy has centered on a flurry of activity designed to demonstrate responsiveness to United States demands but not necessarily to induce adjustment in the bilateral disequilib-rium. From the American viewpoint, the specter of Japan's unbroken winning streak in trade competition was at the focus of virtually every new concept and proposed initiative introduced in United States trade policy in the 1980's. Possible responses to reverse its deteriorating trade position include reciprocity, industrial policy, results-oriented trade talks, and reinvigorated American industrial competitiveness.

There is a serious, systemic trade problem between the two countries that is seriously misunderstood, underestimated and inadequately addressed. It arises from political, cultural and economic forces. The trade disequilibrium is best viewed as the tip of the iceberg, with domestic factors as the main underlying causal factors. With both countries continuing to treat symptoms rather than causes, it is no surprise that trade conflict has occurred on a nonstop basis since 1969. To the extent that the diagnosis offered here is correct, neither an end nor a plateau in trade frictions is in sight.

Economic conflict begins with accusations by the United States and other countries that Japan is an unfair, adversarial trader that does not play by conventional international rules in order to pursue a mercantile policy of self-aggrandizement. Critics allege that Japanese markets remain largely closed, albeit informally, to imports of manufactured goods. Its exporting companies are said to be avaricious predators intent on building market share and destroying their foreign competition. The more rabid critics of Japan accuse it of continuing to fight World War II through economic means.

Japan, in turn, is tired of what has become an unbroken record of United

States whining. It accuses the United States of excessive consumption, an inadequate effort to improve its own industrial productivity, and not trying hard enough to sell in the Japanese market. The boom in Japan's exports to the United States, according to Japanese critics, reflects the preferences of American consumers for low-cost, high-quality goods, some of which are not even manufactured in the United States. The more extreme critics consider the United States to be in permanent decline, a country that is burdened by poor economic policy management, an excessively heterogeneous population, an excessive need for instant gratification, and shockingly bad business practices.

The proximate cause of the trade frictions is the large, seemingly permanent United States bilateral deficits with Japan (see Table 1). It is legitimate to state unequivocally that these deficits have produced a genuine disequilibrium in political terms, that is, an American belief that something is grievously wrong and urgently needs rectification, mainly through adjustments by Japan. It is *not* legitimate to state unequivocally that these deficits represent an absolutely unacceptable economic disequilibrium. Bilateral deficits per se, as the Japanese are quick to point out, are relatively insignificant. It is multilateral trade balances that matter.

It is the sources of the bilateral trade imbalance that must be of central concern. Here again, there are many opinions but no genuine consensus. Conflicting perceptions are an inherent part of bilateral trade disputes. Some argue that the culprit is Japanese industrial policy, in which close government-business relations have built a mighty anti-import fortress known colloquially as Japan, Incorporated. Others contend that the culprit is the simple manufacturing ineptitude of the United States, a country alleged, but not proved, to be in the advanced stages of moving into a postindustrial services-oriented economy.

The systemic source of the imbalance is best viewed as a divergence in ends (priorities and values) and therefore a divergence in means (domestic, economic and trade policies). The American system is weighted in favor of the individual and consumption. The Japanese system is weighted in favor of the corporation and production. American ideology favors the free market and cheap imports. Japanese ideology favors government enhancement of market forces, industrial self-sufficiency, and world-class strength in the manufacturing sector. The United States prints money to finance the world's largest trade deficit and in turn consumes more as a country than it produces. Japan saves like mad, accepts relatively poor housing and an inadequate infrastructure, and continues sending massive amounts of capital earned from its trade surpluses back to the United States, the effect of which is to compensate for this country's inadequate savings rate. American foreign relations for half a century have centered on political and military goals. Since 1945, Japan's foreign relations have sought to maximize exports [see Table 2 for a summary of Japan's trade structure as compared to that of the West]. . . .

ORIGINS OF THE TRADE DISPUTE

As a Japanese surplus became a fixture in the bilateral trade relationship, the United States successfully induced Japan

Table 1

Bilateral United States–Japan Trade Balances, 1981–1990

	U.S. Bilateral Deficit ($ billion)	U.S. Imports From Japan ($ billion)	U.S. Exports to Japan ($ billion)
1981	$15.8	$37.6	$21.8
1982	16.7	37.7	21.0
1983	19.3	41.2	21.9
1984	33.6	57.1	23.6
1985	46.2	68.8	22.6
1986	55.0	81.8	26.9
1987	56.3	84.6	28.2
1988	52.1	89.8	37.7
1989	49.0	93.5	44.5
1990	41.1	89.6	48.6

Source: United States Department of Commerce.

to take sustained actions on two fronts. The first involved additional "voluntary" export restraints in a number of sectors, including textiles, automobiles, steel, color televisions, and machine tools. The second involved Japan's initiation of an unprecedented series of unilateral measures that eliminated or reduced hundreds of overt tariff and nontariff trade barriers. The result was an eventual Japanese contention that it had become the world's most open market (a valid claim, at least in regard to formal import restrictions). This assertion was not widely accepted in the United States, where complaints about the difficulty of succeeding in the Japanese market are still voiced by many American companies.

Bilateral consultations and negotiations continued throughout the 1980's amid continuous proposals by various members of Congress to pass harsh, retaliatory legislation as leverage to force genuine reciprocity in market access. As the "Japan problem" worsened, new forms of agreements were pursued. They included altering macroeconomic policies in an effort to increase the value of the yen's exchange rate relative to the dollar. Instead of a piecemeal approach to addressing United States corporate complaints, market-oriented, sector-selective (MOSS) talks were convened in 1985 to focus on all the alleged market-access problems for four specially designated goods in which the United States retained a comparative advantage (electronics, pharmaceuticals/medical equipment, telecommunications, forestry products, and, later, automobile parts). One year later, the two governments concluded a groundbreaking agreement involving trade in semiconductors; it sought to shelter the American industry from Japanese "dumping" (selling below production cost) of chips both in the United States and in third countries, and it sought to provide the American industry with a specific percentage (20 percent) of the Japanese market in lieu of any further Japanese promises of market-opening measures.

Table 2

Comparing Japan's Trade Structure With the West

Category	Japan				West Germany		United States		North America		European Community	
	1980	1987	1988	1989	1980	1987	1980	1987	1980	1987	1980	1987
Manufactured goods *(as percentage of GDP)*												
Exports	11.9	9.5	9.1	9.6	20.9	24.2	5.5	4.3	4.4	3.0	8.5	8.1
Imports	2.9	2.8	3.2	3.5	13.3	14.8	5.1	7.5	4.3	6.3	5.3	5.3
Balance	9.0	6.7	5.9	6.1	7.6	9.4	0.4	-3.2	0.1	-3.2	2.9	2.3
Non-Manufactured goods *(as percentage of GDP)*												
Exports	0.2	0.1	0.1	0.1	1.6	1.0	1.3	0.7	1.4	0.8	1.0	0.7
Imports	9.0	3.5	3.3	3.6	7.3	3.5	3.6	1.4	3.0	1.1	6.0	2.6
Balance	-8.8	-3.4	-3.2	-3.5	-5.7	-2.5	-2.3	-0.7	-1.6	-0.3	-5.0	-1.9

Source: Organization for European Cooperation and Development, *Summary Report on Trade of Japan* (Paris: OECD, 1990), *Far Eastern Economic Review* (Hong Kong), June 21, 1990, p. 47.

STRUCTURAL IMPEDIMENTS INITIATIVE

More new forms of negotiating modalities were introduced in 1989. The first was a direct outgrowth of Japan's being identified as a "priority" source of foreign-trade barriers against American goods under the Super 301 amendment to the Omnibus Trade and Competitiveness Act of 1988. Acting under the law, the administration of President George Bush named three areas—supercomputers, communications satellites, and wood products—that required either productive bilateral negotiations (read foreign concessions would be forthcoming) or eventual United States retaliation in kind against Japanese goods. The second, the so-called Structural Impediments Initiative (SII), was an indirect outgrowth of the Super 301 and marked a major conceptual breakthrough. The original American idea was to discuss the big picture for the first time by addressing such structural barriers to imports as the Japanese distribution system, the industrial structure (whereby companies in an extended consortium, such as Mitsui or Mitsubishi, tend to buy from one another), and the rigid pricing system for imports. But Japan insisted that the agenda be expanded to include its charges about the structural weaknesses in the United States that are allegedly the principal sources of the trade disequilibrium.

The contradictory positions that were subsequently introduced in the SII are a perfect microcosmic symbol of the near 180-degree difference in the way each country (and Japan's supporters in the United States) apportion blame for generating bilateral economic antagonisms. In this regard, the debate over causality becomes a kind of Rorschach test. Both of the main contending views on causality are rational. But, given the absence of incontrovertible scientific methodology to determine precise cause and effect, individuals unconsciously fall back on previous experiences, prejudices, and preconceived notions in identifying with one side over the other.

While both sides continue hurling charges at each other, the festering trade dispute has begun to spill over into other economic issues. The agenda now includes the concerns of some Americans about Japan's allegedly excessive investment in the United States, its rising political influence in the United States, and the wisdom of Japan's independent development of advanced military weapons like the FSX fighter.

FLAWS IN JAPAN'S ECONOMIC CASE

An economic maxim applies to Japan: for society as a whole, there is no such thing as a free lunch. There can be no denying that Japan has achieved an economic miracle in its industrial sector since the 1950's. The miracle received crucial assistance from a seemingly universal consensus in the country that individual sacrifices had to be made in order to accomplish the priority goal of industrial recovery, a concept that could easily be embraced in a society that emphasized a group orientation. Japan's unprecedented industrial success, the springboard for its unprecedented trade success, also flowed from unexpectedly successful official policies and from unexpectedly brilliant accomplishments by private industry.

The major flaw in Japanese international economic relations continues to be the inhospitable atmosphere accorded to imports of sophisticated manufactured goods. Japan can honestly boast of having the lowest level of overt barriers and point to recent sharp upturns in its level of manufactured imports. Nevertheless, it has a surplus in manufactured goods so large (a world-record-shattering $172 billion in 1988) that it renders absurd the often heard Japanese claim that it must export a lot of manufactured goods in order to pay for its imports of raw materials. Japan's trade pattern continues to be in a class by itself in terms of the low figure for imports of manufactures as a percent of gross national product and its relatively low volume of intraindustry trade, that is, importing the same kinds of products that are exported, such as cars.

Japan poses an extraordinary problem for the United States in that a nearly complete array of the traditional techniques utilized in economics to redress a trade disequilibrium has been tried and has failed: relaxation of import barriers, exchange rate appreciation, accelerated domestic demand, politicians' exhortations to import more, and so on. Japan's argument about the true openness of its markets would be a lot more convincing if most of its trading partners were not voicing the same market-access complaints as the admittedly export-indifferent United States.

Although there is a dearth of smoking guns, circumstantial evidence, anecdotal evidence, and plain common sense collectively suggest that in the case of sophisticated manufactured goods, especially those in the targeted industries of the future, Japanese companies do prefer to keep the market share of imports to a "moderate" level. The market is not closed. It is, however, an extraordinary uphill battle by foreign exporters for more than a nominal market share in Japan. Even foreign companies that have a long-term, strong commitment to doing everything right in selling in Japan encounter levels of difficulty and frustration not experienced in countries with less of a history of keeping the rest of the world at a distance.[1]

Japan's efforts at "internationalization" have fallen far short of the mark. The country's retention of its insular, tradition-bound mentality has collided with the sheer magnitude of its export success, as well as with what is arguably the most pervasive international trend of the late twentieth century: accelerated economic interdependence. With its new role as the world's largest creditor nation come new responsibilities and the need for greater empathy for the economic needs and interests of its major trading partners and the poorer countries of the Southern Hemisphere.

Forecasts of the imminent peaking of Japan's economic success are, as they have been for almost 20 years, more wishful thinking and economic fallacy than truth. Japanese society may be aging, and a new generation born into relative affluence may not retain the same commitment to the work ethic as previous generations. But that will not prevent people from working harder. The idea that Japan has come to a plateau because it is not good at innovation flies in the face of the economic data showing massive outpourings of capital for investment in new plants and for research and development by Japanese corporations, as well as an upsurge in new patent applications.

UNITED STATES ECONOMIC FLAWS

The continuing difficulty in exporting sophisticated capital goods to the Japanese market is the first of two distinct, though interrelated, problems that constitute the essence of contemporary United States–Japan trade relations. The second problem is the inadequacies of both the domestic and external American economic performance. These collective inadequacies would perpetuate a large bilateral trade disequilibrium even if Japan were to undertake a radical restructuring of its attitudes toward dependency on foreigners for key technologies, its distribution system, its industrial structure, its willingness to abandon old business relations just to obtain cheaper products, and so forth.

The counterparts of Japan's record-setting trade surpluses are the unprecedented United States deficits that turned the American trade account in the 1980's into a sea of red ink. An important source of the deficits in the first half of the decade was not of Japanese origin: the overvaluation of the dollar's exchange rate made imports a bargain and reduced the competitiveness of American exports on a global basis. Large federal budget deficits following the tax cut induced by Reaganomics combined with falling savings rates to produce an internal United States disequilibrium that inevitably caused a net inflow of capital from abroad and a deficit in the current account (goods and services) of the balance of payments. Until savings increase or the budget deficit is reduced, a United States trade deficit will remain, not of Japanese doing but one that is largely self-inflicted.

When competing head-on with the industrial giants of Japan, the weaknesses of American management practices and production techniques are painfully magnified. The American reward system, which instills myopia among business executives about the value of immediate profits, does not hold up well against the long-term time horizon of Japanese managers willing to invest years of effort and lose hundreds of millions of dollars to maximize global market share. Ironically, several of the "innovations" of Japanese management, such as statistical procedures to enhance quality control, were devised by Americans whose countrymen originally had no interest in their ideas. It was not until recent years that most American business executives switched from the argument that the Japanese were competing mainly through unfair practices to the position that even the mightiest, proudest American industrial company would do well to replicate the perfectly fair and quite clever strategies being practiced by their Japanese competition. Hence, many American companies learned that assembling goods right the first time is cheaper than repairing defects later on, that is, vigorous quality control is effectively free.

Many American factories have switched to the Japanese system of "just in time delivery," by which inventory costs and the need for storage space are reduced by having suppliers deliver components only hours before they are actually needed on the production line. A number of American manufacturing companies have adopted the Japanese model of minimizing layers of middle management and maximizing attention paid to the ideas of production-line workers.

American companies are slowly absorbing the brilliant approach of their Japanese competitors to "process technology," the art of designing the production line for maximum efficiency. As exemplified by the unsuccessful multibillion-dollar retooling by General Motors in the 1980's, maximum efficiency on the production line means more than simple installation of labor-saving devices. It requires a proper configuration of flexible machinery on the production line and cooperation in the design phase among engineers, assembly-line workers, and even suppliers. Maximum efficiency also requires the ability to adjust machinery quickly and simply to turn out different models of the same products, be they automobiles or household appliances.

However, this is not to suggest the beginning of a turnaround in the bilateral trade disequilibrium. Even a more vigorous turnaround by American industry would be insufficient to overcome the disadvantages imposed by the fact that American economic policymaking does not put nearly enough emphasis on enhancing industrial competitiveness as Japan does. For example, the Japanese government has always put a major emphasis on ensuring that high-growth industries have ample amounts of low-cost capital. In the United States, government and business remain adversaries instead of trying jointly to forecast what goals and important new technologies the country's private sector should be pursuing. The American political establishment remains stubbornly opposed to any form of industrial policy in the increasingly important sector of commercial high technology, while mysteriously embracing it in sectors like agriculture and military aerospace. United States tax laws still encourage companies to go into debt to make acquisitions or engage in leveraged buy-outs.

While those presumed to be America's best and brightest are speculatively buying and selling corporate assets and issuing junk bonds of questionable value, the Japanese methodically go about the business of expanding sales through efficient, high-volume, low-defect production methods. While the United States focuses on how to carve up the existing national economic pie, the Japanese seek to enlarge it. While American executives try to please shareholders and maximize their incomes—admittedly a very efficient system—their Japanese competition is trying to please customers and maximize market share—sometimes an even better system.

The Japanese government has the simpler task in designing an optimal negotiating strategy with its United States counterpart. First, it relies on its vast commercial intelligence network in Washington to determine when United States threats are genuine. Second, the Japanese government relies on an even vaster public relations and lobbying network in the United States to get articulate, highly visible versions of Japanese viewpoints and rebuttals before United States officials as well as the general public. Third, it continues to find scattered import barriers to reduce. Japan's nearly quarter century of import liberalization is unique for more than just its extent; it has had the singular motive of seeking not to give lower prices to Japanese consumers but to please American demands. The potential for cheaper imports has been deemed a sacrifice, not an economic bonanza as it would in the United States. Fourth, when United States pressures intensify, the Japanese government pressures the appropriate Japanese companies to ease off on further export growth.

Japan's official trade agenda is basically reactive; the private sector takes the initiative and sets the tone. Most Japanese are satisfied with their country's trade performance and trade surplus. They prefer to stick with a winning formula, wanting nothing basic to change other than for the United States and other trading partners to be more understanding, to stop making threats, and not to pester them for ever more concessions. Japan's mounting global industrial and technological strength is accomplishing one of the transcendent goals of 2,000 years of Japanese history: retaining its political and cultural independence by carefully controlling and limiting foreign intrusion and leverage.

The United States government has found it much more difficult to set an effective bilateral trade agenda because its industry remains on the defensive. In lieu of adopting a grand strategy of homing in on the systemic problem, however, it has pursued piecemeal tactics aimed at changing trading conditions on a product-by-product basis. It has never known exactly how far to push Japan, fearing the triggering of protectionist trade actions or, even worse, political strains. Internal economic shortcomings have always been recognized as contributing to the trade disequilibrium, but for the past decade most of them have been attributed to government interference, not the lack of effective government initiatives or existing mistakes.

The net result is that United States trade policy toward Japan is the worst of both worlds. On the one hand, strident demands make the United States look like a bully with an unending request list. On the other hand, the lack of determination and consistency in United States policy has yielded wholly inadequate results. American negotiating strategy has been largely reduced to a repeated and somewhat predictable version of the good-cop/bad-cop routine of old Hollywood movies. After a ritualistic warning by the liberal trade-loving executive branch that the protectionist ogres in Congress are on the brink of passing restrictive trade legislation, Japan produces a ritualistic market-opening measure or export-restraint agreement, depending on the situation.

When the administration relies on the "congressional card," it implicitly links itself with purportedly fellow free traders in Japan in order to fight villains in another part of the United States government. In the words of a former United States negotiator: "The negotiation thus changed direction: originally a matter of U.S. government requests, it became one of mutually calibrating just how much action would be necessary to keep Congress leashed. Instead of a negotiator, the U.S. trade team became an adviser to the government of Japan on how to handle the U.S. Congress."[2]

The United States government would be well advised to develop a consensus on its needs and goals in the bilateral trade relationship, as well as how hard it is willing to press to achieve them. A unified strategy must come from the Office of the President, and it is unlikely to be produced by conventional policy-making forums. . . .

The first stage of a more effective United States Japanese trade dialogue would consist of both countries formally acknowledging the applicability of the Japanese proverb that when two men fight, both are at fault. Japan needs to accept the fact that selling advanced manufactured goods to its market still poses extraordinary difficulties to most foreigners. Pointing to its increased imports of consumer goods or to healthy sales and profits by United States corporate subsidiaries producing in Japan is not the same thing as demonstrating that the Japanese market for high-tech goods is "reasonably" open in regard to cost, energy, and effort. Japan's industrial policy tends to target the same high-tech industries—such as computers, semicon-

ductors, telecommunications equipment, and biotechnology—in which the United States has (or had) international competitive strength. The United States should not be content with even a bilateral trade surplus with Japan if it was caused by a boom in exports of agricultural and other primary products. Japan ought to realize that the more it discusses its "internationalization," the less likely it truly exists.

The United States needs to accept the fact that, quite apart from its legitimate complaints about the relative difficulty and cost of exporting to Japan, its lack of competitiveness vis-à-vis Japanese products, especially in its home market, is primarily the result of shortcomings in United States domestic economic policies, management practices, and production skills. The United States needs to accept the costly nature of protectionist trade policies, inasmuch as they tend to dissipate pressures on American producers to continue cutting costs and raising quality. Furthermore, restrictions on Japanese goods have already been shown to be harmful to the increasing number of American companies using Japanese-made capital goods and components. At the same time, the United States government must realize that more of the same is not an optimal strategy.

As long as it avoids the somewhat arbitrary idea of putting specific numbers on what Japan should be buying, the United States would be well advised to follow the basic recommendation of the 1989 report to the United States Trade Representative by the Advisory Committee for Trade Policy and Negotiations: the United States should

> structure a program of action that pursues change on multiple fronts, commits adequate resources over a 4–5-year pe-

riod, is strategically focused, and is re-sults-oriented. This program we see as a natural evolution of U.S. trade policy from a more or less reactive response to the damage wrought by the strong dollar in the early 1980's, to active efforts to create the conditions necessary for the growth of industries and sectors critical to the nation's long-term economic vitality.[3]

Japan should embrace as an integral part of its trade policy the belief that, in the long run, its national security is more likely to be enhanced by the friendship of trading partners than by the size of its trade surplus. The Japanese government needs to promote a whole new mind-set in Japan that encourages more attention to the Japanese consumer. This effort would need to be supported by such reforms as a more vigorous legal challenge to cartels and the easing of restrictions on large chain stores (they are more attracted to imports than the small stores effectively controlled by Japanese manufacturers). Furthermore, the government needs to go beyond slogans to generate a genuine consensus among Japanese industries that it is no longer in the national interest to discriminate against imports.

No matter how open the Japanese market becomes (or how much additional leisure time Japanese workers opt for), there is no reason to expect a diminution of Japan's increasing excellence in advanced technologies. If American exports to Japan are to rise and if American imports from Japan are not to swamp important high-tech industries, the United States clearly needs to improve its business environment. The appropriate starting point is an immediate, genuine (as opposed to accounting smoke and mirrors) reduction in the United States budget deficit. By reducing the government's absorption of the available capital pool, productive investment in the industrial sector would be encouraged by the assumed reduction in interest rates that would occur with a reduced federal budget deficit.

Furthermore, the government needs to realize that the nature of modern economics and the fading dividing line between military and civilian technology justify increased official funding of expensive or risky, but promising, new commercial technologies. While the United States does not need a comprehensive "industrial policy" to replace its basic dependence on corporate investment and venture capital, it does need additional government seed money to help entrepreneurial companies compete with the deep pockets of their larger, better financed, vertically integrated Japanese competitors.

No matter what Washington does to improve the domestic business environment, it will not be enough unless American business executives alter their behavior. They must place less emphasis on short-term profits, year-end bonuses, and wheeling and dealing in mergers, acquisitions and leveraged buy-outs. A significant part of the trade battle with Japan continues to be lost on the factory floor.

Official encouragement of dollar depreciation to an exchange rate of between 100 yen and 200 yen would aid American competitiveness, but it is not a panacea. Yen appreciation has not and will not keep Americans from buying high-quality Japanese goods, nor will it open the floodgates in Japan to imports of American-made manufactured goods.

There are two problems with this list of proposed policy and program reforms.

First, it is far from definitive. At the same time, however, neither country is likely to act quickly on its contents. A resolution in the underlying causes of the trade disequilibrium can only be foreseen by optimists. More likely than not, the systemic causes of frictions will remain unaddressed. United States industry may well do better in the competitiveness race but not as well as Japan in the pursuit of excellence in the important new technologies. There is no reason to expect the industrial competitiveness gap to narrow significantly. It therefore appears that during the 1990's Japan is fated to remain America's number-one foreign competitor, number-one illuminator of shortcomings in United States economic policies and business practices, and the principal source of frustration to American trade policymakers.

Continuation of an inferior industrial performance relative to Japan is not conducive either to the long-term economic prosperity or national security interests of the United States. Regrettably, in its successful but short-sighted pursuit of profit and consumption maximization, America cannot be bothered to respond more effectively to the long-term challenges of the alternative model of capitalist power being pursued in Japan. Also regrettably, Japan is not likely to find increased economic success a reason to become truly less insular. By the turn of the century, the inadequacies of United States trade and economic policies may cause this country to fail two key tests cited by Paul Kennedy in *The Rise and Fall of the Great Powers:*

whether, in the military/strategical realm, it can preserve a reasonable balance between the nation's perceived defense requirements and the means it possesses to maintain those commitments; and

whether, as an intimately related point, it can preserve the technological and economic bases of its power from relative erosion in the face of the ever-shifting patterns of global production.[4]

NOTES

1. See for example the report of the sales failure in high-tech goods by a native-born Japanese émigré sent back to live in Japan by Allied-Signal, Inc., in "Hidden Wall: A Native Son Battles Japan's Trade Barriers," *Washington Post,* June 23, 1989.
2. Clyde Prestowitz, Jr., *Trading Places* (New York: Basic Books, 1988), p. 281.
3. "Analysis of the U.S.-Japan Trade Problem" (Report of the Advisory Committee for Trade Policy and Negotiations, Washington, D.C., February, 1989), p. ix.
4. Paul Kennedy, *The Rise and Fall of the Great Powers* (New York: Random House, 1987), pp. 514–515.

NO

Philip H. Trezise

JAPAN, THE ENEMY?

Does Japanese economic competition present a greater threat to American security than Soviet military power? Is Japan a "systematically predatory actor" on the international economic scene? Is it an authoritarian state under irresponsible and corrupt rule? Must we devise a new policy to "contain" a rogue Japan? Is it time for the Pentagon to draw up plans for an eventual war with Japan?

According to opinion polls, a majority of Americans say yes to the first of these questions. Many supposedly well-informed people also respond affirmatively to the next three. The idea of planning for a war with Japan is no doubt remote from most Americans' minds, but it is said to be whispered among those whose profession is to reflect on the contingencies of the future.

To be sure, the actual state of U.S.–Japan relations is less bleak than the news media or the magazine and book authors would have it. The situation is not analogous to the second half of the 1930s. Japan is not rampaging in China or anywhere else. Official relations between Japan and the United States remain close and in the main cordial. Although squabbles over trade policy are chronic, each side treats the other with reasonable regard for the civilities. The American public may view Japan's economic accomplishments and capacities with alarm, but it does not boycott Japanese goods, rather the contrary.

Still something is very wrong with the domestic dialogue. In Congress Japan-bashing is obviously considered to be an appropriate and electorally risk-free activity. Little consideration seems to be given to the thought that any serious rift between the world's two largest economies would hurt mutual and global welfare. That the U.S.–Japanese military alliance has been a force for stability in East Asia for nearly four decades goes largely unspoken, while Japan's low defense budget is a standard target for attacks. And the current polemics carry an undercurrent of racism, not overwhelming, perhaps, but not pleasant either.

Yet on any rational calculation, economic competition from Japan does not threaten America's national security. If Japanese government and industry

From Philip H. Trezise, "Japan, the Enemy?" *The Brookings Review* (Winter 1989/1990). Copyright © 1989 by The Brookings Institution. Reprinted by permission.

engage in conduct contrary to international rules or norms, ample legal, administrative, and economic remedies are available. Japan's democracy has its warts, as whose does not, but it functions effectively in a society that is in all fundamentals free. "Containing" Japan is the offering of a journalist who sees American vulnerabilities that do not exist. Another Pacific war? More remote eventualities can be imagined, but not readily.

These are assertions. Let us see if they can be fortified with arguments and facts.

DEFICITS AND DEBT

Current problems between the two countries obviously derive principally from their economic relationship. That has been the case virtually since the signing of the peace treaty in 1951. The difference today is that the relations are more complex and the interdependence of the two economies is much greater. Whether this greater involvement threatens our well-being is quite another matter.

Some see a threat in our trade imbalance with Japan. The U.S. external deficit has been running at unprecedented heights. Foreign trade in goods accounts for the largest part, and of that, trade with Japan stands out. The total trade deficit peaked in 1987 at $159.5 billion; 36 percent represented the deficit with Japan. The U.S. trade deficit with the world promises to be more nearly $100 billion in 1989, while Japan's share is likely to be close to 50 percent. Inevitably, the size and the seemingly intractable character of Japan's trade surplus with us has been politicized. Thus Representative Richard A. Gephardt in 1988 almost succeeded in writing into law a

provision penalizing nations with "excessive" trade surpluses, to wit, Japan.

A deficit must be covered by borrowing, and the United States has quickly acquired the world's largest-ever external debt, currently estimated at half a trillion dollars, much of it owed to Japan. A relatively small part of the Japanese-owned assets in the United States is in the form of real estate and industrial plant. It turns out, however, that Americans are no less prone than Europeans, Canadians, Mexicans—and Japanese—to anxieties at observing that land, office buildings, and factories are being bought or built by foreigners. Other, less visceral, concerns arise about the much greater sum of foreign capital invested in Treasury securities and the bond and stock markets. Take together these debts provide another element in what has become, at a minimum, a worrisome matter of international public relations.

Underlying all else is the perception that Japan's trade and economic policies are unfair. It is a perception that finds support in a mass of anecdotal material and in a few more rigorous studies of the trade data. In the popular version, Japan's market is said to be closed to American exports while Japanese exports have flourished in the American market. The government of Japan is supposed to subsidize and otherwise coddle the export industries, with special attention to the now and future high-technology sectors. Credit for business and industry is cheap because the Ministry of Finance and the Bank of Japan will it so, mainly in the interest of exports. Although Japanese firms can readily establish themselves in the United States, American businesses encounter high barriers to entry into Japan. The catalogue of the imputed offenses against fairness is extensive.

It unquestionably has achieved a wide measure of acceptance.

Well, the U.S. external deficit is real, the growing debt to foreigners is breathtakingly large, and critical views of Japanese economic policies and practices are not always, as some Japanese insist, self-serving or based on misunderstandings. The United States does have problems in its economic relations with Japan, not all of them trivial.

But do those problems make Japan a consequential, not to say a mortal, danger to American interests or security? Has the Japanese economic miracle, once looked upon as witness to the wisdom of U.S. postwar policy, brought into being a monster?

If the foreign deficit is part of the case against Japan, then one must ask how it came about and what damage it has wrought.

In a sense the deficit, which began its surge in 1982, was intended by nobody and caused by everybody. Before 1982 U.S. deficits on merchandise trade (themselves a phenomenon that did not appear in this century until the 1970s) normally were balanced or overbalanced by earnings from American investments abroad. After the 1981 tax cuts and the subsequent unplanned federal budget deficits, the overall external deficit—goods and services—soared (from less than $9 billion in 1982 to $153 billion in 1987), driven by a rapidly rising trade imbalance and a declining net position on returns from foreign investments.

Conventional wisdom, which in this case is also true wisdom, says that these developments reflected higher rates of savings and fewer desirable investment opportunities abroad than in the United States. Private savings rates in the United States have been among the lowest in the industrial world. The post-1981 federal budget deficits preempted for government use a historically large part of these savings, three-fifths between 1984 and 1988. Shrinking domestic savings and the growing demand for investment pushed up real interest rates and drew foreign savings to U.S. financial markets. In the predictable course of events, this expanding demand for dollars caused the exchange value of the dollar to rise sharply. Just as predictable, the strong dollar attracted imports and put the export industries at severe disadvantage. Hence the massive trade deficits of the 1980s.

It can be and was argued that this sequence could have been slowed or interrupted if the high-savings countries—particularly Japan and Germany—had chosen to emulate the United States by using more of their peoples' savings for public purposes. Germany with very high unemployment and Japan with manifestly large unfilled needs for public facilities might have attacked these domestic issues by lifting the lid on government spending, at the price of bigger budget deficits. They did not do so, for what they saw as compelling economic and political reasons. Had they indeed opted to absorb more of their nations' savings for domestic use, the U.S. consumption and investment boom could not have run unchecked. The practical choices would have been to do something real about cutting the budget deficit or living with interest rates that would have curbed the expansion.

These reflections are germane to the question of the trade deficit's effect on the national welfare. No one can doubt that the strong dollar of the early 1980s hurt U.S. export and import-competing industries. To workers who lost high-paying jobs in these industries, it is little comfort that the national unemployment rate fell steadily to virtually full employment levels while total civilian employment grew at a very satisfactory pace. Nor, presumably, do managements pressured by foreign competition to restructure their companies look back with undiluted pleasure at the experience.

Nevertheless, it is the fact that the trade and overall deficits were accompanied by strongly rising employment and that the growth of productivity per man-hour in the American manufacturing industry from 1981 through 1987 was roughly one and one-half times the 1948–81 average. The reality is that the capital inflow from Japan and elsewhere served to sustain American levels of investment that could not have been reached otherwise. These were voluntary flows, made in response to explicable economic incentives. In short, the United States is richer and more productive because Japanese and other foreigners found it in their interest to send their excess savings here.

Some observers who are not given to demoniac views of foreign investment nonetheless worry that capital inflows might substantially diminish well before American net savings have recovered. In that event, they speculate, interest rates would have to rise, precipitating a U.S. recession. That has not happened, and fears that it will have subsided. It could occur, though, which is one reason why public policy should be focused more than it is on our low savings.

A nonhypothetical reason for concern about U.S. reliance on foreign capital is the external debt that is the counterpart of the borrowing. Payments of interest and dividends on the debt must come out of current American income. In 1988 these payments exceeded $100 billion, almost equaling receipts from accumulated U.S. investments abroad. This year the payments will exceed receipts. Clearly enough, the nation would be better off if these payments were made to other Americans rather than to foreigners. If Americans can cease accumulating debt —which means, remember, restoring the savings rate to more normal levels— disposable incomes will be the higher for it.

But it is well to recognize that the nation's capital stock is larger than it would have been without the foreign inflows that now constitute the external debt. The income generated by that larger stock provides the wherewithal to meet the costs of servicing the borrowings. While it is anomalous and perhaps immoral for the world's richest country to be absorbing so much of the world's savings, the United States is not in danger of being impoverished by the costs of carrying its debt.

FOREIGN DIRECT INVESTMENT

The presence of visible foreign investment seems to make for domestic uneasiness almost everywhere. What is troubling about that uneasiness in the United States is its focus on Japanese direct investment, which still lags behind the British. Some adverse reaction had to be expected as Japanese investors bought real estate in New York and Los Angeles, built auto plants in Ohio, Tennessee, Illinois, and Michigan, and took over textile mills in the Carolinas. The facts hardly warrant hysteria or even mild worry, however. We are not being "colonized" by Japan or anyone else.

The national wealth of the United States is estimated to be $15 trillion. Assets—securities and direct investments in land, structures, and equipment—owned by foreigners at the end of 1988 were valued at $1.3 trillion, or 8.7 percent. (U.S.–owned assets abroad were valued, actually undervalued, at $700 billion.) Foreign direct investment in the United States was $329 billion (slightly greater than the book value of U.S. direct investment abroad) or 2.2 percent of the nation's stock of resources exclusive of people. Japanese direct investments totalled $53 billion, or slightly more than three-tenths of a percent of our national wealth. These are not numbers that would imply the imminent domination of American economic or political life by Japan or by foreigners generally.

It is not always recognized, either, that foreign firms establishing themselves in the United States become American firms, liable for American taxes, required to observe American laws and regulations, and subject to the peculiarities and pressures of American community life. Their interest is to be seen as good corporate citizens here, as is true of American multinationals abroad. Their interest, and ours, is also that they be profitable, for that is the indicator that their and our resources are being used efficiently.

In 1985 a Japanese investor needed, on average, 238 yen to buy a dollar's worth of U.S. assets. In 1988 he needed only 128 yen. This depreciation of the dollar has led to complaints that Japan is buying into America on the cheap. But as depreciation has lowered the yen cost of acquiring land, facilities, and securities in the United States, it has equally lowered the yen income to be earned here. Japanese investors cannot have failed to observe this relationship. The reasons for the present flow of foreign investment into the United States are its good eco-

nomic performance, its political stability, and, possibly, worries that its xenophobes may eventually succeed in writing laws that would block future inflows of capital.

JAPAN'S ECONOMIC INHOSPITALITY

That Japan itself has been less than hospitable to foreign investment is a further source of grievance—part and parcel of the more general indictment of the Japanese government and its businesses for allegedly ignoring claims to reciprocity and equal treatment or, in the more extreme form, for calculated economic aggression against the United States.

A full treatment of that indictment is beyond the scope or purpose of this essay. Some of its points should be mentioned, however. American direct investment in Japan was valued at $17 billion in 1988. In the United Kingdom it was $49 billion. Of course language and acquaintance favor investment in the U.K. But Japan's postwar economic growth was explosive, while the British economy stagnated. Had entry into Japan been as easy as into the U.K., more American firms would surely have overcome language and like barriers—as, of course, many did.

Japan's tariffs were drastically lowered in the 1970s and 1980s, and quota restrictions, except for agricultural imports, largely removed. Nevertheless, Europeans and Americans say the Japanese market is less open than those of the other major industrial powers. A persuasive piece of evidence is Japan's exceptionally low volume of imports of manufactured goods, relative to gross national product or as a share of total imports. Even after allowing for Japan's dependence on imports of foodstuffs, raw materials, and fuel, and for its distance from suppliers, the comparisons are striking. As recently as 1985, only a quarter of Japanese imports were in manufactures; in contrast, fully 70 percent of U.S. imports were manufactured goods. Japan's ratio of manufactures imports to GNP was 2.6 percent; in West Germany, which is also heavily dependent on imports of primary products, the ratio was 14.9 percent.

Since 1985 the strengthening yen has made foreign manufactures cheaper, and imports have risen; between 1985 and 1988 American exports of manufactures to Japan rose by 79 percent, compared with 49 percent to the rest of the world. Manufactures accounted for almost 50 percent of all of Japan's imports in 1988. Yet the ratio to national expenditure was less than half that of the United States, which itself is a modest importer in relation to GNP.

Why Japan's manufactured imports are comparatively low has been the subject of debate among economists, Japanese and American, with no fully conclusive answers. But anomalies in Japan's trade structure give credibility to the existence of an anti-import bias, whether enforced by custom or by rules and regulations.

An example: Japan is a very large importer of raw logs and a small importer of manufactures of wood, although its wood products manufacturing sector is not an obviously efficient processor of the raw materials; it ranks ahead only of apparel and leather in value added per worker. Similarly, Japan imports metal ores and concentrates in quantity, and metal manufactures and semi-manufactures in comparatively inconsiderable lots; no other industrial country exhibits this pattern of trade.

A reasonable assumption is that these seeming oddities (in economic terms) reflect a reluctance to accept the political costs that a contraction of these processing industries would entail. American admirers of Japan's industrial policies like to cite the readiness of the Ministry of Trade and Industry (MITI) to "phase out" aging, inefficient industries. This readiness is pure myth. Japan is no different from other countries in wishing to preserve established industries, and it may well be more diligent at pursuing that objective.

Japan is the largest foreign market for America's farmers. It is also a closed market for rice and a restricted market for a number of other agricultural commodities. These restrictions are required because most of Japanese agriculture is high cost and must be supported by public subsidies. Unrestricted imports would be budgetarily impossible.

Agricultural policy in Japan is unique only in the sense that the costs to taxpayers and consumers are relatively much higher than in other major countries. In some details it seems unusually excessive, however. Wheat is a crop poorly suited to Japan's small-scale farms. Wheat imports are sizable but in quantities carefully controlled to shield rice from undue competition.

In the 1970s, when surpluses caused a decision to retire land from rice production, the Ministry of Agriculture chose to offer truly extraordinary subsidies to farmers who would convert this land to wheat, soybeans, barley, or sugar beets, all import-displacing crops. In the case of wheat, a farmer eligible for all the available benefits could receive payments equal to 13 or 14 times the cost of foreign wheat delivered in Japan. This policy, which in its essentials continues today, actually brought only rather modest acreage into production of the heavily subsidized crops. What it seems to have represented was an unusually committed mindset against imports.

One of the counts in the foreign indictment of Japanese economic policies is the use of subsidies to foster selected industries, particularly the high-tech sectors. This is a much overdrawn matter. An overwhelming share of public subsidies goes to agriculture, followed, now that the money-draining national railways have been privatized, by energy and small business. The amounts going to industry may have served as useful catalysts for ventures targeted by MITI, semiconductors, for example, but they have been tiny in comparison with, say, the funds lavished on the Airbus or the Concorde in Europe. And a number of MITI's long-term targets have been missed altogether. Still, subsidies, together with other features of industrial policy, doubtless have helped to give some Japanese industries a competitive edge not otherwise attainable.

Other unfair or questionable practices are alleged. The industrial/banking groupings (keiretsu)—Mitsubishi, Mitsui, Sumitomo, et al.—are said to give preference to group members, perhaps particularly when the competing product or firm is foreign. Some people believe that the banking system, at government direction, subsidizes industry, or some sectors of industry, in the form of credit on below-market terms. These accusations are not easily substantiated. The second of them indeed seems to run counter to the increasing practice among major Japanese corporations of borrowing against their own commercial paper or in the Euromarkets rather than from the domestic banks.

THE PRICE OF UNFAIR PRACTICES

Supposing, in any case, that at least a significant part of the total indictment has merit, what conclusions are to be drawn?

One is that the losers include those competitive foreign suppliers who encounter a protected and circumscribed market and would-be investors who are denied potentially profitable opportunities. Americans are very important among these losers, but they also number Europeans, Australians, Koreans, and so on. The economic penalties imposed on all of them detract from global welfare, as does protectionism anywhere.

More substantial losers still are the citizens of Japan. As consumers they pay higher-than-necessary prices and have a more limited range of choice. As taxpayers they are required to help finance activities that use the nation's resources wastefully. If they are among the country's efficient producers, they must absorb costs that reduce their returns and worsen their competitive positions.

An economists' aphorism says that a tax on imports is a tax on exports. The argument in essence says that protection raises general money wages. Sectors producing import substitutes or wholly domestic goods can pass on the higher wage costs to consumers. The export industries, facing a world market, cannot, so profits and employment in the export sector decline. In brief, protection diverts resources from export sectors, actual or potential, to sectors where they are or will be used less efficiently. The long-run effect on economic growth is, of course, negative. As remaining protection comes down, Japan's export industries will be the stronger for it. Any improvement in the U.S. trade balance to be gained from greater access to Japan's market is thus likely to be for the short term. A lasting change in the Japanese trade surplus will depend on changes in relative savings/investment ratios.

Nevertheless, a Japan that imports more and exports more is to be desired. The United States has been right to seek greater market access and not only because U.S. exporters stand to benefit. To the extent that Japan is more protectionist than other countries, its contribution to world economic growth and welfare, considerable as it surely has been, is below potential.

A FITTING TRADE PARTNER?

Some of Japan's critics see in its formidable export performance and its outsized trade surplus a danger to the relatively open trading system that has helped to foster and sustain the remarkable gains made in world economic growth since World War II. They point to the import restrictions already imposed on Japanese goods in North America and Western Europe as indicative of a trend that is bound to take on momentum. The end result, presumably, would be to undo completely the international consensus on liberal trade that is represented by the General Agreement on Tariffs and Trade (GATT). In its extreme form, the argument goes that Japan simply does not fit and that the survival of the trading system would be best ensured by its exclusion.

These views have made little evident impression on the political leaders of Japan's trading partners. Far from seeking to isolate Japan, they have the MITI minister as a charter member of the "Quad," the inner group of the GATT composed of American, European Community, Canadian, and Japanese trade officials. In 1986, when Japan's export surplus was nearing its highest point, the GATT membership agreed at Punta del Este to launch the Uruguay Round, with perhaps the most ambitious agenda of any of the multilateral tariff and trade policy negotiations. The objectives include tightening the GATT rules that have been ignored or evaded by the protective measures taken against Japanese exports. The final returns will not be in until 1990 or later, but the Uruguay Round bargainers thus far have registered anything but despair for the GATT and its future.

One reason may be that the macroeconomic effects of Japan's outsized trade surpluses have been less disruptive than might have been feared. The surplus reached a peak in 1987 at $96 billion. Three quarters of it was with the United States and the European Community. These enormous economies, with a combined GNP of well over $9 trillion, seem to have adjusted quite smoothly to the unprecedentedly large trade deficits. In the United States, where the cumulative trade deficit from 1981 through 1988 was $750 billion (40 percent of it in trade with Japan), the march to virtual full employment went largely unchecked. Europe's troubling employment problems began in the early 1970s, long before the surge in Japan's surpluses, and clearly are caused far more by rigidities in the individual national economies than by imports from Japan. West Germany, which has had trade surpluses that in some years were relatively larger than Japan's, has had unemployment levels comparable to those of its fellow EC members.

Of course Japan's export successes have imposed painful adjustment costs on American firms and their workers in certain industries, among them semiconductors, steel, autos, machine tools, and consumer electronics. Against these costs are arrayed gains to consumers, not only from lower prices but also from advances in quality or performance of the product involved, domestic and Japanese. The case for engaging in trade is that its benefits are widely shared and continuing, whereas the costs are local and temporary.

There remain the arguments that Japan is a predatory trader and that national security is about to be imperiled by U.S. dependence on Japanese high-tech goods.

OVERBLOWN FEARS OF PREDATION . . .

Predation can be defined as a policy aimed systematically at eliminating competitors in order to create the conditions for monopoly pricing. That is the classic case for resisting export dumping. As a defense against this putative threat, the GATT allows, and most trading nations including the United States have, antidumping statutes. Japanese goods offered in the United States at below the home market price or below average cost are liable to penalty duties. The economics of that law are open to debate, but its availability is not in question. Nor is its use. At the end of 1987, 158 antidumping findings and orders were outstanding, covering products from 23 countries, Japan most prominent among them, followed by Canada.

Dumping is typically a marketing decision by a private firm or firms. "Unfair" pricing, with its implications of predatory intent, can be facilitated by official subsidies to producers. Here again the United States has a legal defense. Its countervailing duty law, which is sanctioned by the GATT, provides for penalty duties when foreign government subsidies are found to cause or threaten "material injury" to a domestic industry or to materially retard its establishment. Seventy-four countervailing duty orders were in effect at the end of 1987 on goods from 31 countries, none including Japan.

. . . AND HIGH-TECH DEPENDENCE

The existence of antidumping and countervailing duty laws makes a successful predation policy unlikely, if indeed such a policy ever has been considered to be practicable in the American market. Japan, however, has achieved a dominant position in the U.S. market for three major products: video cassette recorders, facsimile machines, and memory chips. Experience with VCRs and Fax hardly bears out fears about exploitation of American consumers. The Japanese makers have been competing vigorously with one another here, the conclusive manifestation being the steady downward course of prices. Moreover, they have moved some of their production to the United States and have established marketing facilities here, where they unquestionably come under the jurisdiction of the antitrust unit of the Department of Justice.

Memory chips are a different story. U.S. market conditions in 1987 and 1988 give convincing evidence of cartel pricing by the Japanese chip industry, to the considerable unhappiness of U.S. user No sleuthing was necessary to determine the cause. The 1986 Semiconductor

Trade Arrangement (STA) negotiated between the two governments provided that the Japanese authorities would ensure that chip prices would be raised to levels determined by the United States to reflect full, nondumping costs. A leading writer on the economic threat from Japan has described the result: "This [the STA] amounted to getting the Japanese government to force its companies to make a profit and even to impose controls to avoid excess production—in short a government-led cartel."

Memory chips are vital to computers, which in turn have manifold military applications. Japanese advances in this category of semiconductors and in the electronics industry generally have been the grounds for the perceived menace to American national security. The Defense Department's Defense Science Board in 1987 found it "an unacceptable situation" that "U.S. defense will soon depend on foreign sources for state-of-the-art technology in semiconductors." Why such dependence should be unacceptable is arguable. The United States depends on foreign sources for other things important to defense, oil for example. The probability that Japan would withhold its semiconductors from its American ally is extremely small.

Nevertheless, the case has been essentially decided. Government subsidies and freedom from antitrust strictures are now to assist American industry to challenge and outdo its Japanese rivals. If the premise is granted that there is a high-tech problem immediately or predictably related to the nation's security, then a response is warranted. One hopes that the response that has been chosen will succeed. In any event, the most productive country in the world is hardly a helpless giant.

PERSPECTIVE ON SUCCESS

Nor should Americans be mesmerized by Japan's economic successes. In the 1960s when Japan's GNP was growing at 10–11 percent annually, many expected that growth to continue more or less indefinitely. In the 1970s the growth rate fell to an average annual 4.5 percent, and it has slowed further to a little more than 4 percent in the 1980s. Nothing about the slowdown is the least bit mysterious. Japan in the 1950s and 1960s was able to employ a growing labor force, including its otherwise jobless and underemployed workers. Its enterprising business class was investing the nation's high savings in the facilities needed to raise the productivity of these workers. As the pool of unemployed declined and population growth tailed off and as the managerial and technical catch-up with Western Europe and the United States came nearer, growth had to slow.

Catch-up is some distance from being complete, moreover. Japanese workers today produce on average about 70 percent as many real goods and services as do American workers. Canadians are at 95 percent of the U.S. level, while the West Europeans fall between the Japanese and the Canadians. Japan and West Germany—and many others—will probably move closer to the United States and Canada over time. But as they achieve parity or superiority by this measure, Americans will not thereby be poorer—any more than they are less well off because Canadians are almost as productive as they are.

If comfort is needed, Japan has an ongoing, basic, and serious economic (and social) problem: Its population is aging much faster than the population of other major industrialized countries. Demographic projections for the year 2000 put Japan's over-65 population at 16.2 percent (West Germany's is projected at 15.0 percent; the United States' at 12.0 percent). In 1950 the over-65 cohort was 4.9 percent of Japan's population; it is expected to be almost a quarter in 2020. The implications of this for the economic fundamentals—the labor force and the savings rate—have to be negative. Japan's has proven to be a remarkably resilient society, and it can be expected to rise to this new challenge. But a nation with a sharply rising ratio of nonworkers to workers is not likely to have the economic dynamism it had in earlier times.

In the end, however, developments in Japan cannot provide solutions for America's own problems. The United States has had an extended economic expansion, supported in important measure by Japanese and other lenders and investors. The U.S. trade deficit and foreign debt are the counterparts of these investments. Even as rich and reliable a borrower as the United States cannot continue acquiring debt at recent rates indefinitely. Market forces along with federal budget decisions have begun to be registered in a declining trade deficit. This decline needs to be continued for our peace of mind and because we probably have been preempting too much of the world's savings. Japan's cooperation will aid the adjustment process. But the critical choices to be made will be ours.

Meanwhile, separately, we can pursue the microeconomic issues we have with Japan. From the U.S. perspective, these primarily involve Japanese protectionism, in which we have a legitimate interest because we can expect to have a more efficient economy if remaining restrictions on access to Japan's market can be reduced or removed. Since Japan's econ-omy will also be made more efficient, there can be no assurance about the effect on our trade imbalance. But the shared gains will be real—as real and desirable as would be those realizable from a successful attack on the protectionism we have at home.

POSTSCRIPT

Is Japan a Threat to America's Economic and National Security?

In the February 1992 issue of *International Economic Conditions*, published by the Federal Reserve Bank of St. Louis, Alison Butler makes a series of insightful comments. She notes that except for a superficial increase in 1991, Japan's bilateral surplus with the United States decreased throughout the late 1980s and early 1990s. In very large measure this is due to the fact that U.S. exports to Japan have grown about seven times faster than the growth rate of Japan's exports to the United States. If this pattern continues for the next five years, the value of Japan's merchandise exports to the United States will about equal the value of her imports from the United States!

In light of this prediction, we must ask a series of questions: (1) Is a trade deficit between two countries such as the United States and Japan a problem? (2) Does the decline in the U.S. auto industry or electronics industry reflect shifting "comparative advantages," or are these losses reflective of "unfair trade practices"? (3) How can the United States improve its economic performance in light of its experiences with modern-day Japan? (4) Should the United States modify its trade policy toward Japan?

If you have lingering questions, you might care to read other works by the two authors. Trezise has written widely in the area of international economics. One of the several books he has coedited or coauthored is *The Future Course of U.S.–Japan Economic Relations* (Brookings Institution, 1983). Likewise, Cohen has written extensively on various international trade and monetary policy issues. Several of his more important contributions are *The Making of United States International Economic Policy: Principles, Problems, and Proposals for Reform*, 3rd ed. (Praeger, 1988) and *Cowboys and Samurai: Why the United States Is Losing the Industrial Battle and Why It Matters* (1991). But do not limit yourself to only Trezise and Cohen. Tens of thousands of pages have been written about U.S.–Japan economic relations. For example, the April 1991 issue of *Current History* is devoted to a discussion of Japan as a world power and its relations with the United States, the Koreas, the former Soviet Union, and other countries. Alison Butler provides a banker's view in an article entitled "Trade Imbalances and Economic Theory: The Case for a U.S.–Japan Trade Deficit," *Federal Reserve Bank of St. Louis Review* (March/April 1991). Finally we suggest a third-party view of this issue—an Australian's opinion: Aurelia George, "Japan's American Problem: The Japanese Response to U.S. Pressure," *The Washington Quarterly* (Summer 1991).

ISSUE 17

Does Global Warming Require Immediate Government Action?

YES: Cynthia Pollock Shea, from "Protecting Life on Earth: Steps to Save the Ozone Layer," *Worldwatch Paper 87* (1988)

NO: Lester B. Lave, from "The Greenhouse Effect: What Government Actions Are Needed?" *Journal of Policy Analysis and Management* (1988)

ISSUE SUMMARY

YES: Cynthia Pollock Shea, a senior researcher with the Worldwatch Institute, pleads with governments and industries to initiate a "crash program" designed to halt emissions of chemicals that deplete the ozone, such as chlorofluorocarbons, before irreparable damage is done to world agriculture, marine life, and human health.

NO: Professor of economics Lester B. Lave warns against drastic solutions that could themselves be harmful or, at a minimum, "costly if the greenhouse consequences are more benign than predicted."

Few of us can forget the heat wave of the summer of 1988. Electric bills skyrocketed as air conditioners ran day and night. Bright green lawns turned yellow-brown. Lakes, streams, and reservoirs fell to critically low levels; car washing was discouraged, lawn sprinkling was banned, and toilets were bricked. Citizens and policymakers alike were concerned that the world was entering the long-predicted and much-feared period of global warming associated with the greenhouse effect.

As summer turned to fall, then–presidential candidate Bush promised voters that if he were elected, he would become the "environmental president." He would protect the environment from the advancing global warming—at least he would attempt to slow its progress. Once elected he joined other heads of state in a Paris environmental summit. This, in turn, led to the policy prescriptions that he introduced in a speech delivered at Georgetown University in early February 1990. Four broad policies were detailed in this speech:

(1) *Increase the information base.* He proposed a sharp increase in U.S. expenditures on studies focused on "global climate change."

(2) *Redirect and increase expenditures on basic energy research and development from $16.4 billion to $17.5 billion.* This represented a modest 6.4 percent

increase in the Department of Energy's budget and some redistribution of funds from civilian applied research and development programs to grants for basic research.

(3) *A phaseout of most chlorofluorocarbons.* In line with a 1987 international agreement, the Montreal Protocol, President Bush proposed a 50 percent cut in the production of these powerful greenhouse gases that attack the ozone layer.

(4) *A "plant-a-tree" program.* The Bush administration proposed planting a billion trees each year at a cost of $170 million annually.

The question we must ask is whether or not these presidential initiatives are appropriate in light of the costs and benefits of public action to slow or reverse the progress of global warming. Once again we must turn to our marginal analysis to determine how aggressive public policy should be in slowing the progress of global warming. We can anticipate that alternative policies will have increasing marginal costs and decreasing marginal benefits as more ambitious programs are employed. Two views of these costs and benefits are provided in the following essays. Cynthia Pollock Shea warns that if decisive action is not taken immediately to protect the ozone layer, we will face serious health hazards, reduced crop yields, decreased fish populations, and industrial damage. Lester B. Lave, on the other hand, argues that there is too much uncertainty to rush forward with sweeping policy action. He preaches moderation.

Since the consequences of these policy decisions may be irreversible and not fully felt for many decades in the future, extreme care must be taken. Older generations may be totally immune from the consequences. It is the younger generations that will pay for the mistakes made in the early 1990s.

YES

Cynthia Pollock Shea

PROTECTING LIFE ON EARTH: STEPS TO SAVE THE OZONE LAYER

When British scientists reported in 1985 that a hole in the ozone layer had been occurring over Antarctica each spring since 1979, the news came as a complete surprise. Although the theory that a group of widely used chemicals called chlorofluorocarbons (CFCs) would someday erode upper atmospheric ozone had been advanced in the mid-1970s, none of the models had predicted that the thinning would first be evident over the South Pole— or that it would be so severe.

Ozone, the three-atom form of oxygen, is the only gas in the atmosphere that limits the amount of harmful solar ultraviolet radiation reaching the earth. Most of it is found at altitudes of between 12 and 25 kilometers. Chemical reactions triggered by sunlight constantly replenish ozone above the tropics, and global air circulation transports some of it to the poles.

By the Antarctic spring of 1987, the average ozone concentration over the South Pole was down 50 percent. Although the depletion was alarming, many thought that the thinning was seasonal and unique to Antarctica. But an international group of more than 100 experts reported in March 1988 that the ozone layer around the globe was eroding much faster than models had predicted. Between 1969 and 1986, the average concentration of ozone in the stratosphere had fallen by approximately 2 percent.

As ozone diminishes, the earth receives more ultraviolet radiation, which promotes skin cancers and cataracts and depresses the human immune system. As more ultraviolet radiation penetrates the atmosphere, it will worsen these health effects, reduce crop yields and fish populations, damage some materials such as plastics, and increase smog. Compounds containing chlorine and bromine, which are released from industrial processes and products, are now widely accepted as the primary culprits in ozone depletion. Most of the chlorine comes from CFCs; the bromine originates from halons used in fire extinguishers.

Spurred to action by the ozone hole, 35 countries have signed an international agreement—the Montreal Protocol—aimed at halving most CFC emissions by 1998 and freezing halon emissions by 1992. But the agreement is so riddled with loopholes that its objectives will not be met. Furthermore, scientific findings subsequent to the negotiations reveal that even if the treaty's goals were met, significant further deterioration of the ozone layer would still occur.

New evidence that a global warming may be under way strengthens the need to further control and phase out CFC and halon emissions. With their strong heat-absorbing properties, CFCs and halons are an important contributor to the greenhouse effect. Currently available control technologies and stricter standards governing equipment operation and maintenance could reduce CFC and halon emissions by some 90 percent. But effective government policies and industry practices to limit and ultimately phase out chlorine and bromine emissions have yet to be formulated. Just as the effects of ozone depletion and climate change will be felt worldwide, a lasting remedy to these problems must also be global.

THE OZONE DEPLETION PUZZLE

As a result of the efforts of many scientists, the pieces of the ozone depletion puzzle have gradually been falling into place. During the long, sunless Antarctic winter—from about March to August—air over the continent becomes isolated in a swirling polar vortex that causes temperatures to drop below -90 degrees Celsius. This is cold enough for the scarce water vapor in the dry upper atmosphere to freeze and form polar stratospheric clouds. Chemical reactions on the surface of the ice crystals convert chlorine from nonreactive forms such as hydrogen chloride and chlorine nitrate into molecules that are very sensitive to sunlight. Gaseous nitrogen oxides, ordinarily able to inactivate chlorine, are transformed into frozen, and therefore nonreactive, nitric acid.

Spring sunlight releases the chlorine, starting a virulent ozone-destroying chain reaction that proceeds unimpeded for five or six weeks. Molecules of ozone are transformed into molecules of ordinary, two-atom oxygen. The chlorine emerges unscathed, ready to attack more ozone. Diminished ozone in the vortex means the atmosphere there absorbs less incoming solar radiation, thereby perpetuating lower temperatures and the vortex itself.

Paradoxically, the phenomenon of global warming encourages the process. Higher concentrations of greenhouse gases are thought to be responsible for an increase in the earth's surface temperature and a decrease in the temperature of the stratosphere. In addition, methane, one of the primary greenhouse gases, is a significant source of stratospheric water vapor. Colder temperatures and increased moisture both facilitate the formation of stratospheric clouds.

While many of the meteorological and chemical conditions conducive to ozone depletion are unique to Antarctica, ground-based research in Greenland in the winter of 1988 found elevated chlorine concentrations and depressed ozone levels over the Arctic as well. Although a strong vortex does not develop there and temperatures are not as low, polar stratospheric clouds do form.

The theories on how chlorine interacts on the surface of particles in polar stratospheric clouds are leading to worries that similar ozone-depleting reactions may occur around the globe. If chemicals such as sulfate aerosols from volcanoes and human-made sulfurs are capable of hosting the same catalytic reactions, global ozone depletion may accelerate even more rapidly than anticipated.

Consensus about the extent of ozone depletion and its causes strengthened with the release of the NASA Ozone Trends Panel report on March 15, 1988. Ozone losses were documented around the globe, not just at the poles. The blame was firmly placed on chlorofluorocarbons. The panel reported that between 30 and 64 degrees north latitude, where most of the world's people live, the total amount of ozone above any particular point had decreased by between 1.7 and 3 percent in the period from 1969 to 1986 (Table 1). The report further stated that while the problem was worst over Antarctica during the spring, "ozone appears to have decreased since 1979 by 5 percent or more at all latitudes south of 60 degrees south throughout the year." The hole alone covers approximately 10 percent of the Southern Hemisphere.

Within a matter of weeks the report's conclusions were widely accepted, and public debate on the issue began to build. Ozone depletion is occurring far more rapidly and in a different pattern than had been forecast. Projections of the amount and location of future ozone depletion are still highly uncertain. Although the fundamental mechanisms of ozone depletion are generally understood, the effect of cloud surface chemistry, the rate of various chemical reactions, and the specific chemical pathways are still in doubt. According to Sherwood Rowland, one of the first to sound a warning, policy decisions now and for at least another decade must be made without good quantitative guidelines of what the future holds.

Table 1

Global Decline in Atmospheric Ozone, 1969–1986*

Latitude	Year-round decrease (percent)	Winter decrease (percent)
53–64° N	− 2.3	−6.2
40–53° N	− 3.0	−4.7
30–40° N	− 1.7	−2.3
19–30° N	− 3.1	n.a.
0–19° N	− 1.6	n.a.
0–19° S	− 2.1	n.a.
19–29° S	− 2.6	n.a.
29–39° S	− 2.7	n.a.
39–53° S	− 4.9	n.a.
53–60° S	−10.6	n.a.
60–90° S	−5.0 or more	n.a.

*Data for the area 30 to 64 degrees north of the equator are based on information gathered from satellites and ground stations from 1969 to 1986. Data for the area from 60 degrees south to the South Pole are based on information gathered from satellites and ground stations since 1979. All other information was compiled after November 1978 from satellite data alone.

Sources: U.S. National Aeronautics and Space Administration, Ozone Trends Panel; Cass Peterson, "Evidence of Ozone Depletion Found Over Big Urban Areas," *The Washington Post*, March 16, 1988.

EFFECTS OF ULTRAVIOLET RADIATION

At present, ozone absorbs much of the ultraviolet light that the sun emits in wavelengths harmful to humans, animals, and plants. The most biologically damaging wavelengths are within the 290- to 320-nanometer band, referred to as UV-B. But according to uncertain projections from computer models, erosion of the ozone shield could result in 5 to 20 percent more ultraviolet radiation reaching populated areas within the next 40 years—most of it in the UV-B band.

In light of the findings of the NASA Ozone Trends Panel, the U.S. Environmental Protection Agency (EPA) damage projections cited in this section are conservative. Although the EPA ranges are based on current control strategies, they assume ozone depletion levels of 1.2 to 6.2 percent. Yet all areas of the globe have already suffered depletion beyond this lower bound.

Globally, skin cancer incidence among Caucasians is already on the rise, and it is expected to increase alarmingly in the presence of more UV-B. Some 600,000 new cases of squamous and basal cell carcinoma—the two most common but rarely fatal skin cancer types—are reported each year in the United States alone. Worldwide, the number of cases is at least three times as high. Each 1 percent drop in ozone is projected to result in 4 to 6 percent more cases of these types of skin cancer. The EPA estimates that ozone depletion will lead to an additional 31,000 to 126,000 cases of melanoma—a more deadly form of skin cancer—among U.S. whites born before 2075, resulting in an additional 7,000 to 30,000 fatalities.

Under the same EPA scenarios, from 555,000 to 2.8 million Americans born before 2075 will suffer from cataracts of the eyes who would not have otherwise. Victims will also be stricken earlier in life, making treatment more difficult.

Medical researchers also fear that UV-B depresses the human immune system, lowering the body's resistance to attacking micro-organisms, making it less able to fight the development of tumors, and rendering it more prone to infectious diseases. In developing countries, particularly those near the equator that are exposed to higher UV-B levels, parasitic infections could become more common. The response may even decrease the effectiveness of some inoculation programs, such as those for diphtheria and tuberculosis.

Terrestrial and aquatic ecosystems are also affected. Screenings of more than 200 plant species, most of them crops, found that 70 percent were sensitive to UV-B. Increased exposure to radiation may decrease photosynthesis, water-use efficiency, yield, and leaf area. Soybeans, a versatile and protein-rich crop, are particularly susceptible. One researcher at the University of Maryland discovered that a simulated ozone loss of 25 percent reduced the yield of one important soybean species by as much as 25 percent. He also found that plant sensitivity to UV-B increased as the phosphorus level in the soil increased, indicating that heavily fertilized agricultural areas may be the most vulnerable.

Aquatic ecosystems may be the most threatened of all. Phytoplankton, the one-celled microscopic organisms that engage in photosynthesis while drifting on the ocean's surface, are the backbone of the marine food web. Because they require sunlight, they cannot escape incoming ultraviolet radiation and continue to thrive. Yet if they remain at the water's surface, studies show that a 25 percent reduction in ozone would decrease their productivity by about 35 percent. A significant destruction of phytoplankton and its subsequent decomposition could even raise carbon dioxide levels, speeding the warming of the atmosphere.

Zooplankton and the larvae of several important fish species will be doubly strained: Their sole food supply, phytoplankton, will be scarcer. For some shellfish species, a 10 percent decrease in ozone could result in up to an 18 percent increase in the number of abnormal larvae. Commercial fish populations already threatened by overharvesting may have more difficulty rebuilding due to effects of increased UV-B. Some species will undoubtedly be more vulnerable to increased ultraviolet radiation than others, and the changes are likely to be dramatic. Ultimately, entire ecosystems may become more unstable and less flexible.

Increased UV-B levels also affect synthetic materials, especially plastics, which become brittle. Studies conducted for the EPA estimated that without added chemical stabilizers, the cumulative damage to just one polymer, polyvinyl chloride, could reach $4,700 million by 2075 in the United States alone.

Ironically, as more ultraviolet radiation reaches the ground, the photochemical process that creates smog will accelerate, increasing ground-level ozone. Studies show that ground-level ozone retards crop and tree growth, limits visibility, and impairs lung functions. Urban air quality, already poor in most areas of the world, will worsen. In addition, stratospheric ozone decline is predicted to increase tropospheric amounts of hydrogen peroxide, an acid rain precursor.

Despite the many uncertainties regarding the amount of future ozone depletion, rising UV-B levels, and their biological effects, it is clear that the risks to aquatic and terrestrial ecosystems and to human health are enormous. The central conclusion of the EPA studies is that "the benefits of limiting future CFC/halon use far outweigh the increased costs these regulations would impose on the economy."

CHEMICAL WONDERS, ATMOSPHERIC VILLAINS

Chlorofluorocarbons are remarkable chemicals. They are neither toxic nor flammable at ground levels, as demonstrated by their discoverer, Thomas Midgley, Jr., in 1930, when he inhaled vapors from a beaker of clear liquid and then exhaled to extinguish a candle. A safe coolant that was inexpensive to produce was exactly what the refrigeration industry needed. E.I. du Pont de Nemours & Company marketed the compound under the trademark Freon. (In chemical shorthand, it is referred to as CFC-12). International production soared, rising from 545 tons in 1931 to 20,000 tons in 1945. Another use for the chemical, as a blowing agent in rigid insulation foams, was discovered in the late 1940s.

Over time, the versatility of the various CFCs seemed almost endless. CFC-11 and CFC-12 were first used as aerosol propellants during World War II in the fight against malaria. In the postwar economy, they were employed in aerosol products ranging from hairspray and deodorant to furniture polish. By the late 1950s, a combination of blowing agents CFC-11 and carbon dioxide was used to make softer furniture cushions, carpet padding, and automobile seats.

Many social and technological developments in recent decades were assisted by the availability of CFCs. Air conditioners made it possible to build and cool shopping malls, sports arenas, high-rise office buildings, and even automobiles. Artificial cooling brought comfort, business, and new residents to regions with warm climates. And healthier, more interesting diets are now available because food can be refrigerated in the production and distribution chain.

Even the computer revolution was aided by CFCs. As microchips and other components of electronic equipment became smaller and more sophisticated, the need to remove the smallest contaminants became critical. CFC-113 is used as

Table 2

Global CFC Use, by Category, 1985

Use	Share of total (percent)
Aerosols	25
Rigid-foam insulation	19
Solvents	19
Air conditioning	12
Refrigerants	8
Flexible foam	7
Other	10

Source: Daniel F. Kohler and others, *Projections of Consumption of Products Using Chlorofluorocarbons in Developing Countries*, Rand N-2458-EPA, 1987.

Table 3

Per Capita Use of CFC-11, CFC-12, and CFC-113, 1986

(kilograms per capita)

	CFC-11	CFC-12	CFC-113	Total*
United States	.34	.58	.31	1.22
Europe	.47	.34	.12	.93
Japan	.23	.29	.43	.91

*Rows not completely additive due to trade.

Source: U.S. Environmental Protection Agency, *Regulatory Impact Analysis: Protection of Stratospheric Ozone*, 1987.

a solvent to remove glue, grease, and soldering residues, leaving a clean, dry surface. CFC-113 is now the fastest growing member of the CFC family; worldwide production exceeds 160,000 tons per year.

An industry-sponsored group, the Alliance for Responsible CFC Policy, pegs the market value of CFCs produced in the United States at $750 million annually, the value of goods and services directly dependent on the chemicals at $28,000 million, and the end-use value of installed equipment and products at $135,000 million. Around the world, aerosols are still the largest user of CFCs, accounting for 25 percent of the total (Table 2). Rigid-foam and solvent applications, the fastest growing uses for CFCs, are tied for second place.

In 1987, global CFC production (excluding the People's Republic of China, the Soviet Union, and Eastern Europe) came close to 1 million tons. Combined production of CFC-11 and CFC-12 accounts for at least three-fourths of this total. Total per capita use of the three most common CFCs is highest in the United States—at 1.22 kilograms—but

Europe and Japan are not far behind (Table 3).

From 1931 through 1986, virtually all the CFC-11 and CFC-12 produced was sold to customers in the Northern Hemisphere. Since raw chemicals and products made with and containing CFCs were then exported, in part to developing countries, final usage was not quite as lopsided. Indeed, the Third World accounted for 16 percent of global CFC consumption in 1986 (Table 4). As populations, incomes, and the manufacturing base grow in developing countries, CFC use there is projected to rise.

Halons, which are used in fighting fires in both hand extinguishers and total-flooding systems for large enclosed areas, contain bromine, a more effective ozone destroyer than chlorine. Demand for halons, which were developed in the 1940s, quadrupled between 1973 and 1984 and is still growing at a rate of 15 percent annually.

Alarming though the latest ozone measurements are, they reflect only the responses to gases released through the early 1980s. Gases now rising through the lower atmosphere will take up to

Table 4

CFC Consumption by Region, 1986

Region	Share of total (percent)
United States	29
Other industrial countries*	41
Soviet Union, Eastern Europe	14
Other developing countries	14
People's Republic of China, India	2

*The European Community accounts for more than half, followed by Japan, Canada, Australia, and others.

Source: "The Ozone Treaty: A Triumph for All," *Update from State*, May/June 1988.

eight years to reach the stratosphere. And an additional 2 million tons of substances containing chlorine and bromine are still on the ground, trapped in insulation foams, appliances, and fire-fighting equipment.

Chlorine concentrations in the upper atmosphere have grown from 0.6 to 2.7 parts per thousand million in the past 25 years. Under even the most optimistic regulatory scenarios, they are expected to triple by 2075. Bromine concentrations are projected to grow considerably faster. Without a complete and rapid phaseout of CFC and halon production, the real losers will be future generations who inherit an impoverished environment.

REDUCING EMISSIONS

On September 16, 1987, after years of arduous and heated negotiation, the Montreal Protocol on Substances That Deplete the Ozone Layer was signed by 24 countries. Provisions of the agreement include a freeze on CFC production (at 1986 levels) by 1989, a 20 percent decrease in production by 1993, and another 30 percent cut by 1998. Halon production is subject to a freeze based on 1986 levels starting in 1992. . . .

The means to achieve these reductions are left to the discretion of individual nations. Most signatory countries are responding with production limits on chemical manufacturers. Although this approach complies with treaty guidelines, it effectively ensures that only those willing to pay high prices will be able to continue using CFCs. It also places the onus of curbing emissions on the myriad industrial users of the chemicals and on the consumers of products that incorporate them. Moving quickly to protect the ozone layer calls for a different approach—one that targets the largest sources of the most ozone-depleting chemicals.

When concern about the ozone layer first emerged in the 1970s, some industrial country governments responded. Since 56 percent of combined CFC-11 and CFC-12 production in 1974 was used in aerosols, spray cans were an obvious target. Under strong public pressure, Canada, Norway, Sweden, and the United States banned CFC propellants in at least 90 percent of their aerosol products. The change brought economic as well as environmental benefits. Hydrocarbons, the replacement propellant, are less expensive than CFCs and saved the U.S. economy $165 million in 1983 alone. The European Community adopted a different approach. In 1980, the member countries agreed not to increase their capacity to produce these two CFCs and called for a 30 percent reduction in their use in aerosol propellants by 1982 (based on 1976 consumption figures).

Despite rapid growth, CFC-113 emissions may be some of the easiest and most economical to control. The chemical is only used to clean the final product and is not incorporated in it. Thus emissions are virtually immediate; three-fourths result from vapor losses, the remainder from waste disposal. A U.S. ban on land disposal of chlorinated solvents that took effect in November 1986, consideration of similar regulations elsewhere, the high cost of incinerating CFC-113 (because it contains toxic fluorine), and accelerating concern about ozone depletion have all created strong incentives for solvent recovery and recycling.

Since CFC-113 costs about twice as much as other CFCs, investments in recovery and recycling pay off more quickly. Recycling of CFC-113 is now practiced on-site at many large computer companies. Smaller electronics firms, for which in-house recycling is not economical, can sell their used solvents to commercial recyclers or the distributors of some chemical manufacturers.

Capturing CFC emissions from flexible-foam manufacturing can also be accomplished fairly quickly but requires investment in new ventilation systems. New suction systems coupled with carbon adsorption technologies are able to recover from 40 to 90 percent of the CFCs released.

Another area that offers significant savings, at a low cost, is improved design, operating, and maintenance standards for refrigeration and air conditioning equipment. Codes of practice to govern equipment handling are being drawn up by many major trade associations. Key among the recommendations are to require worker training, to limit maintenance and repair work to authorized personnel, to install leak detection systems, and to use smaller refrigerant charges. Another recommendation, to prohibit venting of the refrigerant di-

rectly to the atmosphere, requires the use of recovery and recycling technologies.

Careful study of the automobile air conditioning market in the United States, the largest user of CFC-12 in the country, has found that 34 percent of emissions can be traced to leakage, 48 percent occur during recharge and repair servicing, and the remainder happen through accidents, disposal, and manufacturing, in that order. Equipment with better seals and hoses would reduce emissions and result in less need for system maintenance.

Over the longer term, phasing out the use and emissions of CFCs will require the development of chemical substitutes that do not harm the ozone layer. The challenge is to find alternatives that perform the same function for a reasonable cost, that do not require major equipment modifications, that are nontoxic to workers and consumers, and that are environmentally benign. . . .

The time has come to ask if the functions performed by CFCs are really necessary and, if they are, whether they can be performed in new ways. If all known technical control measures were used, total CFC and halon emissions could be reduced by approximately 90 percent. Many of these control strategies are already cost-effective, and more will become so as regulations push up the price of ozone-depleting chemicals. The speed with which controls are introduced will determine the extent of ozone depletion in the years ahead and when healing of the ozone layer will begin.

BEYOND MONTREAL

An international treaty to halve the production of a chemical feared responsible for destroying an invisible shield is unprecedented. But unfortunately, for several reasons, the Montreal Protocol will not save the ozone layer.

First, many inducements were offered to enhance the treaty's appeal to prospective signatories—extended deadlines for developing and centrally planned economies, allowances to accommodate industry restructuring, and loose definitions of the products that can legitimately be traded internationally. The cumulative effect of these loopholes means that, even with widespread participation, the protocol's goal of halving worldwide CFC use by 1998 will not be met.

Second, recent scientific findings show that more ozone depletion has already occurred than treaty negotiators assumed would happen in 100 years. A recent EPA report concluded that by 2075, even with 100 percent global participation in the protocol, chlorine concentrations in the atmosphere would triple. The agreement will not arrest depletion, merely slow its acceleration.

Third, several chemicals not regulated under the treaty are major threats to the ozone layer. Methyl chloroform and carbon tetrachloride together contributed 13 percent of total ozone-depleting chemical emissions in 1985. As the use of controlled chemicals diminishes, the contribution of these two uncontrolled compounds will grow.

The recognition that global warming may have already begun strengthens the case for further and more rapid reductions in CFC emissions. CFCs currently account for 15 to 20 percent of the greenhouse effect and absorb wavelengths of infrared radiation that other greenhouse gases allow to escape. Indeed, one molecule of the most widely used CFCs is as

effective in trapping heat as 15,000 molecules of carbon dioxide, the most abundant greenhouse gas. In light of these findings, logic suggests a virtual phaseout of CFC and halon emissions by all countries as soon as possible. Releases of other chlorine and bromine-containing compounds not currently covered under the treaty also need to be controlled and in some cases halted.

The timing of the phaseout is crucial. Analysts at EPA examined the effects of a 100 percent CFC phaseout by 1990 and a 95 percent phaseout by 1998. Peak chlorine concentrations would differ by 0.8 parts per thousand million, some one-third of current levels. And under the slower phasedown, atmospheric cleansing would be prolonged considerably: Chlorine levels would remain higher than the peak associated with the accelerated schedule for at least 50 years.

As noted, it is technically feasible to reduce CFC and halon emissions by at least 90 percent. Sweden is the first country to move beyond endorsing a theoretical phaseout. In June 1988 the parliament, after extensive discussions with industry, passed legislation that includes specific deadlines for banning the use of CFCs in new products. Consumption is to be halved by 1991 and virtually eliminated by 1995. Environmental agencies in Britain, the United States, and the Federal Republic of Germany have endorsed emissions reductions of at least 85 percent. Chemical producers in these three countries account for over half the global output of controlled substances.

Levying a tax on newly manufactured CFCs and other ozone-depleting substances is one way governments can cut emissions and accelerate the adoption of alternative chemicals and technologies. If the tax increased in step with mandatory production cutbacks, it would eliminate windfall profits for producers, encourage recovery and recycling processes, stimulate use of new chemicals, and provide a source of funding for new technologies and for needed research. Encouraging investments in recycling networks, incinerators for rigid foams, and collection systems for chemicals that would otherwise be discarded could substantially trim emissions from existing products, from servicing operations, and from new production runs. Research on new refrigeration, air conditioning, and insulation processes is worthy of government support. Unfortunately, international funding for developing such technologies totals less than $5 million.

As mentioned in the text of the Montreal Protocol, results of this research, as well as new technologies and processes, need to be shared with developing countries. Ozone depletion and climate warming are undeniably global in scope. Not sharing information on the most recent developments ensures that environmentally damaging and outdated equipment will continue to be used for years to come, further eroding the Third World technology base. . . .

The scientific fundamentals of ozone depletion and climate change are known, and there is widespread agreement that both have already begun. Although current models of future change vary in their predictions, the evidence is clear enough to warrant an immediate response. Because valuable time was lost when governments and industries relaxed their regulatory and research efforts during the early 1980s, a crash program is now essential. Human health, food supplies, and the global climate all hinge on the support that can be garnered for putting an end to chlorine and bromine emissions.

NO
Lester B. Lave

THE GREENHOUSE EFFECT: WHAT GOVERNMENT ACTIONS ARE NEEDED?

Human beings are causing global-scale changes for the first time. . . . [A]rticles by Gordon MacDonald and Irving Mintzer document the "greenhouse" effect and give some indications of the environmental changes that will result. The possibility of such global changes rouses deep emotions in people: awe that humans have become so powerful, rage that we are tampering with the natural environment on a large scale, and fear that we might create an environment hostile to our progeny. Technologists tend to focus on the first emotion with the optimism that we can also find ways to head off or solve the problems. Environmentalists fix on the second, fearing that humans can only ruin nature. This article focuses on the third, asking what governmental or other social actions are possible and warranted. What should be done now and in the foreseeable future as a result of what is currently known about the atmospheric concentration of greenhouse gases, the resulting climate change, and the consequences for people?

WHY DOES THE GREENHOUSE EFFECT RECEIVE SO MUCH ATTENTION?

Scientists have been giving great attention to the greenhouse effect for more than a decade, despite the vast qualitative and quantitative uncertainties. The public joins scientists in the concern that current activities could create a much less hospitable planet in the future. Congress has also directed its concern to these issues. Congress generally regards programs whose impact is more than three to ten years in the future as hopelessly long term; it seems bizarre that greenhouse effects, which are a century or so into the future, have received major Congressional attention. . . .

Greenhouse effects have the attributes of being (1) global (in the sense that all regions are affected), (2) long term (in the sense that near-term effects are undetectable and important effects on people and their well being are perhaps a century in the future), (3) ethical (in the sense that they involve the preferences and well being of people who have not been born yet, as well as plants, animals, and the environment more generally), (4) potentially catastrophic (in the sense that large changes in the environment might result, as well as massive loss of human life and property), and (5) contentious (in the sense that coming to decisions, translating these into agreements, and enforcing agreements would be difficult due to important "spillover" or external effects, uncertainty, the incentives for individual nations to cheat, the difficulty of detecting cheating, and the difficulty of enforcing agreements even after cheating is detected). In addition, many of the likely public investments such as attempts to substitute for carbon dioxide producing activities would be expensive and disruptive. In other words, this set of issues exercises almost all of the tools of policy analysis and poses deep problems to decision analysts. Below, I point out some particularly attractive research areas, such as behavioral reactions, crucial to formulating policy regarding greenhouse gases.

Uncertainty. A dominant question in formulating greenhouse policy is: What is the uncertainty concerning current statements about emissions, atmospheric accumulation, resulting climate changes, and resulting effects on the managed and unmanaged biospheres? . . .

The Department of Energy has put major resources over the past decade into understanding the carbon cycle, the current sources and sinks of carbon in the environment and the mechanisms that handle increasing carbon emissions into the environment. It is safe to say that the carbon cycle is not understood well, with uncertainty regarding perhaps 20% of total sources and sinks of carbon entering the environment. Con-

troversies surround the importance of deforestation, the amount of carbon retained in the atmosphere, the amount being absorbed by the oceans, and the amount being taken up in plants.

The dynamics can be even more difficult to understand, because the oceans hold less carbon as they warm. Thus, there could be a destabilizing feedback of a warmer atmosphere leading to ocean warming, which induces release of carbon to the atmosphere. With the oceans becoming a net source rather than a sink, atmospheric concentrations would increase more rapidly, leading to rapidly increasing atmospheric temperatures, which induce ocean warming and carbon release. Is this scenario one that leads to disaster—or one where the ocean warming takes so long that fossil fuels are fully used and the increased carbon taken up by plants before the oceans warm enough to release appreciable carbon dioxide to the atmosphere? To what extent, and how quickly, would increased plant growth, due to a warmer climate, more rain, and higher atmospheric concentrations of carbon dioxide, absorb much more of the atmospheric carbon and slow or stop atmospheric warming?

The speed with which natural ecosystems can adapt to climate change is also a matter of concern. A large-scale climate change, comparable to a carbon dioxide doubling, has occurred over the last 18,000 years since the end of the last great ice age. While the temperature changes are comparable, the previous change occurred over 18,000 years while the change due to the greenhouse effect would occur over a century or so, perhaps one-hundred times faster. This rate of change could exceed the abilities of natural ecosystems to adapt. The amount of change is small, however, compared to what is currently experienced for the changes from day to night or season to season.

The issues related to carbon dioxide are much different from the issues related to other greenhouse gases. Neither of the two feedback mechanisms sketched above apply to CFC (chlorofluorucarbons) or methane. The Environmental Protection Agency estimates that about half of the atmospheric warming, after a century, would be attributed to gases other than carbon dioxide—an estimate that is markedly different from those of ten years ago. Much needs to be done to understand feedback mechanisms for the other greenhouse gases and to investigate possible interactions among the gases. For example, atmospheric warming is likely to increase the demand for air conditioning, which would lead to greater electricity use (resulting in increased carbon dioxide emissions) and to greater emissions of CFC from compressor leaks. The warming would also increase the demand for insulation, some of which would be foam insulation made with CFC, releasing much more of this gas to the atmosphere.

The current global circulation models are magnificent examples of technical virtuosity. The physical movements and energy fluxes of the atmosphere are described by partial differential equations that are too complicated to be solved explicitly. Thus the models depend upon expert judgment to decide what aspects of the problem should be treated explicitly within the model and how much attention each aspect should get. The current predictions of the consequences of doubling atmospheric carbon dioxide come mainly from models that treat the oceans as if little mixing occurred and there were no currents. The models also ignore many chemical reactions in the atmosphere. Clearly, these models are "wrong" in the sense of being bad examples of reality. But the central question is whether failing to include these elements results in an error of 10% or whether the models could be wrong to the extent of predicting warming when these gases actually result in atmospheric cooling. . . .

As shown below, exploring the consequences of this warming requires detailed predictions or assumptions for each area about climate, storm patterns, and the length of the growing season. These predictions are little more than educated guesses. For the modelers, this uncertainty is a stimulus to do better. For the policy analyst, the uncertainty must be treated explicitly in deciding what actions are warranted now and in the future.

Even vast uncertainty need not preclude taking preventive action. Uncertainty should induce caution and prevent decision makers from rushing into actions and commitments, however. For example, precipitous action would have led to forbidding military and 747 flights in the stratosphere in the early 1970s. Then, in the late 1970s, precipitous action might have led to building aircraft to fly in the stratosphere as much as possible. Finally, today aircraft flights in the stratosphere are regarded as irrelevant to stratospheric ozone levels.

It is prudent to be concerned about potentially disastrous effects and to be willing to take some actions now, even given the uncertainty. For example, American regulators insisted on building strong containment vessels around civilian nuclear reactors, even though they regarded the chance of a mishap that would require the containment vessel as remote. The USSR regulators did not insist on such safeguards, with quite different results between the problems at Three Mile Island and the tragedy at Chernobyl.

While there is major uncertainty, the policy conclusions about CFC emissions are different today from those about carbon dioxide emissions, as I discuss below.

Accounting for the Uncertainty. The long-term effects of an increase in greenhouse gases are unknown and almost certainly unknowable. The physical changes, such as the gross increase in temperature for each latitude might be predicted, but it is unlikely that the dates of last frost and first freeze and detailed patterns of precipitation will be known for each growing area. Still more difficult to forecast is the adaptive behavior of individuals and governments. The accumulation of greenhouse gases could be enormously beneficial or catastrophic for humans. Or more likely, it would be beneficial at some times and places and catastrophic at others.

Preventive actions are akin to purchasing an insurance policy against potentially catastrophic greenhouse effects. Most people voluntarily purchase life insurance, even though the likelihood of dying in a particular year is very small. I suspect that people would be willing to pay a premium for a policy that would protect against an inhospitable Earth a century or so hence. But, the question is what type of insurance policy is most attractive and how much of a premium are people willing to pay.

Preventing all greenhouse effects is virtually impossible. If the climate changes and resultant human consequences are to be headed off, then heroic actions would be required immediately to reduce emissions of all the greenhouse gases throughout the world. For example, nuclear plants could be built to phase out all coal-burning plants within several decades. The decision to do that would be enormously expensive and disruptive. Such a decision would have to be agreed to in every country and enormous resources would be required to implement it. I would not support such a decision for many reasons.

Short of such heroic measures, are there any actions that might be taken now, even though uncertainty dominates the predictions of effects? Prudence would dictate that we should take actions that might prove highly beneficial, even if they are unlikely to be needed, if their cost is small. Proscribing coal use is not an attractive insurance policy, but we should give serious consideration to limiting the growth rate of coal use. The world discovered after 1974 that there was not a one-to-one coupling of energy use and economic activity. Since then, the developed countries have experienced a considerable increase in economic activity while most countries use little or no more energy than in 1974. Reducing the emissions of other greenhouse gases would be less difficult and disruptive than large reductions in coal use. In particular, it is not difficult or expensive to switch to CFC substitutes that are less damaging and to stop using these chemicals as foaming agents for plastics and in consumer products.

Thus, one of the best ways to deal with uncertainty is to look for robust actions, actions that would be beneficial in the worst case, not harmful in other cases, and not very costly to take. Emphasizing energy conservation is perhaps the best example of a prudent policy. Conservation makes sense without any appeal to greenhouse effects, given the deaths and disease associated with mining, transport, and air pollution from coal. The greenhouse effects simply underline what is already an obvious conclusion, but not one that is being pursued vigorously. So much energy could be saved by adjusting fully to current market prices that sufficient conservation might be attained merely by encouraging this adjustment. In particular, large subsidies to energy use distort resource-allocation decisions significantly.

A second example of an inexpensive insurance policy is switching to less damaging CFCs and using less of them.

Another approach is to develop a strategy of reevaluation at fixed intervals or as new information becomes available. Instead of viewing the current decision as the only opportunity to worry about greenhouse issues, one can attempt to clarify which particular outcomes would cause greatest concern. Then one could revisit the issues periodically to see if uncertainty has been resolved or at least substantially diminished.

SOCIAL AND ECONOMIC CONSEQUENCES OF CLIMATE CHANGE

Announcement of an invention, such as a new drug, is generally greeted with public approval. Certainly there is recognition that innovations may bring undesired consequences, such as occurred with Thalidomide, and so premarket testing and technology assessment have been established and emphasized in many regulatory areas. An innovation seems to be defined in terms of the intent of the inventor to produce something that will make society better or at least to make him richer. On net, it is fair to say that such innovations are viewed positively, with the untoward consequences to be dealt with if they arise.

In contrast, an environmental change such as the greenhouse effect is viewed with horror. Such changes are generally not desired by anyone, but rather emerge as the unintended consequences of society's actions. Those who are horrified might admit that there are some changes that are likely to be beneficial, but they would still regard the overall effect as catastrophic. People tend to be more alarmed by large-scale, rapid environmental changes because the consequences would be important and uncontrollable.

Why are Americans such determined optimists about new technology and such determined pessimists about environmental changes? I suspect that much of the difference is explained by the good intent of the inventor versus the unintended nature of the environmental change. If so, this suggests that people have unwarranted faith in the good intentions of inventors, compared to the unintended changes from taking resources or using the environment as a garbage pail.

Deriving the social and economic consequences of climate change is more difficult than might appear. To be sure, if an area becomes so hot or dry that habitation is impossible, or if an area is under water, the consequences are evident. Thus, if sea level rose, the low-lying parts of Louisiana, Florida, Bangladesh, and the Netherlands would be drastically affected. The vast number of short-term effects are difficult to predict and evaluate. Furthermore, the long-term changes are likely to be less drastic (adjustment occurs to mitigate the difficulties, although this might take a long term for an ecosystem), and so the consequences will be even more difficult to infer.

In particular, a change in climate presents a challenge to farmers. If summers are hotter and drier in the corn belt, then a farmer growing corn in Illinois is going to experience crop failure more frequently, due both to droughts and to heat damage. As the climate changes, rare crop damage will give rise to occasional and then frequent damage. Will the Illinois farmer keep planting corn, surviving with the aid of ever-larger government subsidies? Or will he plant new crops that flourish under the hotter, drier climate?

Climate change also presents an opportunity. Sylvan Wittwer, a noted agronomist, observed that " . . . the present level of atmospheric carbon dioxide is suboptimal, and the oxygen level is supraoptimal, for photosynthesis and primary productivity in the great majority of plants." The increased atmospheric carbon dioxide concentrations would enhance growth and water-use efficiency, leading to more and faster growth. Charles Cooper remarks that a doubled atmospheric concentration of carbon dioxide " . . . is about as likely to increase global food, at least in the long run, as to decrease it. It is certain though, that some nations, regions, and people will gain and others will lose." A new climate regime with more precipitation and a longer growing season bodes well for agriculture—if we figure out what crops to plant and figure out generally how to tailor agriculture to the new climate regime, and how to deal with new pests.

The midcontinental drying, if it occurs, could mean the end of current agricultural practices in the midwest. This climate change might induce more irrigation, dry farming practices such as

have been demonstrated in Israel, new cultivars, different crops, or even ceasing to cultivate this land. The increased rains might mean there was sufficient winter precipitation to provide water for summer irrigation; it would certainly mean that there was sufficient water elsewhere in the country to be transported to the midwest for irrigation. Large dams and canals might be required, but the technology for this is available. Certainly this water would be more expensive than that currently available, but there is no reason to be concerned about starvation or even large increases in food prices for the U.S. On net, food and fibers might be slightly more expensive or less expensive in the U.S. under the new climate, but the change is almost certain to be small compared to other economic changes.

For the U.S., there is no difficulty with finding the appropriate technology for breeding new crops that fit the climate, developing a less water-intensive agriculture, or for moving water for irrigation. The difficulty would be whether agronomists are given the right tasks, whether farmers give up their old crops and farming methods, and whether society can solve the myriad social problems associated with damming newly enlarged rivers and moving the water to where it is needed.

The "less managed" areas, including forests, grasslands, and marsh, might experience large changes and a system far from long-term equilibrium. These effects would be scarcely discernable in measured gross national product, but would be viewed as extremely important by many environmentalists.

Water projects and resources more generally might pose a greater problem. Large-scale water projects, such as dams and canals, are built to last for long periods. Once built, they are not easily changed. Thus, major climate change could lead to massive dams fed by tiny streams or dams completely inadequate for the rivers they are designed to control. Similarly, treaty obligations for the Colorado are inflexible and could pose major problems if there is less water flowing down the river. Similarly, the climate change would induce migration, both across areas in the U.S. and from other countries. The legal and illegal migration could pose major problems. Finally, Americans treasure certain natural resources, such as waterfalls. Climate change that stopped the flow at popular falls would be regarded seriously.

Commenting on energy modeling, Hans Landsberg wrote: " . . . all of us who have engaged in projecting into the more distant future take ourselves too seriously. . . . What is least considered is how many profound turns in the road one would have missed making 1980 projections in 1930! I am not contending that the emperor is naked, but we surely overdress him."

REPRISE: WHY SO MUCH CONCERN FOR THE GREENHOUSE EFFECT?

It is the symbolic nature of the issues that has drawn attention to the greenhouse effect. Anyone who thinks he can see 100 years into the future is mad. If humans have now acquired the power to influence the global environment, then it is likely that we will cause changes even larger than those discussed here within the next century or so. Both the greenhouse effect and other global changes could be predominantly beneficial or harmful to humans and various aspects of the environment, although they are likely to be beneficial in some times and places and detrimental in others. But a large element of the public debate is almost scandalized at the notion that the changes might be beneficial or made beneficial by individual actions and government policies.

The difficulty is public concern that global scale effects are now possible; we have had a "loss of innocence." In the past, if an individual ruined a plot of land, he could move on. If human actions caused major problems such as the erosion of the Dalmatian coast of Yugoslavia, there was always other inviting land. But, if the Earth is made inhospitable, there is no other inviting planet readily at hand.

I share this concern, but find it naive. Having acquired the power to influence the global environment, there is no way to relinquish it. No one intends to change the global environment by emitting greenhouse gases. Rather, the change is an inadvertent consequence of business as usual. The culprit is not a malevolent individual or rapacious company. Instead, it is the scope of human activities stemming from a large population, modern technology, and an unbelievable volume of economic activity. These culprits are not going to disappear, however much we might all wish that people did not have the ability to affect our basic environment. In this sense, the human race has lost its environmental innocence.

The symbolism is important because of the need to educate the public and government and gauge their reactions to this first global environmental issue. If people and governments show themselves to be concerned and willing to make sacrifices, the prospect for the future looks brighter. If instead, each individual and nation regards the effects as primarily due to others, and as someone else's problem, the increases in economic activity and advances in technology promise a future with major unintended changes in the Earth's environment.

Such changes could be dealt with by concerned global action to stop the stimulus and thus the response. Or they could be dealt with by individual and national actions to adapt to the consequences. However much I might wish for concerted action among countries, I do not believe this is likely to occur. There are too many disparate interests, too much to be gained by cheating, too much suspicion of the motives of others, and too little control over all the relevant actors. Thus, reluctantly, I conclude that mitigation through adaptation must be our focus.

For example, within the United States, federal environmental laws have been only a modest success in preventing environmental pollution. Ozone problems have worsened, ground water has become more polluted, and we seem no closer to dealing with radioactive and toxic wastes. When the scope of the problem becomes international, as with acid rain, there is little or no progress. Curtailing sulfur oxides emissions into the air necessarily involves promoting some interests while hurting others. Those who would be hurt are, not surprisingly, more skeptical about whether low levels of acid sulfate aerosols cause disease than those who believe that they would benefit. Getting agreement on action has proven essentially impossible for abating sulfur oxides. It is hard to imagine that a debate among 140 nations on the greenhouse effect would lead to an agreement to adopt binding programs to abate emissions.

A multinational agreement on controlling CFC has been negotiated in 1987. This is an extremely encouraging, and surprising development. There are many obstacles to effective implementation, however, from ratification by each country to best faith efforts to abide by the sense of the agreement.

CONCLUSION

The greenhouse effect is the first of what are likely to be many long-term, global problems. Analysis is difficult because of the vast uncertainty about causes and effects, as well as of the consequences of the resulting climate change. The current uncertainties together with the costs of precipitous action imply that heroic actions to curtail the emissions of all greenhouse gases are not justified. Nonetheless, the current facts support a program of energy conservation, abatement, research, and periodic reconsideration that is far more activist than the current policy of the U.S. government.

I would like to thank Stephen Schneider and Jesse Ausubel for comments. This work was supported in part by the National Science Foundation (Grant No. SES-8715564).

POSTSCRIPT

Does Global Warming Require Immediate Government Action?

The harsh reality is that the environment is deteriorating. Very few, if any, physical scientists dispute this fact. What is disputed is the rate of decline in the global environment and whether or not citizens acting at the end of the twentieth century should try to alter this process. Do we have enough knowledge of the future to take dramatic steps today that will reshape the world of tomorrow? These are hard questions. If we answer incorrectly, our children and our children's children may curse us for our lack of resolve to solve environmental problems that were clear for all to see.

Shea and Lave both agree that there is a clear and present danger associated with ozone-depleting chemicals, such as chlorofluorocarbons, which are also the gases that contribute to the greenhouse effect. What they disagree upon is whether or not we know enough today to take immediate, decisive action. Do *you* know enough? If you do not, we suggest that you read further in this area. *It is your future that is being discussed here.*

A brief history of scientific concerns about the greenhouse effect, which stretches back to the late nineteenth century, is found in Jesse H. Ausubel, "Historical Note," in the National Research Council's *Changing Climate: Report of the Carbon Dioxide Assessment Committee* (National Academy Press, 1983). We should note that there are a number of other essays in *Changing Climate* that may be of interest to you. The Environmental Protection Agency (EPA) has published many studies you might want to examine. See, for example, the EPA's study entitled *The Potential Effects of Global Climate Change on the United States* (December 1989) or *Policy Options for Stabilizing Global Climate* (February 1989). An extensive analysis of the scientific, economic, and policy implications are also found in the *1990 Economic Report of the President.*

ISSUE 18

Should a New Military-Industrial Complex Be Developed?

YES: Mackubin T. Owens, from "Expand the Military-Industrial Complex? Yes—Preparedness Requires It," *Orbis: A Journal of World Affairs* (Fall 1989)

NO: William J. Long, from "Expand the Military-Industrial Complex? No— It's Unnecessary and Inefficient," *Orbis: A Journal of World Affairs* (Fall 1989)

ISSUE SUMMARY

YES: Mackubin T. Owens, a professor of defense economics, warns that the industrial base would be "hard-pressed to support our military needs" without substantial lead time and, therefore, a strategic trade and investments policy should be "enacted as soon as possible."

NO: Associate professor of international affairs William J. Long attacks Owens's military-industrial complex and proclaims that "defense protectionism, like other forms of protectionism, is unnecessary, ineffective, and even dangerous."

The trends in the U.S. defense budget during the 1950s, 1960s, 1970s, and 1980s resemble a roller coaster ride. Driven by foreign and domestic policy considerations within the United States and the pressure of international events, defense expenditures have had an up-and-down pattern and have greatly influenced the economy. Now that the defense budget seems to be in a free-fall because of the remarkable, seemingly overnight collapse of the Soviet Union, questions arise: How far should the defense budget be allowed to fall? Should certain industries critical to defense interests be protected in the event that a massive defense build-up is again determined to be necessary? A review of the ups and downs of the post–World War II defense budgets should help put the current debate over budget cuts into some perspective.

Given the military buildup in the 1940–45 period during World War II, it is not surprising that defense expenditures fell sharply in the postwar period. Defense spending fell nearly 90 percent in the 1945–48 period, yet even after this sharp downsizing, the defense budget remained substantially larger than its prewar level. This reflected the new role the United States had begun to play in the international arena, largely in response to the expansionist policy of the Soviet Union and the Maoist revolution in China.

United States involvement in the Korean War caused defense spending to rise to a record post–World War II level of $395 billion in 1952 (stated in 1991 constant dollars). This represented 60 percent of the federal budget and 12 percent of the gross national product (GNP). As those hostilities receded, defense spending also receded, but a new pattern was established: Defense spending dominated the federal budget even when the United States was not actively engaged in a military conflict. For the remainder of the Eisenhower presidency after the Korean War, peacetime defense spending averaged $216 billion per year (in 1991 constant dollars), which was double the 1945–48 level and equal to 8.5 percent of the GNP. What these numbers could mean in terms of the power and influence of the Department of Defense and defense contractors was a concern of many, and even prompted President Eisenhower, himself a former general, to warn of the dangers of what he called the "military-industrial complex" when he left office in 1961.

This set the stage for the 1960s and 1970s. The first half of the 1960s was peaceful, and defense spending averaged about $240 billion in constant dollars. But once again the Cold War turned into a shooting war with the escalation of U.S. involvement in Vietnam, and defense spending took another long ride upwards, peaking in 1968 at $309 billion. The divisiveness caused by this war in Southeast Asia signaled the Ford and Nixon administrations and later the Carter administration to deemphasize military spending. In the 1973–80 peacetime period, the defense budget fell to its lowest post–World War II level, averaging $220 billion per year in 1991 dollars. In relative terms, this meant that defense spending was not quite 5 percent of GNP and only slightly more than 20 percent of the federal budget.

Was the United States sufficiently prepared militarily if the 1979 Soviet incursion into Afghanistan turned into a full-fledged war? Did the United States respond adequately when Iran seized the U.S. embassy and held the diplomatic staff hostage the same year? Many thought not, including Ronald Reagan, who was then entering the first year of his presidency, and during the years of the Reagan administration, defense spending averaged $310 billion per year. The 1980s witnessed the most extensive peacetime military buildup in U.S. history.

With the dissolution of the Soviet Union in 1991, there is growing political pressure to reduce defense spending. How should this be accomplished without compromising future safety? Two conservatives, Mackubin T. Owens and William J. Long, struggle with this question in the selections that follow. As the military is downsized, does the United States need to "preserve or encourage domestic 'strategic' industries, that is, industries that contribute to technological advancement, national income, or defense programs"?

YES

EXPAND THE MILITARY-INDUSTRIAL COMPLEX? YES—PREPAREDNESS REQUIRES IT

The Department of Defense [DoD] is now emphasizing industrial preparedness not because of a hidden desire to aid inefficient industries, nor because
of grand ambitions to interfere with the U.S. economy. Rather the Pentagon's
concern for industrial preparedness is the result of changes in America's
military circumstances. These have created a demonstrable need for strategic investment and trade policies. While such policies must be limited and
protected by stringent safeguards to prevent abuse, they must be enacted,
and enacted as soon as possible.

Military exercises and war games reveal that in the event of war or even a
protracted low-level conflict, American industry would be hard-pressed to
support the military needs of the United States and its allies without
substantial lead time. Some would argue that military needs already exert a
significant influence on the U.S. economy, to the detriment of other sectors;
and that further steps to direct trade and investment in the interest of
national security, such as those proposed in two recent Pentagon publications, are unnecessary during peacetime. But if American conventional
forces are to provide a credible deterrent (and not just a trip-wire for nuclear
weapons), it is irresponsible to wait for an emergency before undertaking
the many steps necessary to improve the country's military-industrial
base. . . .

AMERICA'S MILITARY-INDUSTRIAL BASE

The U.S. military-industrial base consists of three levels. *Basic industrial
capacity* comprises the foundation industries that produce raw goods necessary for both civilian and military output: metals, chemicals, and energy.
Sub-tier industries produce the components and parts that are put together to

From Mackubin T. Owens, "Expand the Military-Industrial Complex? Yes—Preparedness
Requires It," *Orbis: A Journal of World Affairs* (Fall 1989). Copyright © 1989 by The Foreign Policy
Research Institute. Reprinted by permission. Notes omitted.

create final products. *End-product industries* include those dedicated exclusively to military production, the "defense industries" plus that part of the civilian sector that can be converted to military production.

What the U.S. military requires of this industrial base is to maintain a technological edge over potential adversaries; then, in time of war, to meet the needs of national security in a timely and economical manner. At minimum, this means efficient peacetime production, support for the military's existing force structure and war reserve, and a surge capacity (rapidly expanded production within the existing industrial plant). In the event of a major conventional war, U.S. industry would also have to be mobilized (a structured, systematic increase in production rates over one to two years). Mobilization requires a major expansion of industrial capacity; circumstances may require not only that wartime losses be replaced, but also that support be provided for significantly enlarged forces.

At present, U.S. industry cannot meet the minimum requirement, much less mobilize in response to a global crisis. Problems exist at all three levels. With regard to *basic industrial capacity*, structural changes in the U.S economy and increased foreign competitiveness have caused much traditional heavy industry to move overseas. While this de-industrialization is probably the American economy's most-highly publicized problem, it is in fact the least troubling. The shift of heavy industry to countries such as Japan, South Korea, and Taiwan reflects the workings of comparative advantage, and so reinforces economic efficiency. This international division of labor means that the remaining American producers of such products as steel

are more efficient. Excessive attention to the changing structure of America's heavy industry obscures a critical point: in time of crisis, the United States would have access to an alliance-wide industrial base. While this global industrial base has obvious vulnerabilities, for a maritime nation the advantages of exploiting an international division of labor far outweigh the costs.

Problems at the level of *sub-tier industries* are much more severe. Resources have been diverted from military production because of the sustained growth of the U.S. economy since 1983, leading to heightened civilian demands, and declining real military budgets after 1985. This combination has resulted in increased lead times, rising costs, and bottlenecks. In some cases, the military depends on a unique producer—who may not wish to do business with the U.S. government. The army's attempt in the 1970s to surge tank production was frustrated because the lone producer of tank castings could not meet the increased demand. In 1988, the sole producer of aerospace-grade continuous filament rayon yarn, a material critical to space and strategic missile systems, announced that it was closing and filing for bankruptcy.

Sub-tier production has also been affected by increased foreign competitiveness; much of the U.S. productive capacity has shifted overseas—especially in such areas as electronics, machine tools, fasteners, and precision optics. Although the alliance industrial base partially offsets that shift, the erosion of the traditional U.S. edge in technology remains a legitimate concern. American planners seek to offset the Soviets' numerical superiority with technological superiority. In this critical area, a balance must exist between cooperation with allies and the need to avoid over-dependence on foreign sources for critical technologies during a crisis.

A different set of problems exists at the *end-product* level, where the free market hardly exists. Because the federal government is the sole buyer, the market is monopsonistic. Washington also imposes the regulations under which the sellers must operate. This relationship between supplier and consumer tends to build their initial interests and to de-emphasize their concern with price. Industries serving the military face many barriers to entry, including overly exact specifications, purchases of small quantities, annual procurements, high uncertainty of project funding, long gestation periods, a likelihood of low profits, and the highly specialized nature of military research and development. Other barriers to entry reinforce inefficiencies and make it difficult to match the lower cost practices of the commercial sector. These include government sponsorship of research and development, high overhead, specialized capital equipment and labor, and military specifications. Such problems are exacerbated by stop-and-go funding, excessive government regulations and inflexible contracting and acquisition policies.

A recent study shows the decline in firms willing to do business with the Department of Defense. In 1982, more than 118,000 firms provided manufactured goods to the military; in 1987, fewer than 40,000 remained. Some of the 80,000 went out of business, including about 20,000 small firms. Most, however, simply gave up on the Pentagon and sought out other customers. This is remarkable because, using constant fiscal year (FY) 1989 dollars, the military procurement budget grew from $54.9 billion in 1982 to $87.0 billion five years later. Of course, not every company's capacity is completely lost to the military-industrial base. In time of emergency or war, many would be available for military production, though in a less timely manner. Still, the movement of firms away from military production has exacerbated the structural distortions that characterize the U.S. military industry.

Even greater shortcomings affect the U.S. ability to surge production in times of emergency. Indeed, the lead times and the unit costs of producing weapon systems, resulting from such distortions in the peacetime acquisition process as the extension of programs (increasing the time over which a system will be produced in order to reduce expenditures during a particular fiscal year), stop-and-go funding by Congress, and constant tinkering with military specifications, have increased so dramatically that one can question the whole concept of surge capacity in the production of weapons platforms such as tanks and aircraft. Accordingly, the Department of Defense has focused its attempts to improve surge capacity in the area of sustainability items (spare parts and munitions), especially precision guided munitions, short-range missiles, and other ordnance. While improvements have been made, major deficiencies remain. For example, surging ammunition production would be tethered by a number of sub-tier constraints, leading to possible bottlenecks. Rolling mill and metal-forming firms are already operating at high levels of capacity. In the absence of action before an emergency, it would be difficult to shift some of this capacity to ammunition production. Similar problems would constrain the ability of sub-tier firms to produce ammonium perchlorate. Finally, many guidance systems and explosives are produced overseas.

CURRENT CIRCUMSTANCES

To understand the current problem, several points need to be established. First, the international division of labor is an irreversible fact. Strengthening the U.S. industrial base, therefore, does not mean seeking economic self-sufficiency, much less autarky. Even if this were a good idea, it is not affordable. Fortunately, the loss of U.S. industries to the international division of labor does not necessarily mean that their output is unavailable to the United States, even in time of war. An alliance military-industrial base exists, making it unnecessary to replicate the U.S. industrial base of the 1940s and 1950s, characterized by basic heavy industry. Making use of this alliance base, of course, places a premium on cooperation with the allies. As Robert Costello, former under secretary of defense for acquisition, has said about co-development of the FSX fighter with Japan: "We have to be tied to the Japanese in very direct ways because they have some things that we do not." It also points to the importance of strong naval forces; the navy protects those allies that provide critical materiel as well as the sea lanes of communications to them. But, while disruptions are always possible, overseas suppliers are by and large very reliable, and exercises and war games indicate that U.S. naval power is sufficient to serve its protective function.

Of course, an alliance industrial base has its limits. Vulnerabilities arising from interdiction of trade constrain the global base. But there are also political problems that arise in any alliance. For instance, as Edward Olsen has pointed out, a given country may not mind if its military alliance with the United States involves mutual economic dependence. But how pleased will that ally be if such an alliance involves U.S. economic dependence on a third state? Japan, for example, produces high-technology components for the U.S. military, and thereby accepts a partial U.S. dependency—but how would the Japanese feel about having the U.S. dependent on a third state for a critical part of the military-industrial base? In addition, economic interdependence grants an ally in disagreement with a particular policy the means to put economic pressure on the United States.

Second, the market alone cannot meet all the requirements of national security, primarily for the structural reasons discussed above. This issue was argued at length at the beginning of the Reagan administration, as part of the debate between the Pentagon and the Office of Management and Budget (OMB). The former proposed an "Action Plan for Improvement of Industrial Readiness," calling for expanded use of Title III of the Defense Production Act, as amended. Specifically, the Defense Department wanted Congress to amend the Act to reinstate DoD's authority to borrow directly from the Treasury, as had been the case before 1974. OMB argued that the marketplace, stimulated by the military build-up, by reductions in tax rates, and by changes in depreciation schedules, would improve the military-industrial base without any help from the government. The result was a compromise between the Pentagon and OMB, weighted more favorably toward the latter's position. Unfortunately, the compromise did not have the intended effect, for the increase in expenditures did nothing to change industry structure, the crux of the matter.

More spending only served to conceal industry problems, and, in the long run, to make matters worse.

Finally, caution is required with regard to the Soviet Union, even in an era of reduced tensions. In the early 1980s, the Soviets sharply increased military investment, as a percentage of their gross national product, over what was already a very high level. Combined with an increased stockpiling effort, that added investment has actually improved the ability of the Soviet command economy to meet the demands of protracted war. Thus, Moscow still has the potential, should its interests warrant, to increase military output and that is what, with all its problems, the Soviet economy does best. Even if East-West negotiations should lead to a shift away from a U.S. defense based on forward deployment and high levels of operational readiness, industrial preparedness remains a hedge against a return to business as usual by the Soviets. [In 1991–1992, the United States did reduce substantially its land-based operation in Western Europe.— Eds.]

FORMULATING POLICY

What should be done to improve industrial preparedness? The answer depends on one's perspective. Those who focus on the advantages of free trade tend to conclude that the U.S. government may have done too much already, and would reduce its role further. On the other side, those who mistrust the market would nationalize defense industries, or at least subject major segments of U.S. industry to the vagaries of government planning. But the most prudent approach to im-

proving the military-industrial base lies between these poles, in the development of strategic policies.

Strategic trade and investment policies allocate resources during peacetime to enhance national security in the event of an emergency. These policies acknowledge that the free market normally does not direct resources into the military sector during peacetime, and that waiting until emergency strikes is too late.

Strategic trade policy ensures that the United States does not become overly dependent on foreign suppliers—as might occur were the international division of labor to operate freely—and that it does not lose its technology base. One may disagree over the proper balance between economic efficiency and requirements of trade restrictions in the interest of national security, but national security does have a legitimate claim on the formulation of trade policy.

Strategic investment policy channels, in peacetime, economic assets into areas underfunded by the free market. It involves government allocation of resources into military-oriented research and development and the purchase of items with long lead times (such as tank and aircraft engines, and specialized machine tools). It also directs resources into advanced manufacturing technology, such as flexible manufacturing systems, which are computerized production assemblies (machine tools, a material handling system, a computer control system) that can be programmed to manufacture a variety of products, making it easy to shift from civilian to military production.

A prudent approach to industrial preparedness must include several elements. The U.S. government should:
Establish a forum to address emergency preparedness and mobilization, then con-

nect these requirements to strategic investment and trade policy. At present, no single group accomplishes this goal. The Reagan administration made major advances by reversing the trend that had moved coordination of emergency preparedness out of the White House (the Office of Emergency Preparedness was abolished in 1973). In 1981, President Ronald Reagan created the Emergency Mobilization Preparedness Board (EMPB) and later folded its functions into the National Security Council. In 1988, Reagan further signaled presidential concern about emergency preparedness by issuing Executive Order 12656, which assigned responsibilities to Federal departments and agencies and strengthened the role of the National Security Council as the "principal forum for consideration of national security emergency preparedness policy."

Implement the Graduated Mobilization Response Plan, released by President Reagan in 1988. The plan gives the president options for gradually increasing U.S. military-industrial preparedness in response to increasing international tension. Because of the perception that mobilization is provocative (recalling World War I), it is often treated as a measure of last resort. But if mobilization does not occur until the emergency is in full swing, it may be too late. The Graduated Mobilization Response [GMR] Plan allows the president to take carefully weighted, incremental steps toward an improved state of preparedness, avoiding the extremes of provocation and inaction.

For instance, he can direct an increase in the purchase of long lead-time items or strategic minerals; direct certain industries to surge production to support requirements for existing forces; enhance production capacity by letting contracts to expand physical plant or by opening "cold" standby production lines; and review standby legal authorities. Such steps, taken before a crisis develops into a full-scale conflict, would signal U.S. resolve and could help defuse the emergency. At a minimum, steps taken under this plan would reduce lead times.

Use Title III of the Defense Production Act to carry out the strategic investment policy to ensure that the government can fulfill all phases of the GMR Plan. Investment should be limited to those cases where ordinary market mechanisms cannot meet national military needs, such as the advanced manufacturing technologies private corporations are unwilling or unable, due to structural distortions within the military-industrial base, to employ. Several programs already exist to invest government funds along these lines, including the Industrial Modernization Incentives Program (which provides incentives to contractors to make capital investments that improve productivity), the Manufacturing Technology Program (which invests in advanced production technologies), and the semiconductor Manufacturing Technology Program, known as Sematech.

Build surge capacity into the acquisition process; push so-called surge funding, in effect requiring a contractor to pay for his own surge capacity as part of a contract with DoD.

Improve government-industry cooperation. The first step is to establish forums for cooperation such as a Manufacturing Advisory Council and a Defense Manufacturing Board. Next, antitrust policies should be relaxed, especially those that impede cooperative research and development. Joint ventures between government, industry, and the military should be permitted, even encouraged. This will speed conversion of industrial capacity to wartime requirements.

CONCLUSION

While some of the fears expressed by opponents of strategic trade policy are misguided, their instincts are not. Government intervention in the economy on behalf of national security must be done carefully, for it is fraught with dangers.

Not least is the danger that national security may become a Trojan horse. Writings of the left, such as Robert Reich and Ira Magaziner in *Minding America's Business*, have for some time advocated an industrial policy that seeks to substitute government decisions for those of the market. This approach has often been discredited, and never more dramatically than during the 1980s, when planners (even Japanese planners) could not predict future trends, much less individual winners. Free-market economists, who have to battle with these left-wing partisans of industrial policy, are wary of having to battle also with an industrial policy of the right, introduced as an adjunct to national security.

This is understandable. Already, domestic producers hide behind the banner of national security to achieve protection against more efficient foreign competitors (as in the case of some electronics components, or previously, steel). Usually these producers can count on the support of members of Congress, who see protection of domestic jobs as an irresistible political issue. Moreover, even some economists (notably Jacques Gansler) explicitly advocate military-industrial preparedness as the leading edge of a wider industrial policy.

But legitimate concerns about industrial policy do not undo the serious problems in the American economy that hamper the government's ability to provide for the common defense. The U.S. government in general and the Department of Defense in particular have important, if limited, roles to play in alleviating those problems.

NO

William J. Long

EXPAND THE MILITARY-INDUSTRIAL COMPLEX? NO—IT'S UNNECESSARY AND INEFFICIENT

Although the United States has traditionally pursued a policy of relatively free trade and investment, many are now calling for a more managed approach to defense-related industries. In large measure, these calls have been provoked by America's unprecedented trade deficits, by foreign challenges to its technological lead, and by the sudden reversal in its status from the world's leading creditor to the leading debtor. Should these voices be heeded? Should an effort be made to preserve or encourage domestic "strategic" industries, that is, industries that contribute to technological advancement, national income, or defense programs? The issue breaks down into three component questions. Do imperfections in the market (such as industry concentration or export targeting by foreign governments) demand remedial U.S. action that departs from free trade norms? If so, are government agencies capable of discovering the remedies that will nurture the appropriate industries? And can the political process produce appropriate and effective policies?

The Department of Defense (DoD), among others, already has answered all three of these questions in the affirmative, and its decisions could profoundly affect the course of U.S. trade and investment policy. In so deciding, however, the DoD has ignored basic objections to so major a shift in America's economic stance. And a close look at those objections suggests that defense protectionism, like other forms of protectionism, is unnecessary, ineffective, and even dangerous.

FREE TRADE VERSUS STRATEGIC TRADE

American free-trade liberalism holds that the distribution of resources should be left to market mechanisms and that the provision of collective

From William J. Long, "Expand the Military-Industrial Complex? No—It's Unnecessary and Inefficient," *Orbis: A Journal of World Affairs* (Fall 1989). Copyright © 1989 by The Foreign Policy Research Institute. Reprinted by permission. Notes omitted.

goods (such as stable exchange rates) should be the province of international organizations. Although the United States has never completely realized this ideal, its postwar trade and investment policy has usually favored free trade. The reason for this policy was stated by President Reagan in September 1983, and it is a reason that would have been given by any of his predecessors: "The United States believes that international direct investment flows should be determined by private market forces. . . . We believe there are only winners, no losers, and all participants gain from it." Thus, with regard to capital barriers, the United States has maintained an open-door policy that has few exceptions. With regard to trade barriers, it has led an international movement away from high tariffs and toward a more open international trading system. To be precise, it has stood for the principle of negotiating diffuse, reciprocal trade liberalization through multilateral institutions such as the General Agreement on Tariffs and Trade.

Within the U.S. government, however, support for this policy has not been unanimous. Congress often has opposed free trade and investment policies, while the president and executive branch agencies held the bulwark. Repeatedly, since the Reciprocal Trade Agreements Act of 1934 provided for the reduction of tariff levels by executive decree, the executive branch has held at bay congressional attempts to pass protectionist legislation. This resistance usually has taken the form of offering partial relief to politically important groups suffering from foreign competition (such as the steel and auto industries) in exchange for congressional support for international free trade and open capital markets. The pattern has been clear: Congress makes the noise, the executive branch takes the heat, and a deal is struck.

This system of relatively open trade and investment has unquestionably served U.S. and Western interests well. The increase in global trade and capital flow since the days of the Smoot-Hawley Tariff Act (1930) has been dramatic and unprecedented. Between 1933 and 1980, for example, real, price-adjusted U.S. exports more than doubled as a share of U.S. goods production. With expanded trade and investment has come an era of global and national prosperity.

Nevertheless, the argument that free trade and investment policies best serve the nation is presumptive only. It can and should be overridden by an argument for government intervention where compelling evidence in a particular case supports the need for national security. Indeed, U.S. trade and investment policy has long recognized such conflicts. Perhaps the best known departure from free trade liberalism is embodied in the Export Administration Act, under which the Commerce Department, in consultation with other agencies, grants or denies export licenses for reasons of national security or foreign policy. The Department of Defense is entitled to review these license applications for the export or re-export of specified commodities and technical data to communist countries, or to certain non-communist countries thought to pose a significant risk of diversion.

Nor are export controls the only justifiable limits that national security can impose on free trade. Even in the nuclear age, it makes sense for the United States to safeguard select production capacities from economic, political, or military disruption.

But in terms of large-scale economic policy, the Defense Department traditionally has held that open trade and investment policies were vital to maintaining the U.S. technological advantage over the Soviet Union, and in this way nade an essential contribution to U.S. defense. The Defense Department also opposed import restrictions because it wished to maintain the option of procuring goods and components on a worldwide market and because it viewed its ability to deal with economic competitors as more important than securing domestic suppliers. The department's support for the co-development of the FSX aircraft with Japan indicates that this view still predominates, on occasion. These premises are now changing rapidly, however, and the changes mark a turning point in the executive branch's approach to trade and investment.

THE NEW DEFENSE PROTECTIONISM

Increasingly, the argument is heard in defense circles that a sound strategic trade and investment policy entails governmental protection of, or encouragement for, certain industries. In the narrow version of this argument, the industries are said to be vital to U.S. defense programs. In the broad version, they are merely linked to the economic health upon which U.S. military power is based.

During the 1980s, such notions of a strategic trade and investment policy spread quickly from the academic to the policy-making realm and took institutional root at the Department of Defense. This change was prompted in part by the precipitous decline in the fortunes of the U.S. high-technology sector, once a showcase of the U.S. economy and a prime source of America's defense superiority. From 1980 to 1985, America's high-technology trade balance declined drastically, from a surplus of $27 billion to less than $4 billion. In 1986, the United States incurred its first high-technology trade deficit. As a result, a fissure developed in the executive branch's traditionally solid support for liberal free trade and investment policies. Elements in DoD began to argue that "strategic industries"—semiconductors, numerically controlled machine tools, high-speed computers, telecommunications equipment, and a variety of other sophisticated technology products—should be protected from foreign competition and acquisition because of their role in . . . the industrial requirements of the U.S. military. . . .

In mid-1988, the department released *Bolstering Defense Industrial Competitiveness*, an important examination of the U.S. defense industrial base that outlined a general strategy for preserving and strengthening domestic industries of strategic importance. Focusing on America's increasing dependence on foreign hardware and technology and on the erosion of U.S. competitiveness in defense-related industries, the report concluded that "United States institutions have not responded adequately or quickly enough to basic shifts in economic or manufacturing power among nations." It recommended a more active role for the Defense Department in U.S. foreign and domestic economic policy, the establishment of internal DoD mechanisms for addressing defense manufacturing issues, and the formation of a Defense Manufacturing Strategy Committee at the National Academy of Sciences to undertake a comprehensive analysis of the interplay between foreign trade and domestic defense procurement policies.

A more recent study, *Final Report on the Defense Industrial and Technology Base*, issued by the Defense Science Board study group (which consists of defense contractors and university officials), reinforced this view. It found the U.S. industrial and technological base ever less capable of meeting national security needs. Consistent with DoD inclinations, the report called on the president to create an Industrial Policy Committee, chaired by the national security adviser, to assess and eliminate the gap between military needs and industrial capabilities. It also recommended the inclusion of the secretary of defense in the Cabinet-level Economic Policy Council.

Then, in March 1989, in consultation with the Energy Department, DoD released its *Critical Technologies Plan*, which lists twenty-two technologies considered essential to ensuring the "long-term qualitative superiority of U.S. weapons systems." Many of the listed technologies are in important commercial sectors. Further, in presenting the list for review by the Congress, Deputy Undersecretary of Defense for Acquisition Milton Lohr noted that the list is not comprehensive, nor does it include all the important supporting technologies.

The Defense Department's new-found interest in the economy is of truly staggering scope. It has begun to advocate active government participation in the market through trade and investment policies that protect and promote those industries it believes are strategic. Clearly, the time has come to raise hard questions about DoD's understanding of its role in a free economy.

IS DEFENSE PROTECTIONISM NECESSARY?

To be sure, the presumption in favor of free trade can be overridden when that policy potentially endangers vital national security concerns. But such a move presumes that the proposed intervention is necessary, that it will be effective, and that it can be accomplished in a way that yields more benefit than harm. Does DoD's campaign for a strategic trade and investment policy meet these three criteria?

Like most major industrial countries, the United States already protects essential military, food, energy, communications, transport, and core production needs through a host of selective measures. The U.S. government promulgates over 600 pages of regulations governing strategic exports. It prohibits or limits foreign acquisitions in the atomic energy, airline, and communication industries. It stockpiles and subsidizes food and energy, and protects such manufactures as steel, automobiles, textiles, semiconductors, and machine tools. It finances research and development in national defense, aerospace, health, and medicine. The cost of protecting and promoting these many "strategic" sectors already amounts to an enormous burden. DoD efforts to identify new strategic industries will further add to these costs without significantly improving national security.

The argument for an expanded DoD role in managing the U.S. economy ignores certain basic realities. First, contrary to the assumption underlying the new DoD economic interventionism, U.S. national security does not require total reliance on domestic supplies. In an era of growing economic and technological interdependence and transnational corporations, the industrial base of American security must to some degree depend on the resources of U.S. allies and on companies not completely under U.S. national control. Indeed, sensible procurement of manufacturing equipment, weapons, and technology should exploit the innovation and competitive discipline that foreign suppliers can provide.

Undoubtedly, domestic or accessible foreign supplies could meet U.S. security needs for nearly all products under a wide variety of wartime scenarios. Invariably, in the past, U.S. industries petitioning for import protection on national security grounds have failed to prove that competing foreign suppliers would be unavailable sources in wartime. One reason is that the proliferation of technological competence throughout the West means alternative suppliers can be found in Western Europe, Japan, and elsewhere.

Second, a reduction in conventional forces—and hence the economic resources needed to sustain them—is at the top of both the U.S. and Soviet arms control agendas. Success in controlling arms will allow the DoD to shift funds from present expenditures to building reserve capacity and mobilization potential. Too, should there be similar progress in lessening the probability of a major and protracted conventional war, the U.S. force structure will shift accordingly, and the structure of the U.S. defense industry with it. Almost certainly, this will mean a move away from large-scale production capacity.

Third, many problems thought to require government's intervention could be better resolved by getting the government out of the marketplace. As one

study of a defense industrial policy put it:

> The government should stop taking actions that work against . . . market trends. Overly stringent antitrust policies work against the cooperative development and subsequent diffusion of new technologies. Overly zealous export restrictions prevent U.S. firms from reaping the profits from proprietary-product development.

Similarly, a government effort to put its fiscal affairs in order and to increase the rate of domestic savings might go far toward improving America's industrial base.

Fourth, DoD already spends some $300 billion dollars a year, approximately 5 to 6 percent of the gross national product. Nearly 85 percent of this money is spent in the realm of non-nuclear defense. Properly spent, that sum could be a tremendous tool in shaping the U.S. industrial capacity, both active and latent, that national security requires. Clearly, this is not how it has been used. But flaws in the Pentagon's management of its budget should not excuse disruptions of the free market. It will be time for such disruptions only when DoD has done all it can working with the free market.

To be specific on this score, the Defense Department should seek innovative measures to serve U.S. defense needs efficiently. It should re-examine its procurement practices and undertake additional farsighted projects in basic science and engineering to improve U.S. security and technological abilities. For example, the Office of Technology Assessment recently found that the Pentagon's complex procurement process inhibits commercial exploitation of new developments, and that DoD strategy for developing critical technologies often lacks coordination. Further, as a consequence of funding demonstration-and-development projects, and supporting technology commercialization proposals, the Pentagon's funding of basic research as a percentage of total DoD expenditures has declined dramatically, from 5.2 percent in 1965 to an estimated 2.2 percent in 1990. Similarly, the budget share for basic research at DoD's Defense Advanced Research Projects Agency (DARPA) has fallen from 20 percent in 1980 to 7 percent in 1989. This atrophy of support for basic research and the lack of policy coordination, if left uncorrected, are sure to affect defense preparedness and the U.S. ability to maintain its technological advantage over potential adversaries.

IS DEFENSE PROTECTIONISM EFFECTIVE?

Strategic trade and investment policy is fraught with uncertainty. The United States has no tradition of successful government involvement in economic decision making, and no evidence suggests that the U.S. government as a whole, let alone the Department of Defense, knows how to improve national welfare and security by developing sectors of the economy that will produce higher rates of return on investment or extraordinary technological benefits.

For example, government intervention in the semiconductor market yielded less than optimal results. This is not for lack of trying. In addition to supporting voluntary export restraints, DoD involvement in the semiconductor industry has included the funding, research, and development of semiconductor manufacturing techniques through Sematech; opposing in late 1986 Fujitsu Corporation's acquisition

of Fairchild Semiconductor (a U.S. firm owned by a French parent company); and, recently, committing itself to operate its own semiconductor manufacturing plant under a contract with National Semiconductor.

The Pentagon has little to show for these efforts. The voluntary restraint agreement with Japan raised the costs and reduced the competitiveness of U.S. semiconductor-using industries; drove Japan toward the high end of the semiconductor market, where it will compete more directly with U.S. manufacturers; encouraged Japan to build sophisticated micro-processors not covered by the agreement; and created a market niche for Korea's nascent semiconductor industry. It is too early to assess the outcome of the Sematech project, but it does mark a major departure from traditional American reliance on the market to allocate capital for commercial undertakings, and may set an ominous precedent.

DoD's track record on export controls, another area where industrial competitiveness must be balanced against national security, offers little reason for optimism regarding trade and investment policy. The Pentagon consistently has shown that it is not sufficiently sensitive to free trade's benefits, either economic or military. Thus, a special panel sponsored by the National Academies of Sciences and Engineering found that the Defense Department's efforts to reinvigorate security export controls have skewed the balance in favor of military security and against economic vitality, at considerable cost to U.S. competitiveness. This willingness to forego the contribution that free trade makes to economic vitality, scientific and technological advancement, and ultimately military security suggests that the strategic trade initiative also is likely to be overly protectionist.

Ironically, then, more DoD involvement in the commercial sector could retard, rather than accelerate, the pace of technological advancement essential to America's defense. It would shelter U.S. industry from the consequences of inefficiency and inertia, and limit the potential for Western collaboration.

IS DEFENSE PROTECTIONISM PRUDENT?

Policy making on such issues as trade and investment is highly diffuse in Washington, with no single congressional committee or executive agency in firm control. In Congress, the splintering of jurisdiction over trade and investment issues has recently reached unprecedented levels. During the 100th Congress, more than a dozen committees shared jurisdiction over trade and competitiveness legislation in the Senate, and a similar number of committees shared jurisdiction in the House. The Omnibus Trade and Competitiveness Act of 1988 required a conference committee composed of 199 members!

In the executive branch, authority also is decentralized. Although the key players vary with the issue, they usually include the Treasury, Commerce, State, Agriculture, and Labor departments, the Office of the U.S. Trade Representative, and the Council of Economic Advisers. A bid by the Department of Defense for ascendancy in trade and investment policy in broadly defined national security-related areas poses a considerable risk. Even assuming DoD could successfully balance security and free trade considerations, political realities could easily undermine the most thoughtful policies.

Once DoD weakens the executive branch's commitment to open trade and capital markets, large and powerful industries are likely to wrap themselves in the banner of strategic trade to obtain preferential treatment. For, as Jacques S. Gansler, a former Pentagon procurement officer, puts it: "National security sells. Industrial policy doesn't."

It appears this process is already under way. Buoyed by its intervention in the machine tool and semiconductor cases, the Defense Department announced in December 1988 that it plans to devote $30 million to the development of high-definition television (HDTV). DARPA, which is in charge of the undertaking, maintains that U.S. manufacture of HDTV will increase the demand for semiconductors, since high-definition television is projected to consume up to 40 percent of the dynamic random-access memory chip market. This investment is supposed to assist the profitability and innovativeness of U.S. semiconductor manufacturers, and of course semiconductors are at the heart of computers, jet fighters, and sophisticated defense systems. This logic ends up making a consumer electronic item the Pentagon's concern.

Seizing on the government's rationale, the American Electronics Association (AEA) asked Congress for $1.35 billion in grants, loans, and guarantees to promote HDTV. The association's proposal specifically requests $300 million in grants over three years from DARPA. Yet the firms sponsoring the AEA study and pleading for government support had investment funds totaling $24 billion in 1988. More peculiar still, DoD seems intent on helping American manufacturers prevail in their rivalry with Japanese companies.

Not only has this nothing to do with DoD's mission, but such intervention will inevitably lead America's trading partners to construe the whole strategic trade policy as a form of hostile economic nationalism. This perception might then produce a harsh response from the Japanese, who have a strong protectionist tradition of their own. The sobering experience of the Smoot-Hawley measure should be remembered: within a year of the tariff's enactment, twenty-six governments had retaliated against the United States.

CONCLUSIONS

Profound economic changes and intractable political problems rightly challenge existing policy assumptions and institutional patterns. The devastation of the Great Depression and World War II delegitimized U.S. high tariff policy and galvanized American support for open international markets. As one consequence of these crises, executive branch institutions acquired unprecedented capacity to effect liberal free trade and investment policy.

Today, huge and enduring trade deficits and the sudden reversal in the U.S. credit position in the 1980s confront policy makers with a crisis that may reshape the norms and institutional arrangements governing trade and investment policy in the 1990s and beyond. The Department of Defense has taken this opportunity to advocate active government participation in the market through trade and investment policies that protect and promote those industries it believes are strategic in one or several meanings of that term. DoD argues (as do others) that such interventions are required because other countries are un-

dermining U.S. security and exploiting the United States economically through their own interventions. Further, DoD has offered itself a lead role in identifying potentially necessary government involvement. Its interests are already reflected in new statutory provisions and new institutions such as Sematech.

For those concerned with the future course of U.S. trade and investment policy, Department of Defense activism in the economic arena should be worrisome. The Defense Department's institutional weight and influence may overwhelm other institutions in the highly decentralized and delicately balanced economic policy-making process and foreclose effective debate. Moreover, the manifold benefits of economic freedom, and the potential for harm in economic interventionism, make government policies to shelter defense industries prima facie unwise. A defense industrial policy should therefore not be launched until thorough study has proven that national security requirements make it unavoidable.

POSTSCRIPT

Should a New Military-Industrial Complex Be Developed?

As we have noted, the demise of the USSR and the cumulative effects of the military buildup during the Reagan years, have set the stage for the current debate over the need for reductions in U.S. defense spending. Adding urgency to the debate is that just as defense budgets are being cut and further sharp reductions are being proposed, *postponed* expenditures are coming due: Under pressure of the spending restrictions in the Gramm-Rudman-Hollings Act, which was designed to reduce the federal budget deficit and required by law a balanced budget by 1992, President Reagan was forced to slow military spending in his second term. However, instead of cutting programs and not initiating new programs, the Reagan administration and Congress responded by stretching out programs in the hope that funding would become available at a later date. That later date is here.

Owens's concern is that, in the rush to cut military spending, care must be taken not to jeopardize the military-industrial base. A smaller defense budget means that fewer resources will be directed toward military use. In the event of war, private industry may not be able to respond quickly enough to prevent disaster. Owens therefore asks for increased government participation in the marketplace through a series of "trade and investment policies" that are designed to protect industries that he feels are strategic. Long flatly rejects this interventionism. For him, the "manifold benefits of economic freedom" are "prima facie" evidence that interventionism is wrong.

Since the defense industry is so important in the economy, much has been written about it. You might start with Lawrence J. Korb's "The 1991 Defense Budget," in Henry J. Aaron, ed., *Setting National Priorities* (Brookings Institution, 1990). Two articles that share Owens's view are Jacques S. Gansler, "Needed: A U.S. Defense Industrial Strategy," *International Security* (Fall 1987), and Edward A. Olsen, "A Case for Strategic 'Protectionism,'" *Strategic Review* (Fall 1987). As you no doubt realize, Long's argument is really a "free trade" argument. There are numerous essays written in defense of free trade. A few articles that touch on the issues raised here are *Balancing the National Interest: U.S. National Security Export Controls and Global Economic Competition* (National Academy Press, 1987); Judith Goldstein, "The Political Economy of Trade: Institutions of Protection," *American Political Science Review* (March 1986); and Robert Pastor, "The Cry-and-Sigh Syndrome: Congress and Trade Policy," in Alan Schick, ed., *Making Economic Policy in Congress* (American Enterprise Institute, 1983).

CONTRIBUTORS
TO THIS VOLUME

EDITORS

THOMAS R. SWARTZ was born in Philadelphia in 1937. He received a B.A. from LaSalle University in 1960, an M.A. from Ohio University in 1962, and a Ph.D. from Indiana University in 1965. He is currently a professor of economics at the University of Notre Dame and the director of the Notre Dame Center for Economic Education. He writes in the areas of urban finance and economic education, and his most recent publication is *The Changing Face of Fiscal Federalism* (M. E. Sharpe Press, 1990), coedited with John E. Peck. He has worked on several books with Frank J. Bonello; in addition to six *Taking Sides* volumes, they have coedited *Alternative Decisions in Economic Policy* (Notre Dame Press, 1978) and *The Supply Side: Debating Current Economic Policies* (The Dushkin Publishing Group, 1983).

FRANK J. BONELLO was born in Detroit in 1939. He received a B.S. in 1961 and an M.A. in 1963 from the University of Detroit and a Ph.D. in 1968 from Michigan State University. He is currently an associate professor of economics and the Arts and Letters College Fellow at the University of Notre Dame. He writes in the areas of monetary economics and economic education, and, in addition to those publications he has coedited with Thomas R. Swartz, he is the author of *The Formulation of Expected Interest Rates* and the coauthor, with William I. Davisson, of *Computer-Assisted Instruction in Economic Education: A Case Study* (University of Notre Dame Press, 1976). He and Professor Swartz are also currently editing a new book entitled *Urban Finance Under Seige*, to be published by M. E. Sharpe.

STAFF

Marguerite L. Egan   Program Manager
Brenda S. Filley   Production Manager
Whit Vye   Designer
Libra Ann Cusack   Typesetting Supervisor
Juliana Arbo   Typesetter
David Brackley   Copy Editor
David Dean   Administrative Assistant
Diane Barker   Editorial Assistant

AUTHORS

ROBERT ALMEDER is a professor of philosophy at Georgia State University and a member of the editorial board for the *Journal of Business Ethics*. He is the coeditor of *Business Ethics* (Prometheus Books, 1987).

RICHARD P. APPELBAUM is a professor in and the chairman of the Department of Sociology at the University of California, Santa Barbara. He is the author of *Karl Marx* (Sage Publications, 1988) and the coauthor, with John I. Gilderbloom, of *Rethinking Rental Housing* (Temple University Press, 1988).

DICK ARMEY, congressman (R) from Texas, 26th District (1985–present; term ends 1993), is the ranking Republican on the Joint Economic Committee. He is also a member of the House Education and Labor Committee and of the Banking, Finance, and Urban Affairs Committee. Before running for Congress, he was the chairman of the economics department at the University of North Texas.

DOUG BANDOW is a senior fellow of the CATO Institute and a member of the State of California Bar Association and the U.S. Court of Appeals for the District of Columbia. He is the author of *The Politics of Plunder: Misgovernment in Washington* (Transaction, 1990).

FRED BLOCK is a professor of sociology at the University of California, Davis. His publications include *Post-Industrial Possibilities: A Critique of Economic Discourse* (University of California Press, 1990).

SAMUEL BOWLES is a professor of economics at the University of Massachusetts–Amherst, and he also teaches economics at the Center for Popular Economics. He is a coauthor, with David M. Gordon and Thomas E. Weisskopf, of *After the Waste Land: A Democratic Economics for the Year 2000* (M. E. Sharpe, 1991).

DAVID CAREY, a former financial planner for the investment firm Allegheny Financial Group, Ltd., is an assistant professor of philosophy at Whitman College in Walla Walla, Washington. He has written extensively on the topic of business ethics.

JOHN E. CHUBB is a senior fellow of the Governmental Studies Program at the Brookings Institution, a private nonprofit organization devoted to research, education, and publication in economics, government, foreign policy, and the social sciences. His publications include *Politics, Markets, and America's Schools* (Brookings Institution, 1990), coauthored with Terry M. Moe.

STEPHEN D. COHEN, a former international economist for the U.S. Treasury Department, is a professor of international economic relations in the School of International Service at American University in Washington, D.C. He has also been a Visiting Fulbright Professor at the London School of Economics. His publications include *Cowboys and Samurai: Why the United States Is Losing the*

Battle with the Japanese, and Why It Matters (HarperCollins, 1991).

MICHAEL DOLNY is a doctoral student in sociology at the University of California, Santa Barbara.

PETER DREIER is the director of housing at the Boston Redevelopment Authority and a board member of the National Low-Income Housing Coalition.

ROBERT EISNER, a former president of the American Economic Association, is the William R. Kenan Professor of Economics at Northwestern University in Evanston, Illinois. He is a fellow of the American Academy of Arts and Sciences and of the Econometric Society. His publications include *The Total Incomes System of Accounts* (University of Chicago Press, 1989).

RANDALL K. FILER is an associate professor of economics at Hunter College, City University of New York, as well as in the university's Graduate Center. He has also taught at Brandeis University, and his research focuses on wages, employment, discrimination, and financial markets.

MILTON FRIEDMAN, a former chairman of the president's Council of Economic Advisers and the recipient of the 1976 Nobel Prize in economic science, is a senior research fellow of the Stanford University Hoover Institution on War, Revolution, and Peace. His publications include *Tyranny of the Status Quo* (Harcourt Brace Jovanovich, 1984), coauthored with Rose Friedman.

JOHN I. GILDERBLOOM is an associate professor of urban policy and the director of research in the Urban Center on Aging at the University of Louisville in Louisville, Kentucky.

DAVID M. GORDON is a professor of economics at the New School for Social Research in New York City, where he has been teaching since 1973. He is a coauthor, with Samuel Bowles and Thomas E. Weisskopf, of *After the Waste Land: A Democratic Economics for the Year 2000* (M. E. Sharpe, 1991).

PETER GORDON is a professor of planning and economics at the University of Southern California and the director of research at the Planning Institute of the University of Southern California School of Urban and Regional Planning. His recent work concerns the interaction of urban settlement patterns and travel demand.

ALAN GREENSPAN is the chairman of the Board of Governors of the Federal Reserve System and the chairman of the Federal Open Market Committee, the Federal Reserve System's principal monetary policymaking body. He has served in a number of corporate and governmental positions, including chairman of the President's Council of Economic Advisers under former president Ford.

BILL HONIG is the superintendent of public instruction for California's State Department of Education in Sacramento.

W. LEE HOSKINS is the president and chief executive officer of the Huntington National Bank. He has also been president of the Federal Reserve Bank of Cleveland, a chief economist and senior vice president of PNC Financial Corporation, and a vice president and director of research at the Federal Reserve Bank of Philadelphia.

JERRY A. JACOBS is an associate professor of sociology and the chairman of the graduate program in sociology at the University of Pennsylvania in Philadelphia, Pennsylvania. His current projects include a study of women's entry into management, research on part-time employment, and an analysis of trends in sexual segregation in 56 countries. He is also editing a special issue of the sociology journal *Work and Occupations*.

ROBERT W. KASTEN, JR., senator (R) from Wisconsin (1980–present; terms ends 1993), is the ranking member of the Senate Small Business Committee. He is also the ranking member of the Appropriations Committee's Foreign Operations Subcommittee and the Commerce, Science, and Transportation Committee's Surface Transportation Subcommittee.

JEFFREY R. KENWORTHY is a professional officer in environmental science at Murdoch University in Perth, Western Australia, where he completed his doctorate. He has also worked on an Australian government-funded project to examine urban land use policies for transportation energy conservation.

MICHAEL KINSLEY is a senior editor for *The New Republic* magazine and the author of *Curse of the Giant Muffins and Other Washington Maladies* (Summit Books, 1987).

ROBERT KUTTNER is a contributing editor for *The New Republic* magazine. He has written numerous books and articles on social and political subjects, and his publications include *The Life of the Party: Democratic Prospects in 1988* (Penguin, 1988).

ANDREW LARKIN is a professor of economics at Saint Cloud State University in St. Cloud, Minnesota. He received his Ph.D. in economics from the University of Nebraska.

LESTER B. LAVE is the James H. Higgins Professor of Economics at Carnegie Mellon University in Pittsburgh, Pennsylvania, with appointments in the Graduate School of Industrial Administration, the School of Urban and Public Affairs, and the Department of Engineering and Public Policy. He was also a senior fellow of the Brookings Institution from 1978 to 1982.

WILLIAM J. LONG is an associate professor of international affairs at the Georgia Institute of Technology. His most recent book is *U.S. Export Control Policy: Executive Autonomy Versus Congressional Reform* (Columbia University Press, 1989).

LAWRENCE M. MEAD is an associate professor of politics at New York University, where he teaches public policy and American government. He has conducted extensive research on federal welfare and employment programs, which is reflected in such publications as *The New Politics of Poverty: The Nonworking Poor in America* (Basic Books, 1992).

MICHAEL MEEROPOL is a professor of economics at Western New England College in Springfield, Massachusetts, and a staff economist at the Center for Popular Economics in Amherst, Massachusetts.

JOHN MILLER is a former professor of economics at Wheaton College in Norton, Massachusetts, and a member of the National Steering Committee of the Union for Radical Political Economics.

TERRY M. MOE is a professor of political science at Stanford University, where he has been teaching since 1981. His book, *Politics, Markets, and America's Schools* (Brookings Institution, 1990), coauthored with John E. Chubb, has received national attention for its institutional critique of the American school system.

CHARLES MOSKOS is a professor of sociology and the chairman of the intervarsity seminar on armed forces and society at Northwestern University in Evanston, Illinois. He also serves on the board of advisers of the Democratic Leadership Council. His publications include *A Call to Civic Service: National Service for Country and Community* (Free Press, 1988).

PETER W. G. NEWMAN is an associate professor in environmental science at Murdoch University in Perth, Western Australia. He has studied the city planning implications of transportation as an academic at Stanford University and as a local government councillor and community representative on Perth's metropolitan planning council.

LISA NEWTON is a professor of philosophy and the director of the Program in Applied Ethics at Fairfield University in Fairfield, Connecticut. She is the president of the Society for Business Ethics and a member of the American Philosophical Association and the American Society of Law and Medicine.

WILLIAM D. NORDHAUS is the John Musser Professor of Economics and the chairman of the Department of Economics at Yale University. He is also a staff member of Yale University's Cowles Foundation for Research in Economics and a member and sometime senior adviser of the Brookings Panel on Economic Activity. His publications include *The Efficient Use of Energy Resources* (Yale University Press, 1979).

MACKUBIN T. OWENS is a professor of defense economics at the U.S. Naval War College. He has served as a national security adviser to Senator Robert W. Kasten, Jr., and as the director of legislative affairs for the nuclear weapons programs of the Department of Energy.

HARRY W. RICHARDSON is a professor of planning and economics at the University of Southern California, Los Angeles. He is also a member of the editorial boards for *Regional Studies* and *International Regional Science Review.*

PAUL CRAIG ROBERTS, chairman of the Institute for Political Economy, holds the William E. Simon Chair at the Center for Strategic and International Studies in Washington, D.C. He was awarded the French Legion of Honor in 1987 for his contributions to "the renewal of economic science and policy."

CYNTHIA POLLOCK SHEA is a senior researcher with the Worldwatch Institute and a coauthor of its *State of the World* publication. Her principal interests include ozone depletion and energy and waste management technologies and policies.

MORTON H. SKLAR served as legal counsel to and the director of Job Watch, a public interest project providing information and support services related to employment.

RONNIE J. STEINBERG is an associate professor of sociology at Temple University in Philadelphia, Pennsylvania. She is the editor of a book series entitled *Women in the Political Economy* for Temple University Press, and her other publications include *Job Training for Women: The Promise and Limits of Public Policies* (Temple University Press, 1989), coedited with Sharon Harlan.

CHRISTOPHER D. STONE is the Roy P. Crocker Professor of Law at the University of Southern California, where he has been teaching since 1965. He served as a fellow of law and economics at the University of Chicago from 1962 to 1963, and his publications include *Earth and Other Ethics: The Case for Moral Pluralism* (Harper & Row, 1987).

PHILIP H. TREZISE, a former assistant secretary of state for economic affairs, is a senior fellow of the Brookings Institution. He received the President's Award for Distinguished Federal Civilian Service and the Distinguished Honor Award from the U.S. Department of State. His publications include *Building a Canadian-American Free Trade Area* (Brookings Institution, 1987), coedited with Edward R. Fried and Frank Stone.

WILLIAM TUCKER, a writer and social critic, is a staff writer for *Forbes* magazine. His publications include *The Excluded Americans: Homelessness and Housing Policies* (Regnery Gateway, 1989), which won the 1991 Mencken Award for best nonfiction.

THOMAS E. WEISSKOPF is a professor of economics at the University of Michigan. He is a coauthor, with Samuel Bowles and David M. Gordon, of *After the Waste Land: A Democratic Economics for the Year 2000* (M. E. Sharpe, 1991).

INDEX